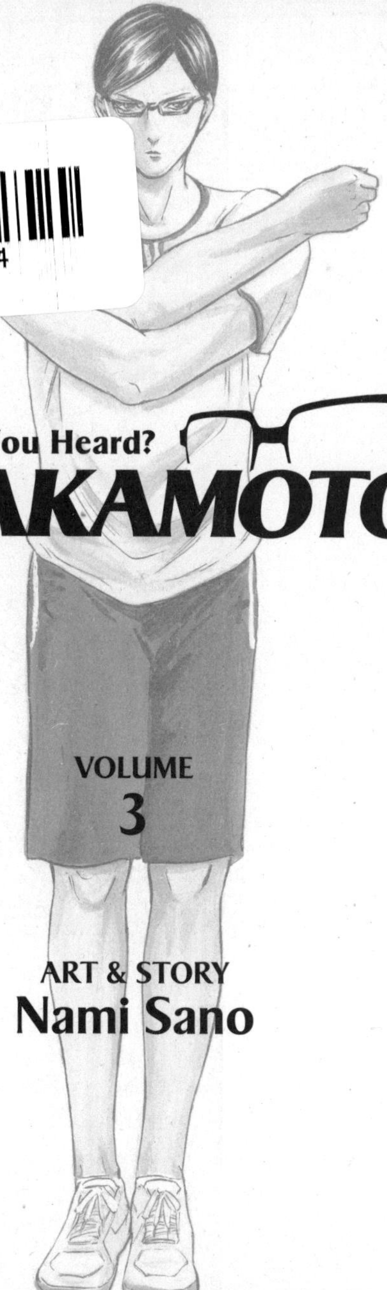

Haven't You Heard?
I'M SAKAMOTO

VOLUME
3

ART & STORY
Nami Sano

SEVEN SEAS ENTERTAINMENT PRESENTS

Haven't You Heard? I'M SAKAMOTO

story and art by **NAMI SANO** **VOLUME 3**

TRANSLATION
Adrienne Beck

ADAPTATION
Karis Page

LETTERING AND LAYOUT
Lys Blakeslee

COVER DESIGN
Nicky Lim

PROOFREADER
Shanti Whitesides

PRODUCTION MANAGER
Lissa Pattillo

EDITOR-IN-CHIEF
Adam Arnold

PUBLISHER
Jason DeAngelis

Sakamoto Desuga? Vol.3

First published in Japan in 2014 by KADOKAWA CORPORATION ENTERBRAIN.
English translation rights arranged with KADOKAWA CORPORATION ENTERBRAIN through TOHAN CORPORATION., Tokyo.

ISBN: 978-1-626922-51-8

Printed in Canada

First Printing: March 2016

10 9 8 7 6 5 4 3 2 1

FOLLOW US ONLINE: ***www.gomanga.com***

READING DIRECTIONS

This book reads from ***right to left***, Japanese style. If this is your first time reading manga, you start reading from the top right panel on each page and take it from there. If you get lost, just follow the numbered diagram here. It may seem backwards at first, but you'll get the hang of it! Have fun!!

1
2
3
4
5
6
7
8
9

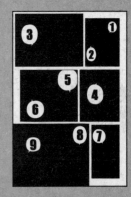

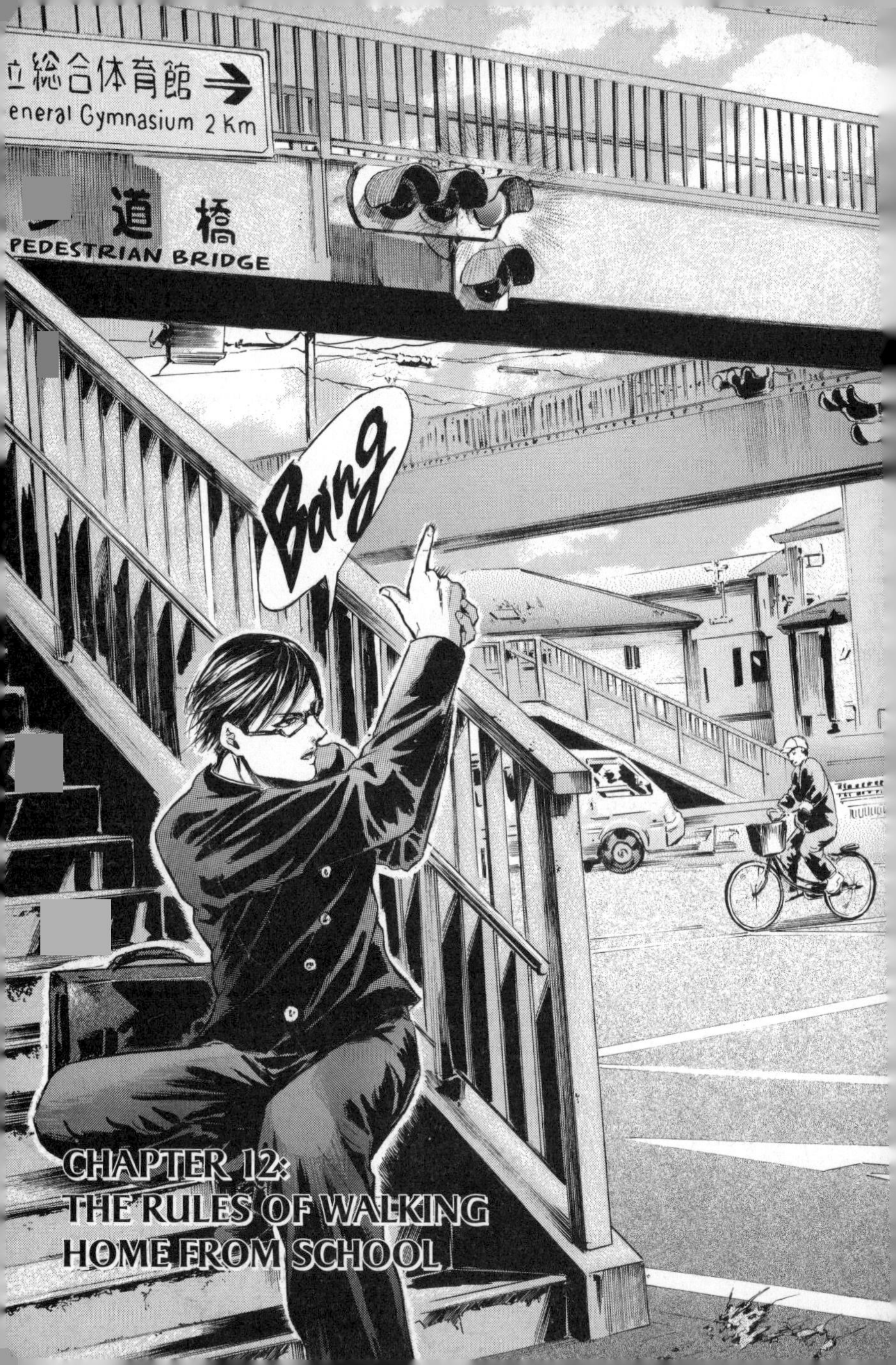
立総合体育館 →
eneral Gymnasium 2 Km
道 橋
PEDESTRIAN BRIDGE
Bang
CHAPTER 12:
THE RULES OF WALKING
HOME FROM SCHOOL

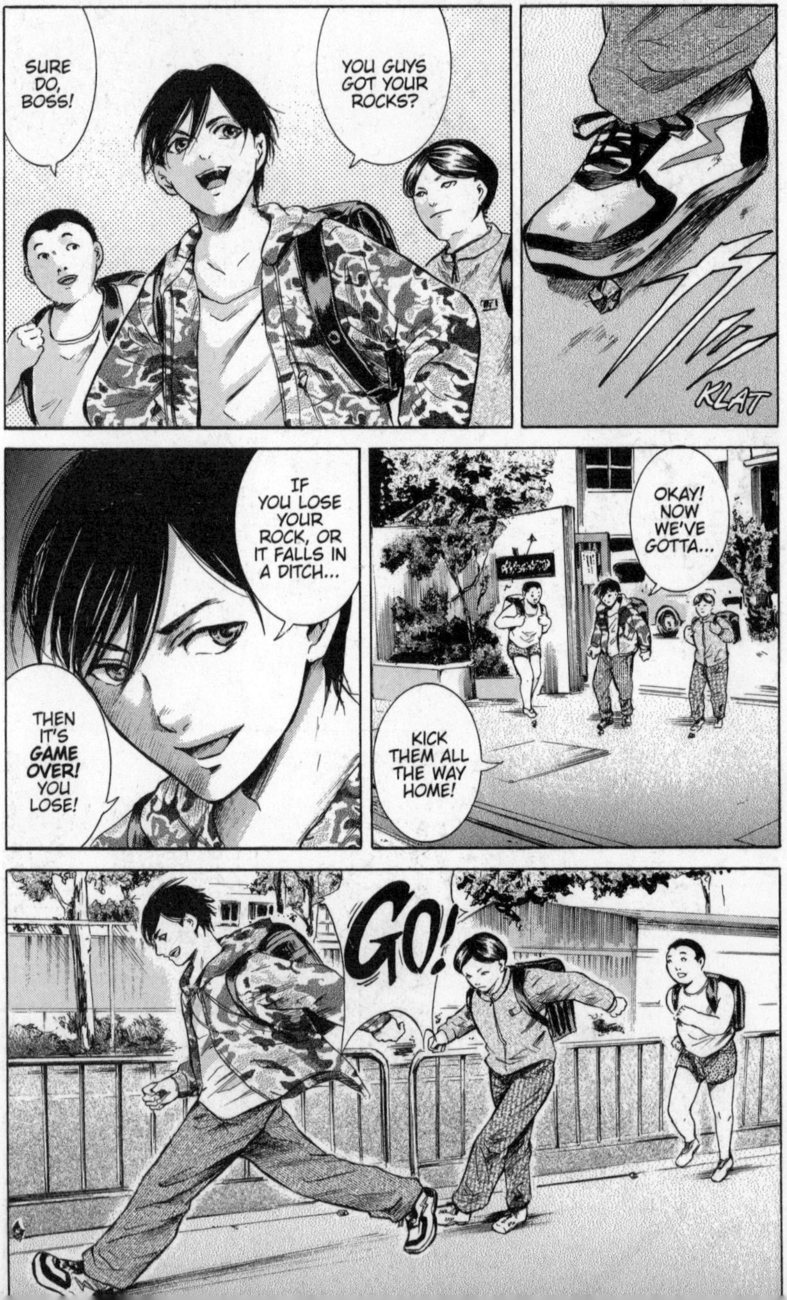
KLAT
YOU GUYS GOT YOUR ROCKS?
SURE DO, BOSS!
OKAY! NOW WE'VE GOTTA...
KICK THEM ALL THE WAY HOME!
IF YOU LOSE YOUR ROCK, OR IT FALLS IN A DITCH...
THEN IT'S **GAME OVER!** YOU LOSE!
GO!

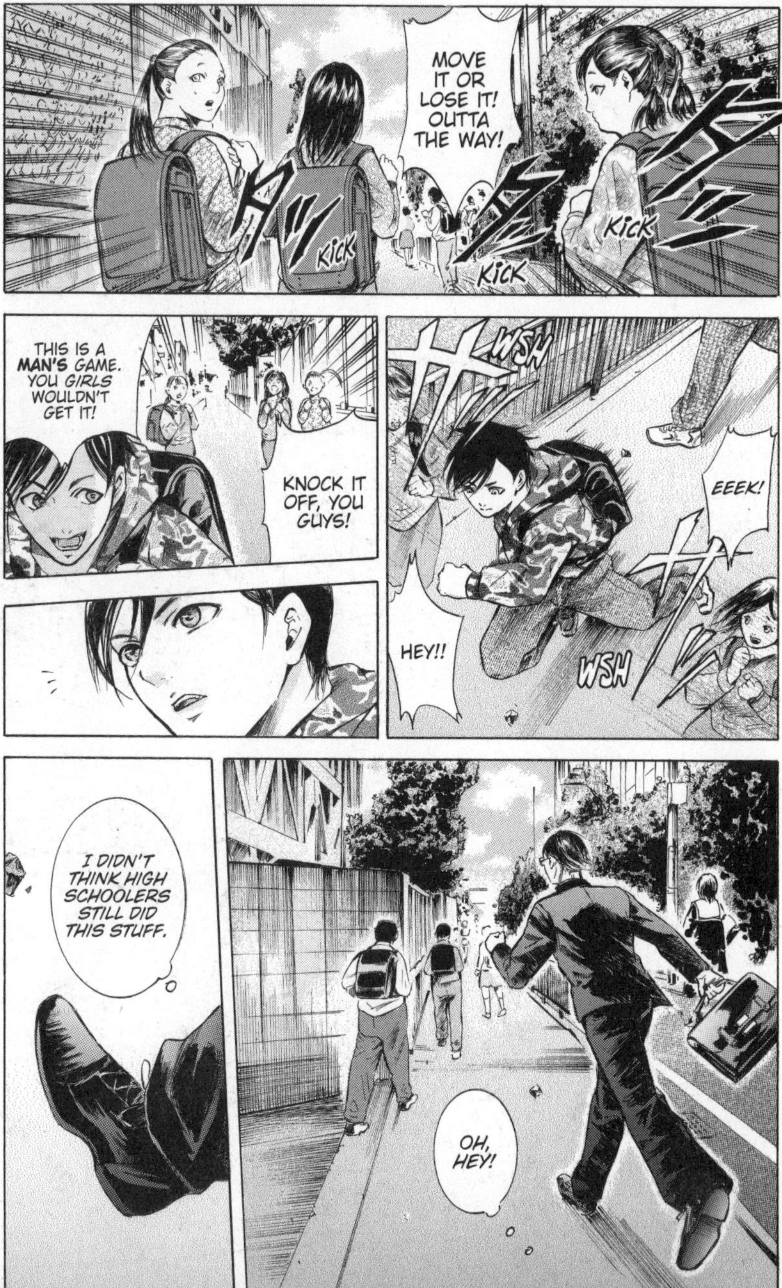
MOVE IT OR LOSE IT! OUTTA THE WAY!
KICK
KICK
KICK
WSH
EEEK!
HEY!!
WSH
KNOCK IT OFF, YOU GUYS!
THIS IS A MAN'S GAME. YOU GIRLS WOULDN'T GET IT!
OH, HEY!
I DIDN'T THINK HIGH SCHOOLERS STILL DID THIS STUFF.

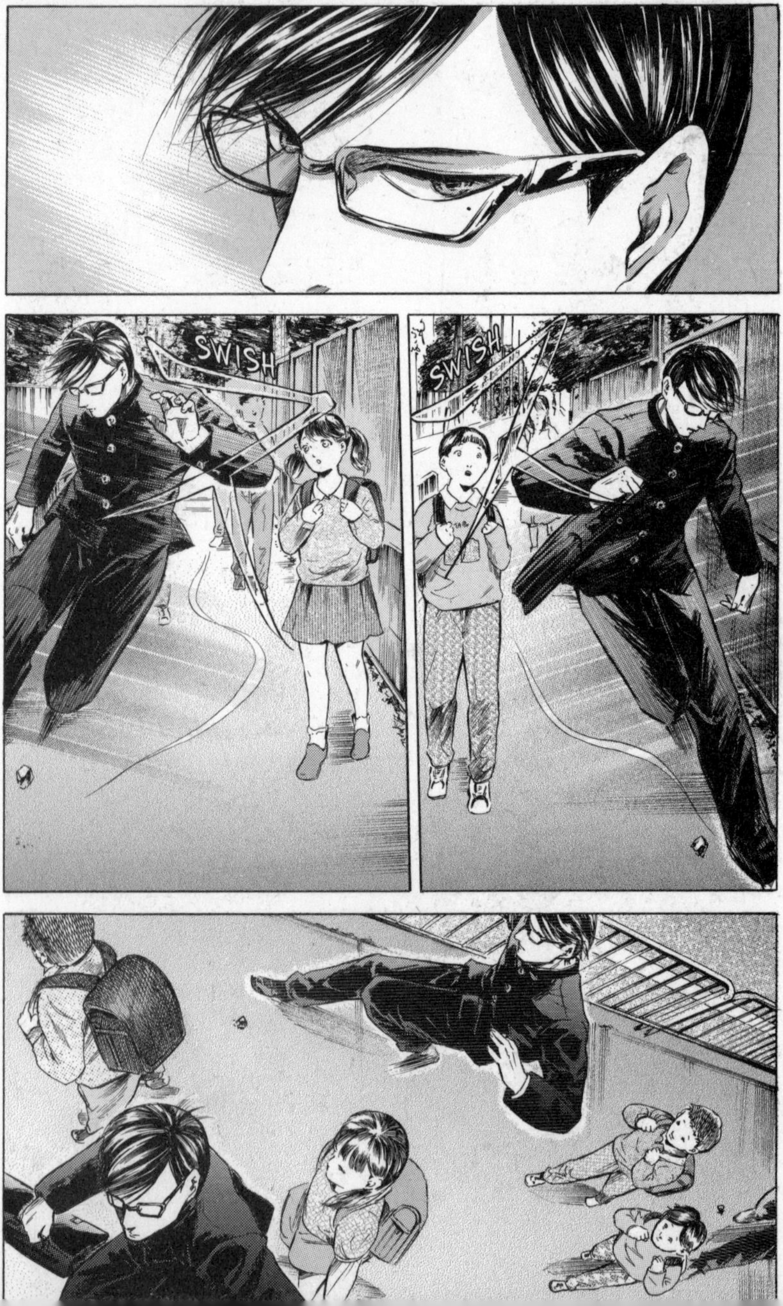
SWISH
SWISH

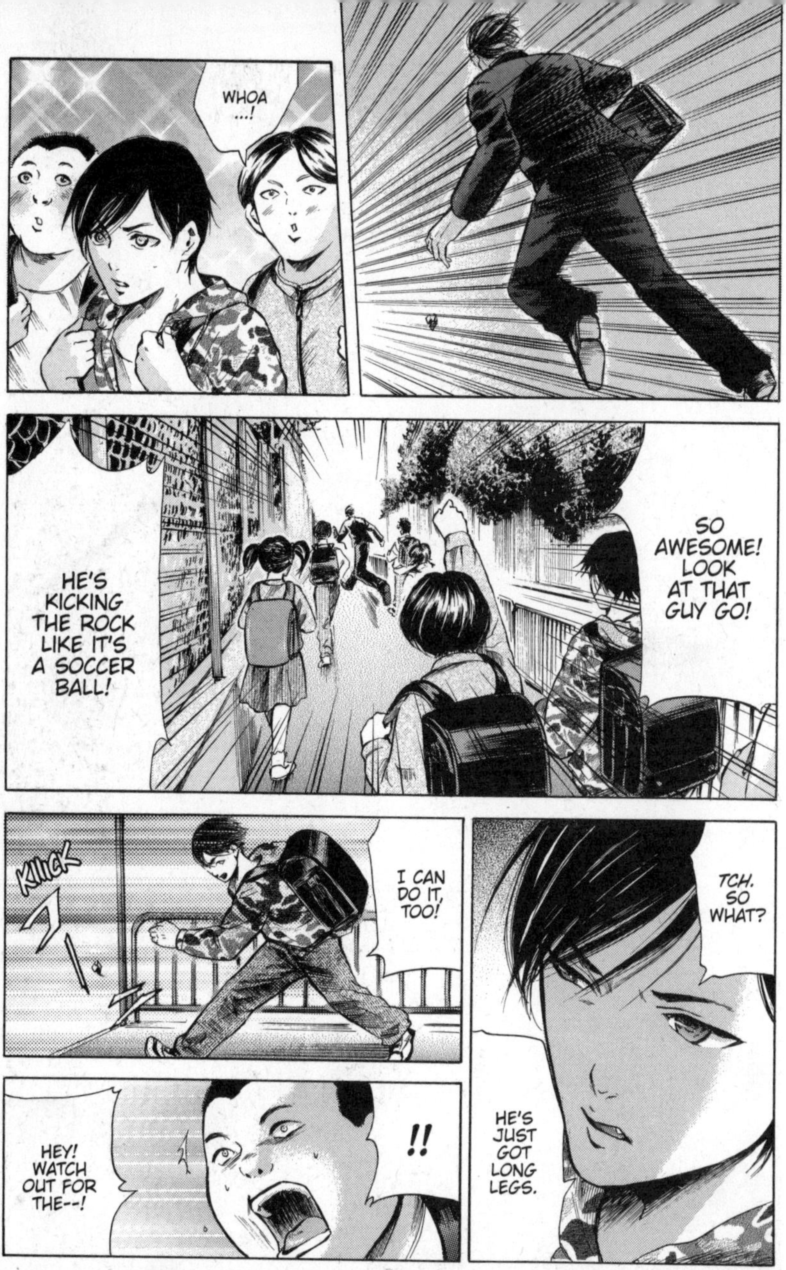
WHOA ...!
SO AWESOME! LOOK AT THAT GUY GO!
HE'S KICKING THE ROCK LIKE IT'S A SOCCER BALL!
TCH. SO WHAT?
HE'S JUST GOT LONG LEGS.
I CAN DO IT, TOO!
KIIICK
!!
HEY! WATCH OUT FOR THE--!

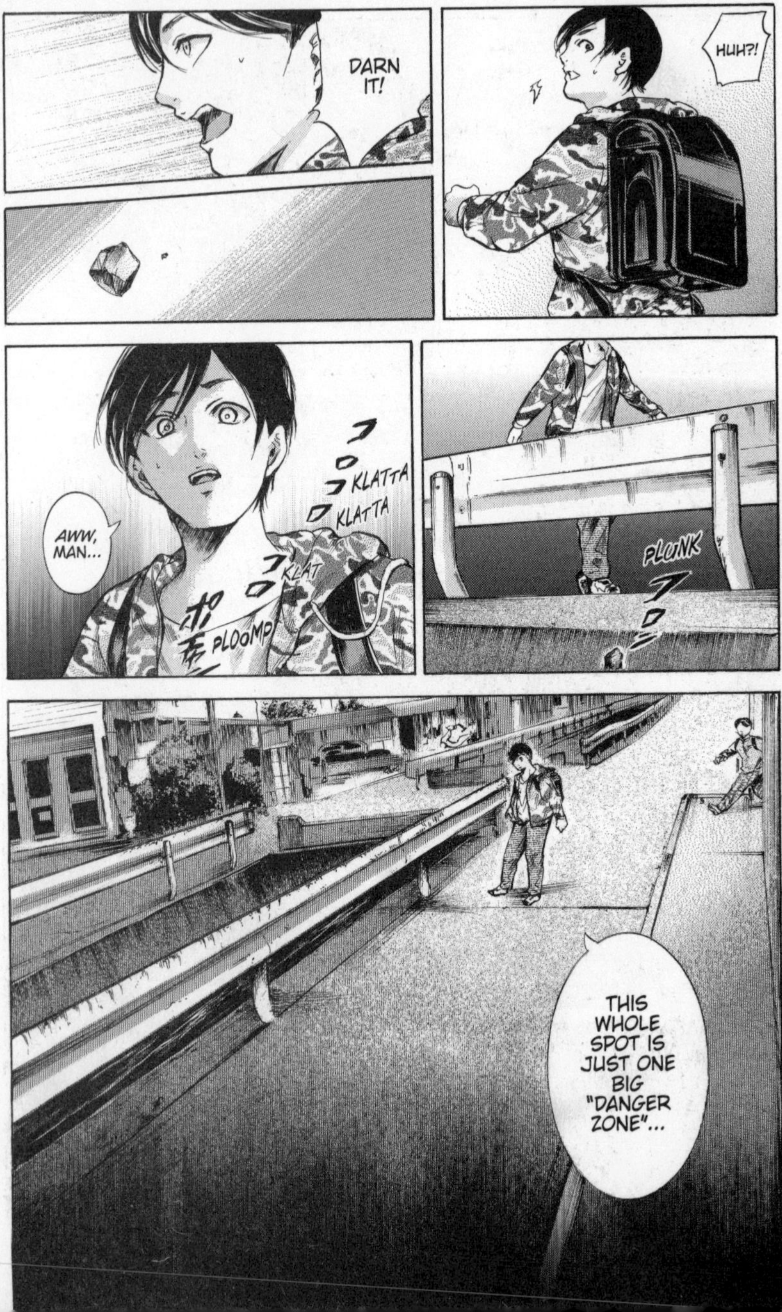
HUH?!
DARN IT!
PLUNK
KLATTA
KLATTA
AWW, MAN...
KLAT
PLOOMP
THIS WHOLE SPOT IS JUST ONE BIG "DANGER ZONE"...

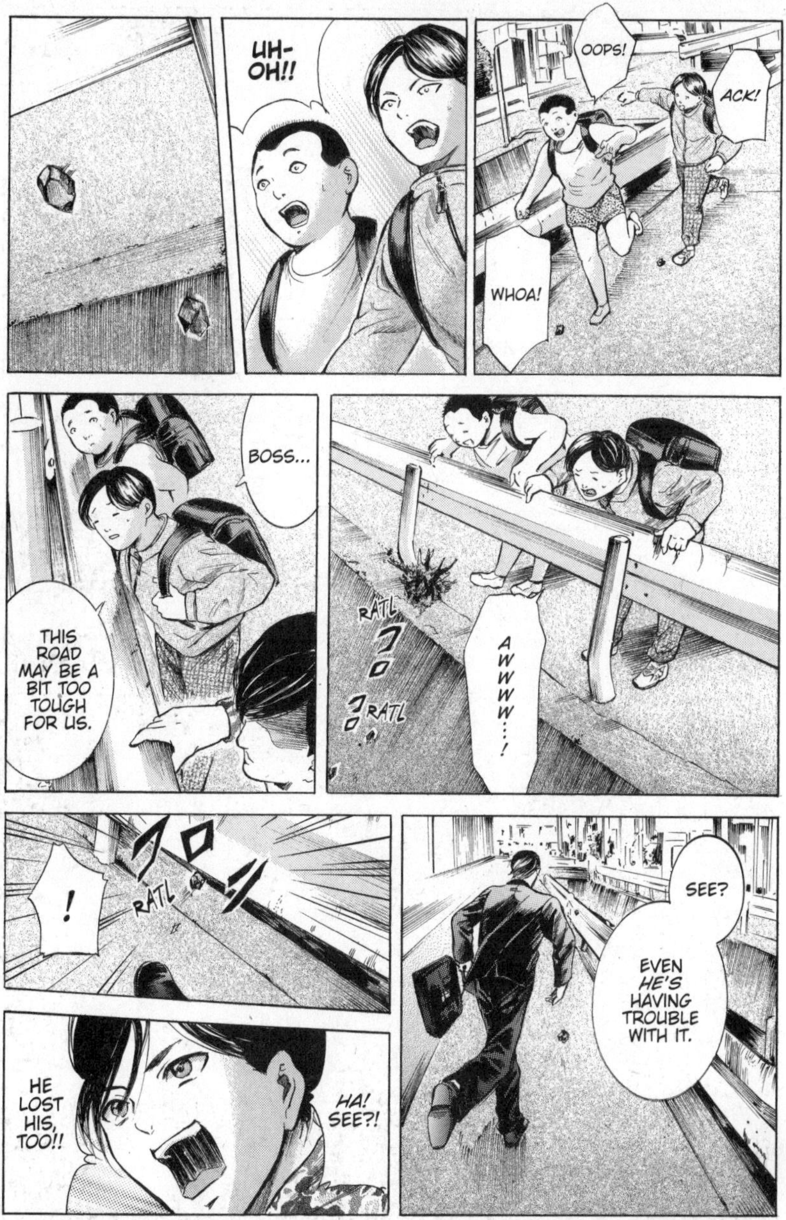
ACK!
OOPS!
WHOA!
UH-OH!!
AWWWW...!
RATL
RATL
BOSS...
THIS ROAD MAY BE A BIT TOO TOUGH FOR US.
SEE?
EVEN HE'S HAVING TROUBLE WITH IT.
!
RATL
HA! SEE?!
HE LOST HIS, TOO!!

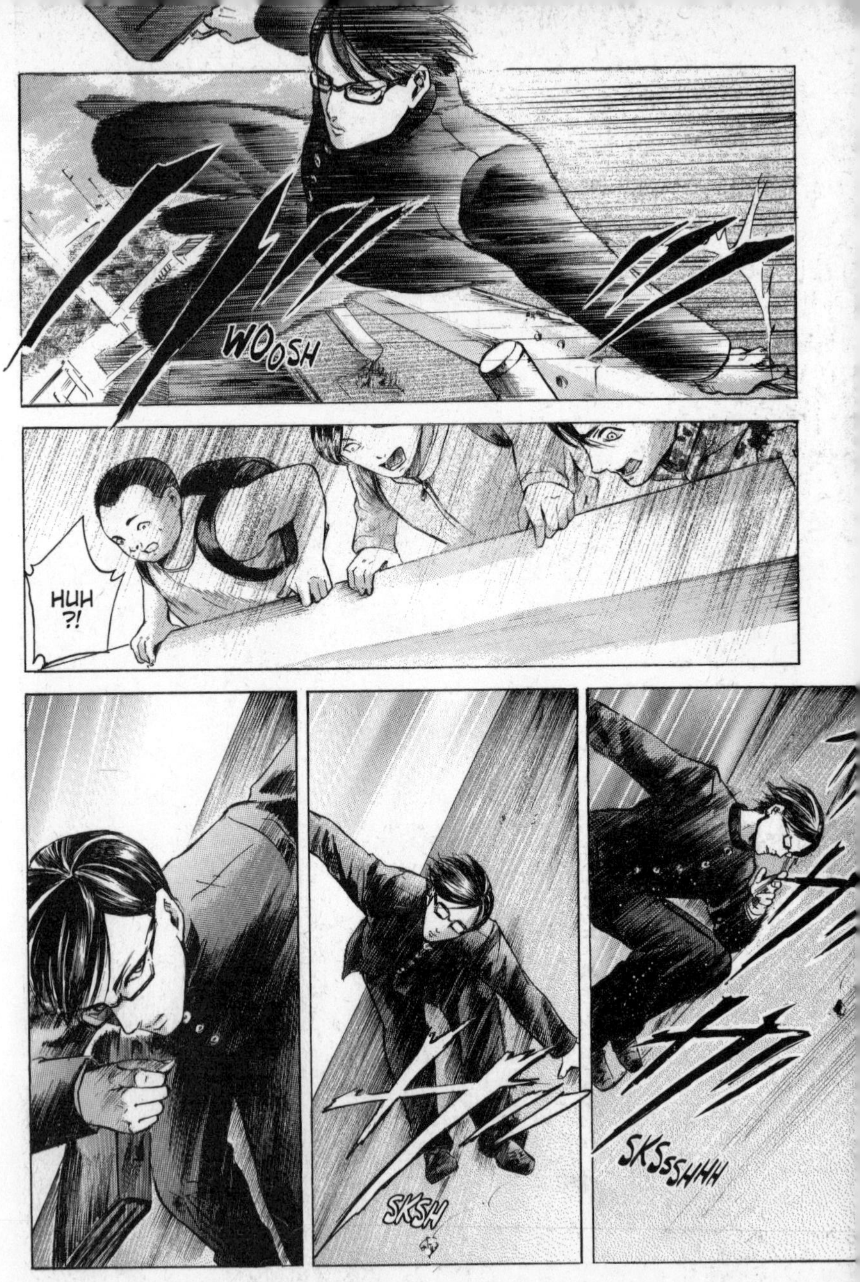
WOOSH
HUH ?!
SKSSSHHH
SKSH

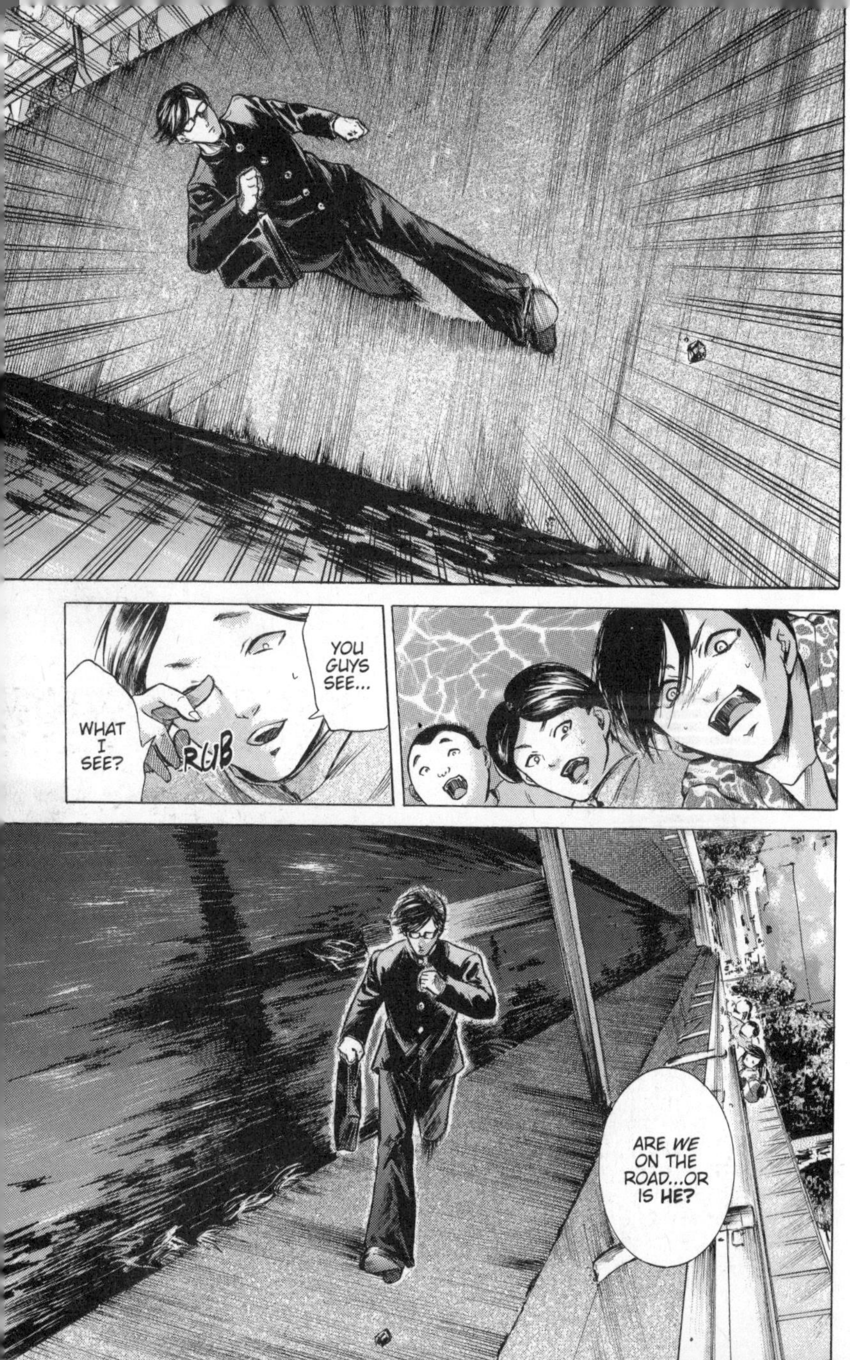
YOU GUYS SEE...
WHAT I SEE?
RUB
ARE WE ON THE ROAD...OR IS HE?

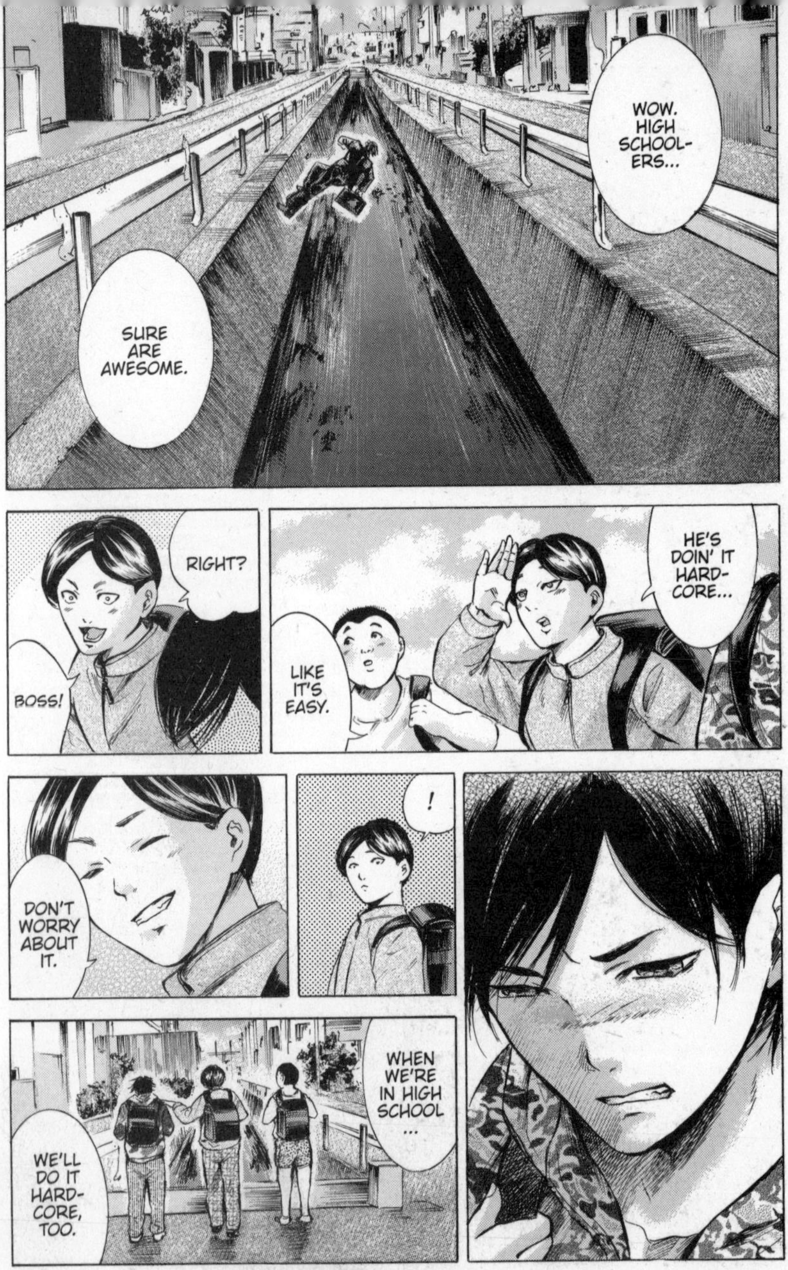

WOW. HIGH SCHOOLERS...
SURE ARE AWESOME.
HE'S DOIN' IT HARDCORE...
LIKE IT'S EASY.
RIGHT?
BOSS!
!
DON'T WORRY ABOUT IT.
WHEN WE'RE IN HIGH SCHOOL ...
WE'LL DO IT HARDCORE, TOO.

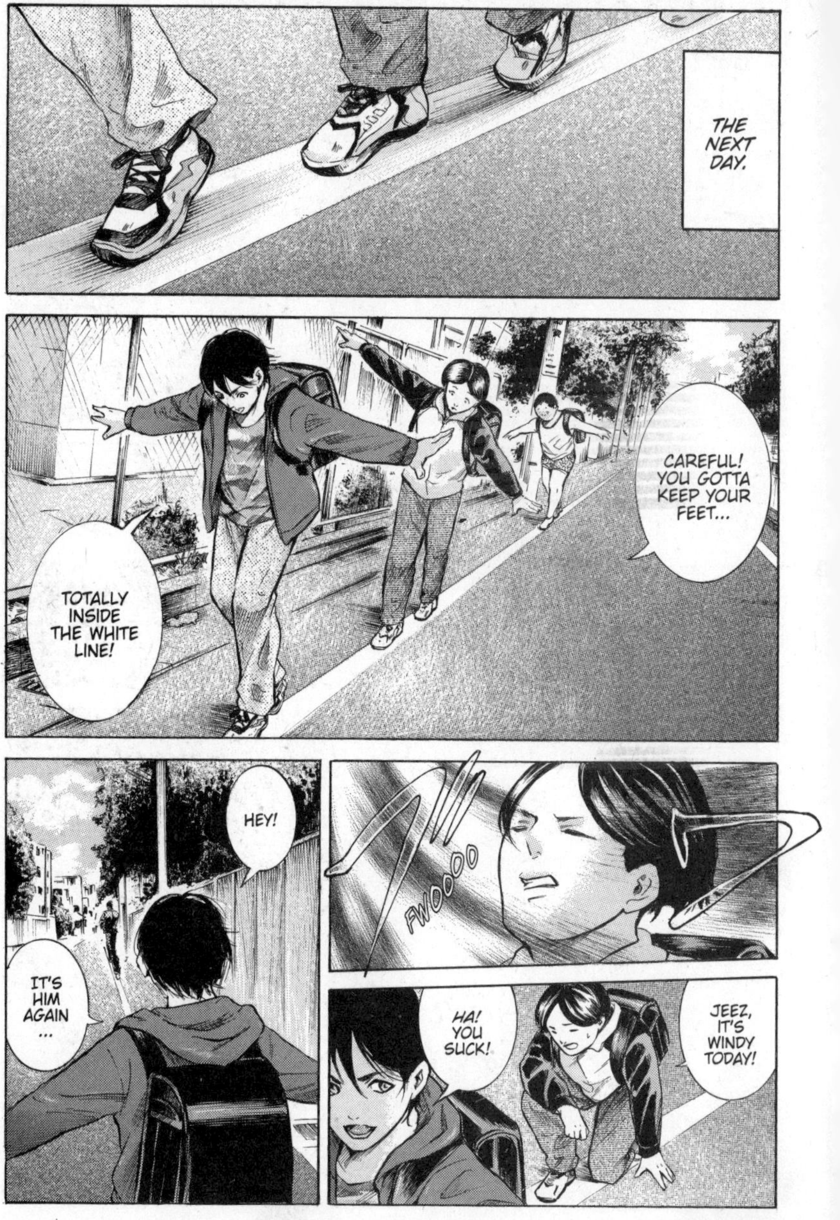
THE NEXT DAY.
CAREFUL! YOU GOTTA KEEP YOUR FEET...
TOTALLY INSIDE THE WHITE LINE!
FWOOOO
JEEZ, IT'S WINDY TODAY!
HA! YOU SUCK!
HEY!
IT'S HIM AGAIN...

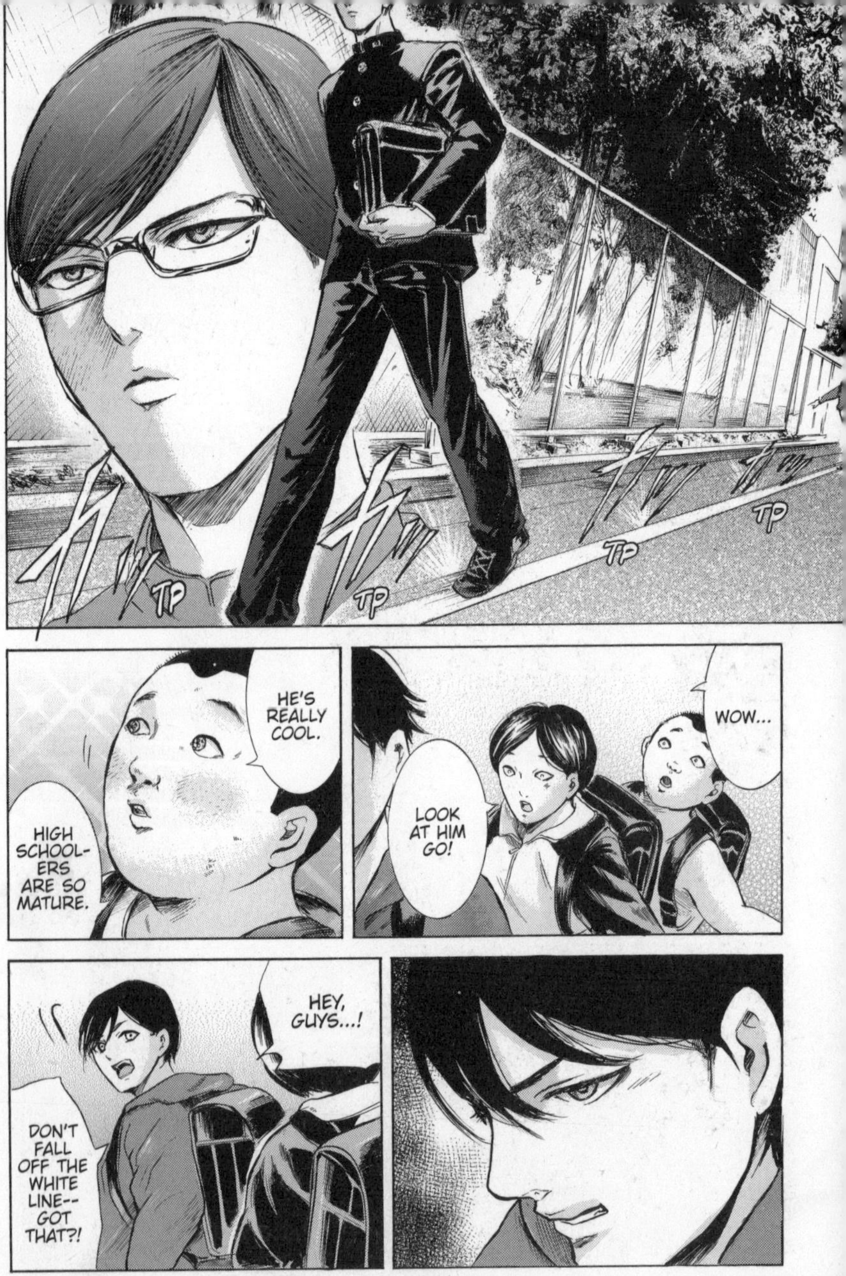
TP
TP
TP
TP
WOW...
LOOK AT HIM GO!
HE'S REALLY COOL.
HIGH SCHOOL-ERS ARE SO MATURE.
HEY, GUYS...!
DON'T FALL OFF THE WHITE LINE--GOT THAT?!

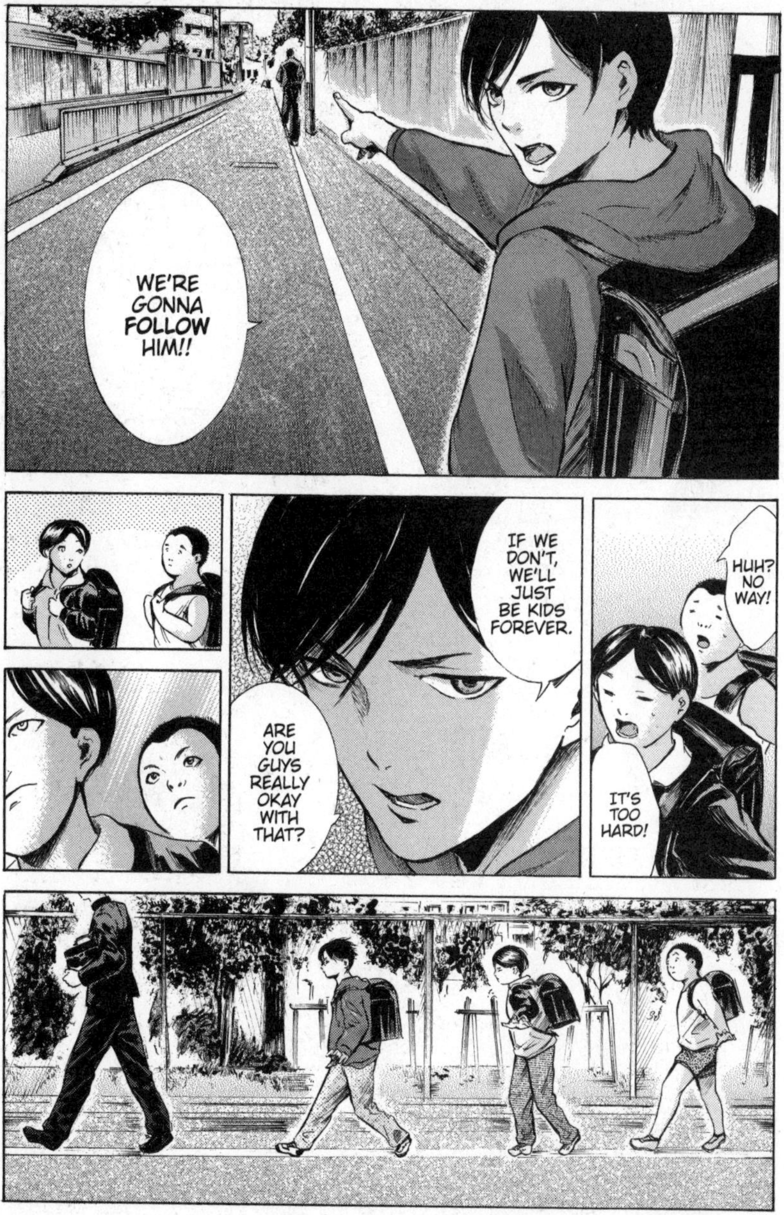
WE'RE GONNA FOLLOW HIM!!
HUH? NO WAY!
IT'S TOO HARD!
IF WE DON'T, WE'LL JUST BE KIDS FOREVER.
ARE YOU GUYS REALLY OKAY WITH THAT?

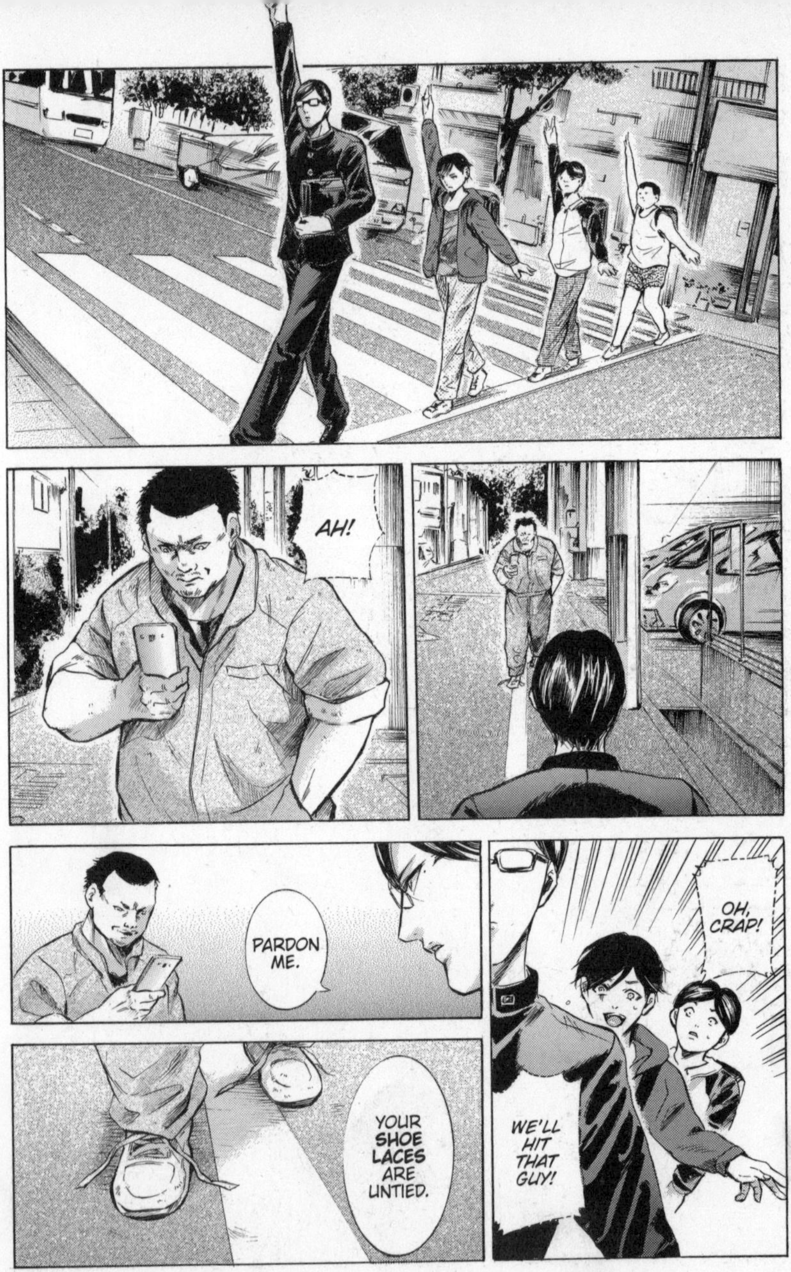
AH!
OH, CRAP!
WE'LL HIT THAT GUY!
PARDON ME.
YOUR SHOE LACES ARE UNTIED.

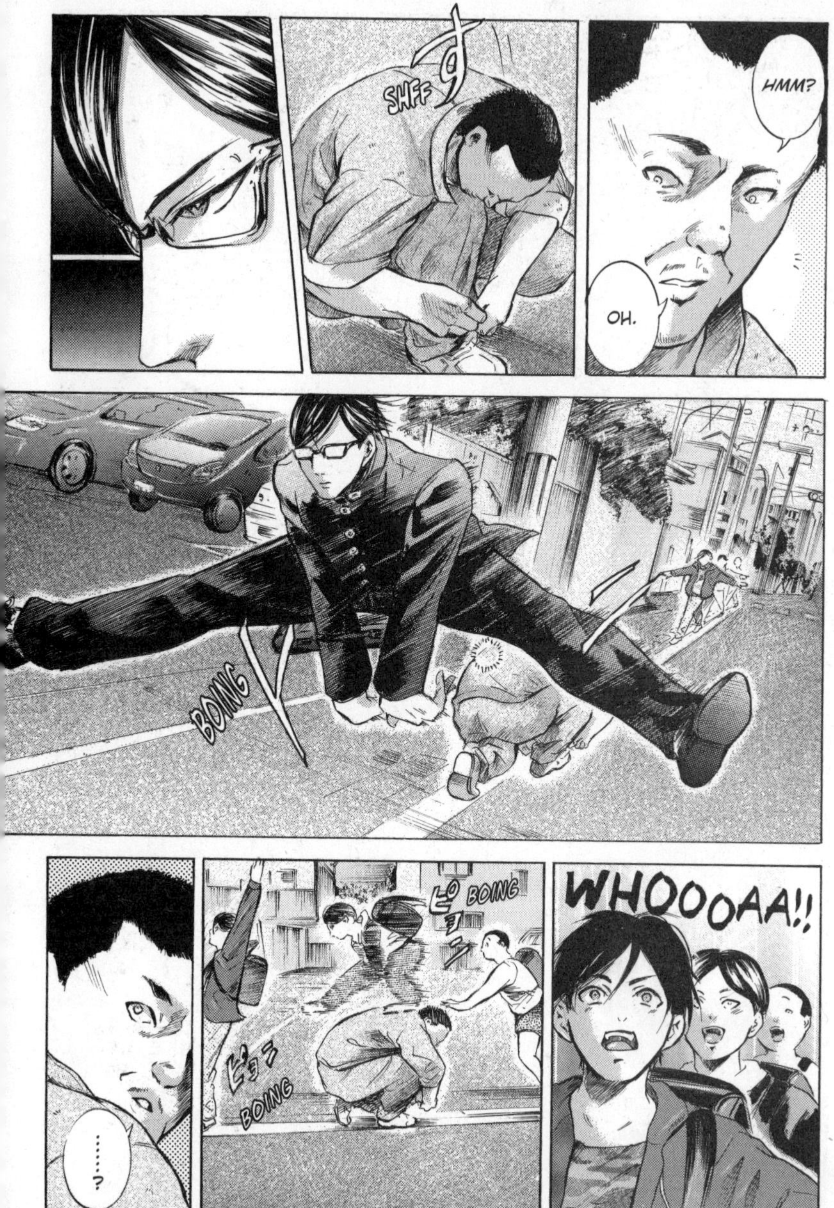
HMM?
OH.
SHFF
す
BOING
WHOOOAA!!
BOING
BOING
......?

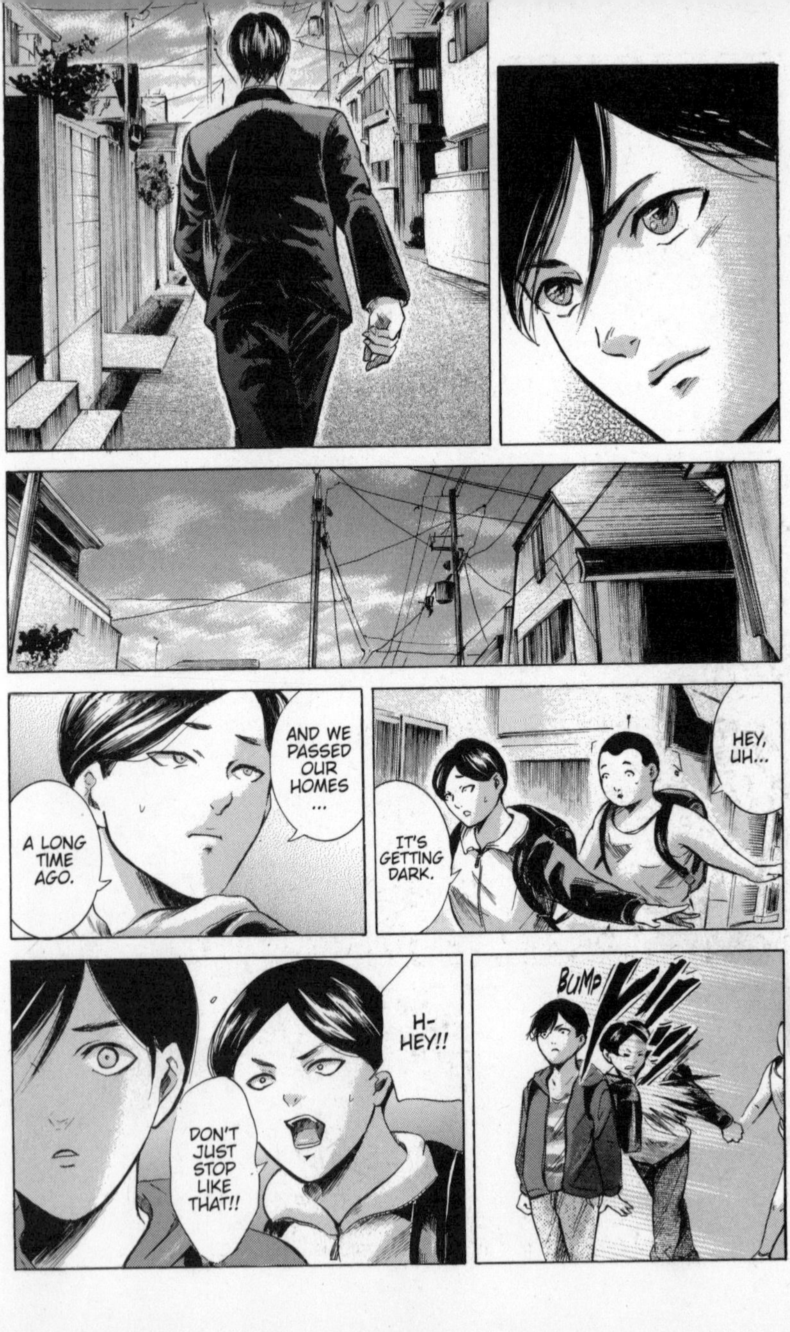
HEY, UH...
IT'S GETTING DARK.
AND WE PASSED OUR HOMES...
A LONG TIME AGO.
BUMP
H-HEY!!
DON'T JUST STOP LIKE THAT!!

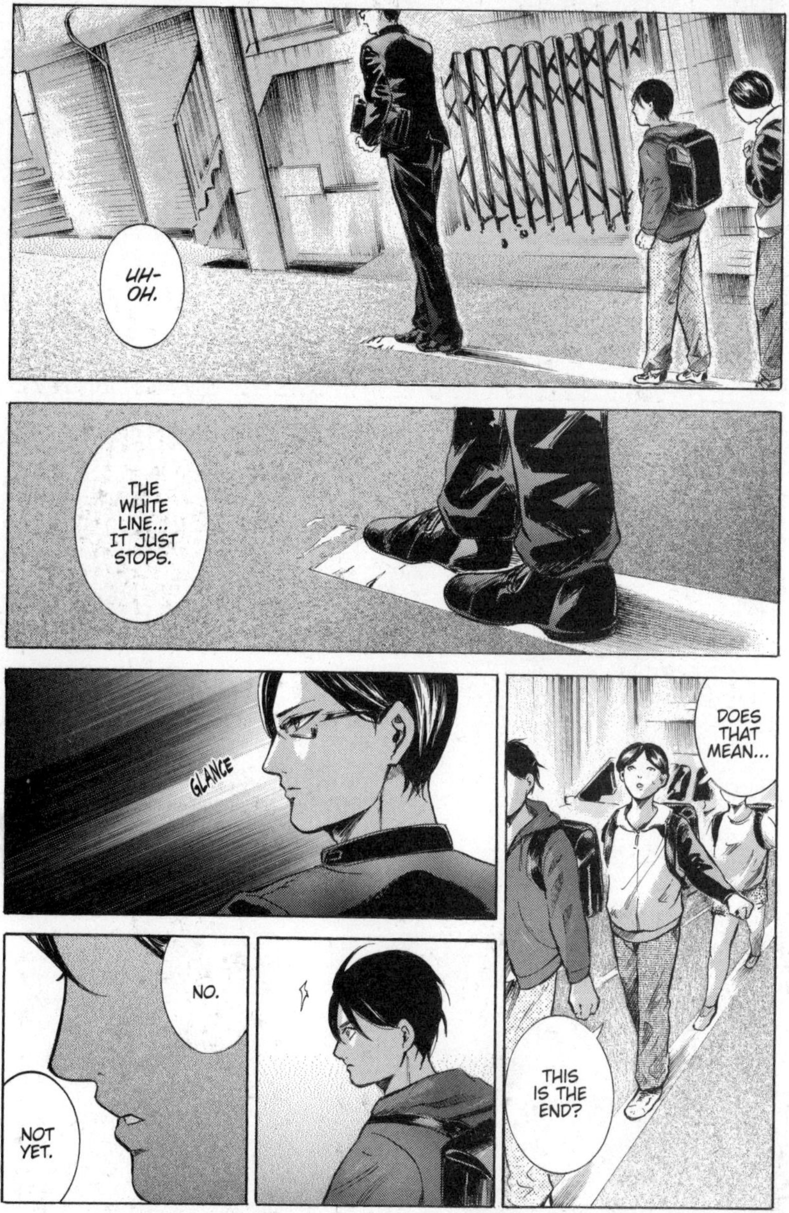
UH-OH.
THE WHITE LINE... IT JUST STOPS.
DOES THAT MEAN...
THIS IS THE END?
GLANCE
NO.
NOT YET.

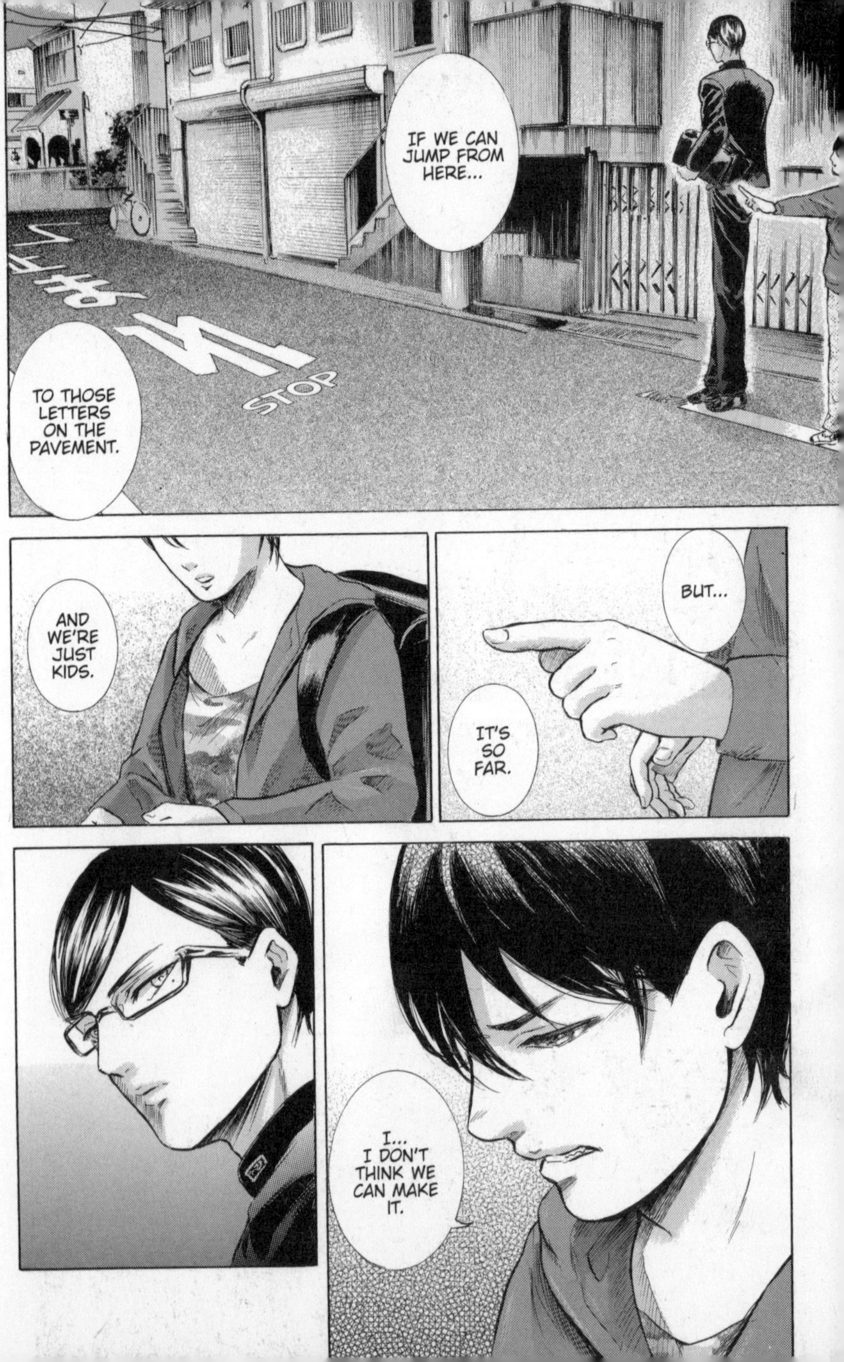
IF WE CAN JUMP FROM HERE...
TO THOSE LETTERS ON THE PAVEMENT.
STOP
BUT...
IT'S SO FAR.
AND WE'RE JUST KIDS.
I... I DON'T THINK WE CAN MAKE IT.

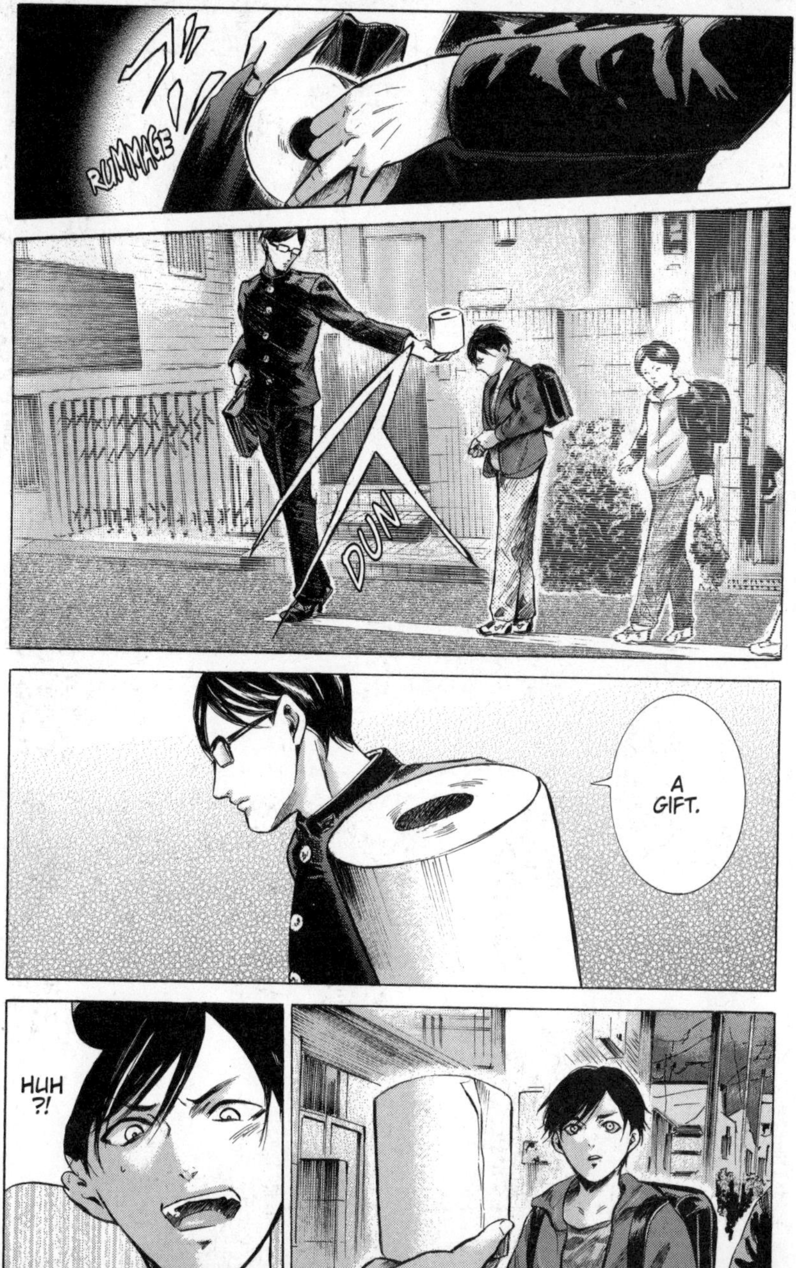
RUMMAGE
DUN
A GIFT.
HUH ?!

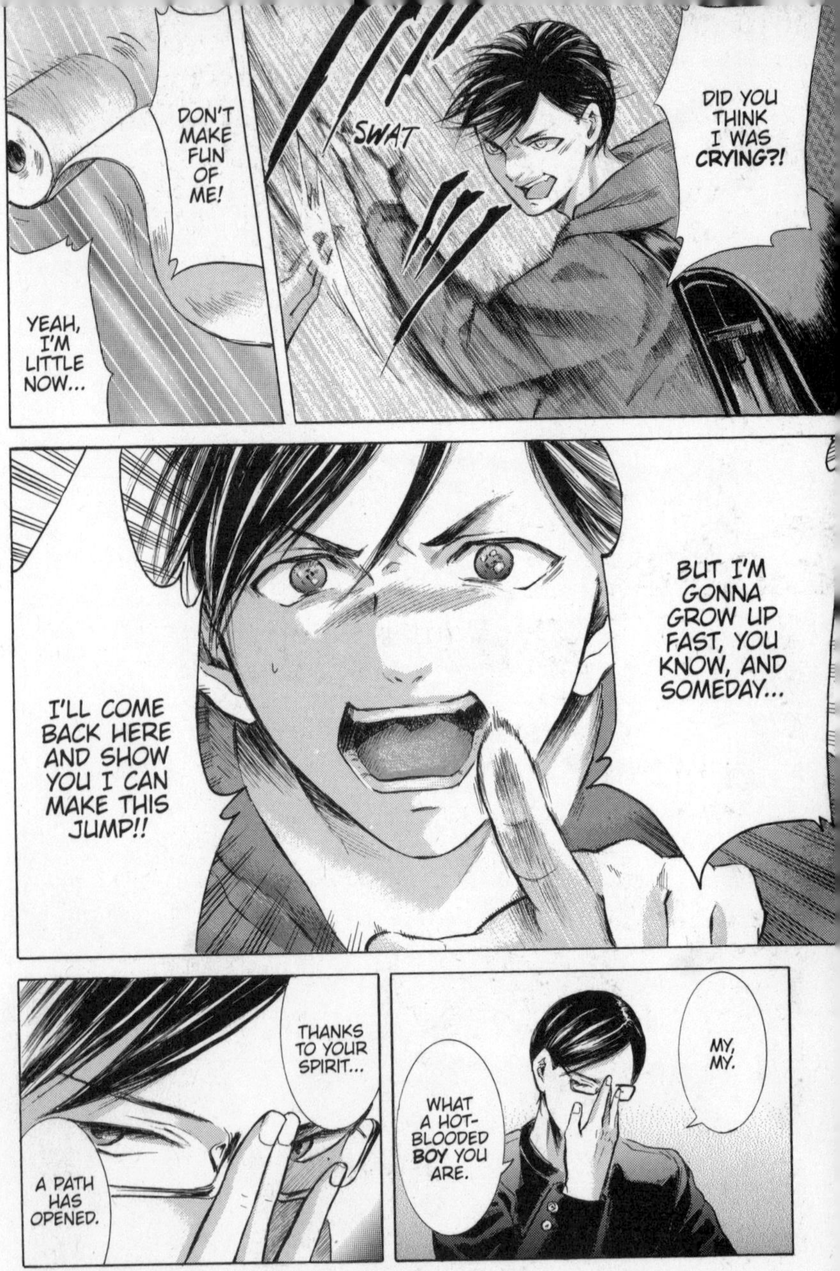
DID YOU THINK I WAS CRYING?!
SWAT
DON'T MAKE FUN OF ME!
YEAH, I'M LITTLE NOW...
BUT I'M GONNA GROW UP FAST, YOU KNOW, AND SOMEDAY...
I'LL COME BACK HERE AND SHOW YOU I CAN MAKE THIS JUMP!!
MY, MY.
WHAT A HOT-BLOODED BOY YOU ARE.
THANKS TO YOUR SPIRIT...
A PATH HAS OPENED.

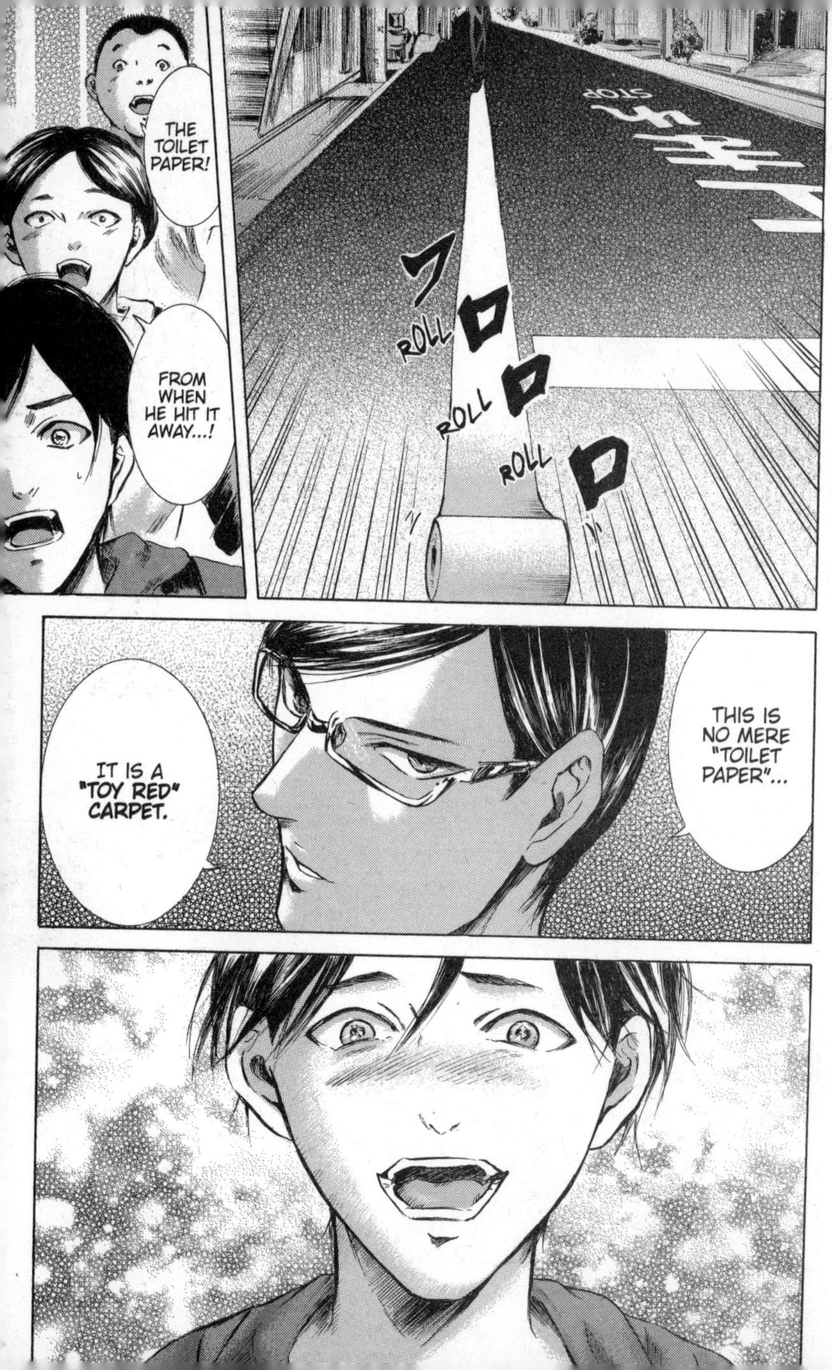
STOP
ROLL
ROLL
ROLL
THE TOILET PAPER!
FROM WHEN HE HIT IT AWAY...!
THIS IS NO MERE "TOILET PAPER"...
IT IS A "TOY RED" CARPET.

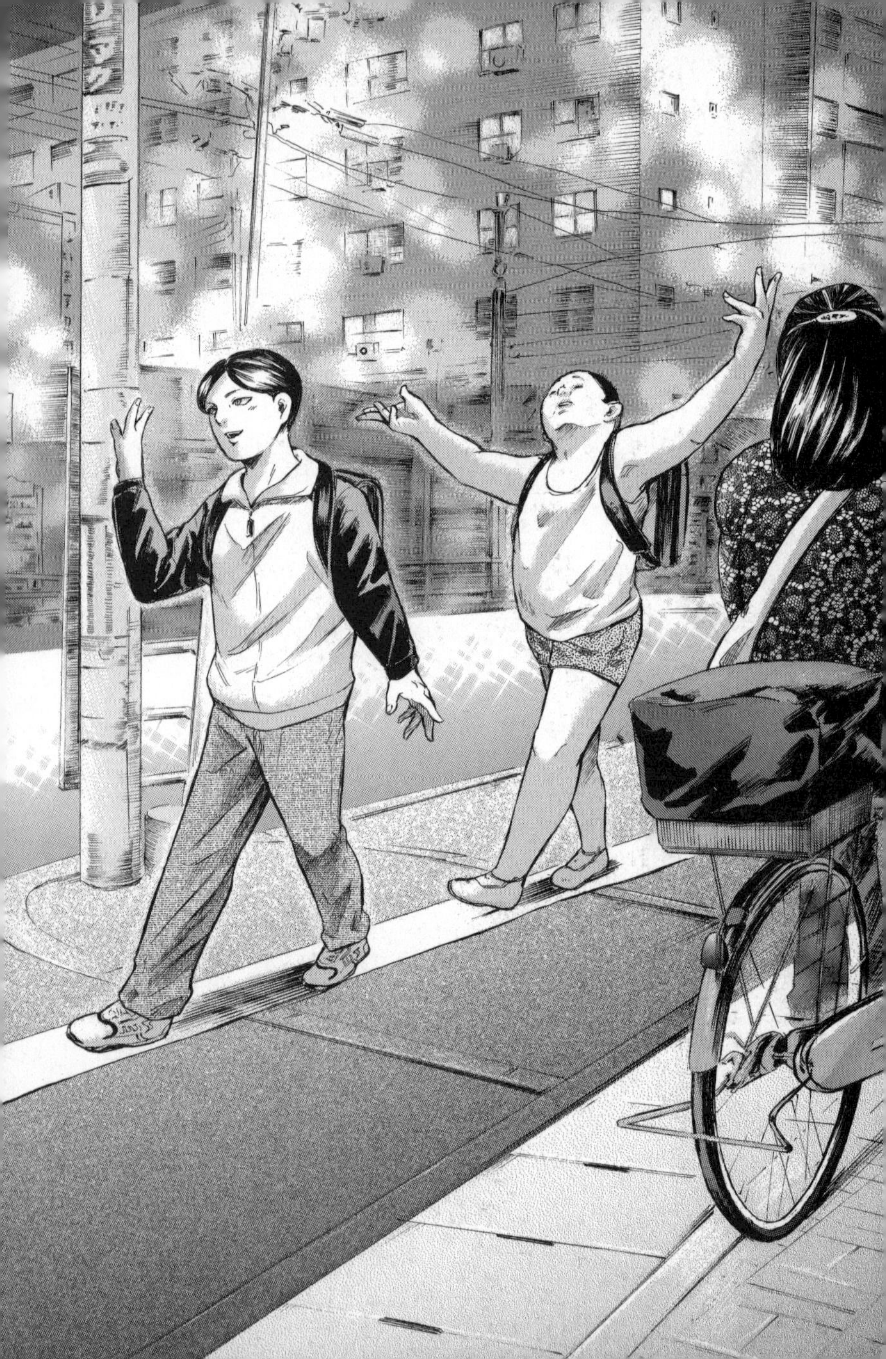

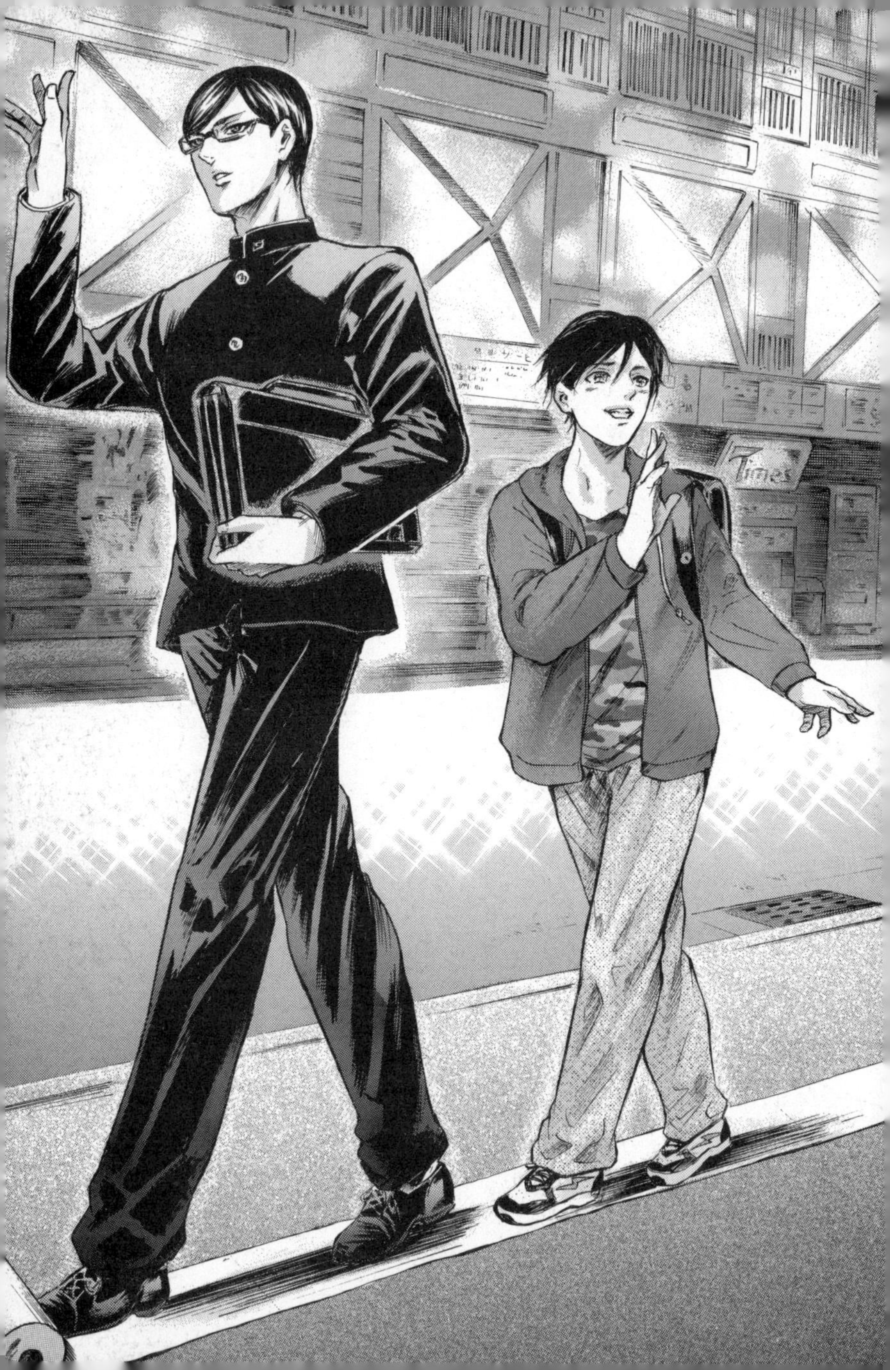
Times

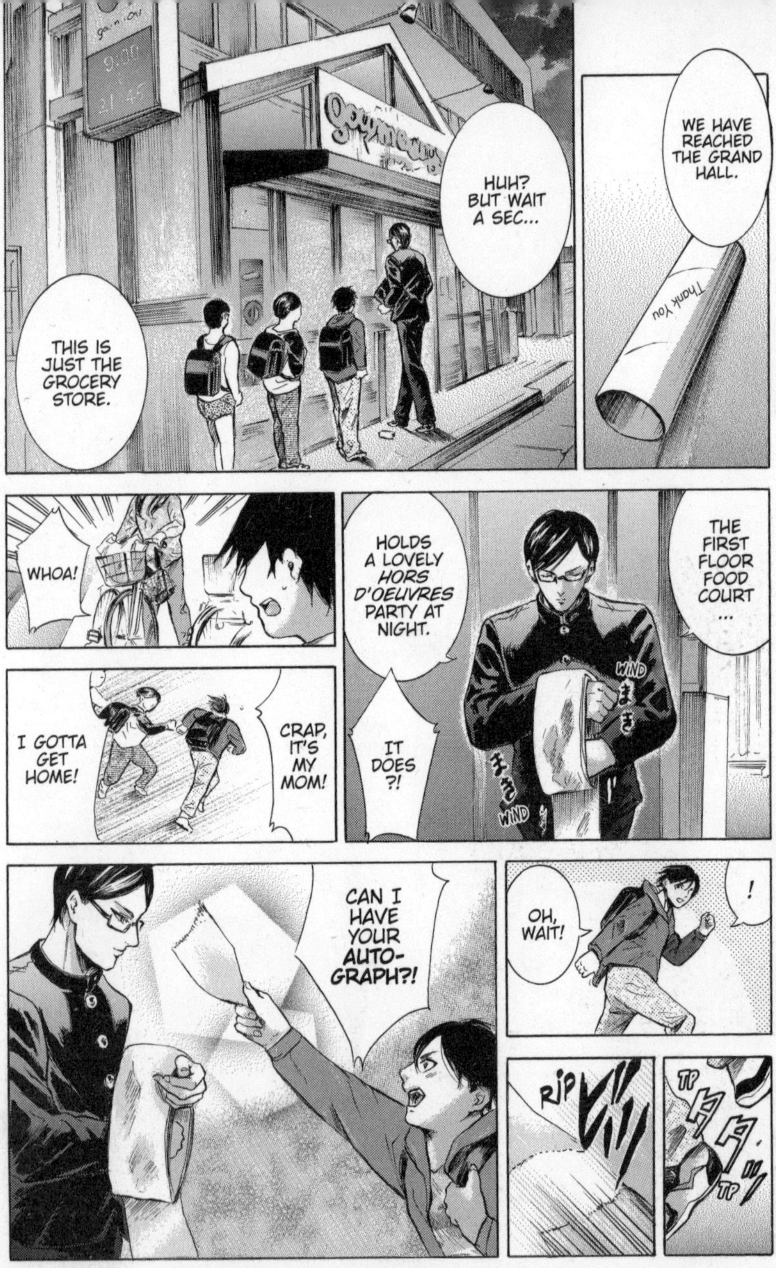
WE HAVE REACHED THE GRAND HALL.
Thank You
HUH? BUT WAIT A SEC...
THIS IS JUST THE GROCERY STORE.
THE FIRST FLOOR FOOD COURT...
HOLDS A LOVELY *HORS D'OEUVRES* PARTY AT NIGHT.
WIND
WIND
IT DOES?!
WHOA!
CRAP, IT'S MY MOM!
I GOTTA GET HOME!
!
OH, WAIT!
TP
TP
RIP
CAN I HAVE YOUR AUTOGRAPH?!

End of Chapter 12

Break Time #1:
Courtyard

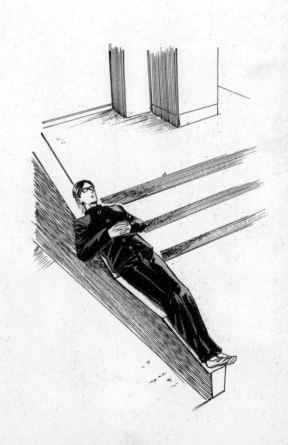

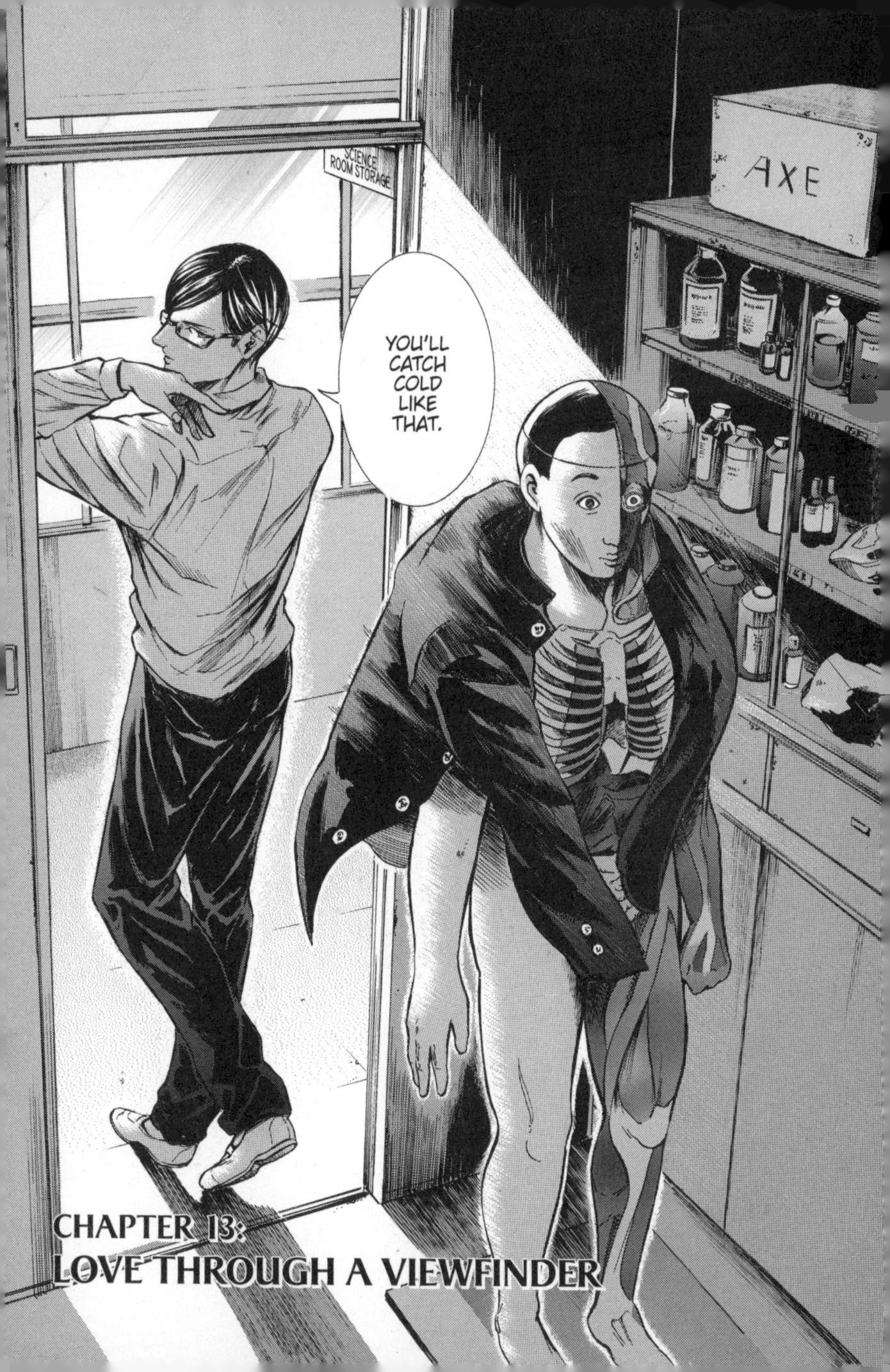
SCIENCE ROOM STORAGE
YOU'LL CATCH COLD LIKE THAT.
AXE
CHAPTER 13:
LOVE THROUGH A VIEWFINDER

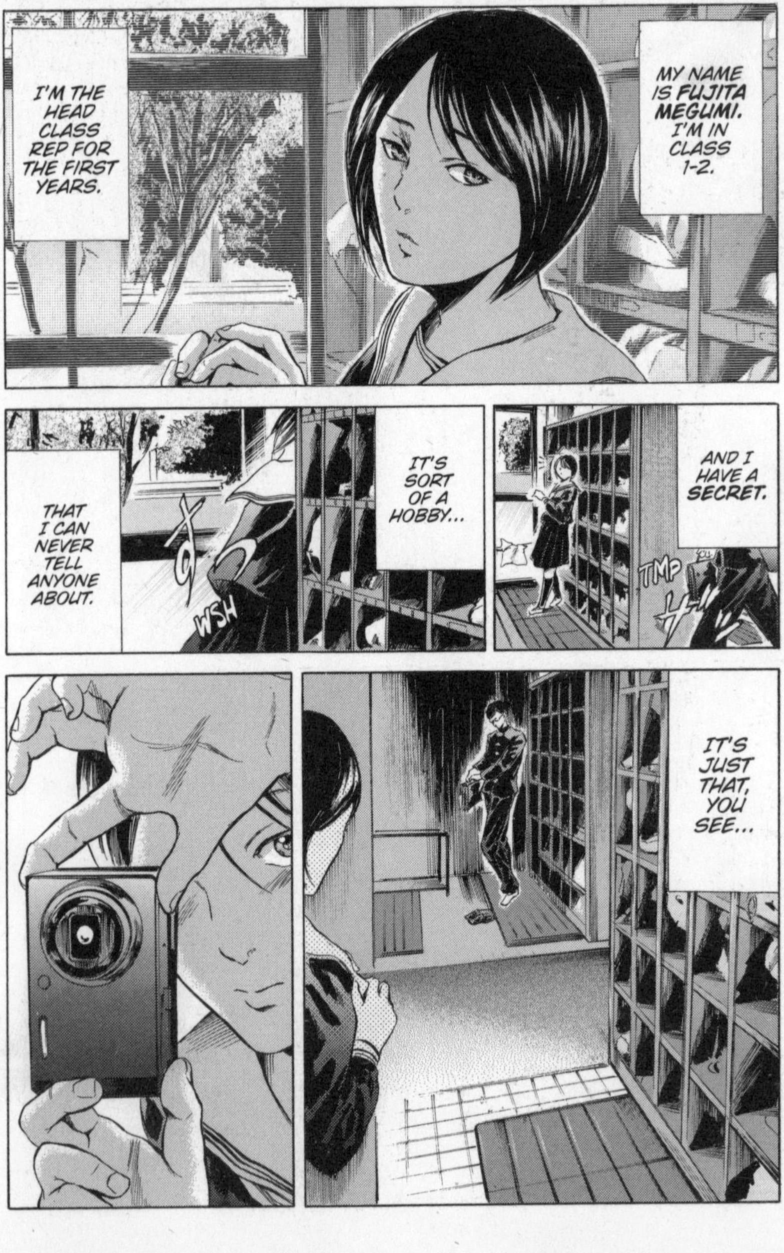
MY NAME IS **FUJITA MEGUMI.** I'M IN CLASS 1-2.
I'M THE HEAD CLASS REP FOR THE FIRST YEARS.
AND I HAVE A **SECRET.**
TMP
IT'S SORT OF A HOBBY...
THAT I CAN NEVER TELL ANYONE ABOUT.
WSH
IT'S JUST THAT, YOU SEE...

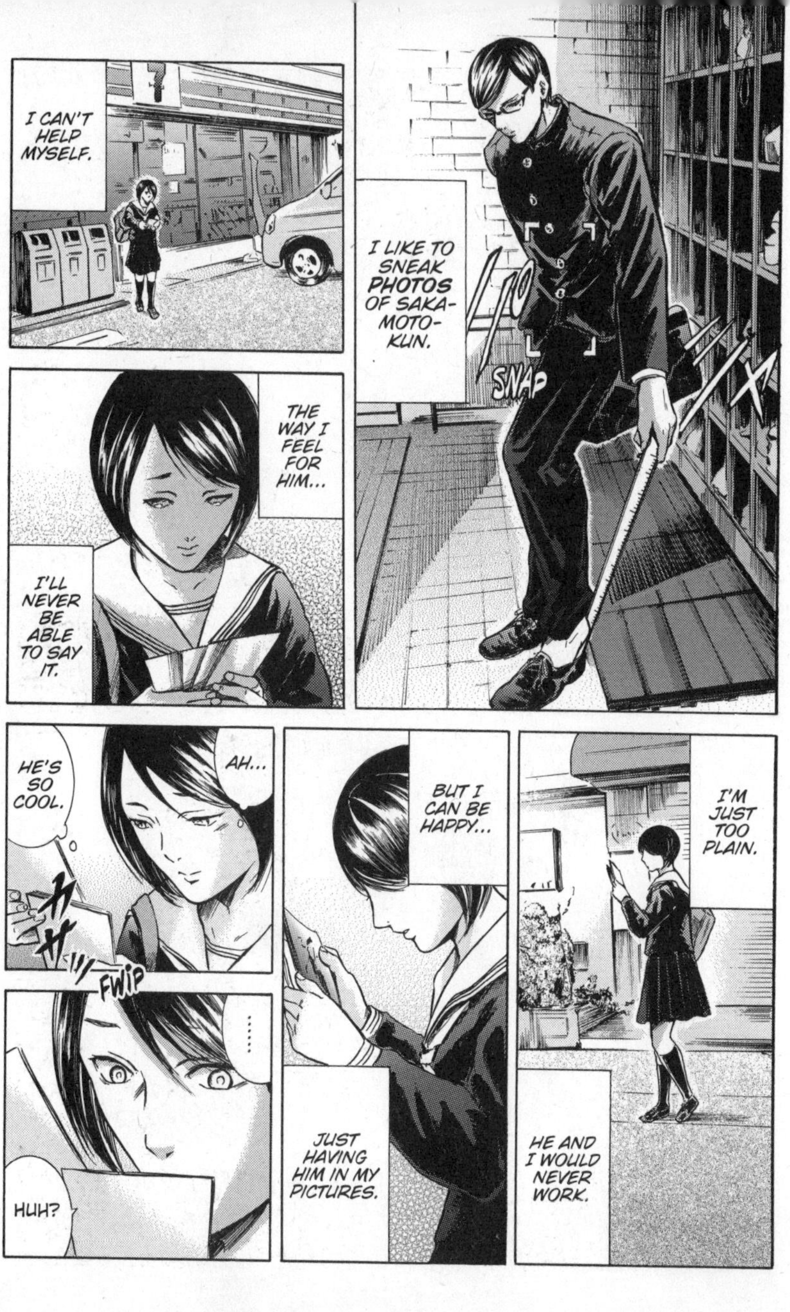

I LIKE TO SNEAK PHOTOS OF SAKA-MOTO-KUN.
SNAP
I CAN'T HELP MYSELF.
THE WAY I FEEL FOR HIM...
I'LL NEVER BE ABLE TO SAY IT.
I'M JUST TOO PLAIN.
HE AND I WOULD NEVER WORK.
BUT I CAN BE HAPPY...
JUST HAVING HIM IN MY PICTURES.
AH...
HE'S SO COOL.
FWIP
......
HUH?

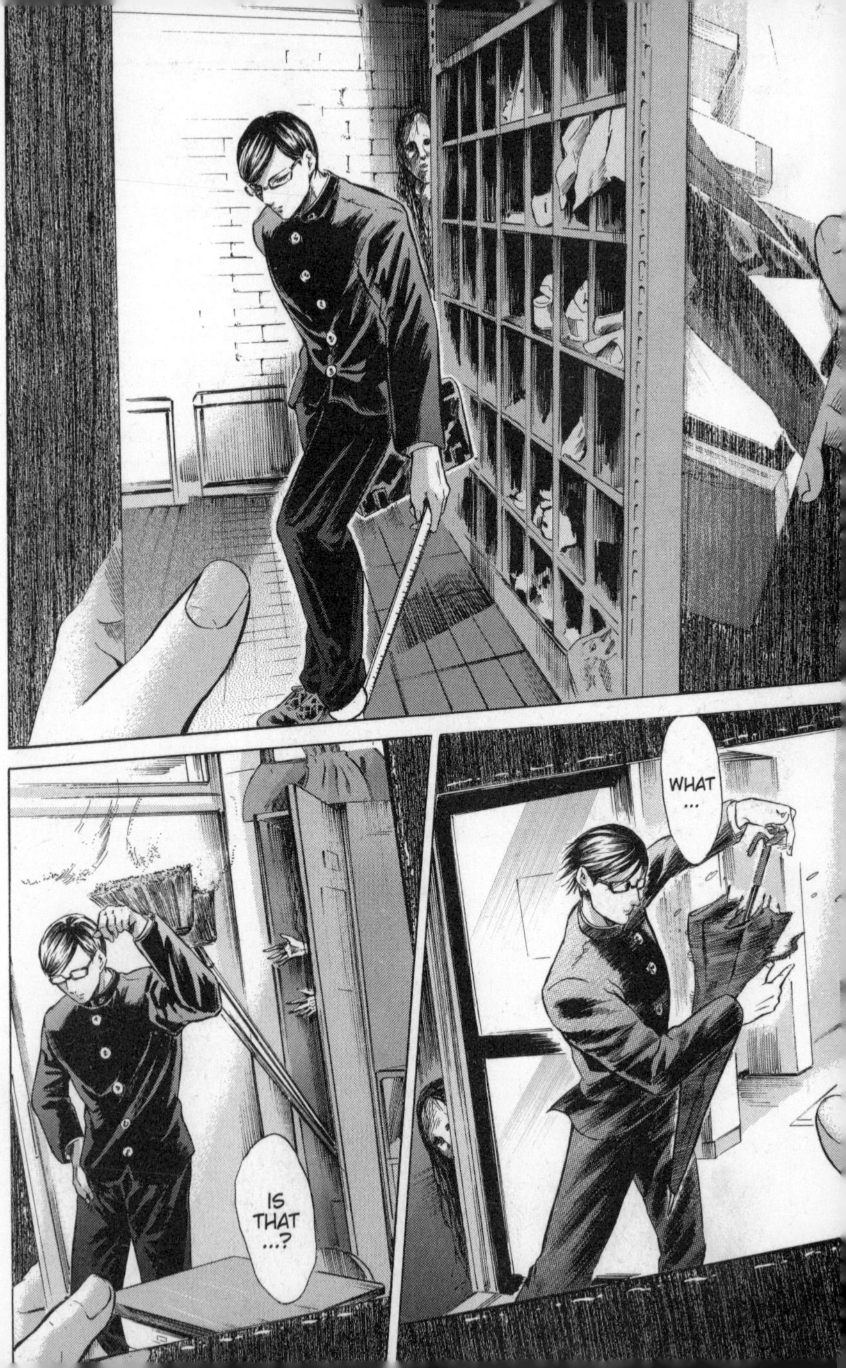
WHAT ...
IS THAT ...?

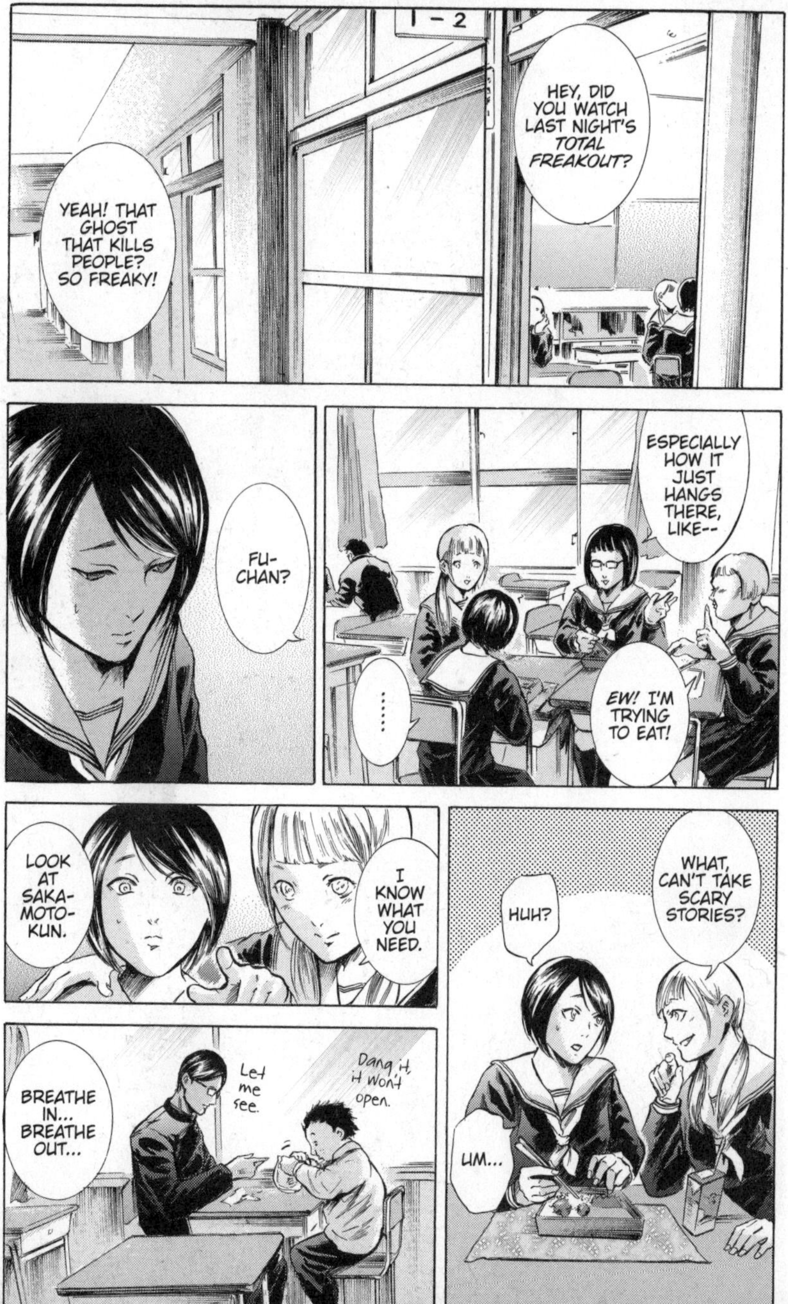
1 – 2
HEY, DID YOU WATCH LAST NIGHT'S *TOTAL FREAKOUT*?
YEAH! THAT GHOST THAT KILLS PEOPLE? SO FREAKY!
ESPECIALLY HOW IT JUST HANGS THERE, LIKE--
EW! I'M TRYING TO EAT!
......
FU-CHAN?
WHAT, CAN'T TAKE SCARY STORIES?
HUH?
UM...
I KNOW WHAT YOU NEED.
LOOK AT SAKAMOTO-KUN.
Dang it, it won't open.
Let me see.
BREATHE IN... BREATHE OUT...

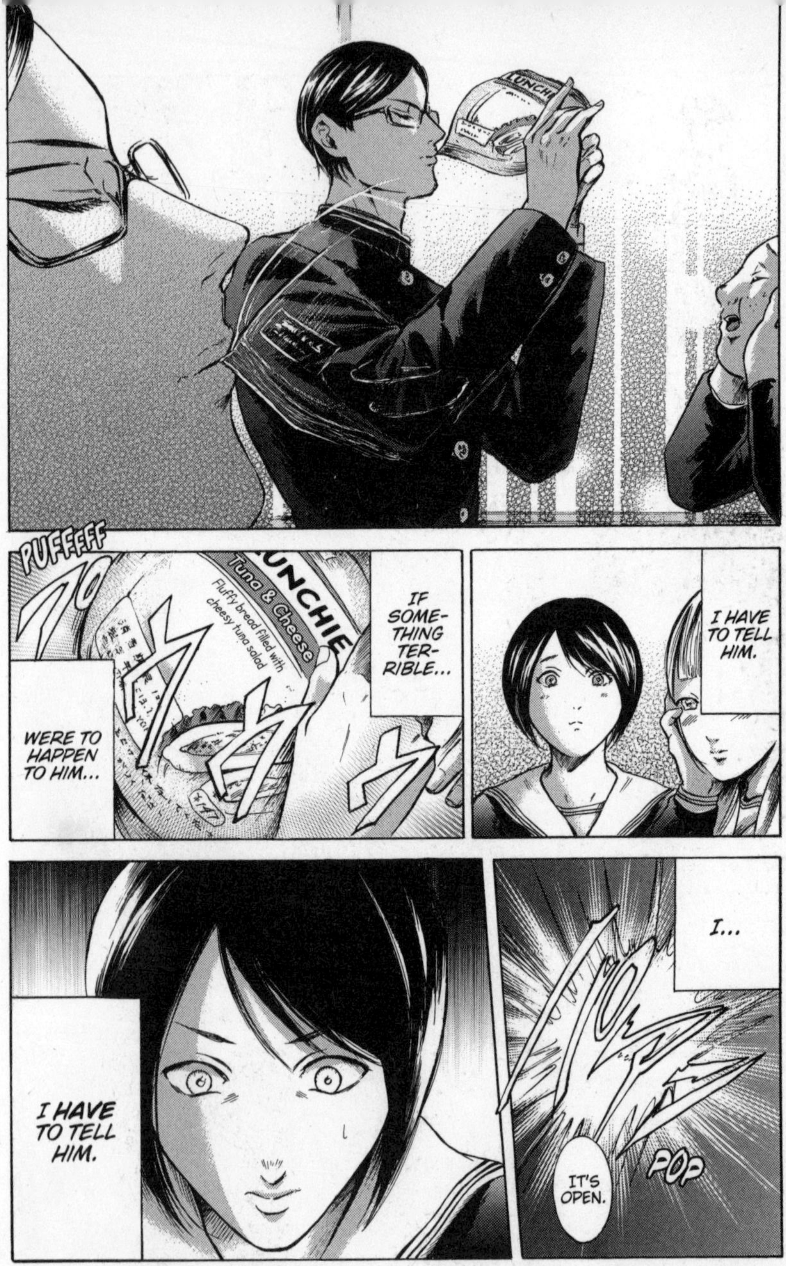
I HAVE TO TELL HIM.
IF SOME-THING TER-RIBLE...
PUFFFFF
LUNCHIE
Tuna & Cheese
Fluffy bread filled with cheesy tuna salad
WERE TO HAPPEN TO HIM...
I...
POP
IT'S OPEN.
I HAVE TO TELL HIM.

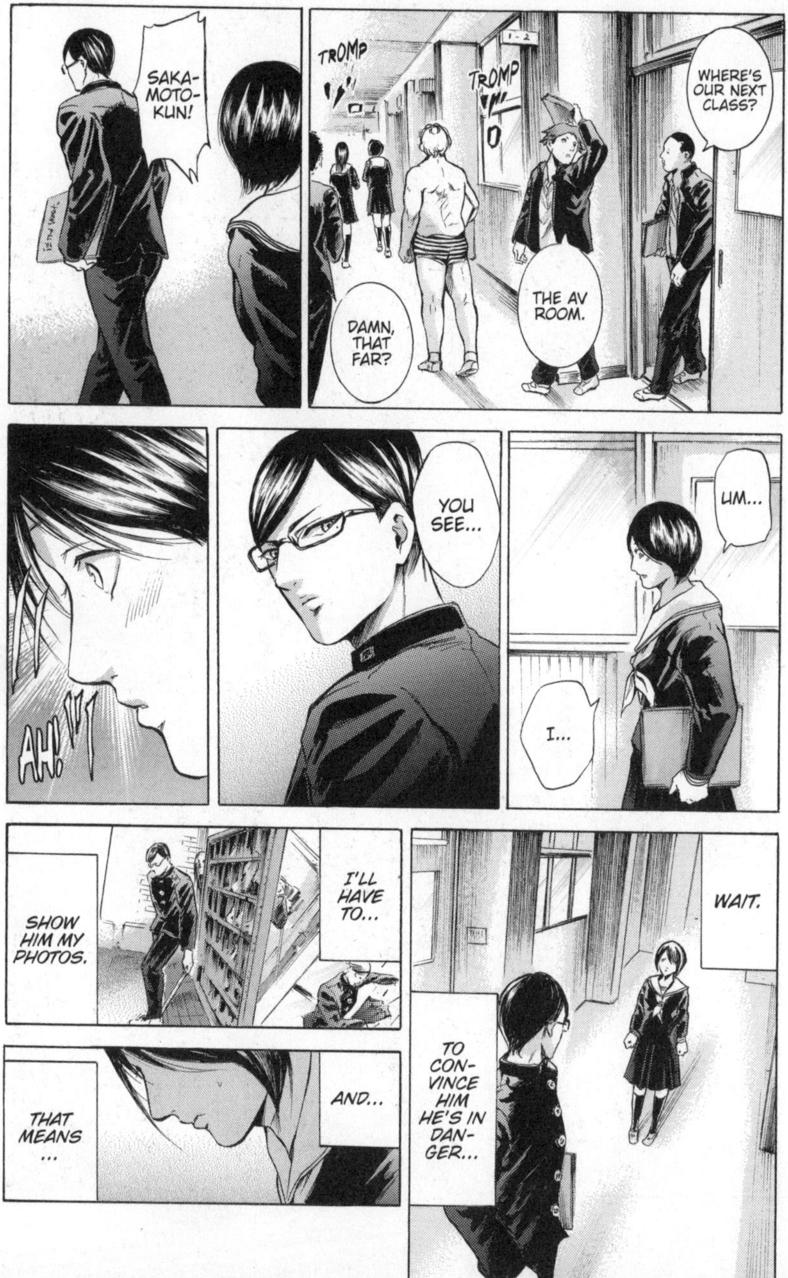
WHERE'S OUR NEXT CLASS?
TROMP
TROMP
THE AV ROOM.
DAMN, THAT FAR?
SAKA-MOTO-KUN!
UM...
I...
YOU SEE...
AH!
WAIT.
TO CON-VINCE HIM HE'S IN DAN-GER...
I'LL HAVE TO...
SHOW HIM MY PHOTOS.
AND...
THAT MEANS ...

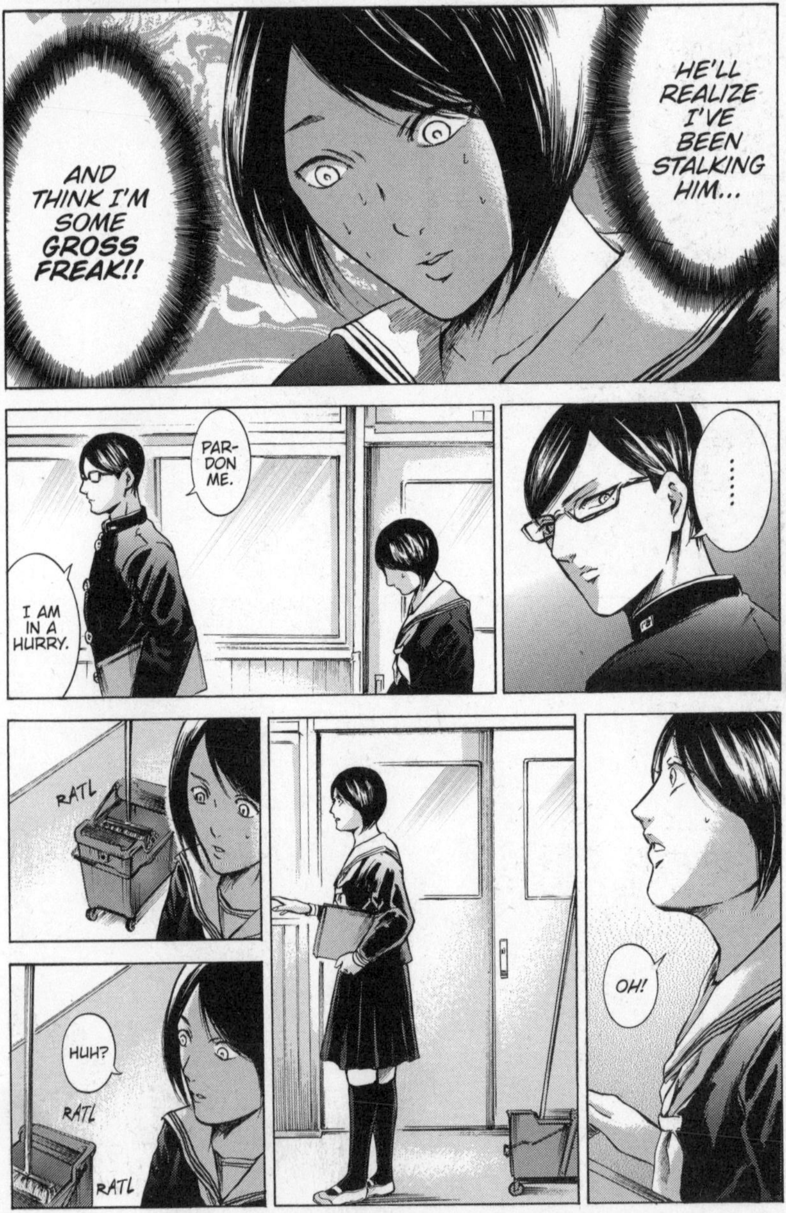
HE'LL REALIZE I'VE BEEN STALKING HIM...
AND THINK I'M SOME GROSS FREAK!!
......
PAR-DON ME.
I AM IN A HURRY.
OH!
RATL
HUH?
RATL
RATL

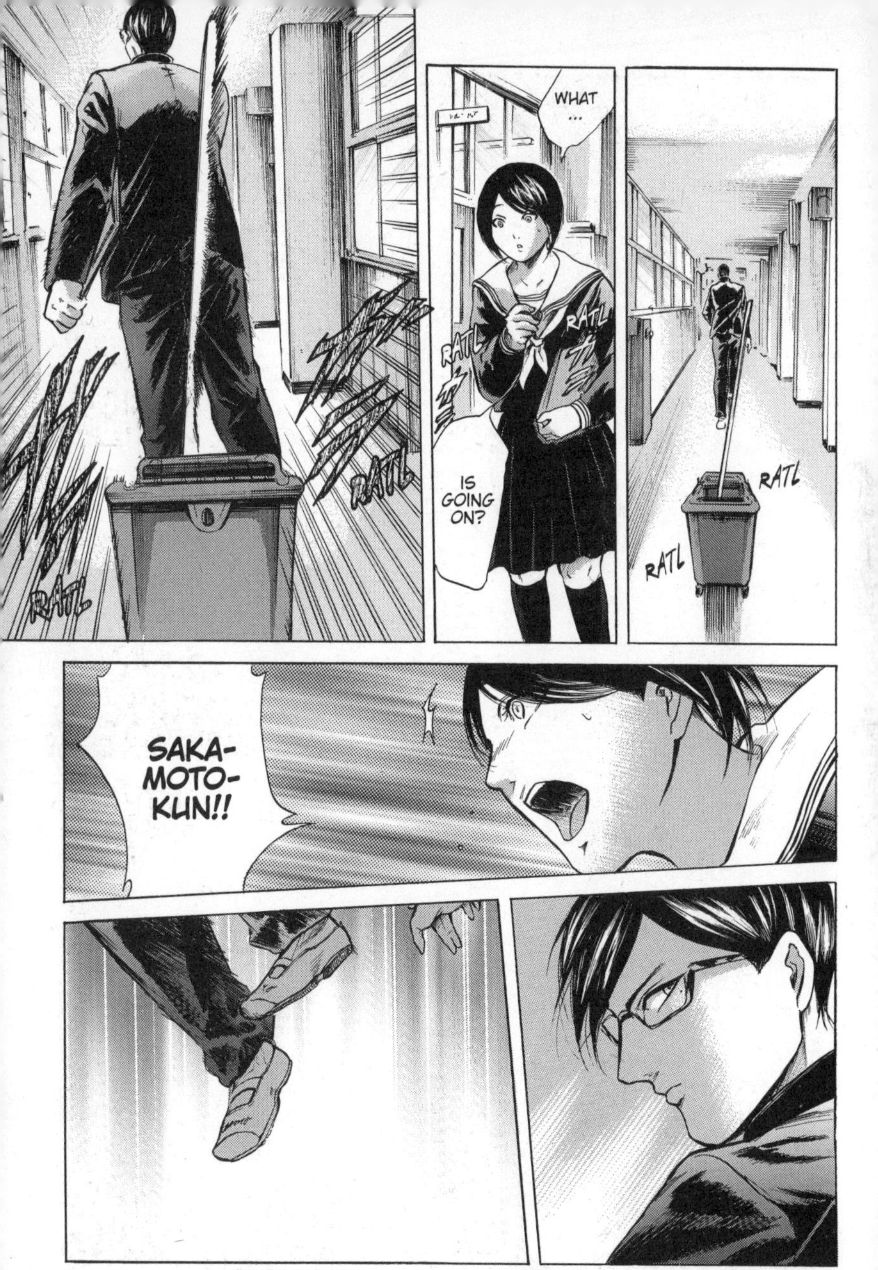
RATL
RATL
WHAT ...
IS GOING ON?
RATL
RATL
RATL
RATL
SAKA-MOTO-KUN!!

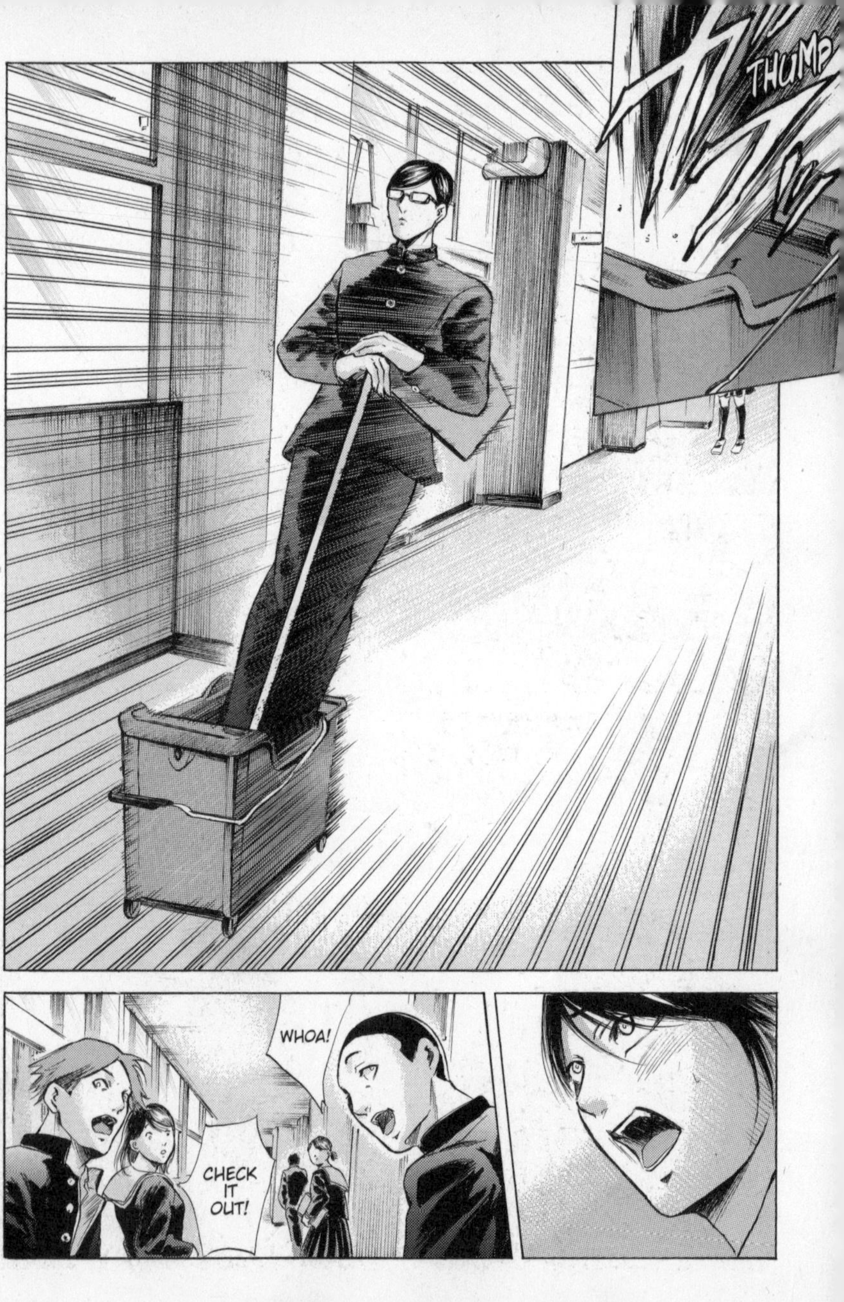
THUMP
WHOA!
CHECK IT OUT!

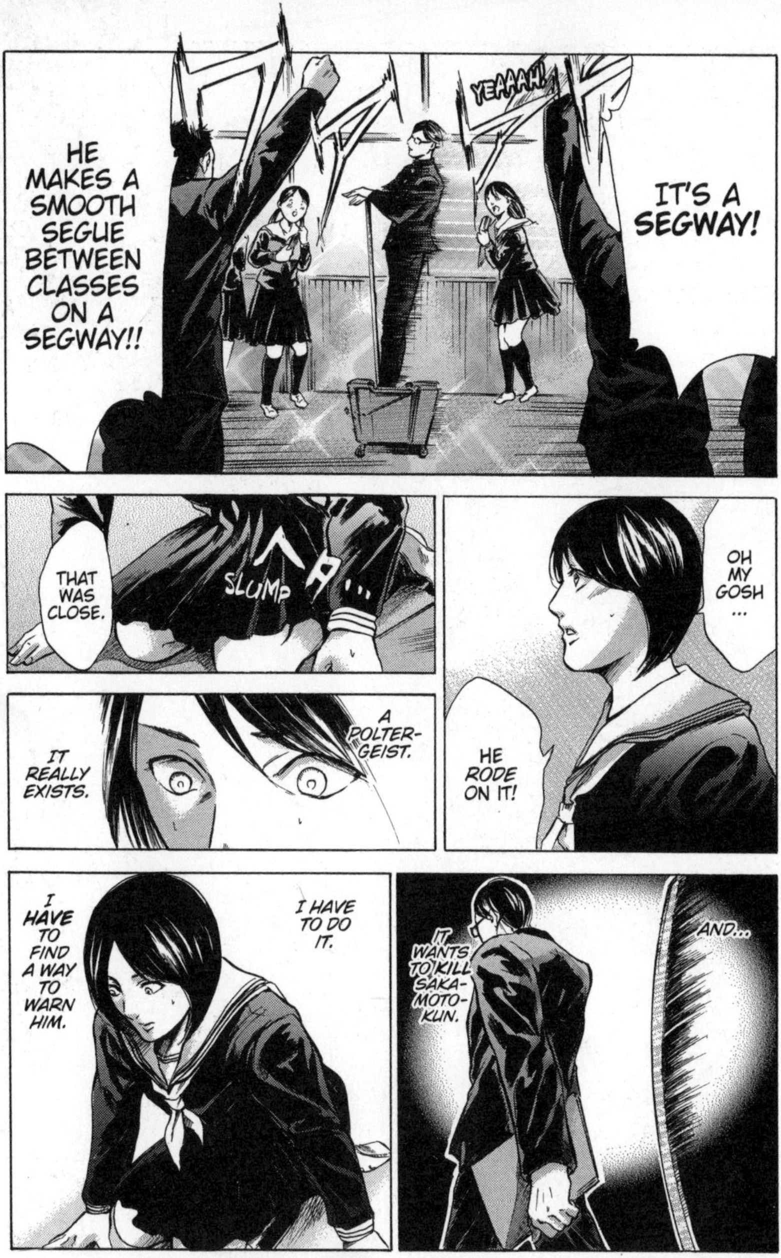
YEAAAH!
IT'S A SEGWAY!
HE MAKES A SMOOTH SEGUE BETWEEN CLASSES ON A SEGWAY!!
OH MY GOSH ...
HE RODE ON IT!
SLUMP
THAT WAS CLOSE.
A POLTER-GEIST.
IT REALLY EXISTS.
AND...
IT WANTS TO KILL SAKA-MOTO-KUN.
I HAVE TO DO IT.
I **HAVE** TO FIND A WAY TO WARN HIM.

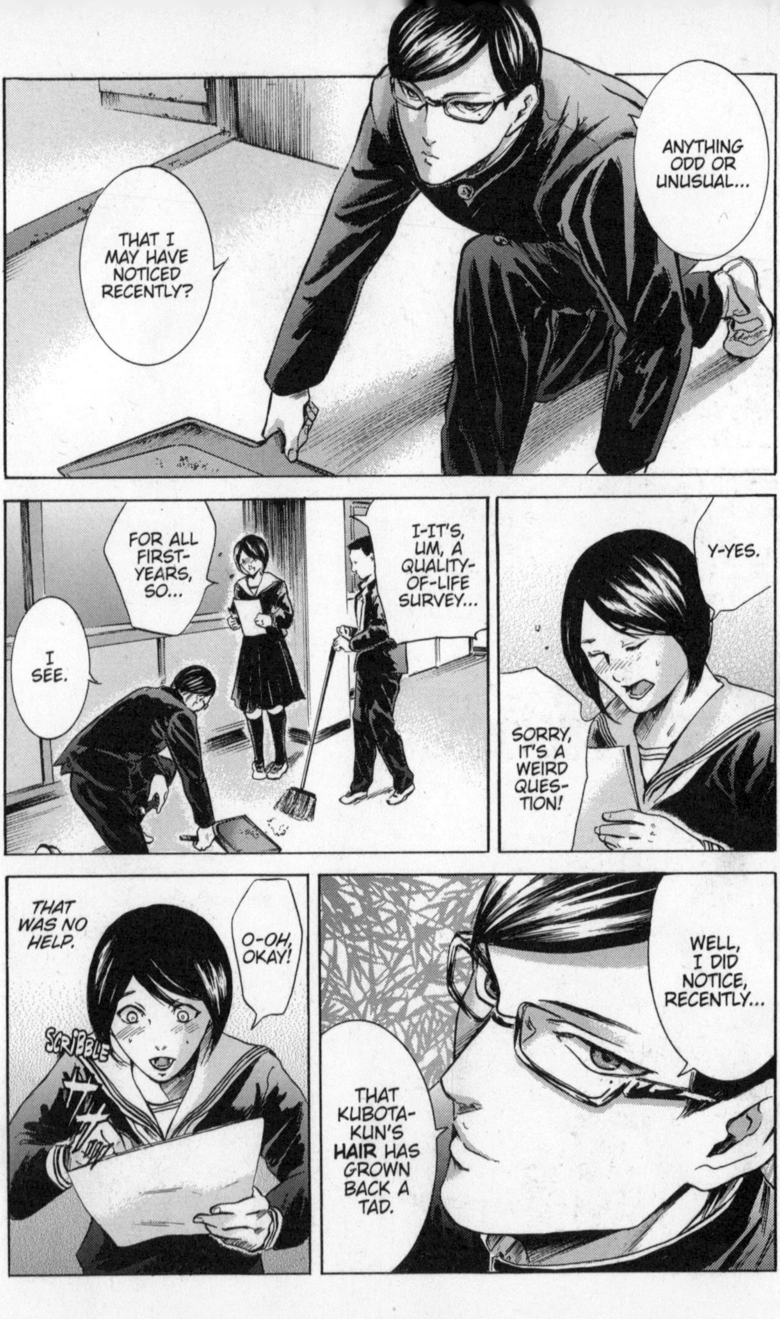
ANYTHING ODD OR UNUSUAL...
THAT I MAY HAVE NOTICED RECENTLY?
Y-YES.
SORRY, IT'S A WEIRD QUESTION!
I-IT'S, UM, A QUALITY-OF-LIFE SURVEY...
FOR ALL FIRST-YEARS, SO...
I SEE.
WELL, I DID NOTICE, RECENTLY...
THAT KUBOTA-KUN'S **HAIR** HAS GROWN BACK A TAD.
O-OH, OKAY!
THAT WAS NO HELP.
SCRIBBLE

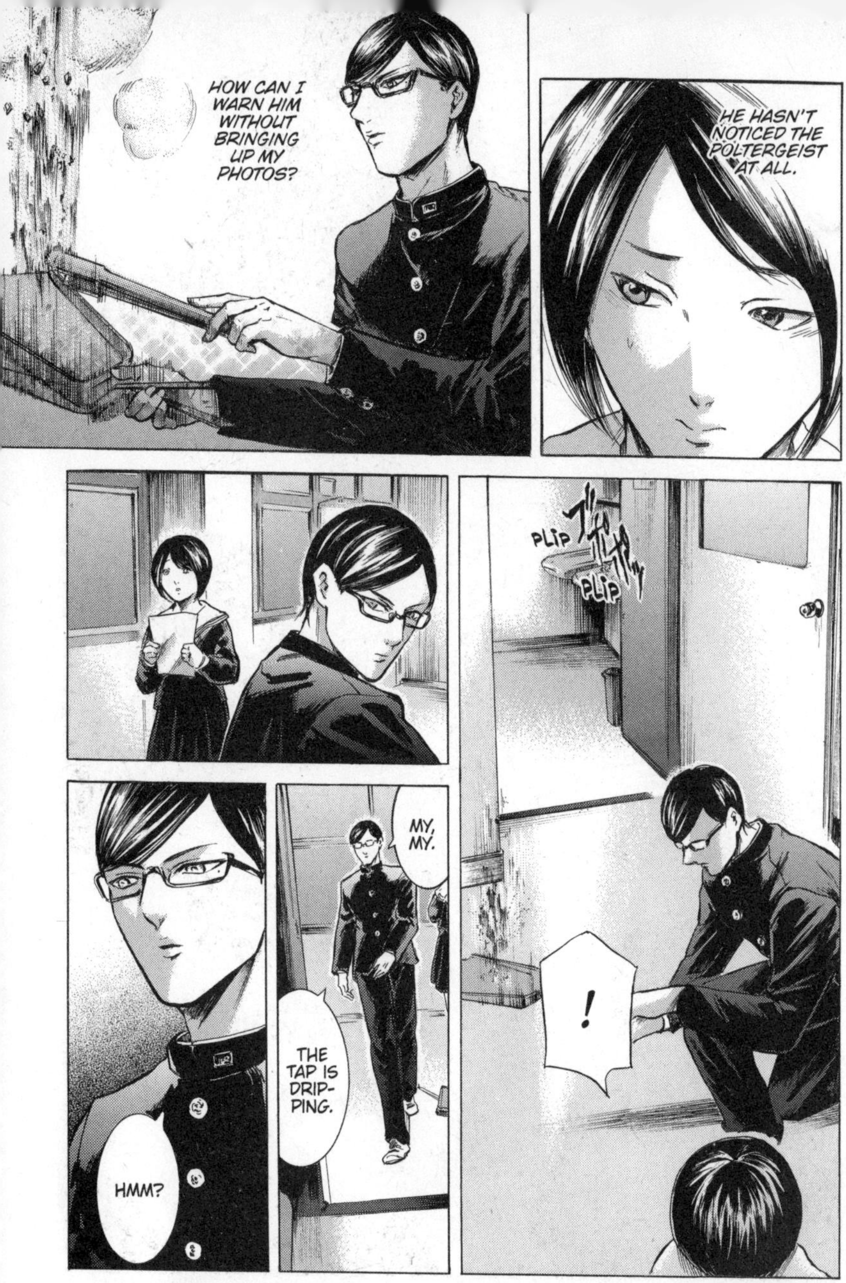
HE HASN'T NOTICED THE POLTERGEIST AT ALL.
HOW CAN I WARN HIM WITHOUT BRINGING UP MY PHOTOS?
PLIP
PLIP
!
MY, MY.
THE TAP IS DRIP-PING.
HMM?

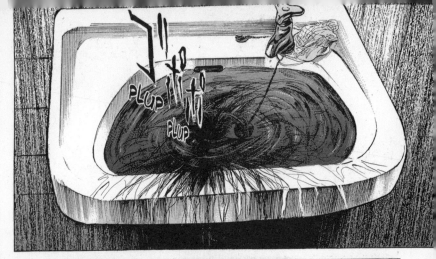

EW
!!

I-IS
THAT...
HAIR?!

?!

SPLOOSH

SWFF

BLOOSH

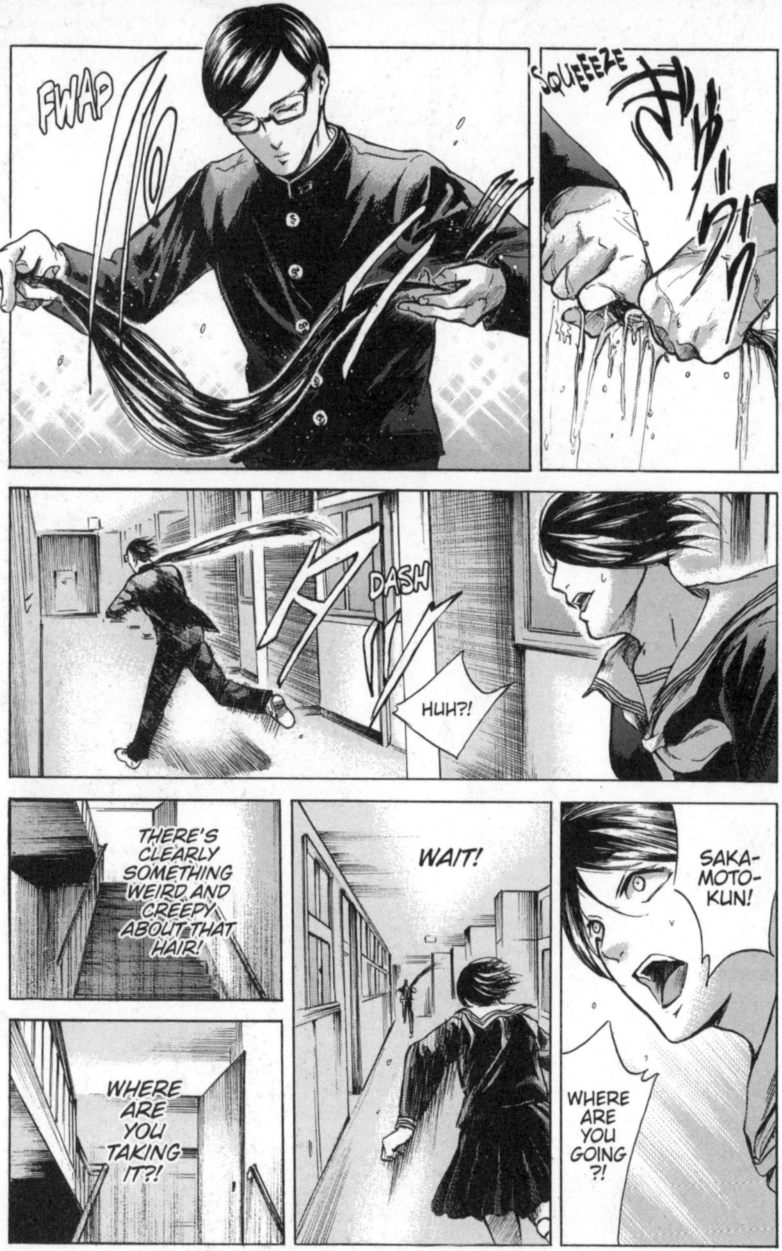
SQUEEEZE
FWAP
DASH
HUH?!
SAKA-MOTO-KUN!
WHERE ARE YOU GOING?!
WAIT!
THERE'S CLEARLY SOMETHING WEIRD AND CREEPY ABOUT THAT HAIR!
WHERE ARE YOU TAKING IT?!

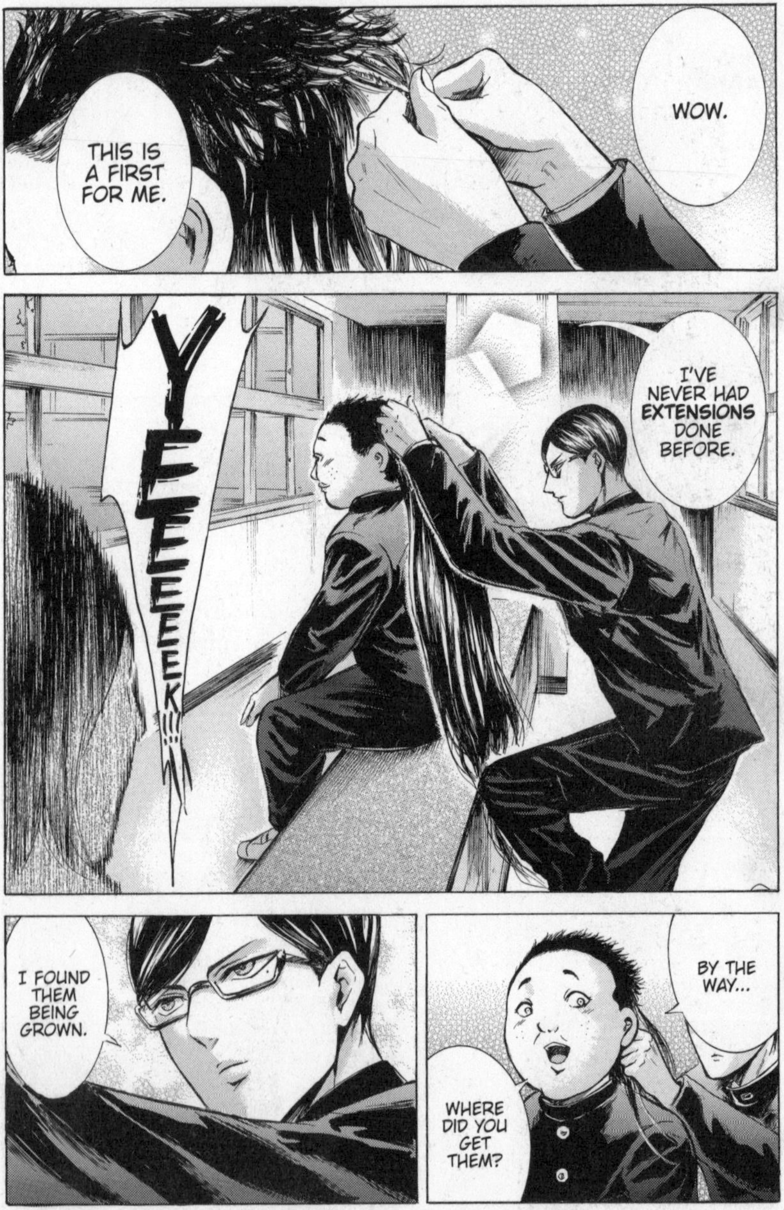
WOW.
THIS IS A FIRST FOR ME.
I'VE NEVER HAD EXTENSIONS DONE BEFORE.
YEEEEEEEK!!!
BY THE WAY...
WHERE DID YOU GET THEM?
I FOUND THEM BEING GROWN.

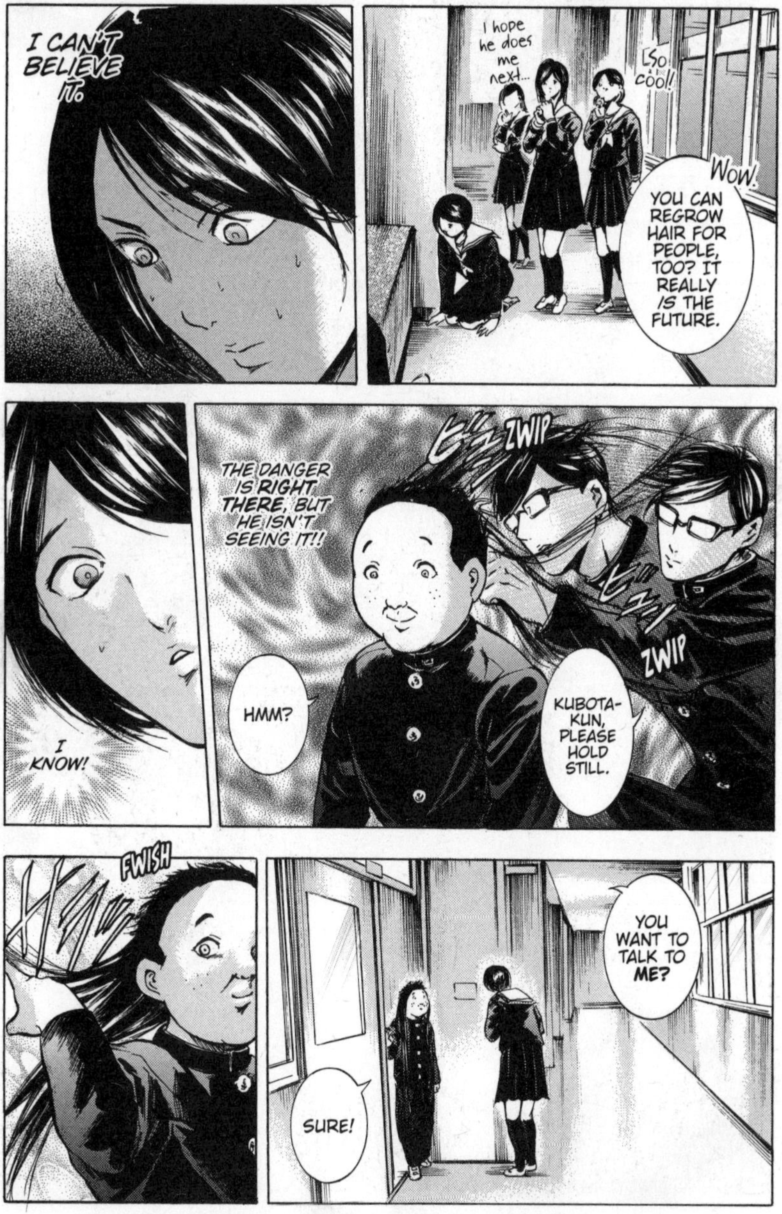
So cool!!
I hope he does me next...
WOW.
YOU CAN REGROW HAIR FOR PEOPLE, TOO? IT REALLY IS THE FUTURE.
I CAN'T BELIEVE IT.
ZWIP
THE DANGER IS RIGHT THERE, BUT HE ISN'T SEEING IT!!
ZWIP
KUBOTA-KUN, PLEASE HOLD STILL.
HMM?
I KNOW!
YOU WANT TO TALK TO ME?
SURE!
FWISH

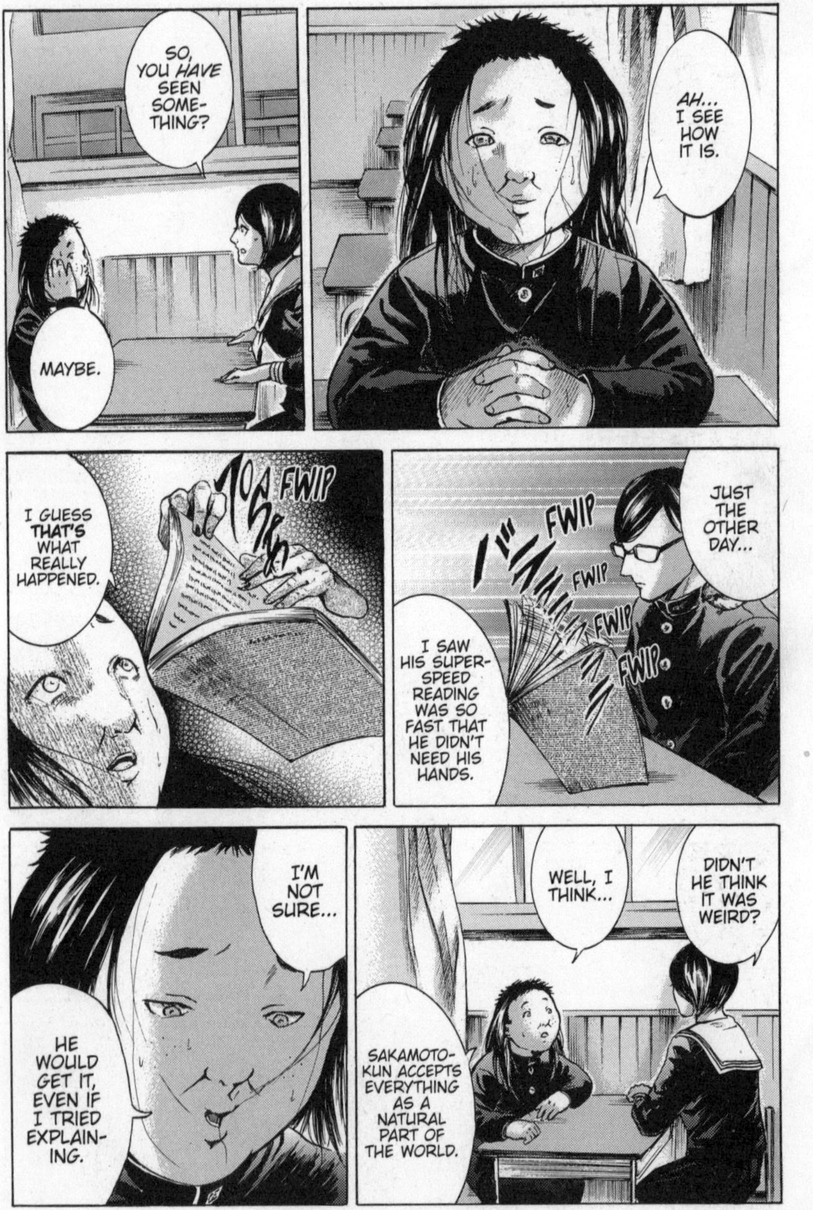
AH... I SEE HOW IT IS.
SO, YOU HAVE SEEN SOME-THING?
MAYBE.
JUST THE OTHER DAY...
FWIP
FWIP
FWIP
FWIP
I SAW HIS SUPER-SPEED READING WAS SO FAST THAT HE DIDN'T NEED HIS HANDS.
FWIP
I GUESS THAT'S WHAT REALLY HAPPENED.
DIDN'T HE THINK IT WAS WEIRD?
WELL, I THINK...
SAKAMOTO-KUN ACCEPTS EVERYTHING AS A NATURAL PART OF THE WORLD.
I'M NOT SURE...
HE WOULD GET IT, EVEN IF I TRIED EXPLAIN-ING.

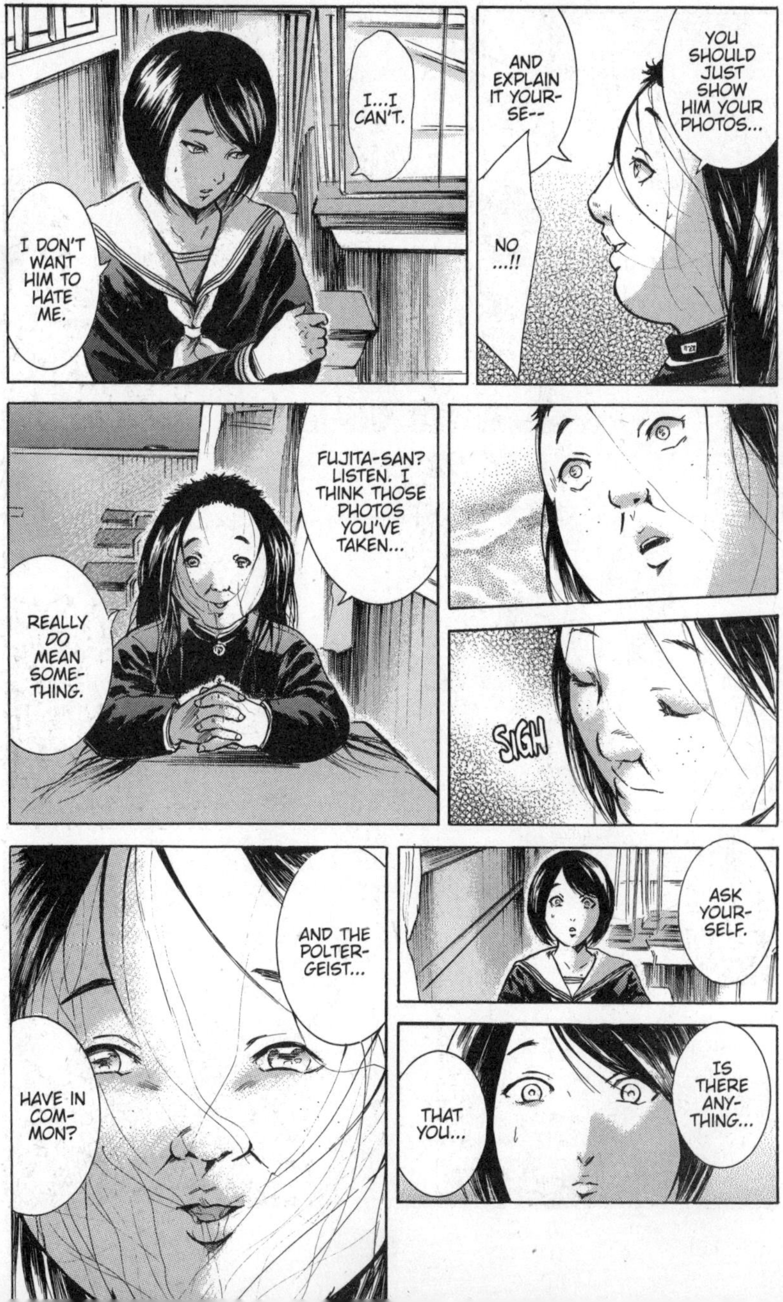
YOU SHOULD JUST SHOW HIM YOUR PHOTOS...
AND EXPLAIN IT YOURSE--
NO ...!!
I...I CAN'T.
I DON'T WANT HIM TO HATE ME.
SIGH
FUJITA-SAN? LISTEN. I THINK THOSE PHOTOS YOU'VE TAKEN...
REALLY *DO* MEAN SOMETHING.
ASK YOURSELF.
IS THERE ANYTHING...
THAT YOU...
AND THE POLTERGEIST...
HAVE IN COMMON?

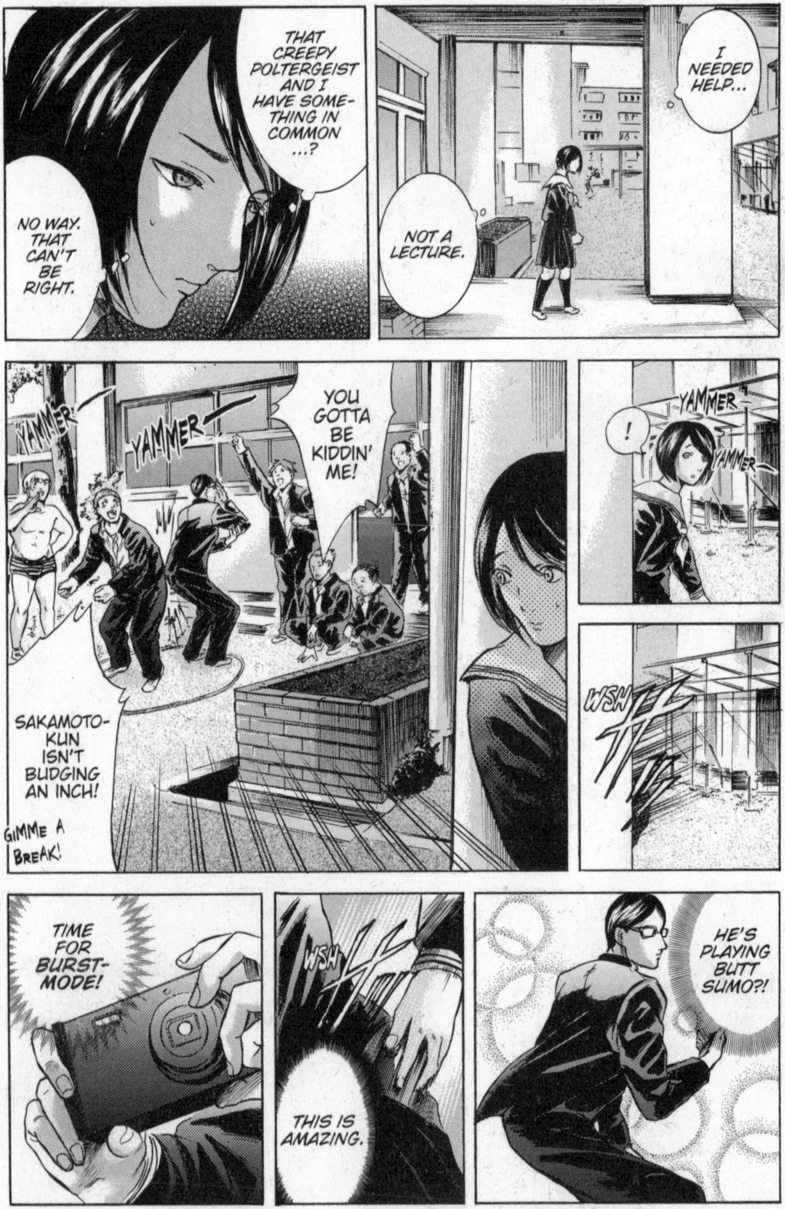
I NEEDED HELP...
NOT A LECTURE.
THAT CREEPY POLTERGEIST AND I HAVE SOMETHING IN COMMON ...?
NO WAY. THAT CAN'T BE RIGHT.
!
YAMMER
YAMMER
WSH
YOU GOTTA BE KIDDIN' ME!
YAMMER
YAMMER
SAKAMOTO-KUN ISN'T BUDGING AN INCH!
GIMME A BREAK!
HE'S PLAYING BUTT SUMO?!
WSH
THIS IS AMAZING.
TIME FOR BURST-MODE!

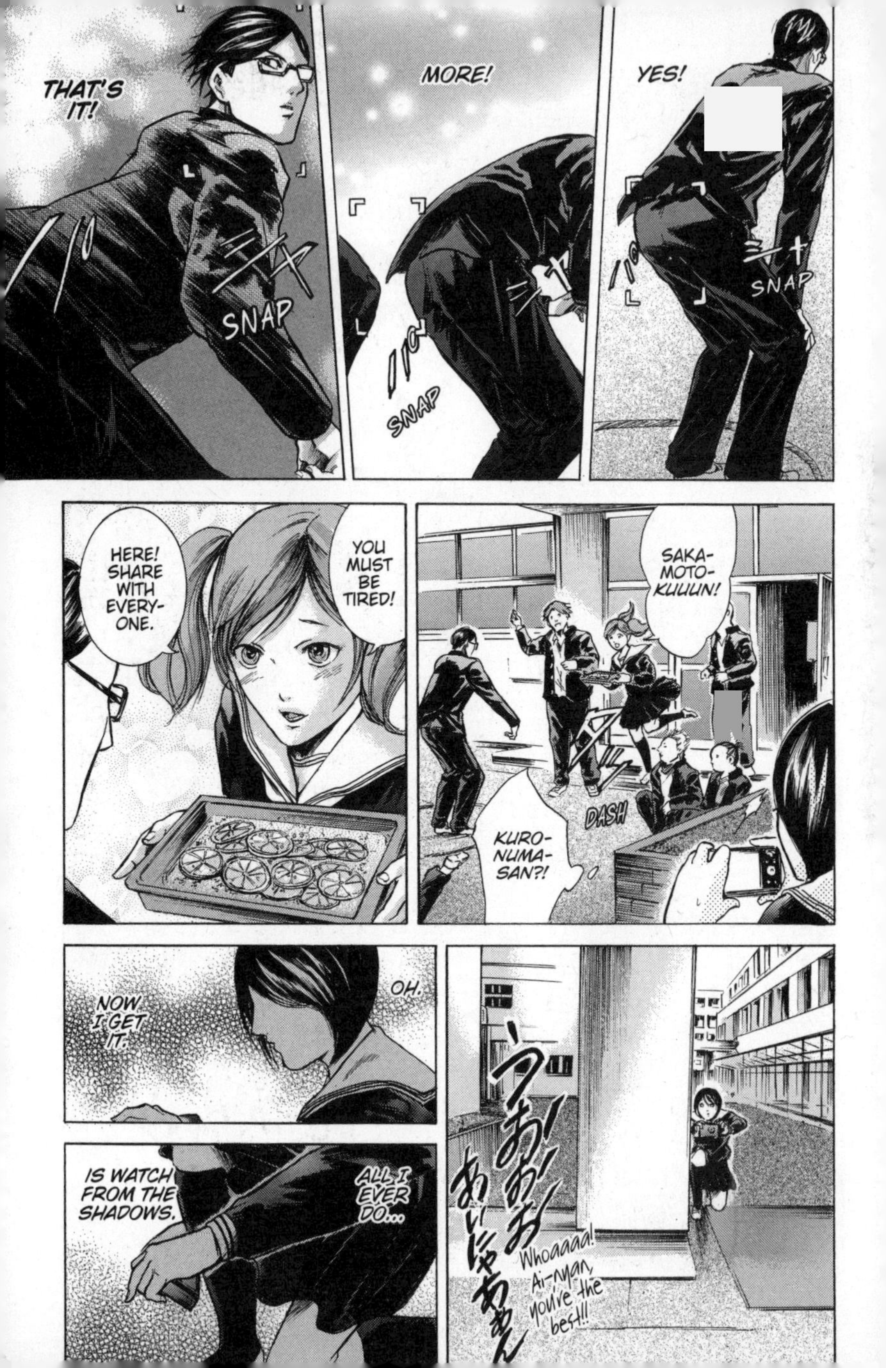
YES!
SNAP
MORE!
SNAP
THAT'S IT!
SNAP
SAKA-MOTO-KUUUN!
DASH
KURO-NUMA-SAN?!
YOU MUST BE TIRED!
HERE! SHARE WITH EVERY-ONE.
Whoaaaa! Ai-nyan, you're the best!!
OH.
NOW I GET IT.
ALL I EVER DO...
IS WATCH FROM THE SHADOWS.

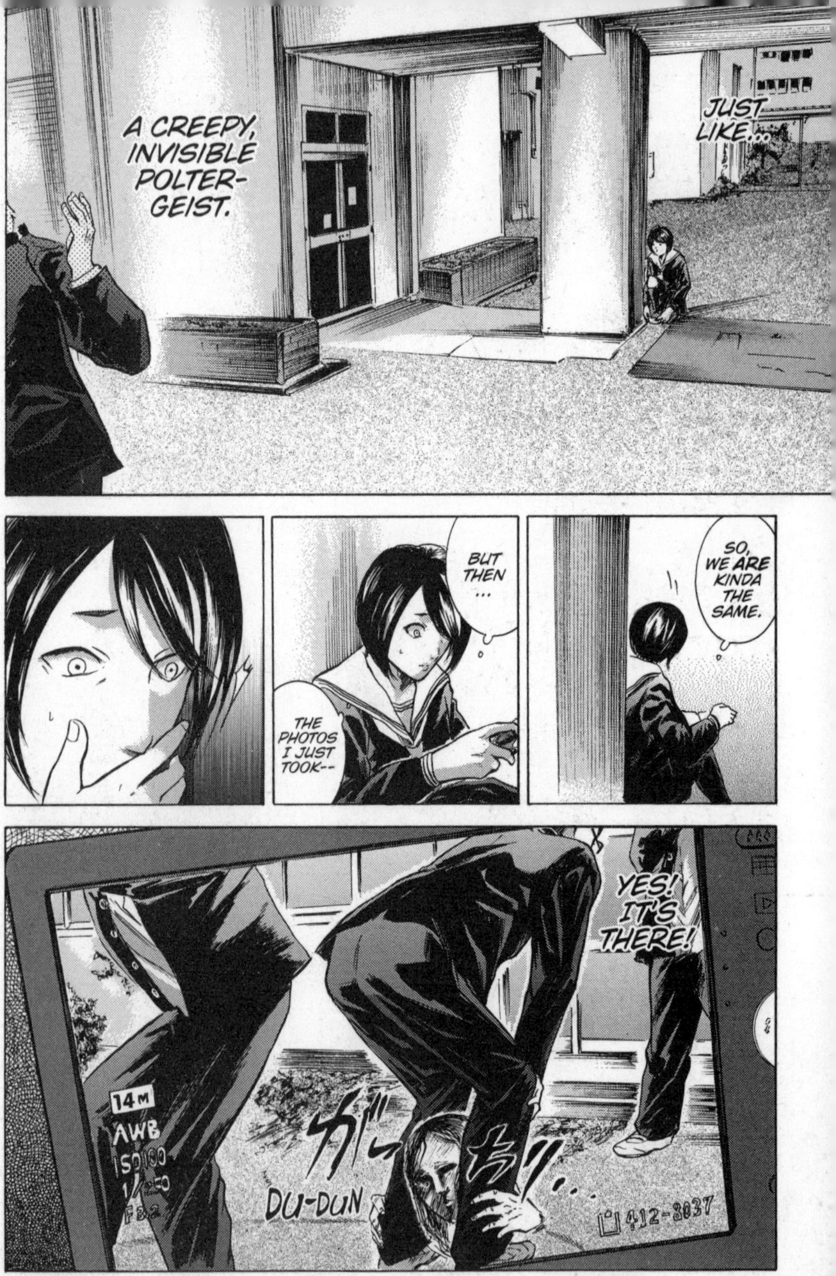
JUST LIKE...
A CREEPY, INVISIBLE POLTER-GEIST.
SO, WE ARE KINDA THE SAME.
BUT THEN ...
THE PHOTOS I JUST TOOK--
YES! IT'S THERE!
14M
AWB
412-3037
DU-DUN

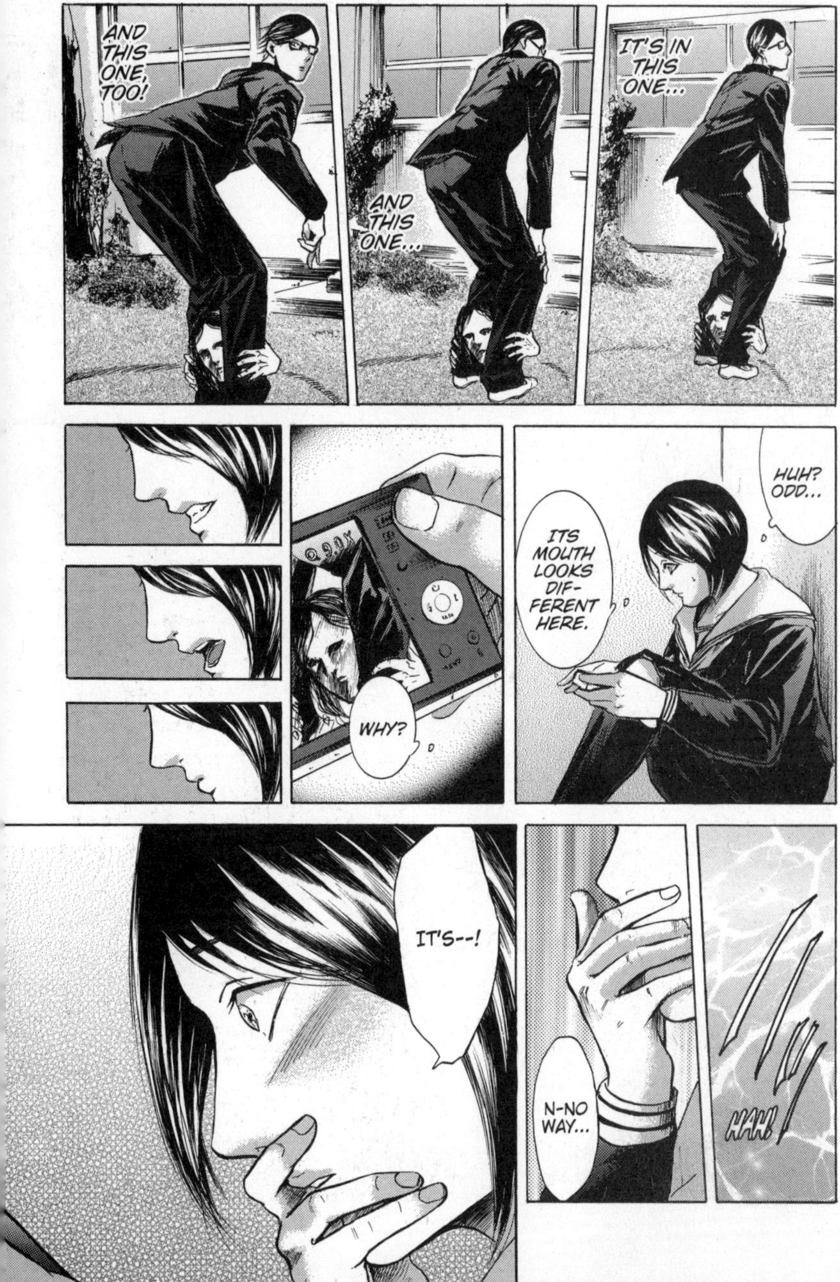
IT'S IN THIS ONE...
AND THIS ONE...
AND THIS ONE, TOO!
HUH? ODD...
ITS MOUTH LOOKS DIF-FERENT HERE.
WHY?
HAH!
N-NO WAY...
IT'S--!

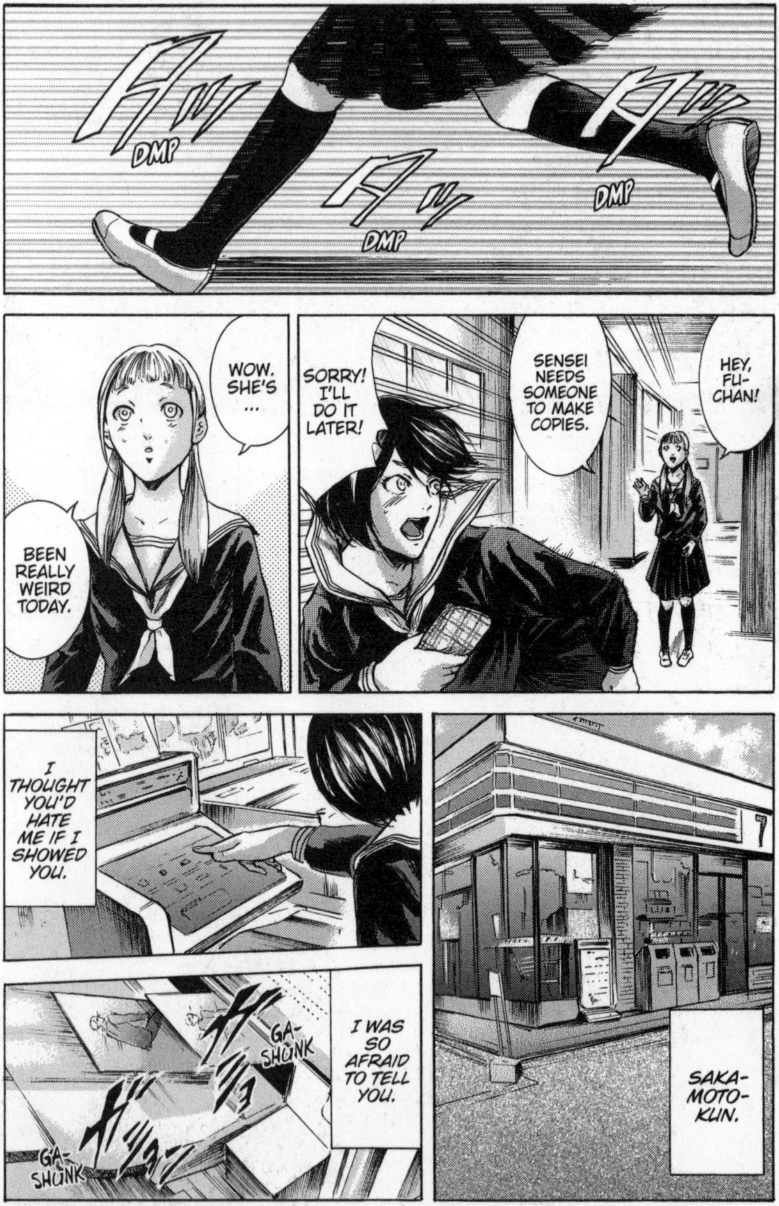
DMP
DMP
DMP
HEY, FU-CHAN!
SENSEI NEEDS SOMEONE TO MAKE COPIES.
SORRY! I'LL DO IT LATER!
WOW. SHE'S ...
BEEN REALLY WEIRD TODAY.
SAKA-MOTO-KUN.
I THOUGHT YOU'D HATE ME IF I SHOWED YOU.
I WAS SO AFRAID TO TELL YOU.
GA-SHUNK
GA-SHUNK

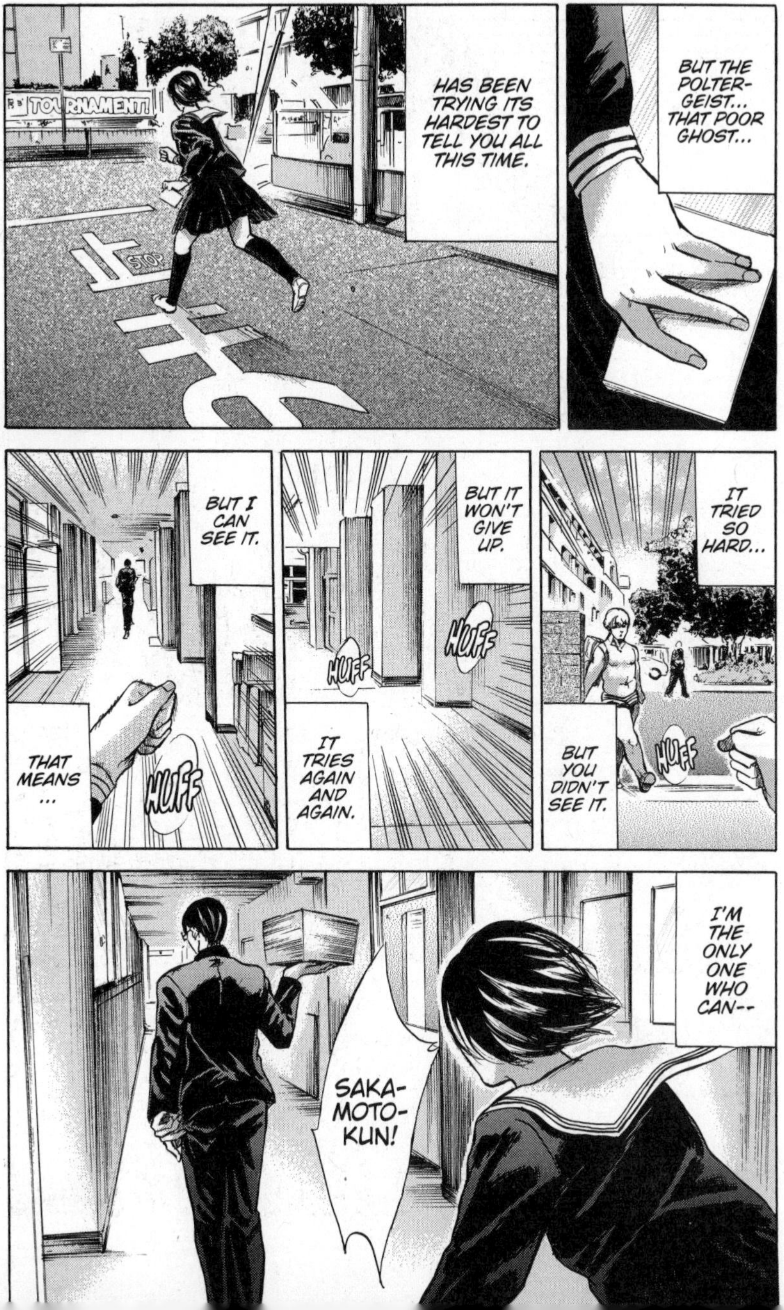
BUT THE POLTER-GEIST... THAT POOR GHOST...
HAS BEEN TRYING ITS HARDEST TO TELL YOU ALL THIS TIME.
TOURNAMENT!
STOP
IT TRIED SO HARD...
HUFF
BUT YOU DIDN'T SEE IT.
BUT IT WON'T GIVE UP.
HUFF
HUFF
IT TRIES AGAIN AND AGAIN.
BUT I CAN SEE IT.
THAT MEANS ...
HUFF
I'M THE ONLY ONE WHO CAN--
SAKA-MOTO-KUN!

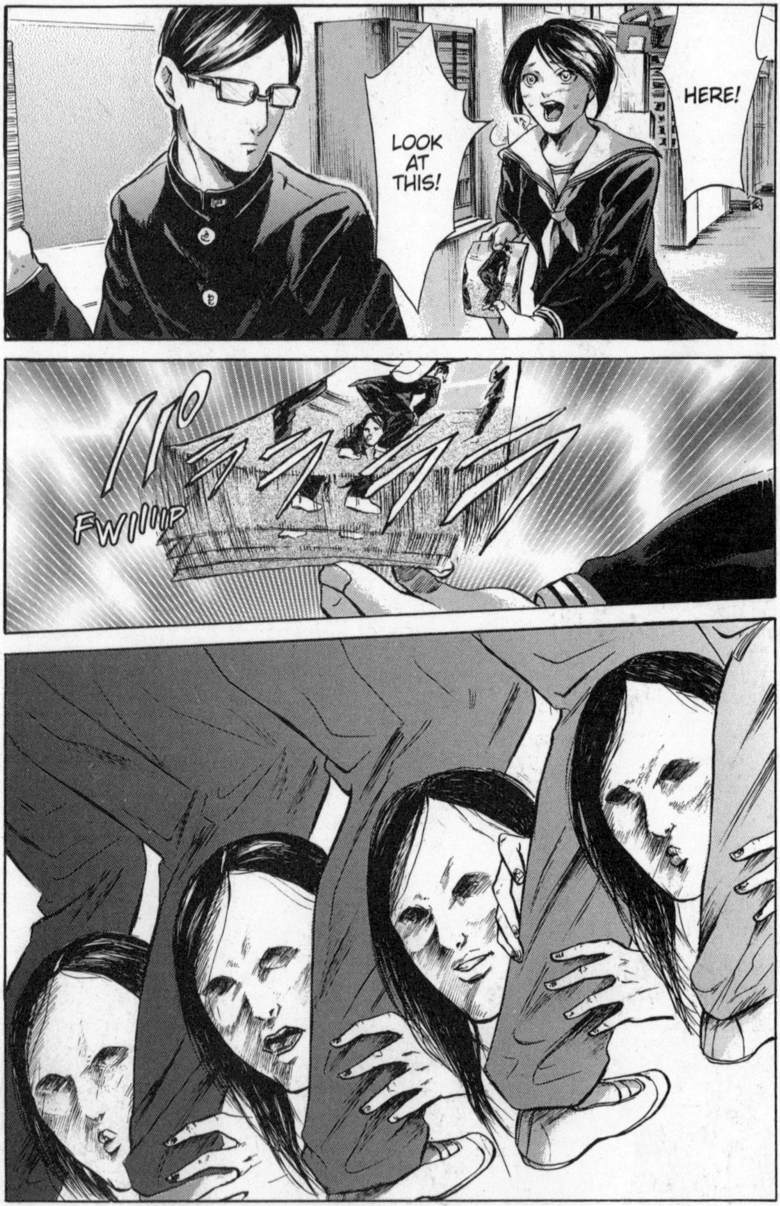
HERE!
LOOK AT THIS!
パララララ
FWIIIIP

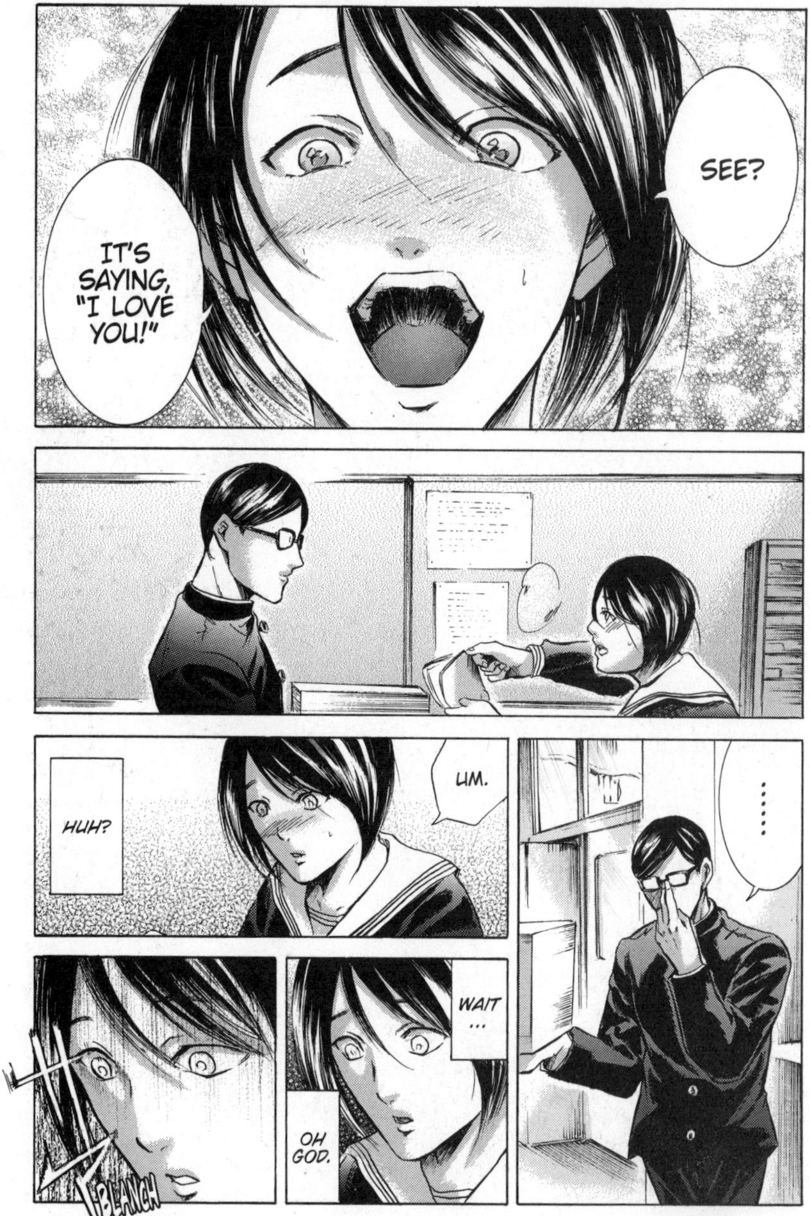
SEE?
IT'S SAYING, "I LOVE YOU!"
......
UM.
HUH?
WAIT ...
OH GOD.
BLANCH

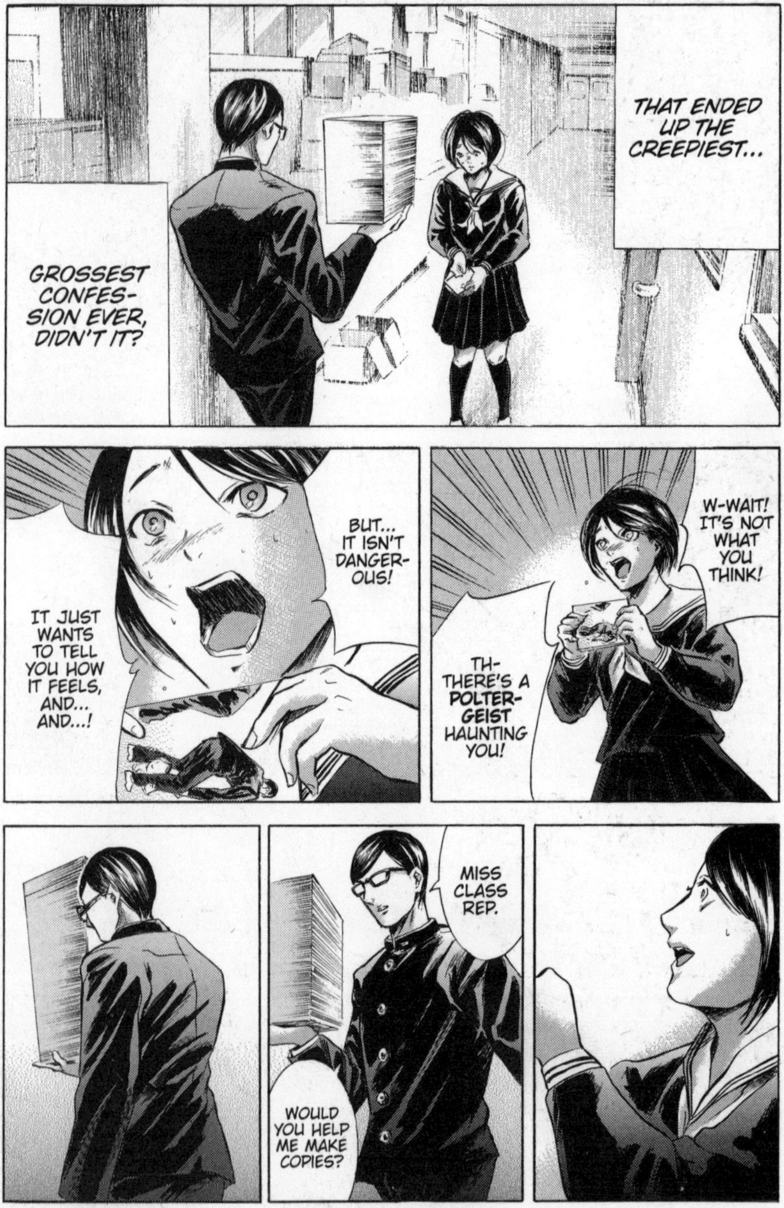
THAT ENDED UP THE CREEPIEST...
GROSSEST CONFESSION EVER, DIDN'T IT?
W-WAIT! IT'S NOT WHAT YOU THINK!
TH-THERE'S A **POLTERGEIST** HAUNTING YOU!
BUT... IT ISN'T DANGEROUS!
IT JUST WANTS TO TELL YOU HOW IT FEELS, AND... AND...!
MISS CLASS REP.
WOULD YOU HELP ME MAKE COPIES?

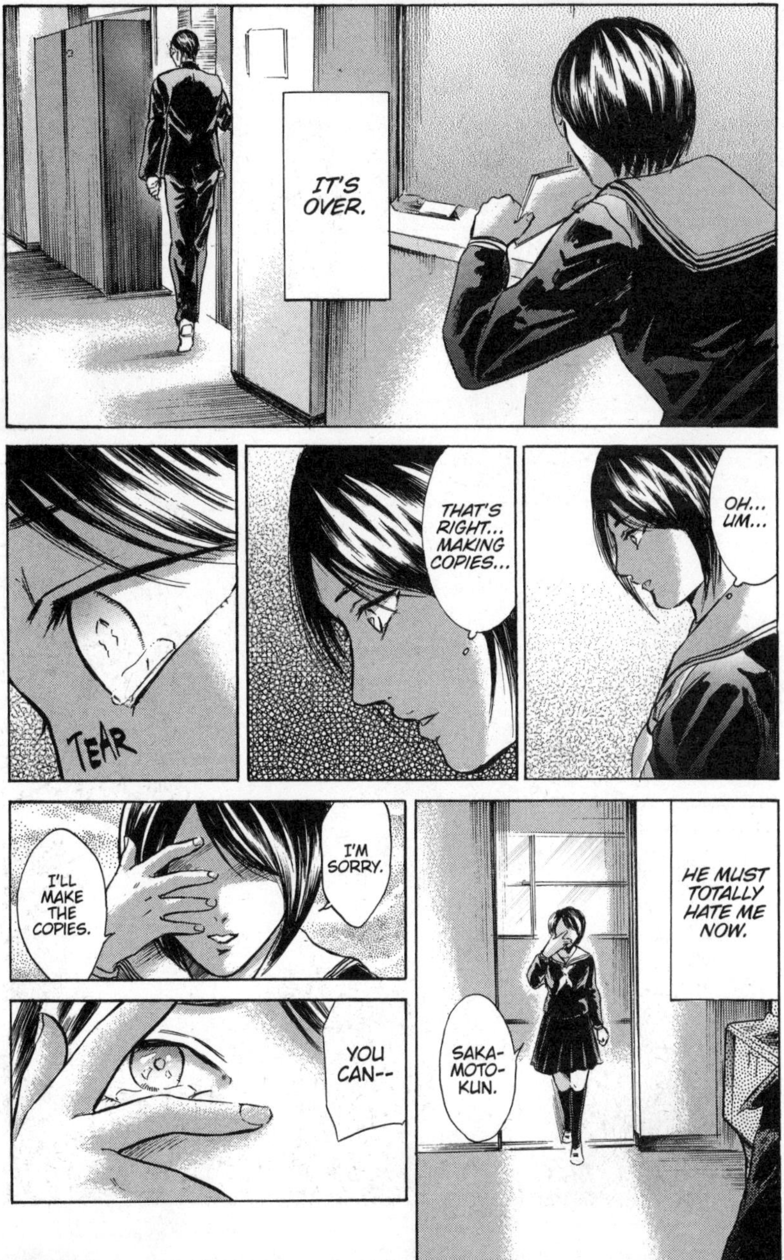
IT'S OVER.
OH... UM...
THAT'S RIGHT... MAKING COPIES...
TEAR
HE MUST TOTALLY HATE ME NOW.
SAKA-MOTO-KUN.
I'M SORRY.
I'LL MAKE THE COPIES.
YOU CAN--

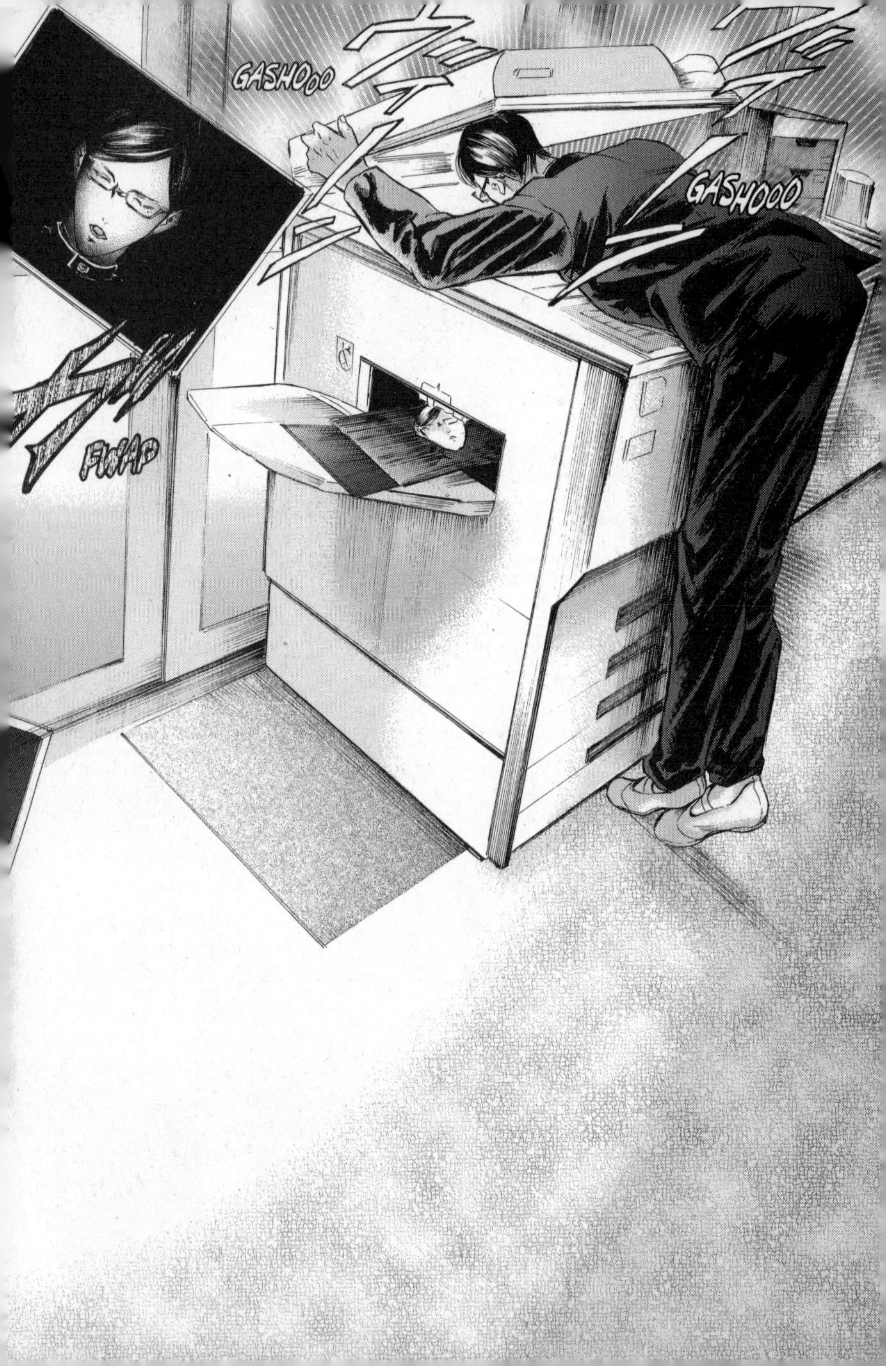
GASHOOO
GASHOoo
FWAP

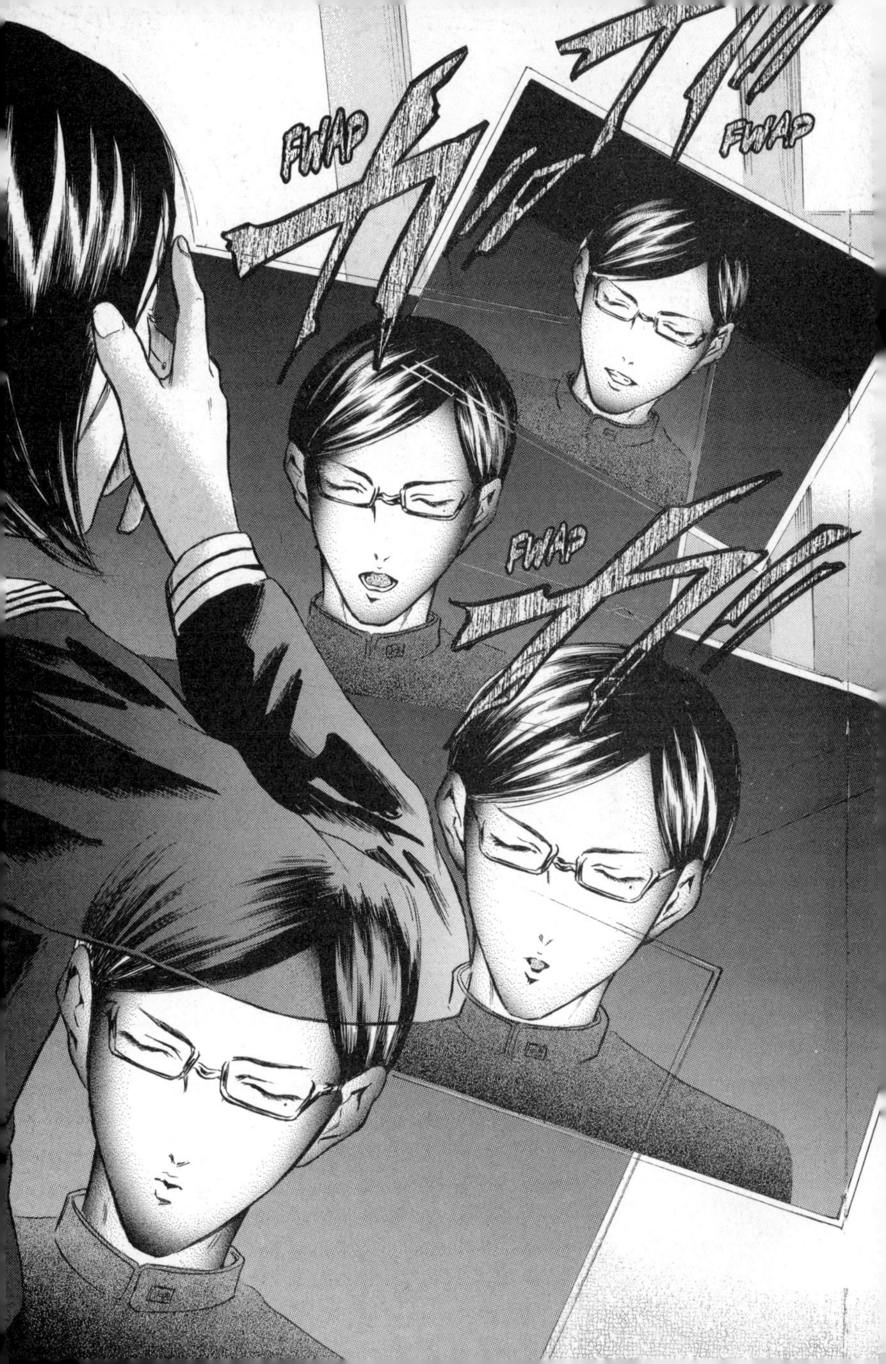
FWAP
FWAP
FWAP

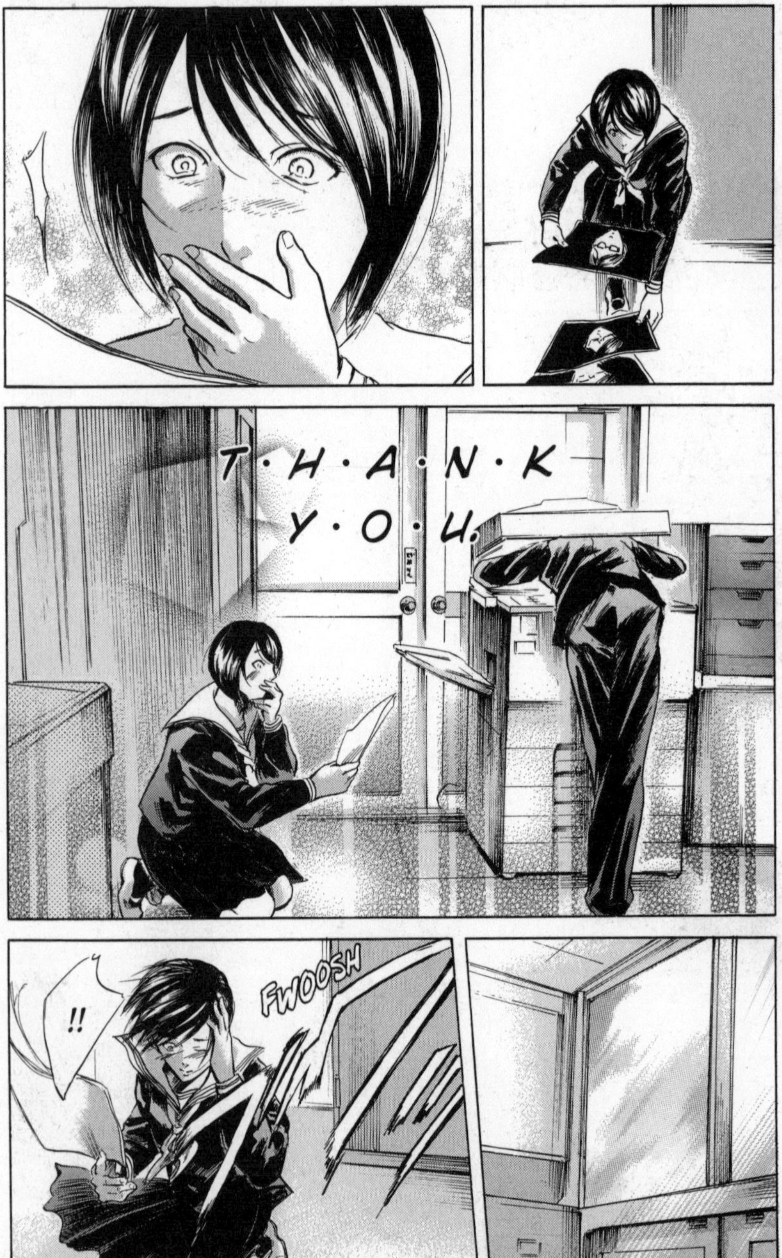
T·H·A·N·K Y·O·U.
FWOOSH
!!

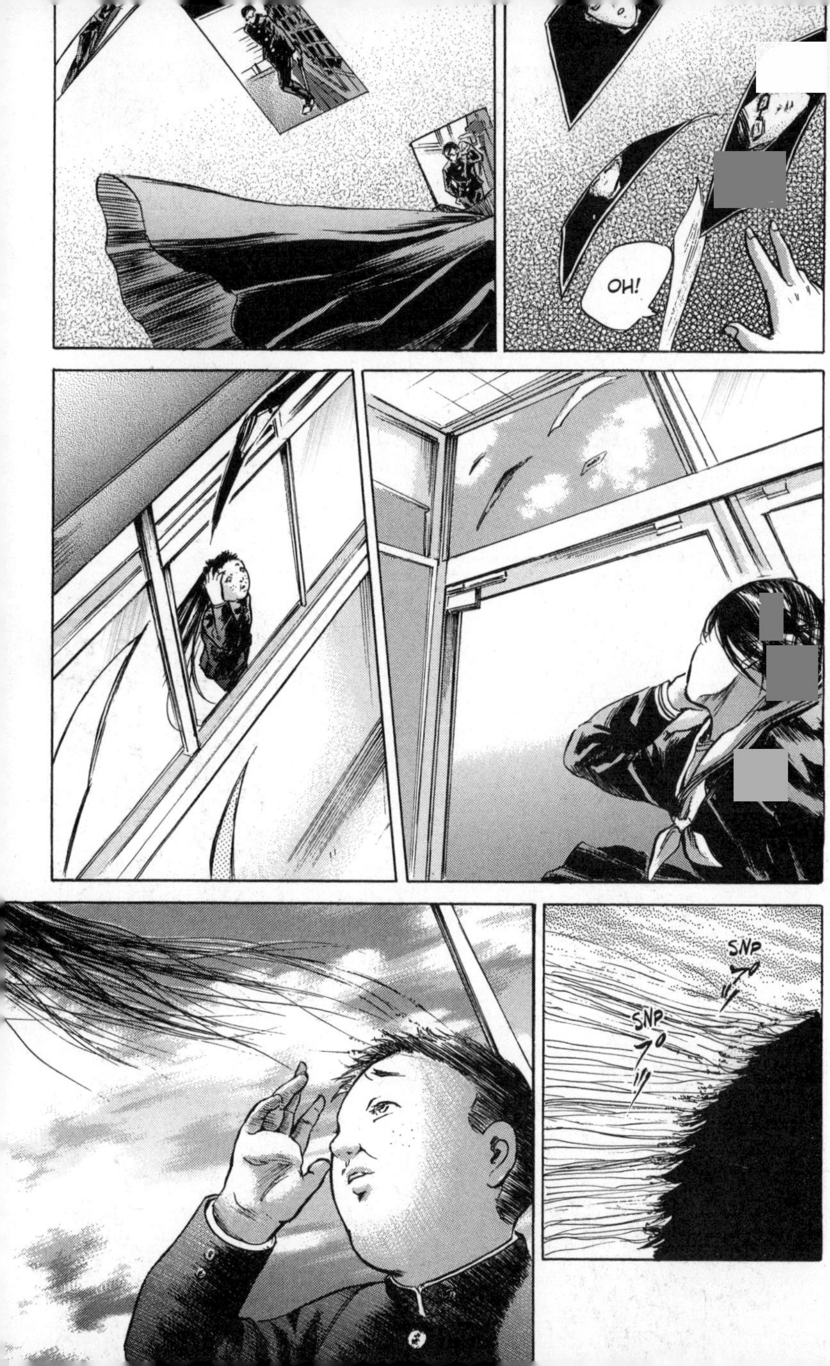
OH!
SNP
SNP

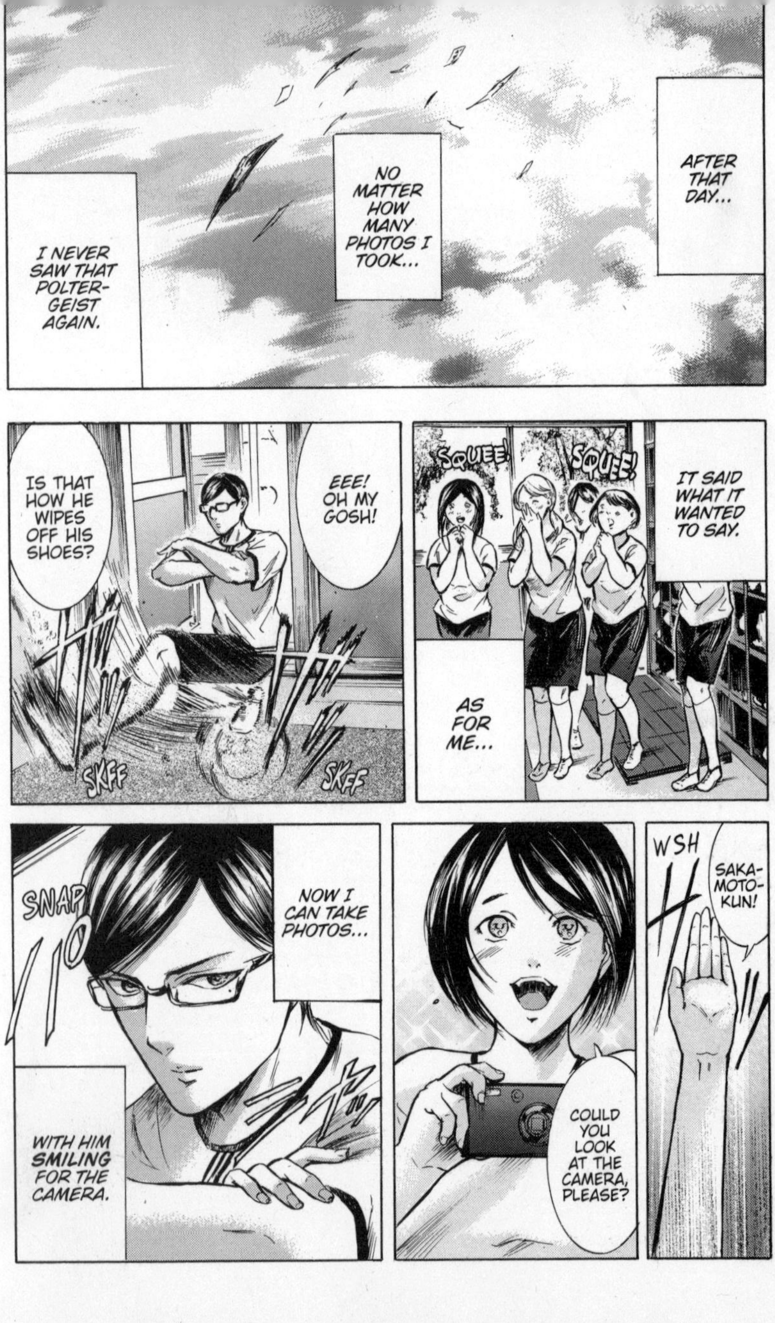
AFTER THAT DAY...
NO MATTER HOW MANY PHOTOS I TOOK...
I NEVER SAW THAT POLTER-GEIST AGAIN.
IT SAID WHAT IT WANTED TO SAY.
SQUEE!
SQUEE!
AS FOR ME...
EEE! OH MY GOSH!
IS THAT HOW HE WIPES OFF HIS SHOES?
SKFF
SKFF
WSH
SAKA-MOTO-KUN!
COULD YOU LOOK AT THE CAMERA, PLEASE?
NOW I CAN TAKE PHOTOS...
SNAP
WITH HIM SMILING FOR THE CAMERA.

End of Chapter 13

Break Time #2:
    Pool

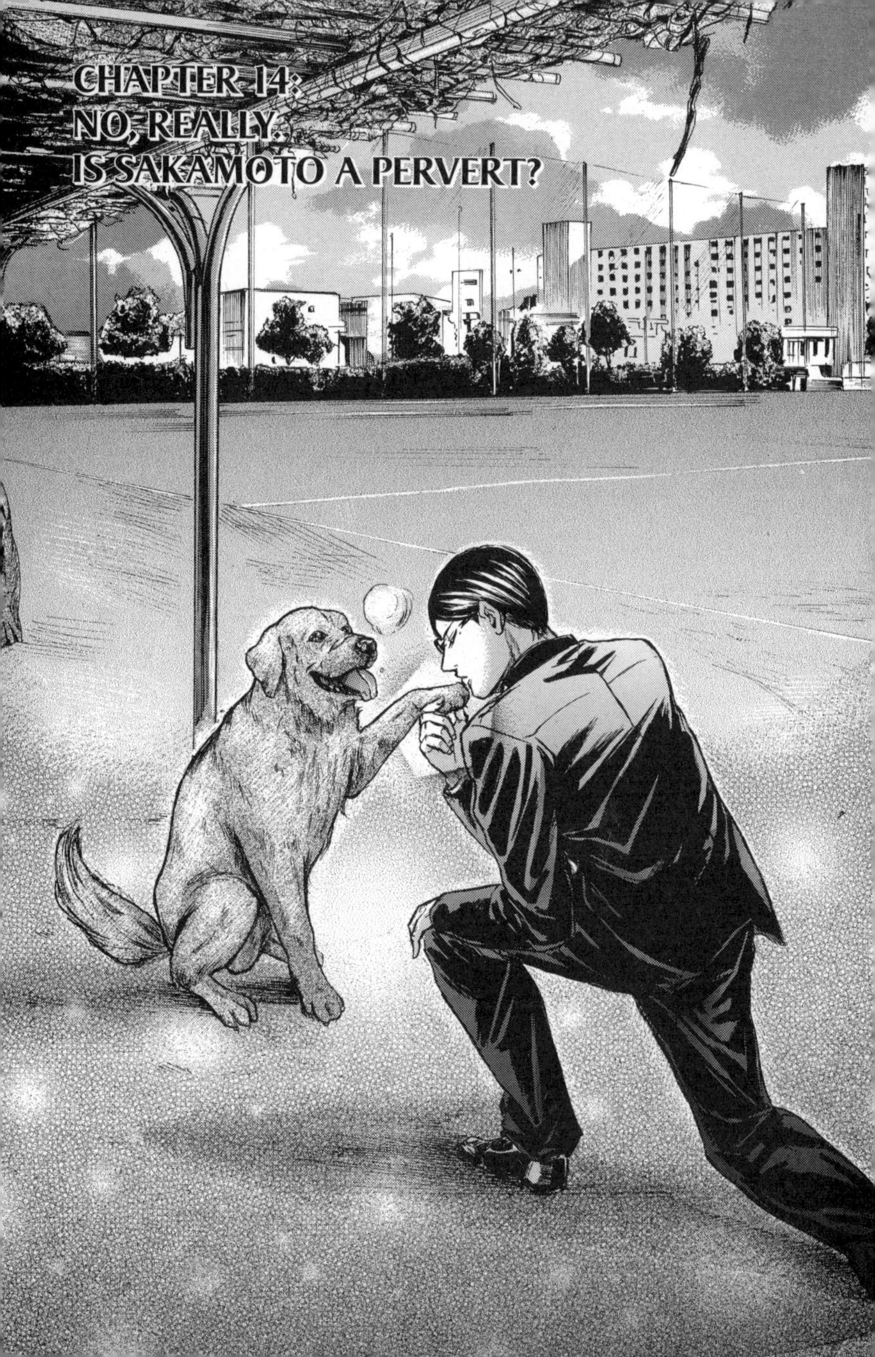
CHAPTER 14:
NO, REALLY.
IS SAKAMOTO A PERVERT?

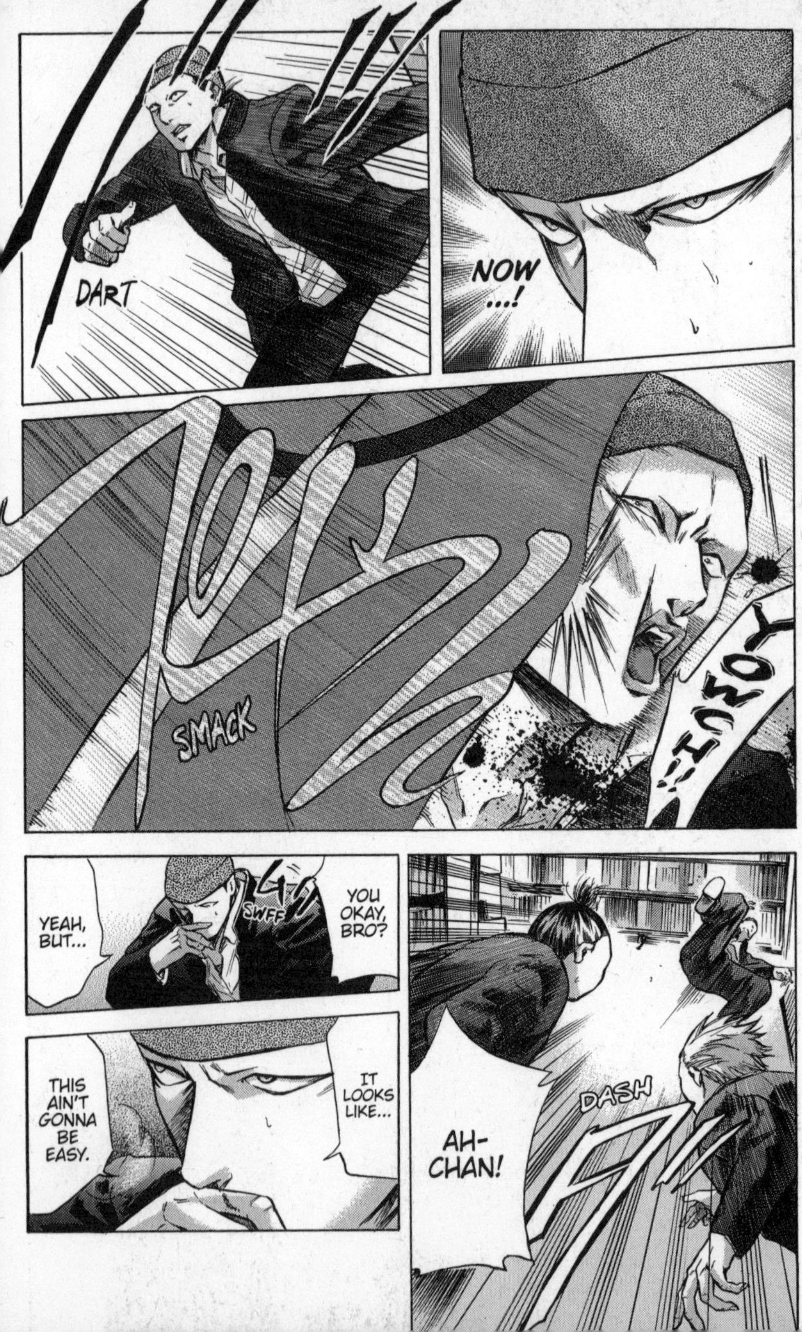
NOW ...!
DART
YOWCH!!
SMACK
DASH
AH-CHAN!
YOU OKAY, BRO?
SWFF
YEAH, BUT...
IT LOOKS LIKE...
THIS AIN'T GONNA BE EASY.

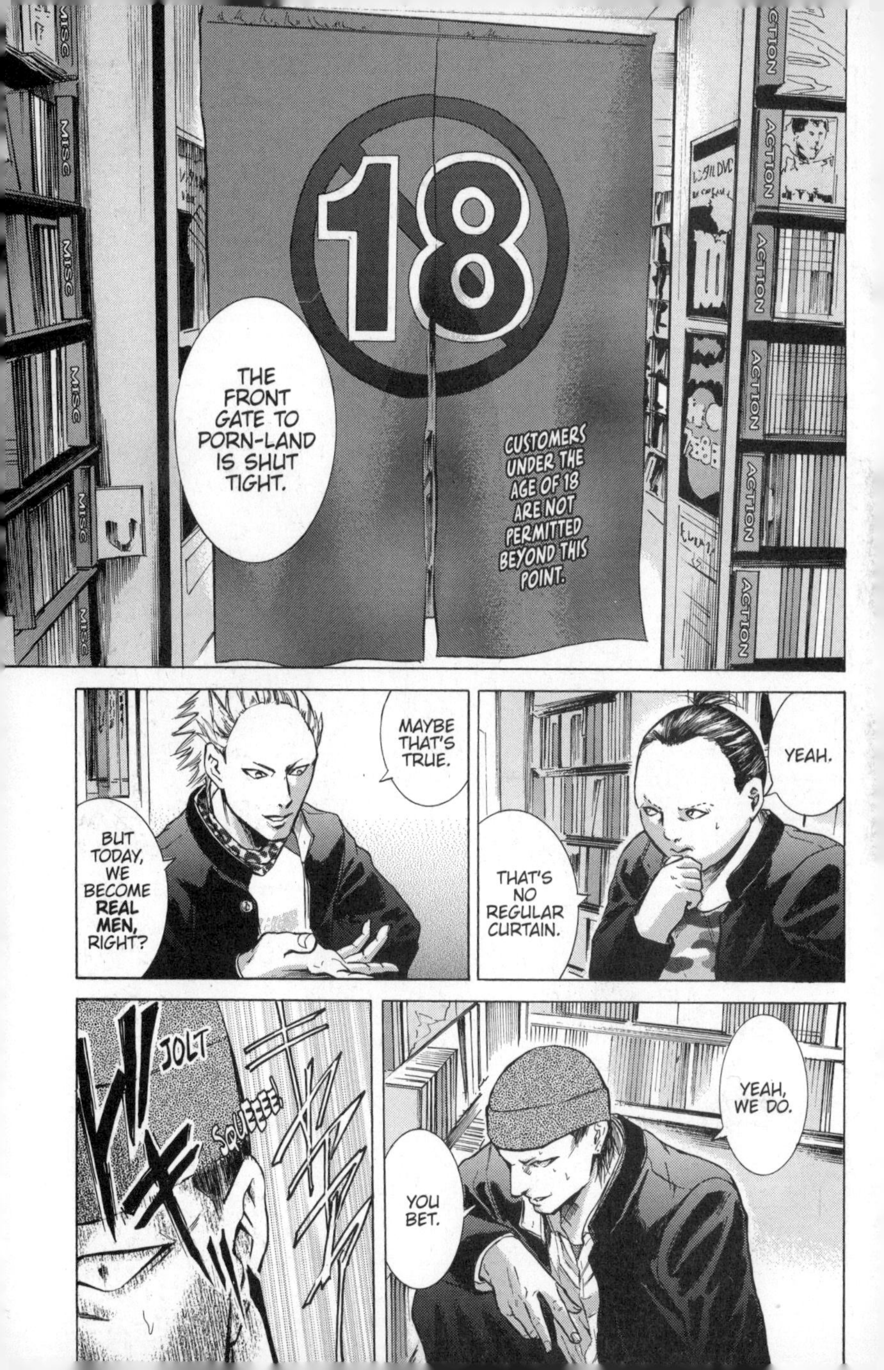
18
CUSTOMERS UNDER THE AGE OF 18 ARE NOT PERMITTED BEYOND THIS POINT.
THE FRONT GATE TO PORN-LAND IS SHUT TIGHT.
YEAH.
THAT'S NO REGULAR CURTAIN.
MAYBE THAT'S TRUE.
BUT TODAY, WE BECOME **REAL MEN**, RIGHT?
YEAH, WE DO.
YOU BET.
JOLT
SQUEEEEE

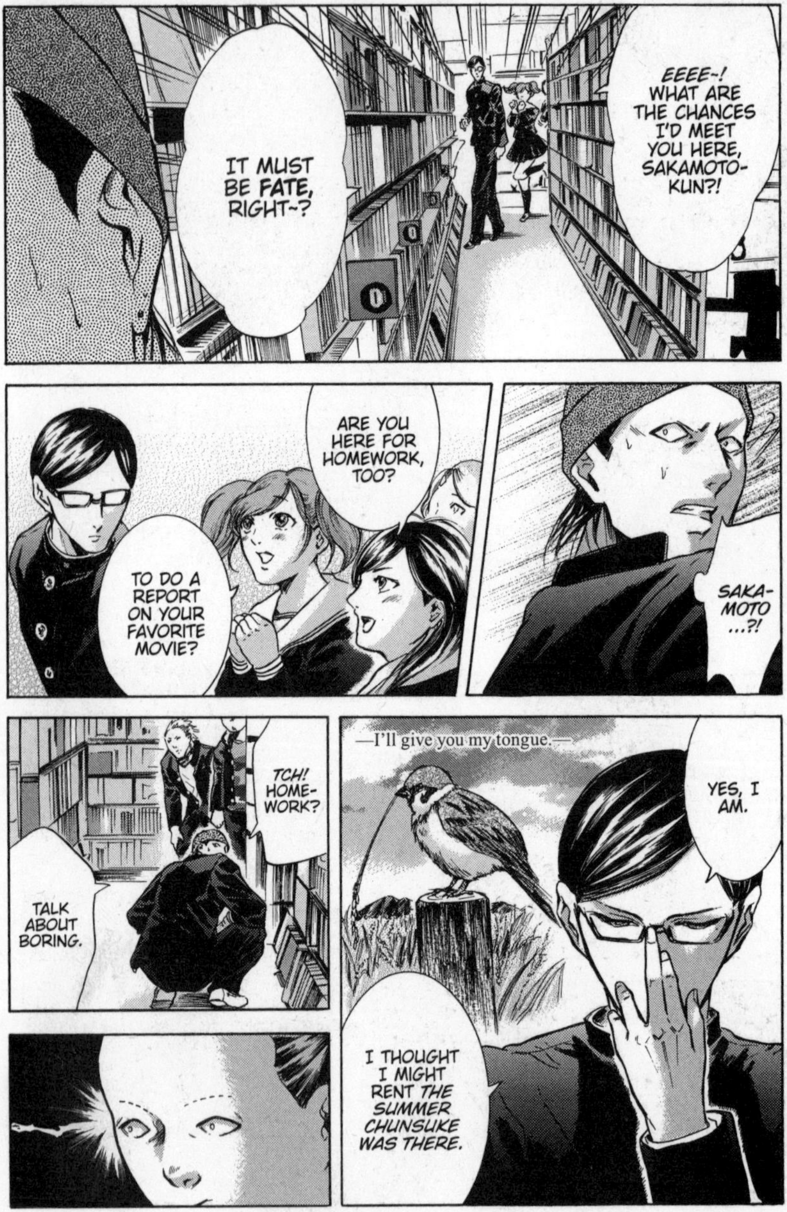
EEEE~! WHAT ARE THE CHANCES I'D MEET YOU HERE, SAKAMOTO-KUN?!
IT MUST BE FATE, RIGHT~?
SAKA-MOTO ...?!
ARE YOU HERE FOR HOMEWORK, TOO?
TO DO A REPORT ON YOUR FAVORITE MOVIE?
—I'll give you my tongue.—
YES, I AM.
I THOUGHT I MIGHT RENT THE SUMMER CHUNSUKE WAS THERE.
TCH! HOMEWORK?
TALK ABOUT BORING.

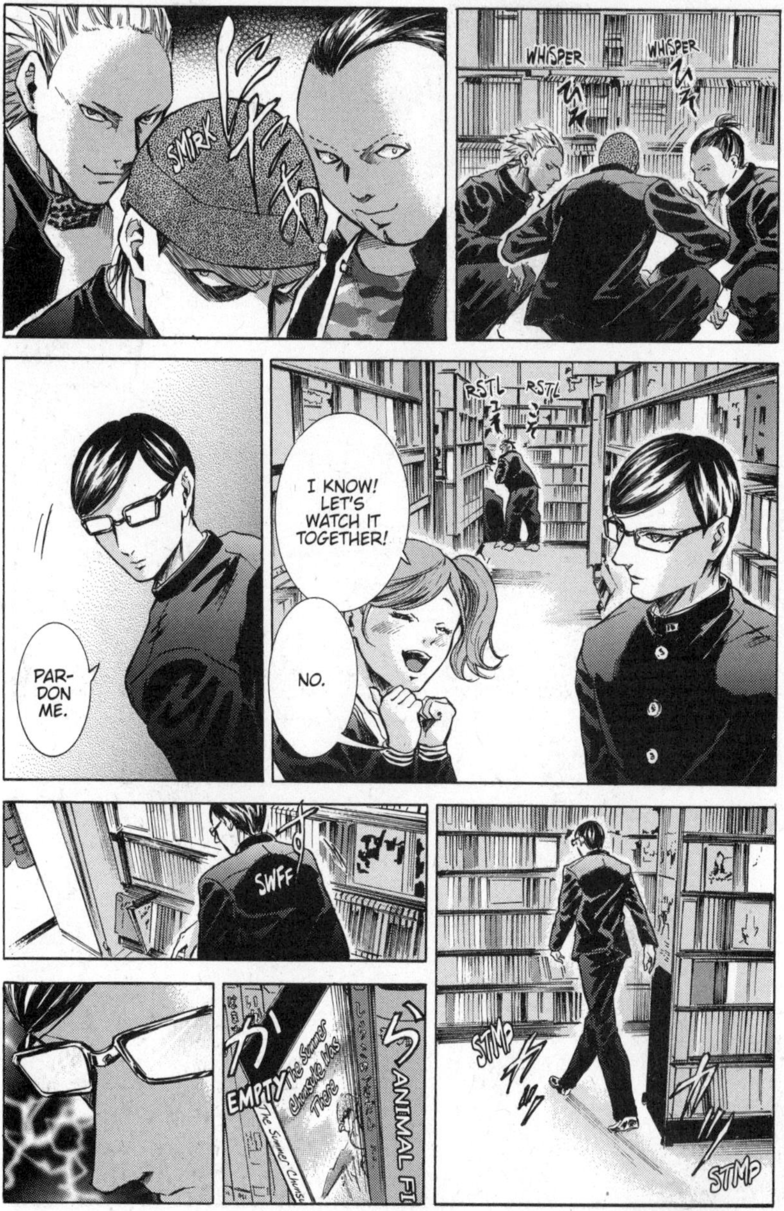
WHISPER
WHISPER
SMIRK
RSTL
RSTL
I KNOW! LET'S WATCH IT TOGETHER!
NO.
PARDON ME.
STMP
STMP
SWFF
EMPTY
ANIMAL

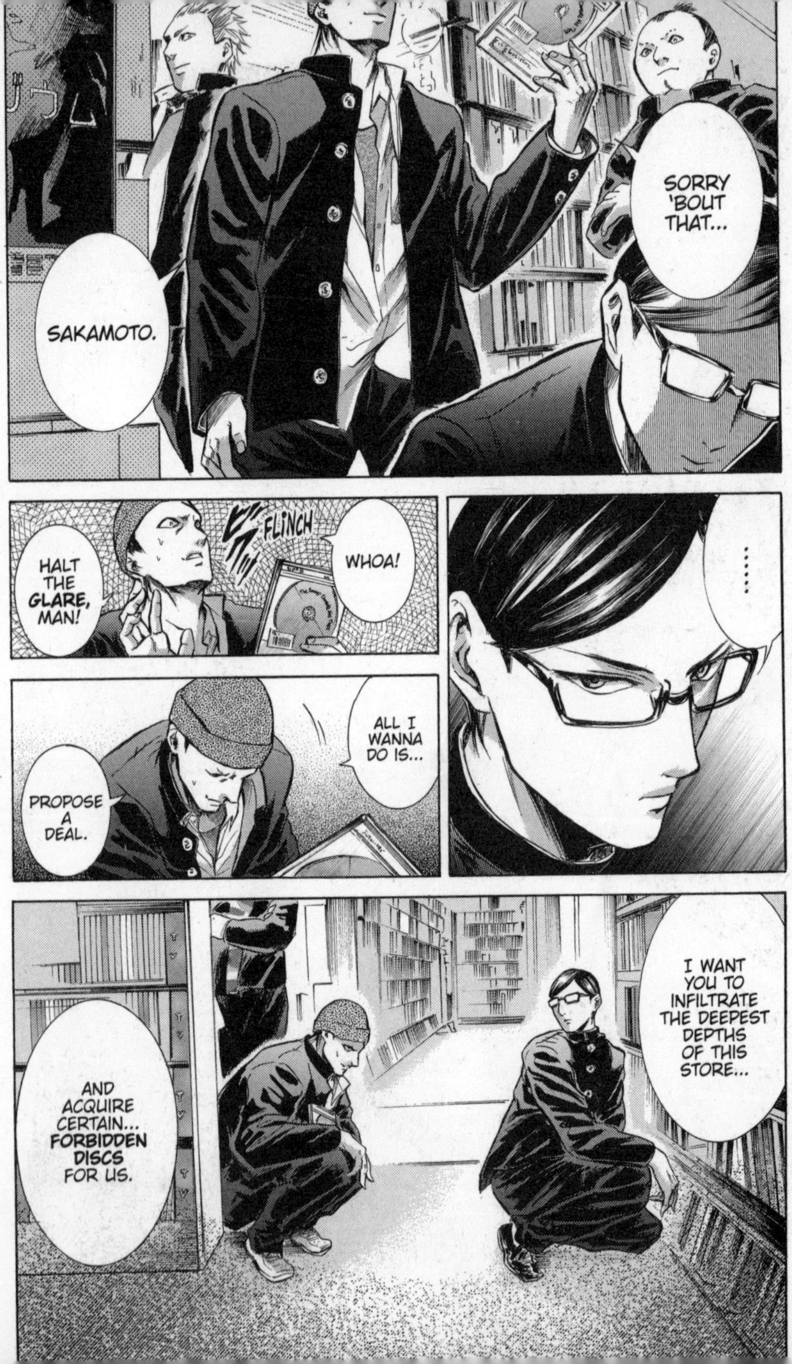
SORRY 'BOUT THAT...
SAKAMOTO.
......
WHOA!
FLINCH
HALT THE GLARE, MAN!
ALL I WANNA DO IS...
PROPOSE A DEAL.
I WANT YOU TO INFILTRATE THE DEEPEST DEPTHS OF THIS STORE...
AND ACQUIRE CERTAIN... FORBIDDEN DISCS FOR US.

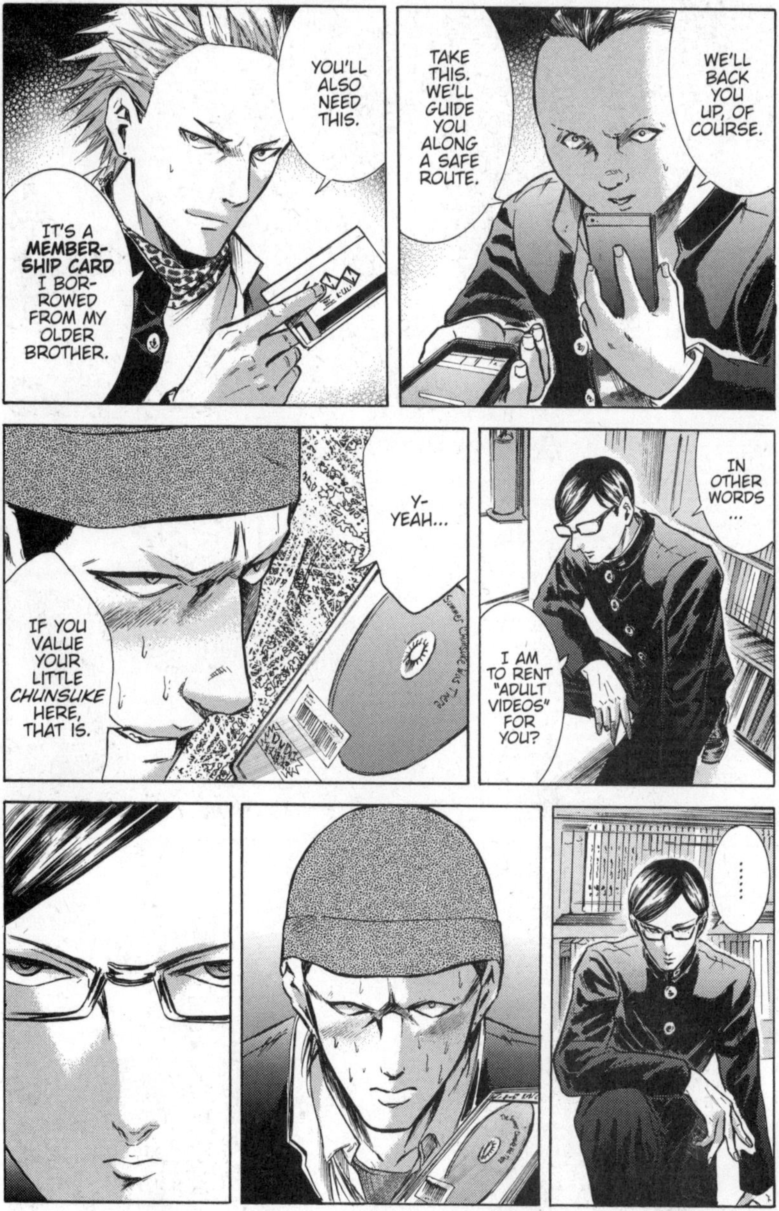
WE'LL BACK YOU UP, OF COURSE.
TAKE THIS. WE'LL GUIDE YOU ALONG A SAFE ROUTE.
YOU'LL ALSO NEED THIS.
IT'S A MEMBER-SHIP CARD I BOR-ROWED FROM MY OLDER BROTHER.
IN OTHER WORDS ...
I AM TO RENT "ADULT VIDEOS" FOR YOU?
Y-YEAH...
IF YOU VALUE YOUR LITTLE CHUNSUKE HERE, THAT IS.
......

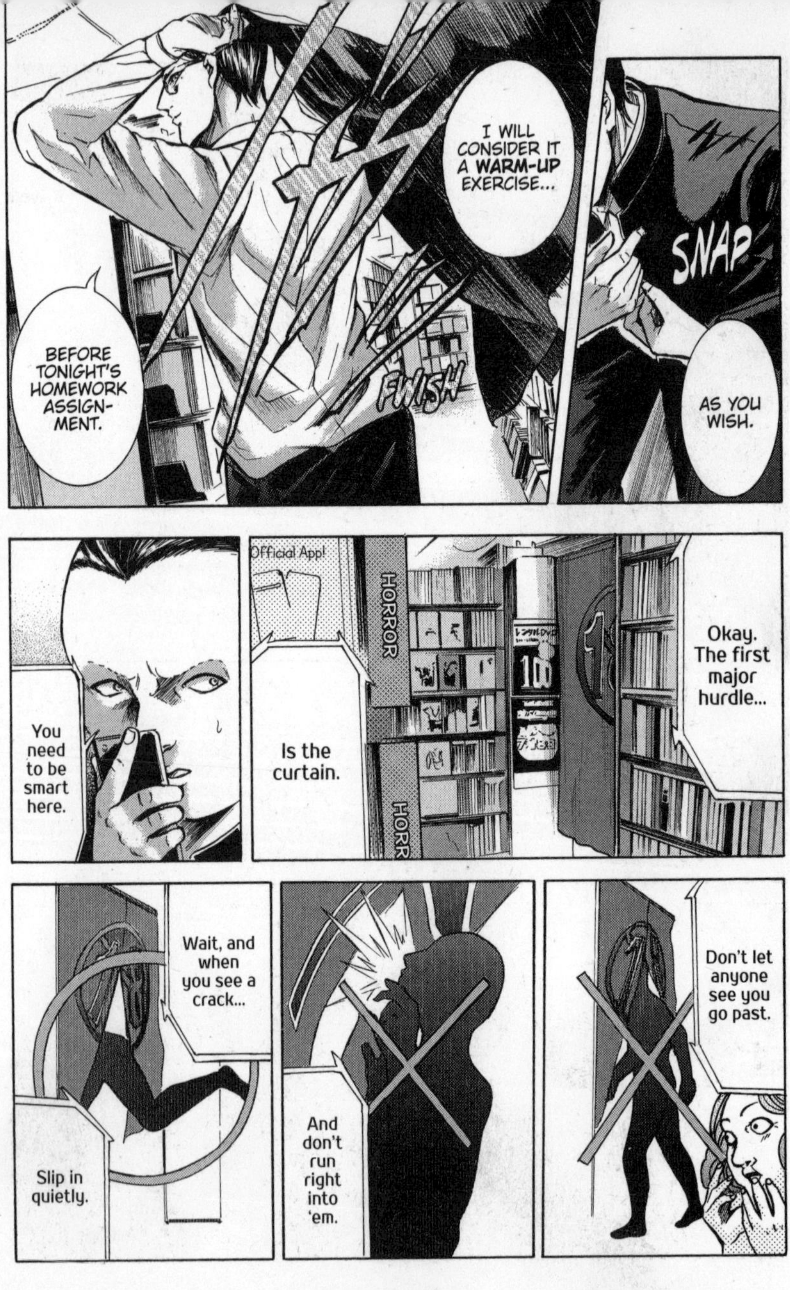
SNAP
AS YOU WISH.
I WILL CONSIDER IT A **WARM-UP** EXERCISE...
BEFORE TONIGHT'S HOMEWORK ASSIGN-MENT.
FWISH
Official App!
Okay. The first major hurdle...
HORROR
HORROR
Is the curtain.
You need to be smart here.
Don't let anyone see you go past.
And don't run right into 'em.
Wait, and when you see a crack...
Slip in quietly.

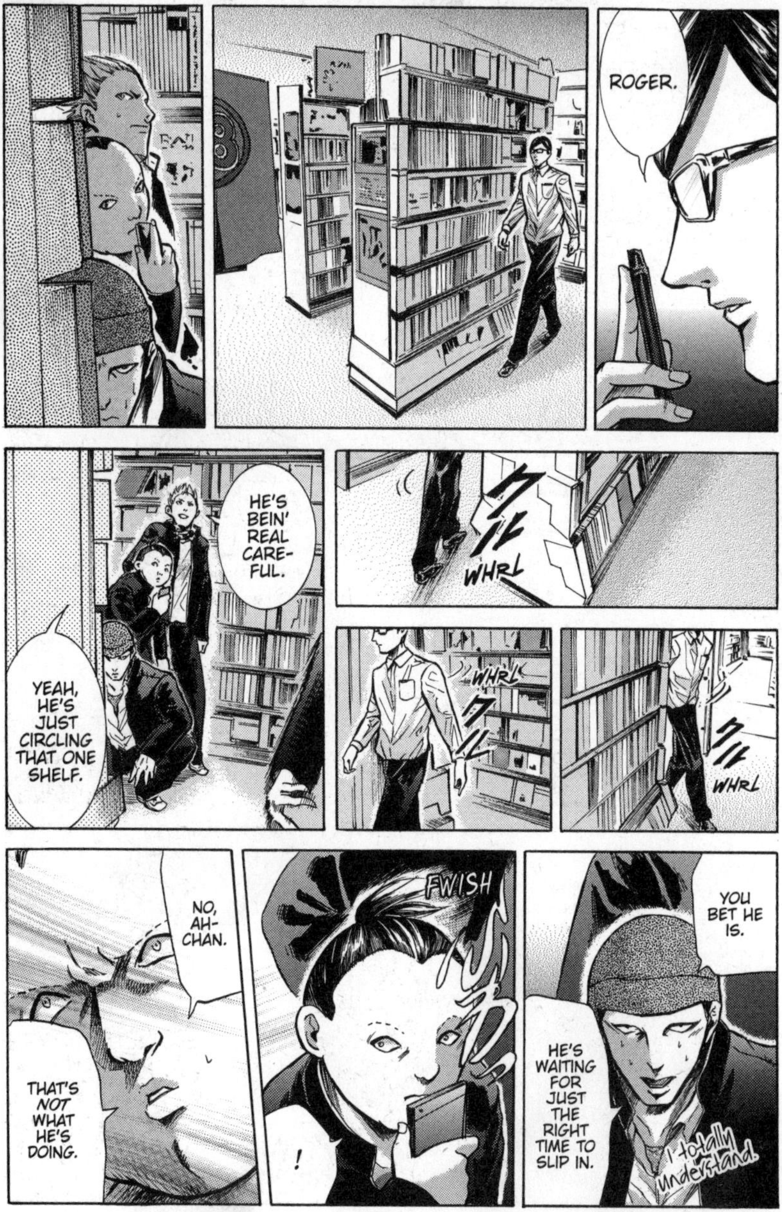
ROGER.
WHRL
WHRL
WHRL
HE'S BEIN' REAL CAREFUL.
YEAH, HE'S JUST CIRCLING THAT ONE SHELF.
YOU BET HE IS.
HE'S WAITING FOR JUST THE RIGHT TIME TO SLIP IN.
I totally understand.
FWISH
!
NO, AH-CHAN.
THAT'S *NOT* WHAT HE'S DOING.

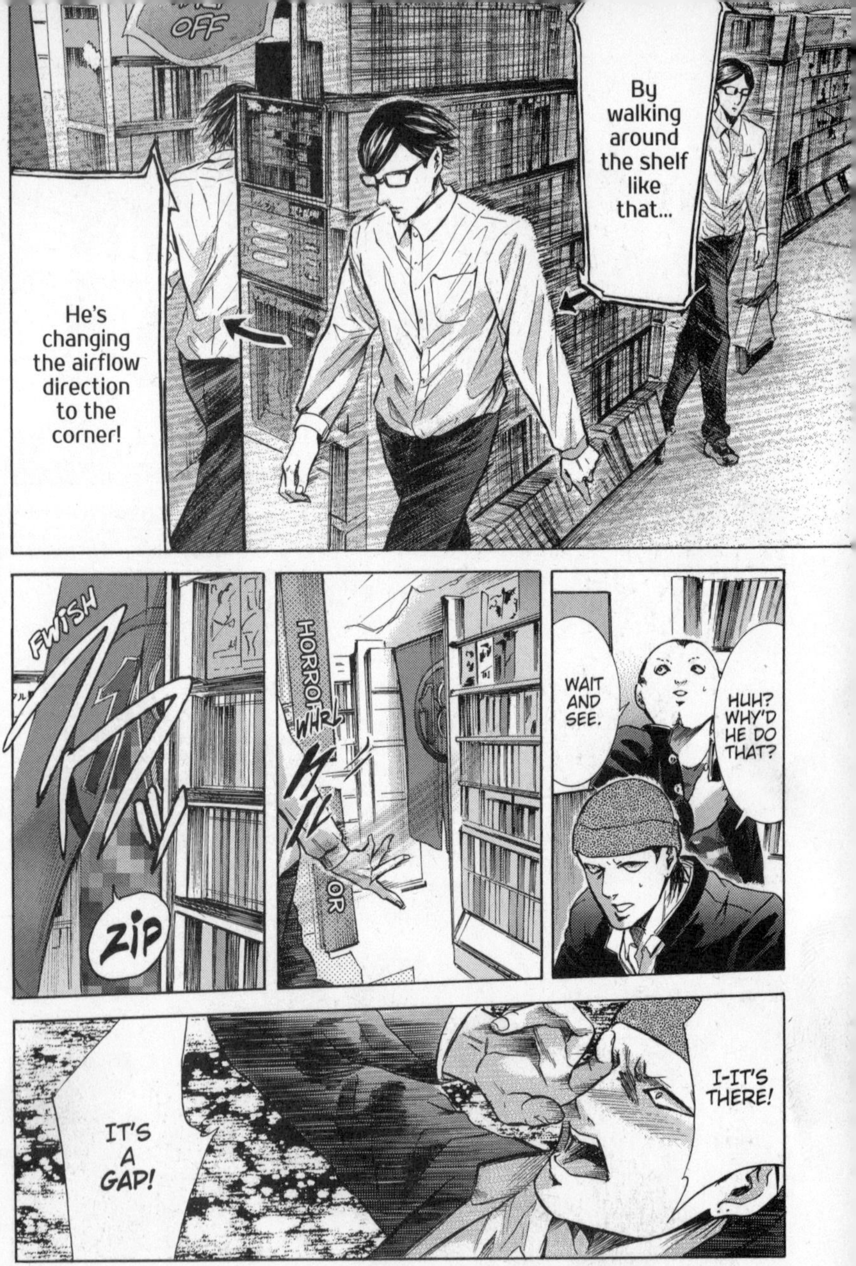
OFF
By walking around the shelf like that...
He's changing the airflow direction to the corner!
HUH? WHY'D HE DO THAT?
WAIT AND SEE.
WHRL
FWISH
ZIP
I-IT'S THERE!
IT'S A GAP!

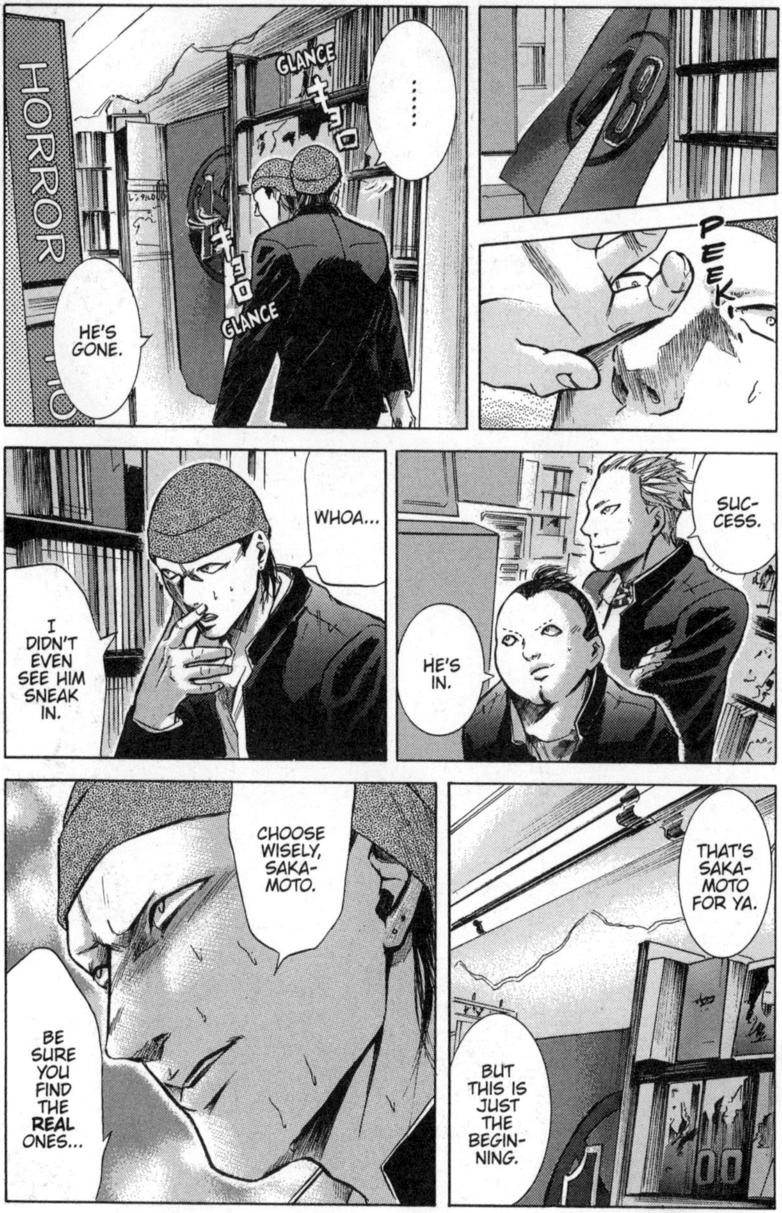
PEEK
......
GLANCE キョロ
HORROR
キョロ GLANCE
HE'S GONE.
SUC-CESS.
HE'S IN.
WHOA...
I DIDN'T EVEN SEE HIM SNEAK IN.
THAT'S SAKA-MOTO FOR YA.
BUT THIS IS JUST THE BEGIN-NING.
CHOOSE WISELY, SAKA-MOTO.
BE SURE YOU FIND THE **REAL** ONES...

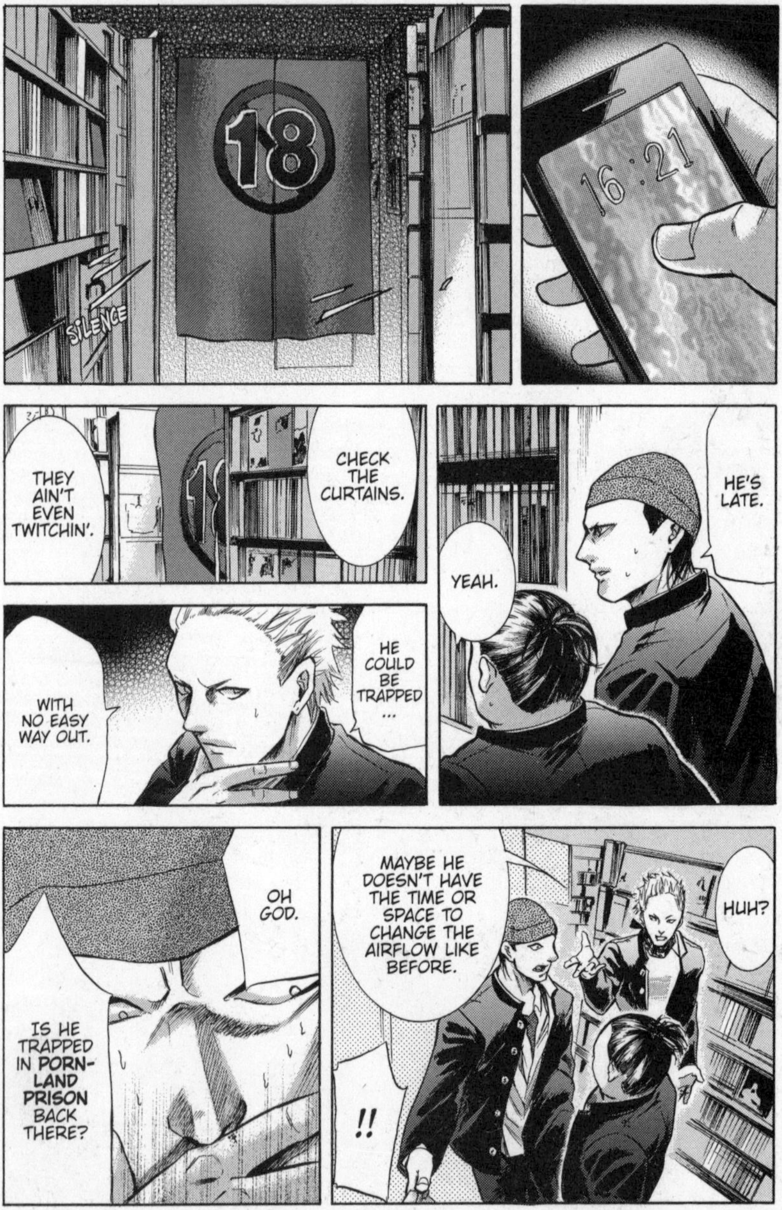
16:21
SILENCE
HE'S LATE.
YEAH.
CHECK THE CURTAINS.
THEY AIN'T EVEN TWITCHIN'.
HE COULD BE TRAPPED ...
WITH NO EASY WAY OUT.
HUH?
MAYBE HE DOESN'T HAVE THE TIME OR SPACE TO CHANGE THE AIRFLOW LIKE BEFORE.
!!
OH GOD.
IS HE TRAPPED IN **PORN-LAND PRISON** BACK THERE?

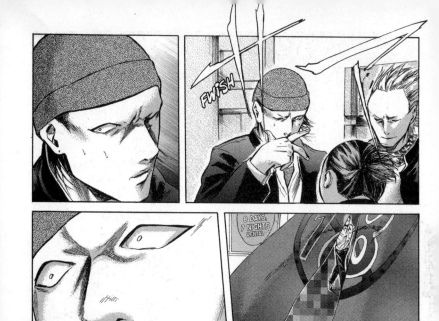

FWISH

8 DAYS 7 NIGHTS RENTAL

JIGGLE
MY CRUSH
NO NOT HERE
A LADY SPEAKS

STREETS OUT
BORN HOUSEWIFE
MY MISTRESS' BATHTIME
A LADY SPEAKS
BUTTS

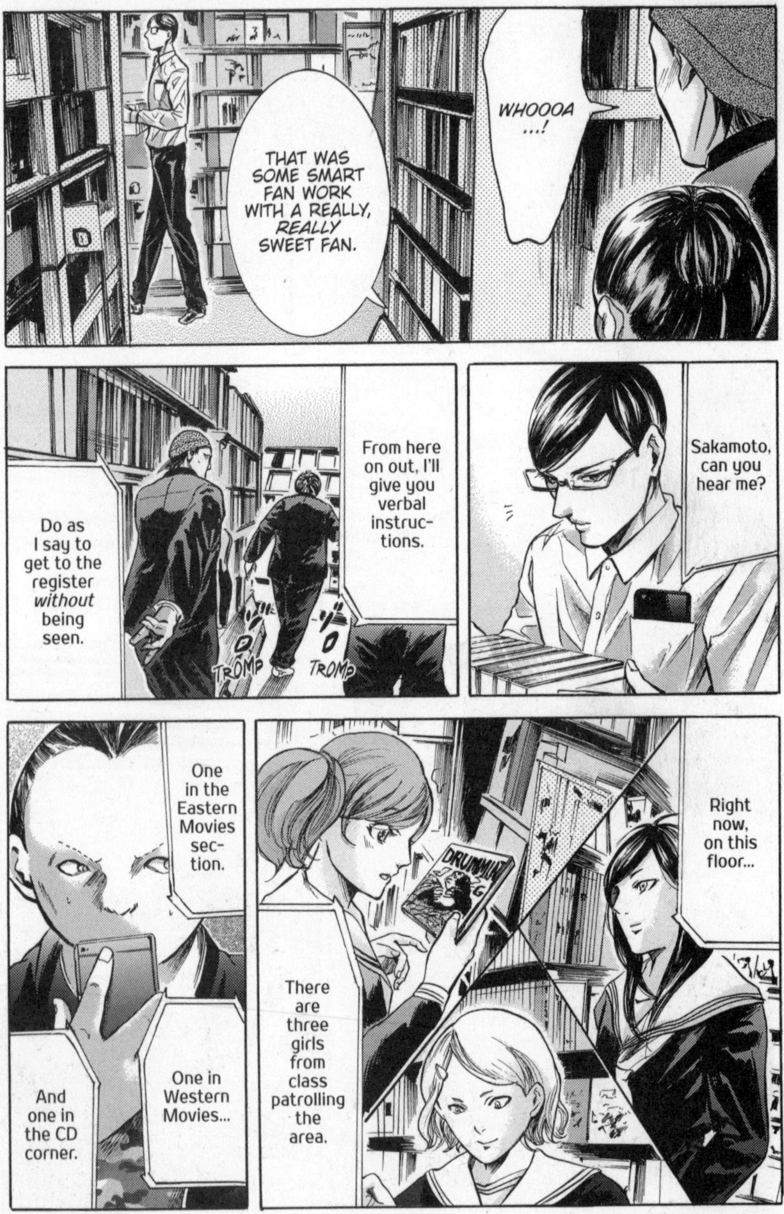
WHOOOA ...!
THAT WAS SOME SMART FAN WORK WITH A REALLY, *REALLY* SWEET FAN.
Sakamoto, can you hear me?
From here on out, I'll give you verbal instructions.
Do as I say to get to the register *without* being seen.
TROMP
TROMP
Right now, on this floor...
There are three girls from class patrolling the area.
One in the Eastern Movies section.
One in Western Movies...
And one in the CD corner.

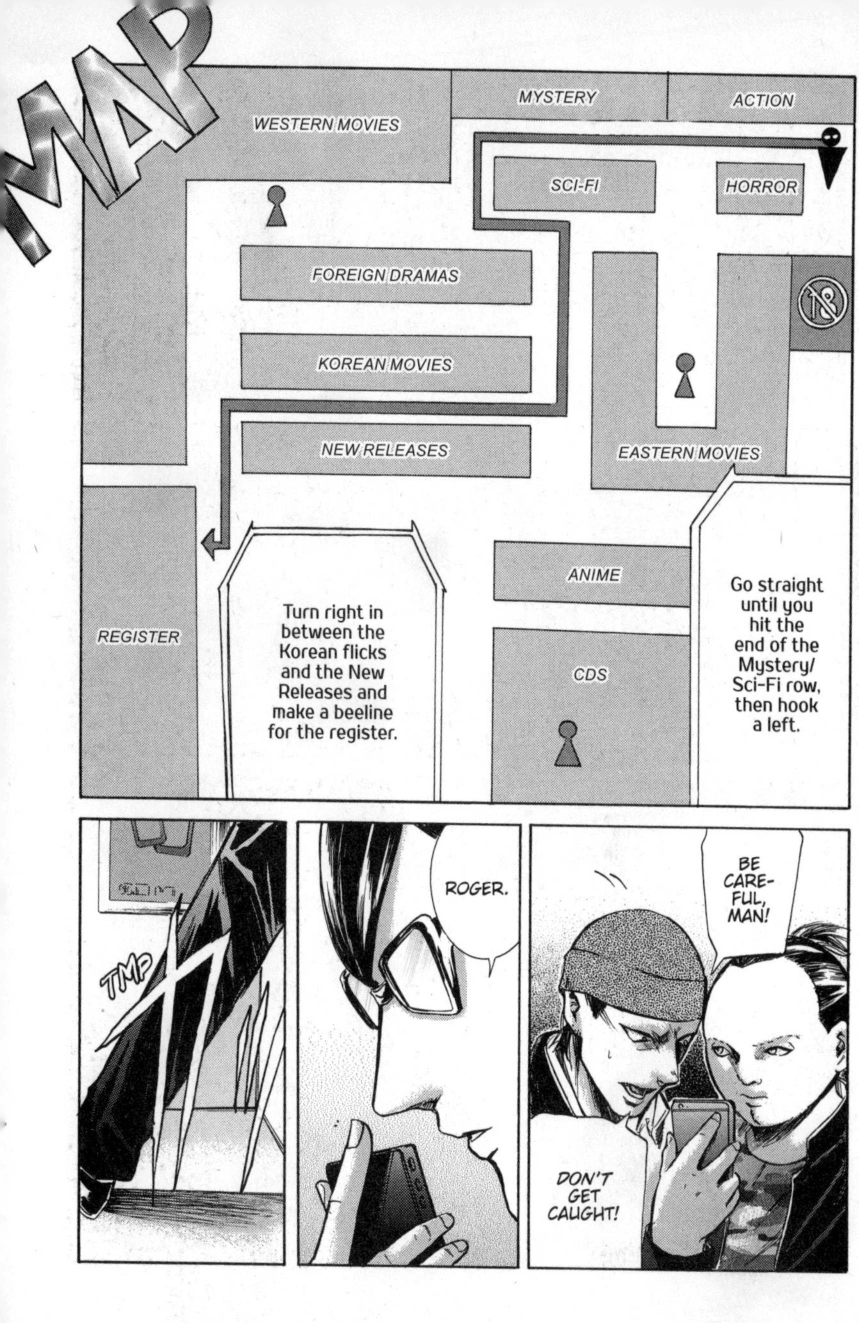
MAP
ACTION
MYSTERY
WESTERN MOVIES
HORROR
SCI-FI
FOREIGN DRAMAS
KOREAN MOVIES
NEW RELEASES
EASTERN MOVIES
Go straight until you hit the end of the Mystery/ Sci-Fi row, then hook a left.
ANIME
CDS
Turn right in between the Korean flicks and the New Releases and make a beeline for the register.
REGISTER
BE CAREFUL, MAN!
DON'T GET CAUGHT!
ROGER.
TMP

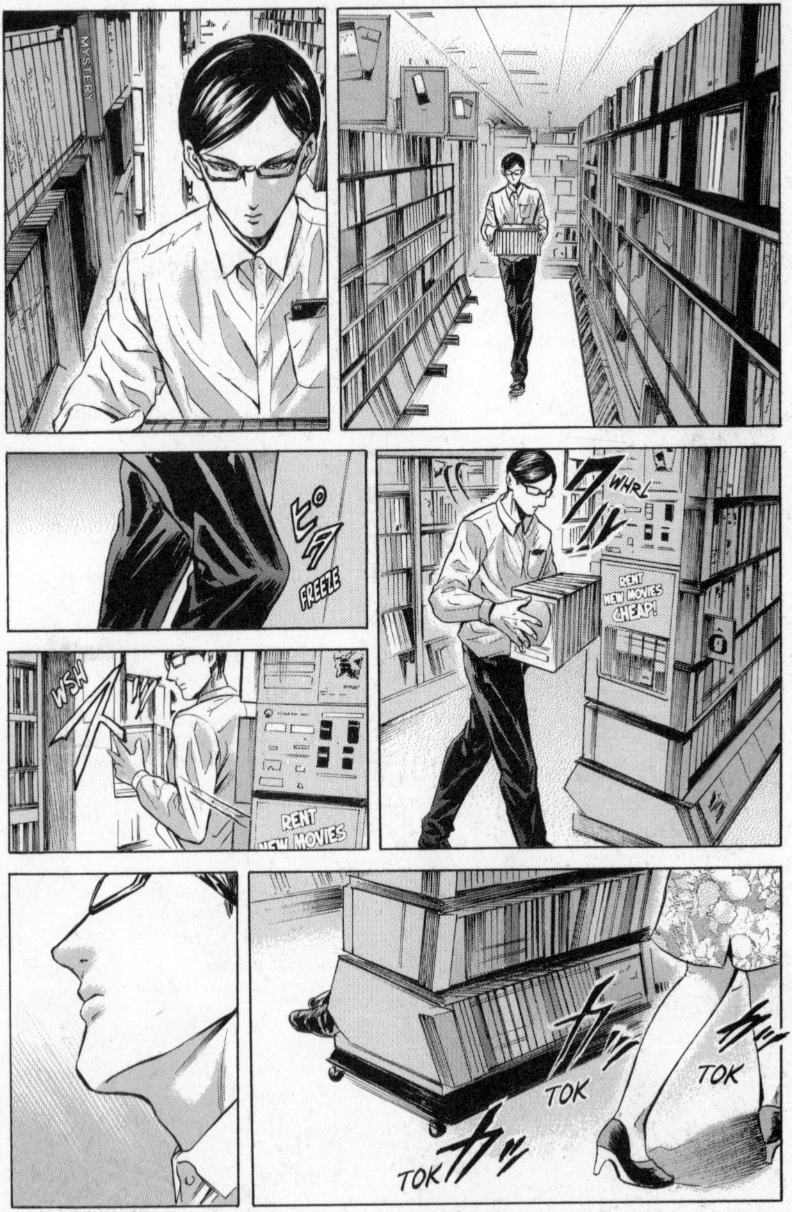

MYSTERY
WHRL
RENT NEW MOVIES CHEAP!
FREEZE
WSH
RENT NEW MOVIES
TOK
TOK
TOK

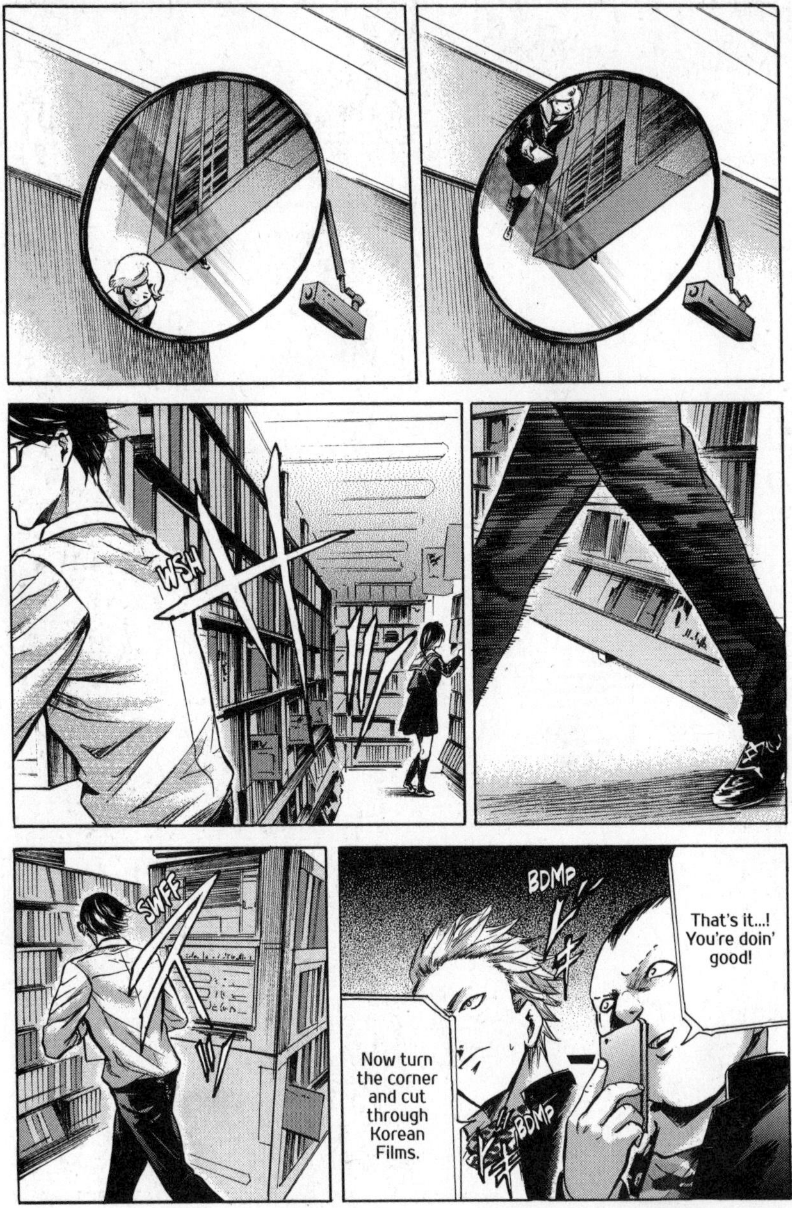
WSH
That's it...! You're doin' good!
BDMP
Now turn the corner and cut through Korean Films.
BDMP
SWFF

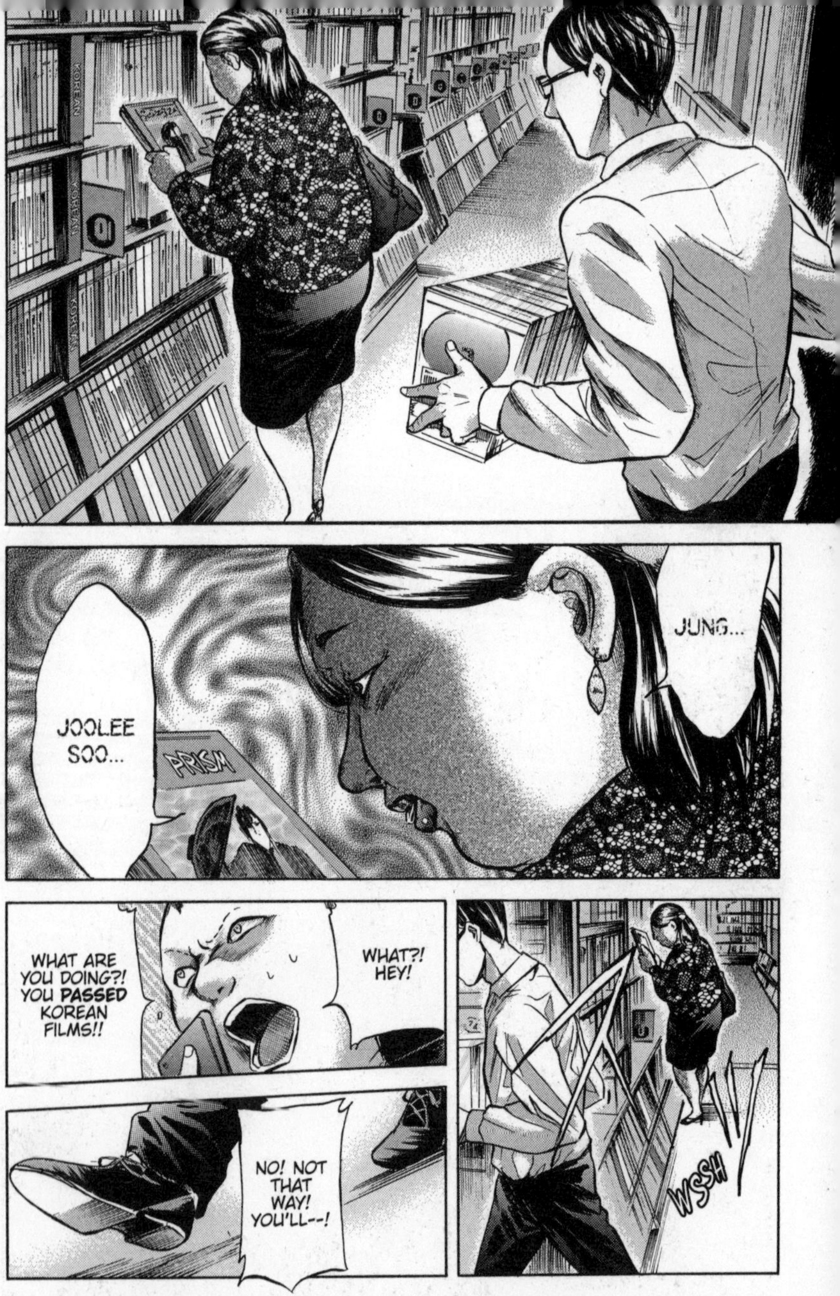
JUNG...
JOOLEE SOO...
WSSH
WHAT?! HEY!
WHAT ARE YOU DOING?! YOU **PASSED** KOREAN FILMS!!
NO! NOT THAT WAY! YOU'LL--!

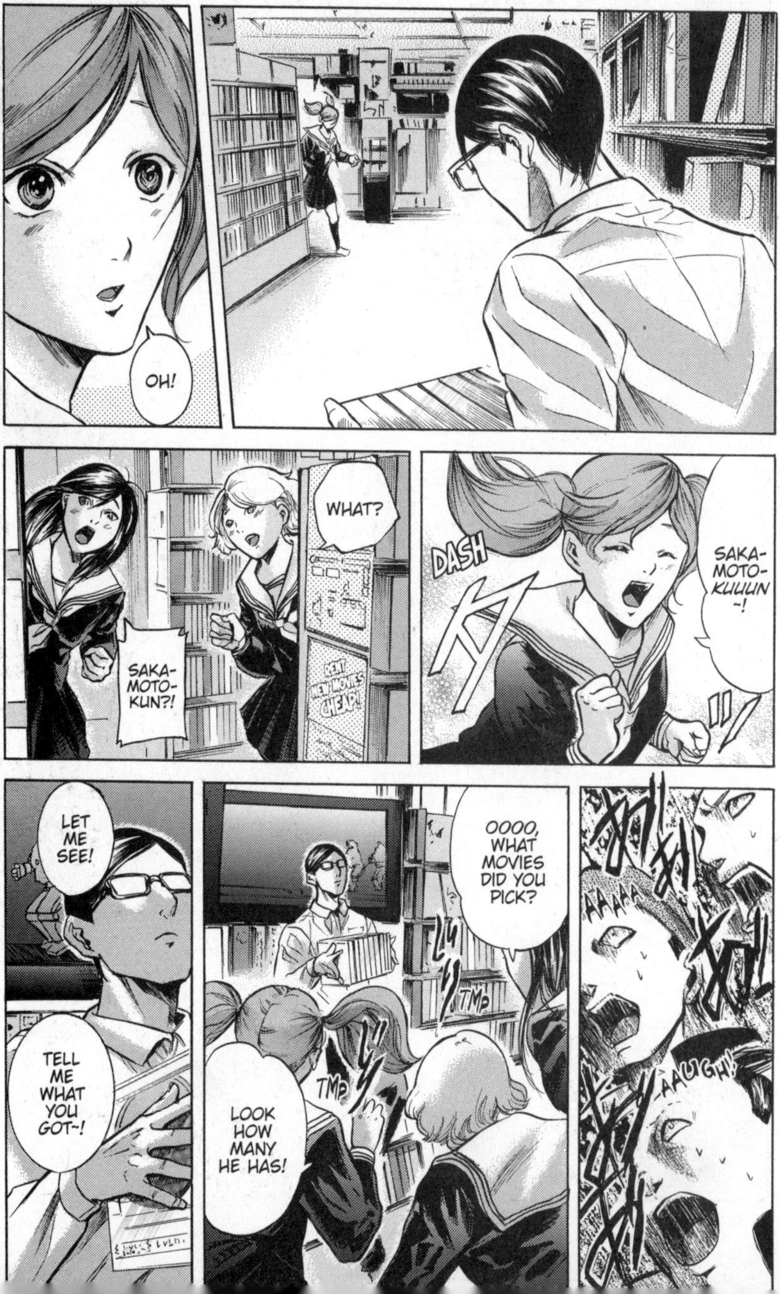
OH!
DASH
SAKA-MOTO-KUUUN~!
WHAT?
SAKA-MOTO-KUN?!
RENT NEW MOVIES CHEAP!
AAAA
AAUGH!
OOOO, WHAT MOVIES DID YOU PICK?
TMP
TMP
LOOK HOW MANY HE HAS!
LET ME SEE!
TELL ME WHAT YOU GOT~!

SECRET SKILL...

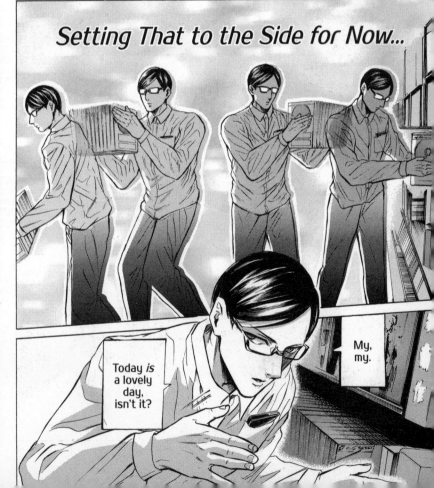

Setting That to the Side for Now...

Today *is* a lovely day, isn't it?

My, my.

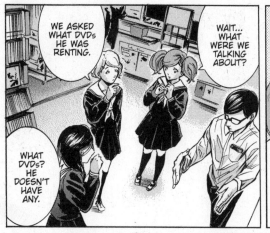

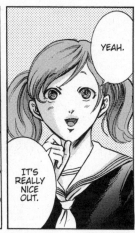

YEAH.
IT'S REALLY NICE OUT.
WAIT... WHAT WERE WE TALKING ABOUT?
WE ASKED WHAT DVDs HE WAS RENTING.
WHAT DVDs? HE DOESN'T HAVE ANY.
YESSS!! HE BROKE OUT A ROBOT DANCE...
AND MOVED THE CONVERSATION ALONG LIKE IT WAS ON A CONVEYOR BELT!
OH, THAT'S RIGHT!
I TOTALLY FOUND A CD THAT, LIKE, PERFECTLY FITS SAKAMOTO-KUN.
c'mon, I'll show you!
!!
Now, Sakamoto!
GO!
WSH

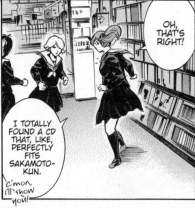

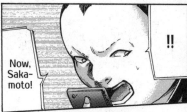

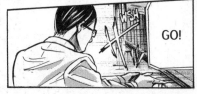

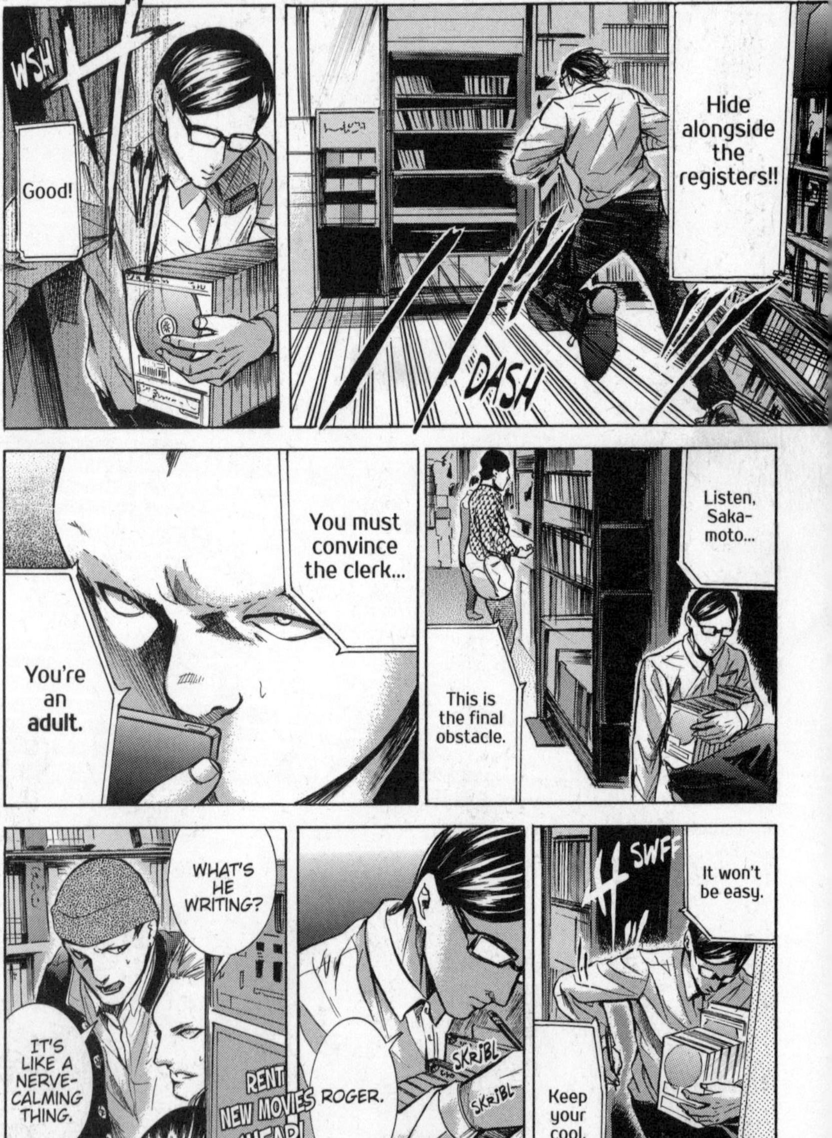
Hide alongside the registers!!
DASH
WSH
Good!
Listen, Sakamoto...
This is the final obstacle.
You must convince the clerk...
You're an **adult.**
SWFF
It won't be easy.
Keep your cool.
SKRIBL
SKRIBL
ROGER.
RENT NEW MOVIES CHEAP!
WHAT'S HE WRITING?
IT'S LIKE A NERVE-CALMING THING.

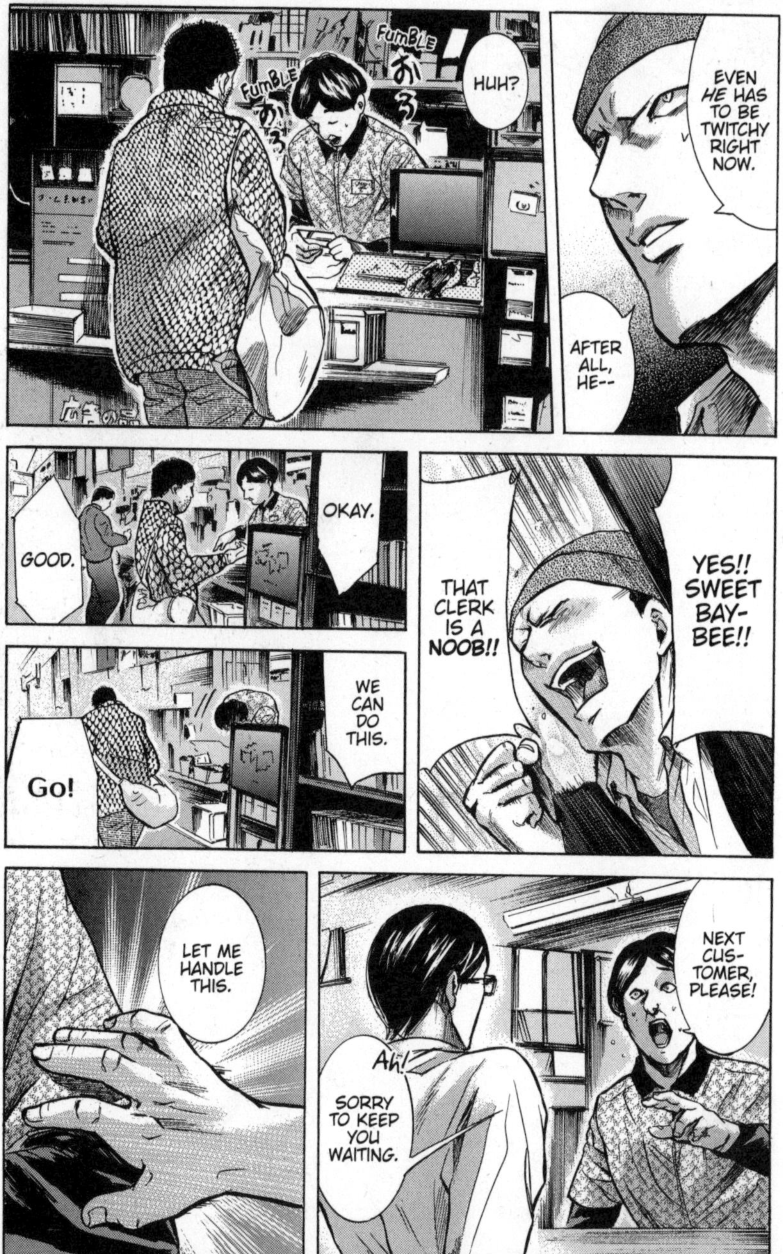
EVEN HE HAS TO BE TWITCHY RIGHT NOW.
AFTER ALL, HE--
HUH?
FUMBLE
FUMBLE
YES!! SWEET BAYBEE!!
THAT CLERK IS A NOOB!!
OKAY.
GOOD.
WE CAN DO THIS.
Go!
NEXT CUS-TOMER, PLEASE!
Ah!
SORRY TO KEEP YOU WAITING.
LET ME HANDLE THIS.

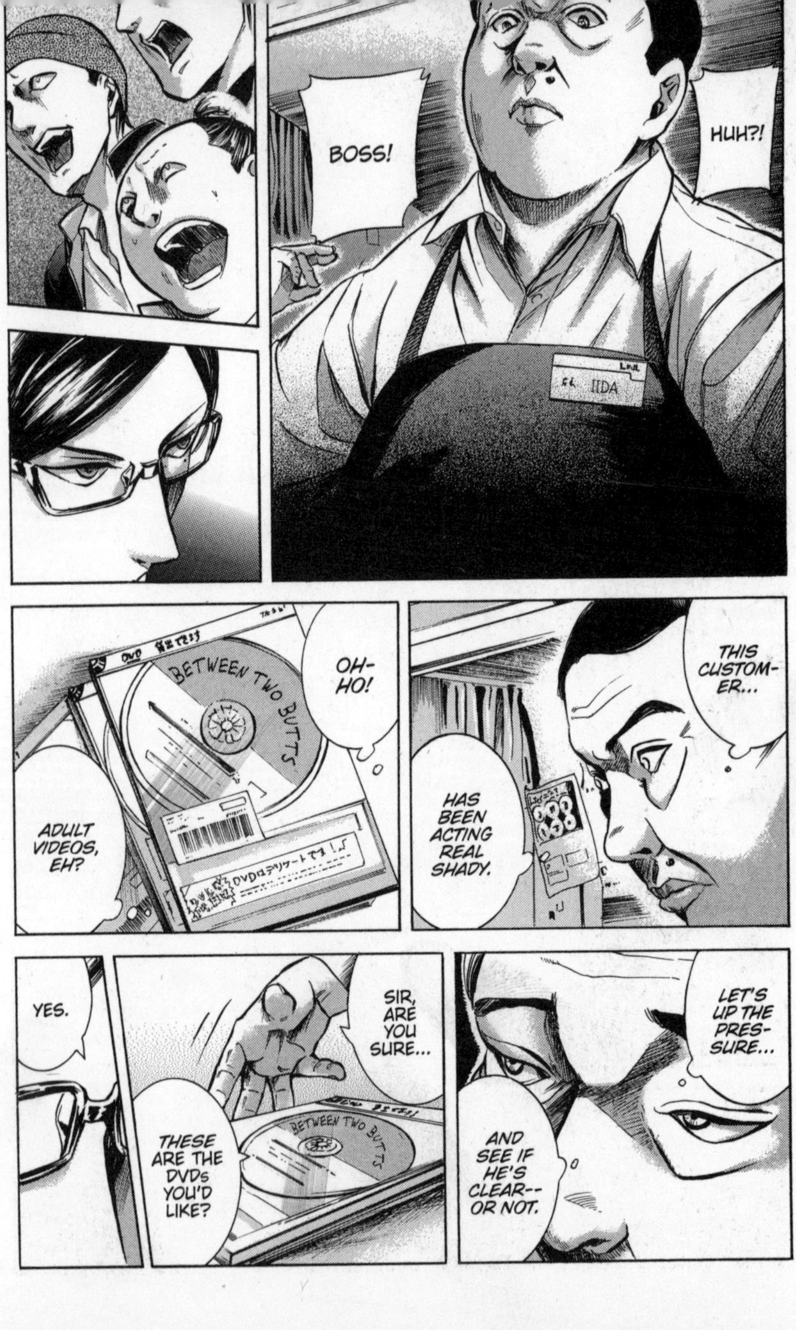
BOSS!
HUH?!
IIDA
THIS CUSTOMER...
HAS BEEN ACTING REAL SHADY.
BETWEEN TWO BUTTS
OH-HO!
ADULT VIDEOS, EH?
LET'S UP THE PRESSURE...
AND SEE IF HE'S CLEAR--OR NOT.
SIR, ARE YOU SURE...
THESE ARE THE DVDs YOU'D LIKE?
BETWEEN TWO BUTTS
YES.

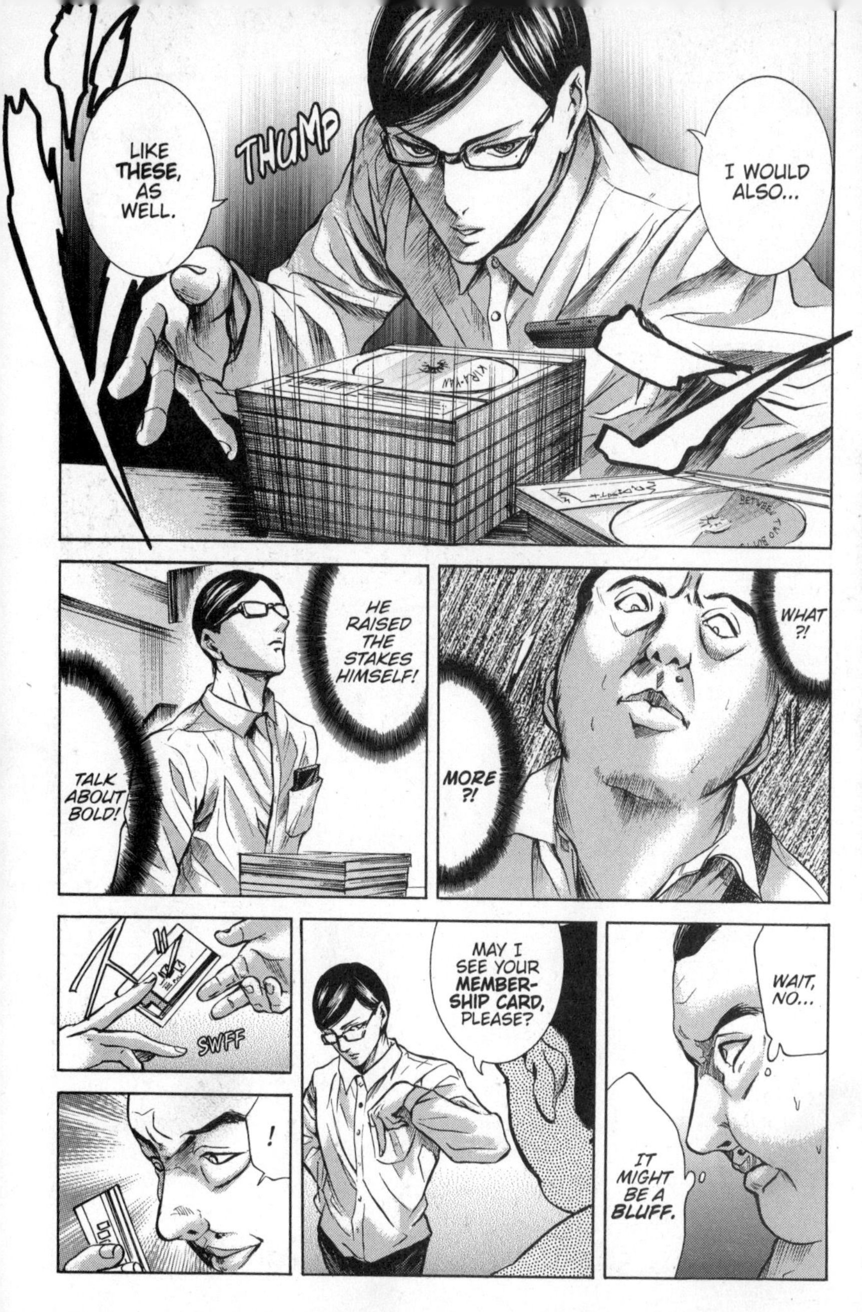
I WOULD ALSO...
THUMP
LIKE THESE, AS WELL.
WHAT?!
MORE ?!
HE RAISED THE STAKES HIMSELF!
TALK ABOUT BOLD!
WAIT, NO...
IT MIGHT BE A BLUFF.
MAY I SEE YOUR MEMBER-SHIP CARD, PLEASE?
SWFF
!

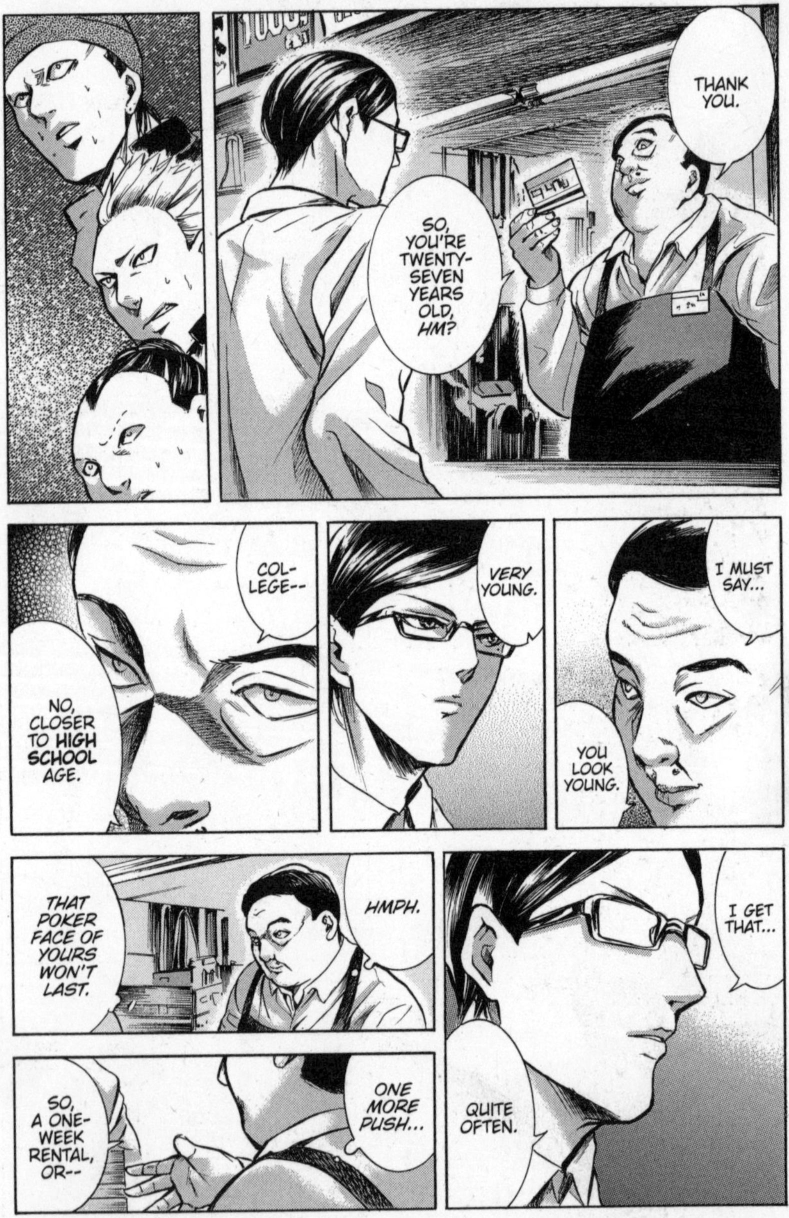
THANK YOU.
SO, YOU'RE TWENTY-SEVEN YEARS OLD, HM?
I MUST SAY...
YOU LOOK YOUNG.
VERY YOUNG.
COL-LEGE--
NO, CLOSER TO **HIGH SCHOOL** AGE.
I GET THAT...
QUITE OFTEN.
HMPH.
THAT POKER FACE OF YOURS WON'T LAST.
ONE MORE PUSH...
SO, A ONE-WEEK RENTAL, OR--

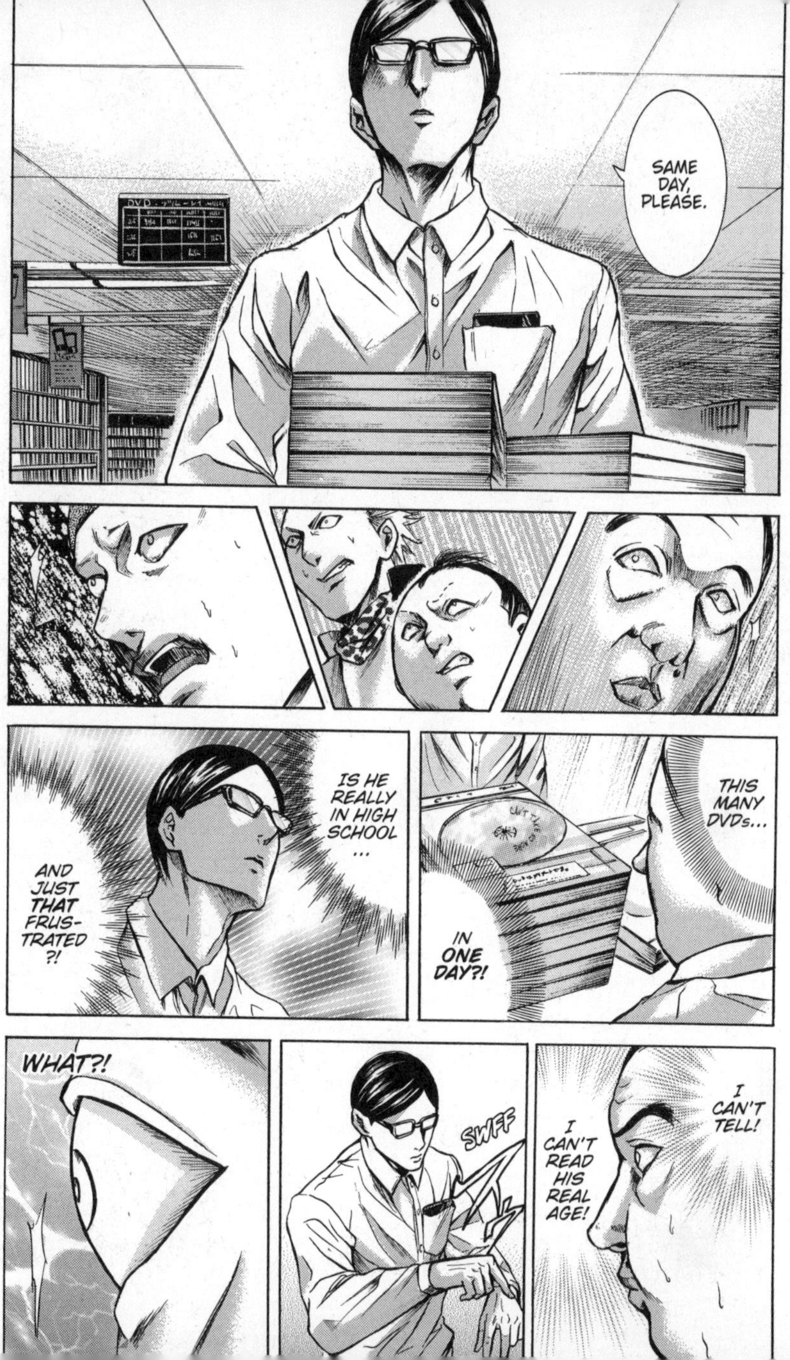
SAME DAY, PLEASE.
THIS MANY DVDs...
IN ONE DAY?!
IS HE REALLY IN HIGH SCHOOL ...
AND JUST THAT FRUS-TRATED ?!
I CAN'T TELL!
I CAN'T READ HIS REAL AGE!
SWFF
WHAT?!

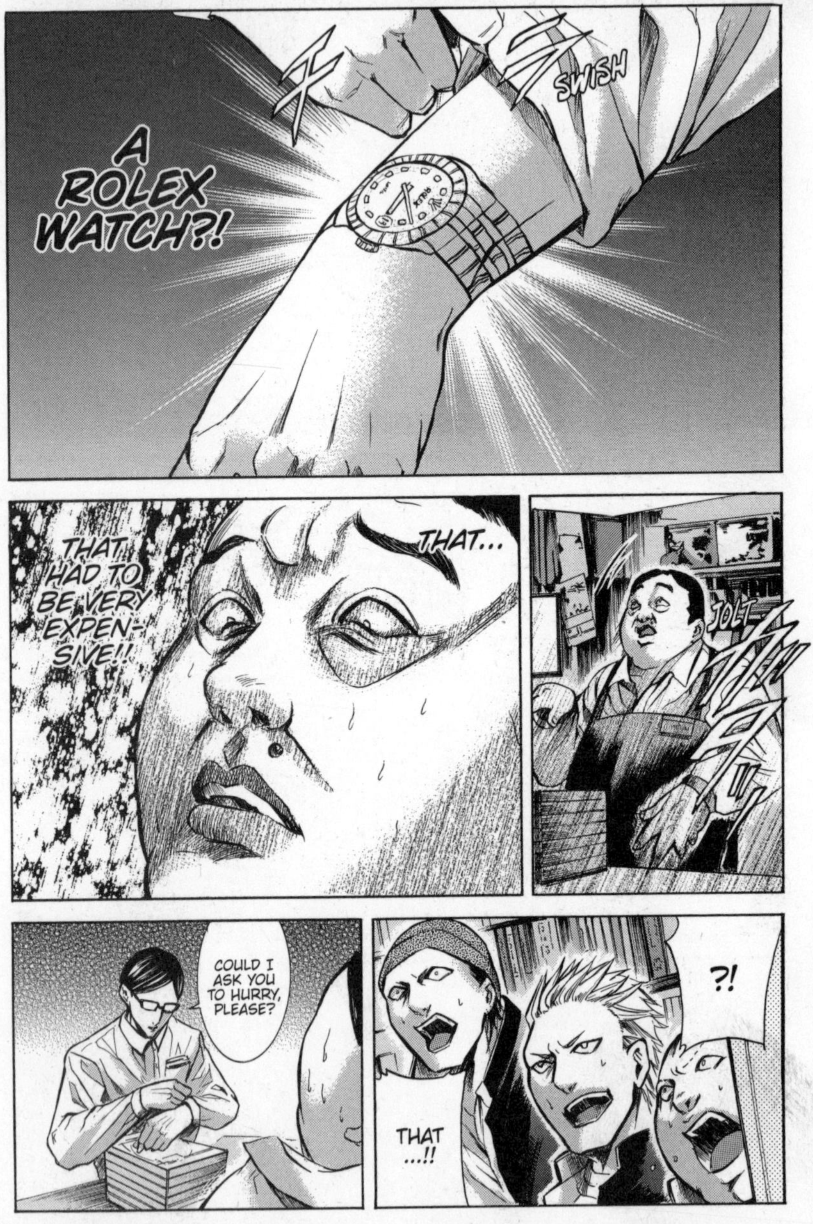
SWISH
A ROLEX WATCH?!
JOLT
THAT...
THAT HAD TO BE VERY EXPEN-SIVE!!
?!
THAT ...!!
COULD I ASK YOU TO HURRY, PLEASE?

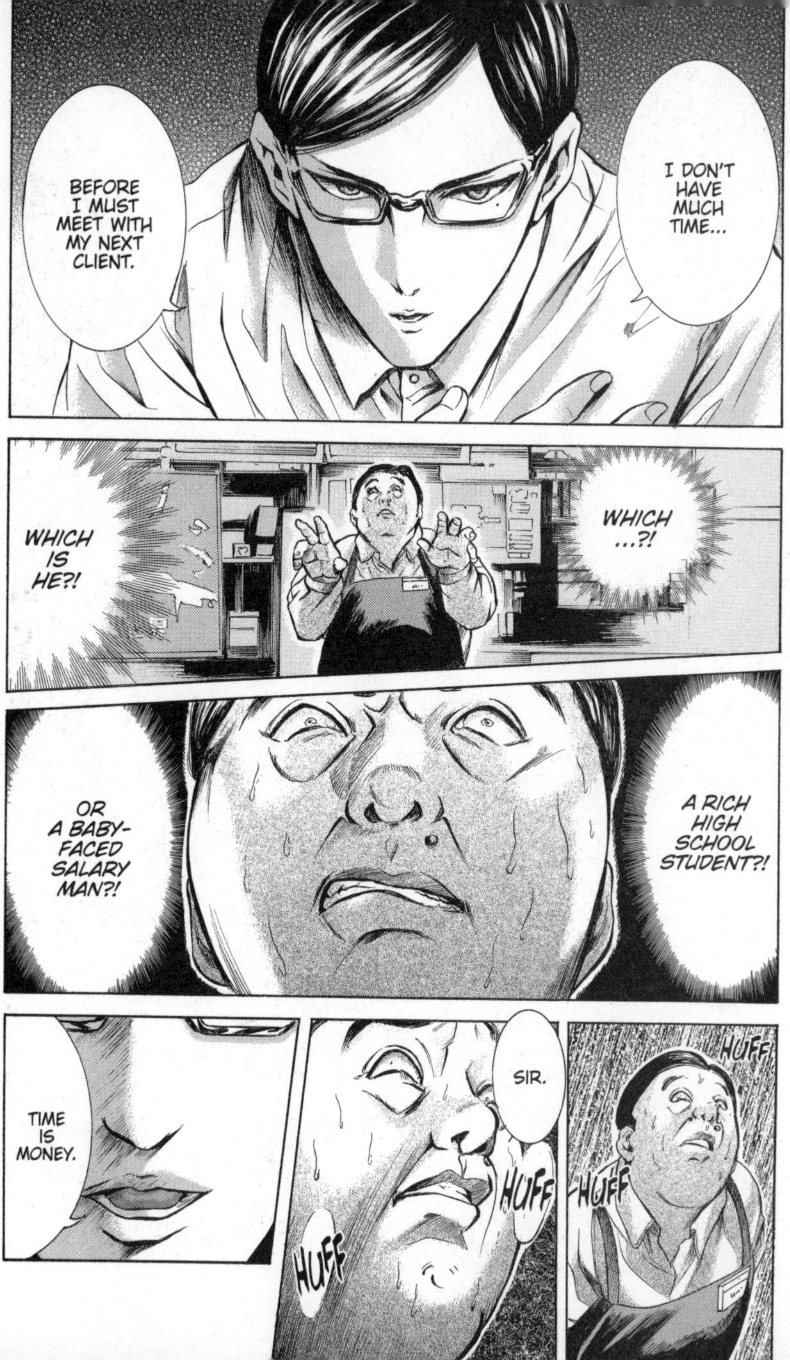

I DON'T HAVE MUCH TIME...
BEFORE I MUST MEET WITH MY NEXT CLIENT.
WHICH ...?!
WHICH IS HE?!
A RICH HIGH SCHOOL STUDENT?!
OR A BABY-FACED SALARY MAN?!
HUFF
HUFF
SIR.
HUFF
HUFF
TIME IS MONEY.

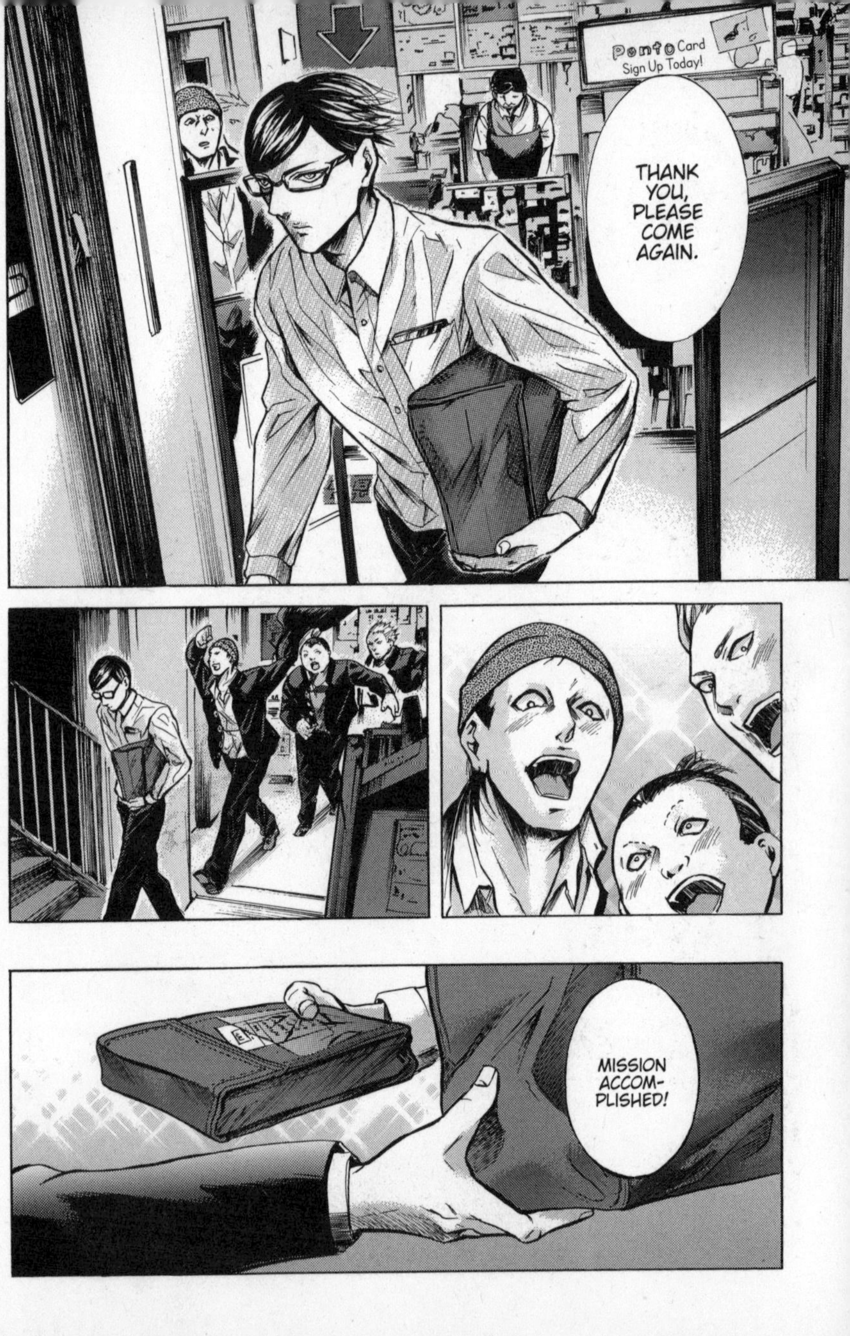
Ponto Card
Sign Up Today!
THANK YOU, PLEASE COME AGAIN.
MISSION ACCOM-PLISHED!

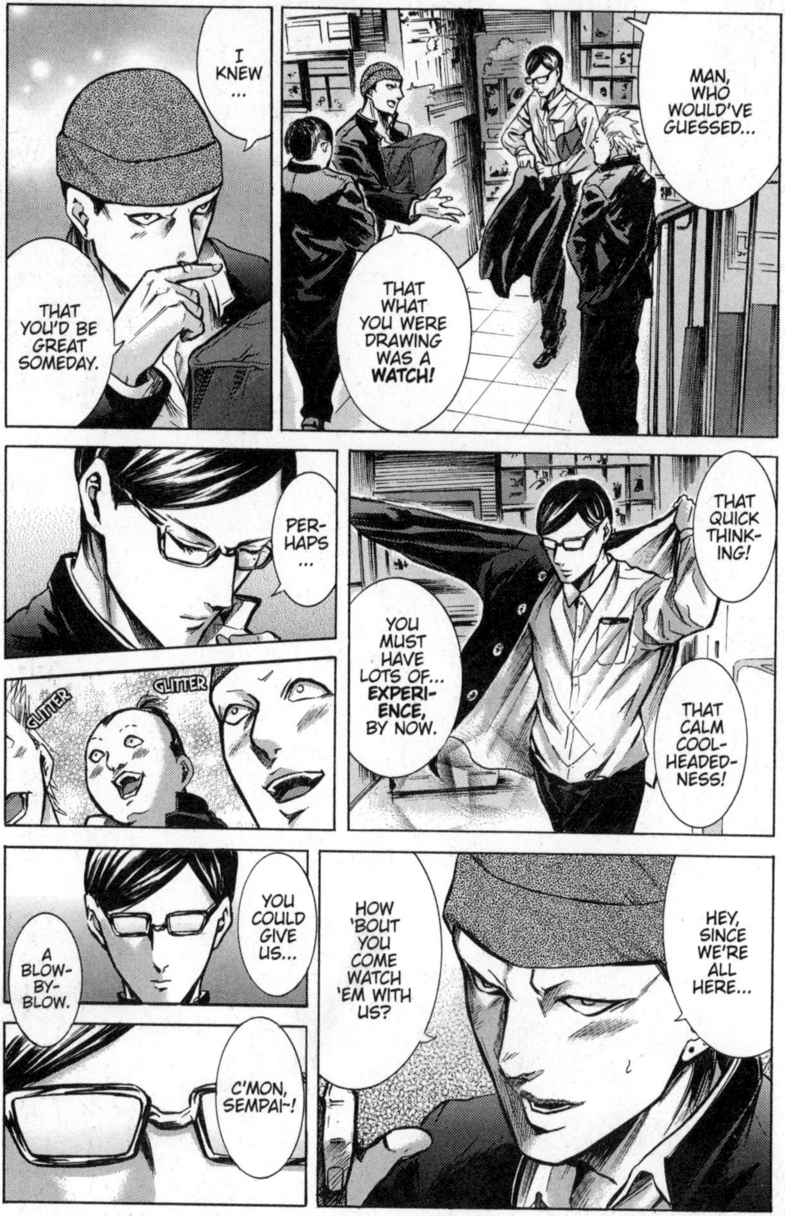
MAN, WHO WOULD'VE GUESSED...
THAT WHAT YOU WERE DRAWING WAS A **WATCH!**
I KNEW ...
THAT YOU'D BE GREAT SOMEDAY.
THAT QUICK THINKING!
THAT CALM COOL-HEADED-NESS!
YOU MUST HAVE LOTS OF... **EXPERIENCE,** BY NOW.
PER-HAPS ...
GLITTER
GLITTER
HEY, SINCE WE'RE ALL HERE...
HOW 'BOUT YOU COME WATCH 'EM WITH US?
YOU COULD GIVE US...
A BLOW-BY-BLOW.
C'MON, SEMPAI~!

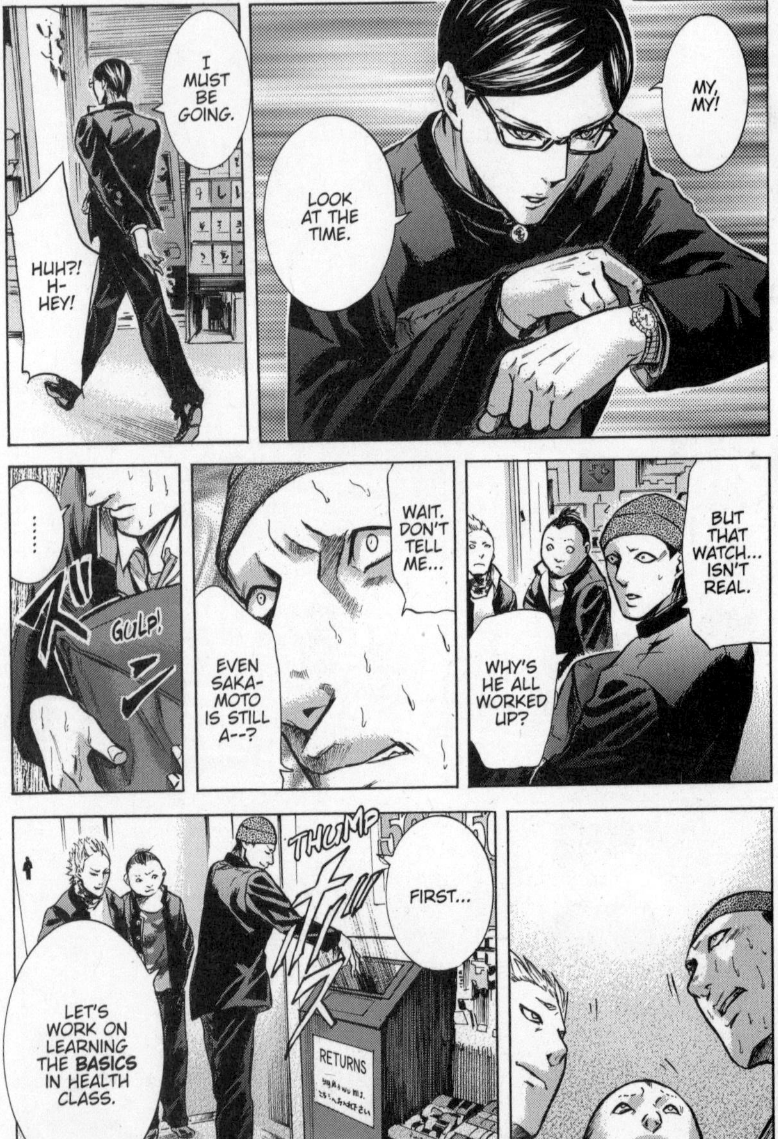
MY, MY!
LOOK AT THE TIME.
I MUST BE GOING.
HUH?! H- HEY!
BUT THAT WATCH... ISN'T REAL.
WHY'S HE ALL WORKED UP?
WAIT. DON'T TELL ME...
EVEN SAKAMOTO IS STILL A--?
......
GULP!
THUMP
FIRST...
LET'S WORK ON LEARNING THE **BASICS** IN HEALTH CLASS.
RETURNS

End of Chapter 14

Break Time #3:
Tennis Court

CHAPTER 15:
SERA'S FRENCH REVOLUTION

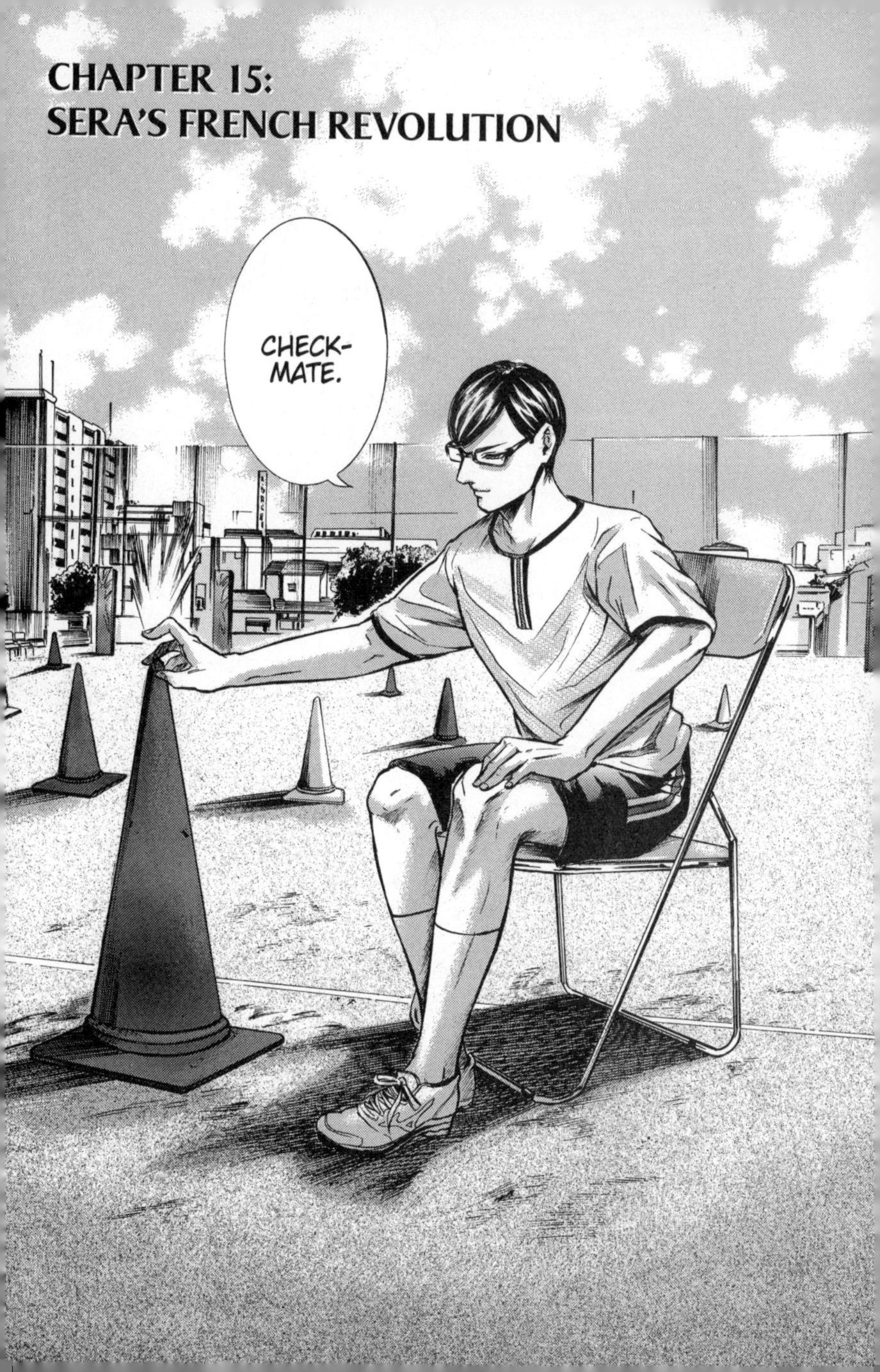
CHECK-
MATE.

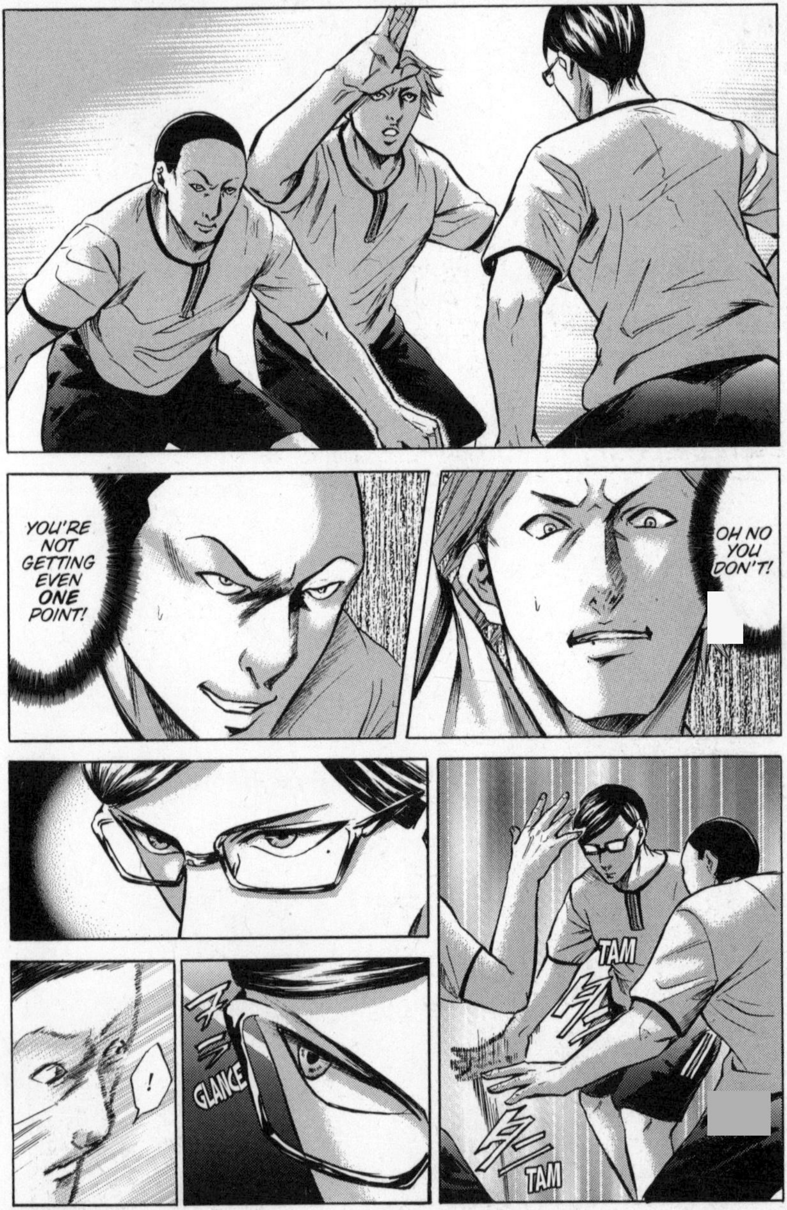
OH NO YOU DON'T!
YOU'RE NOT GETTING EVEN ONE POINT!
TAM
TAM
GLANCE
!

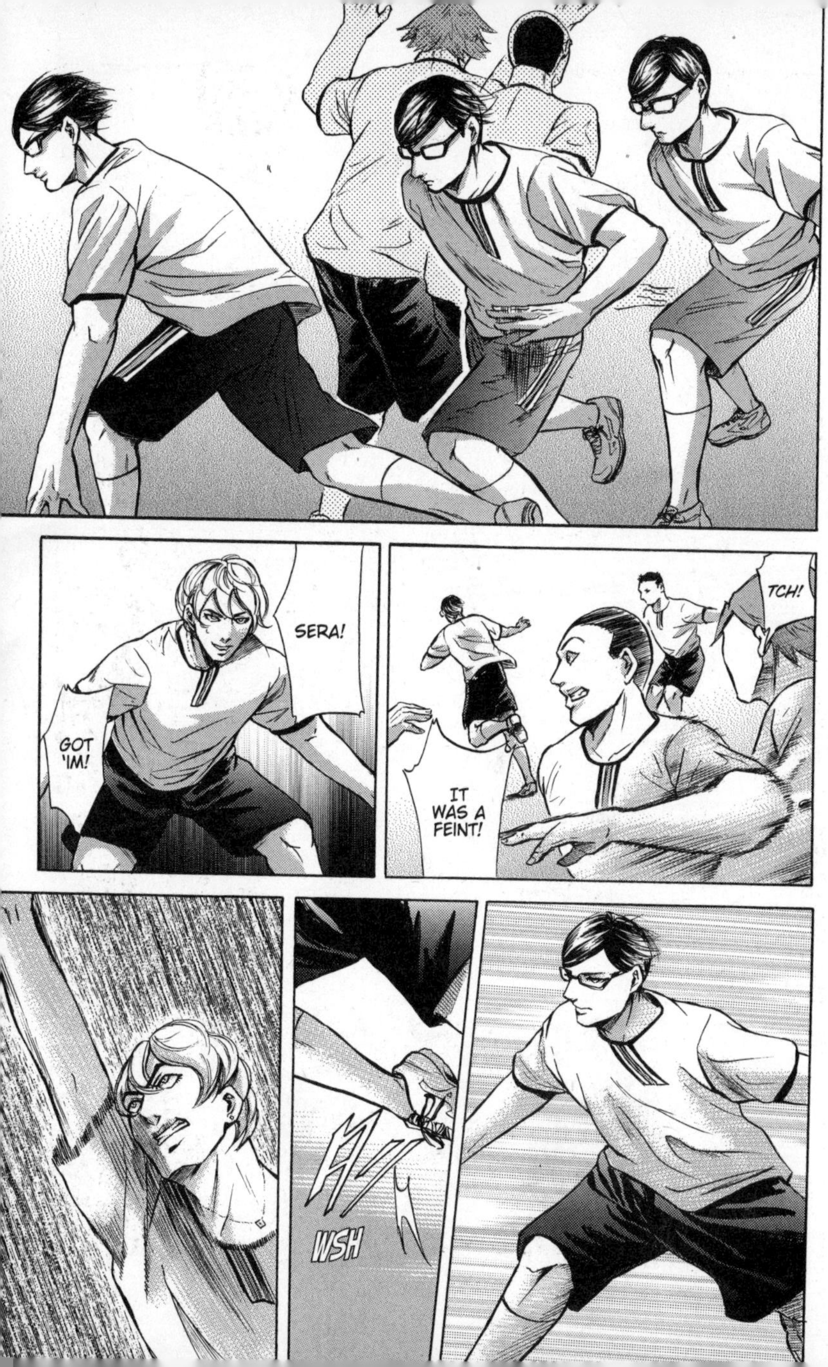
TCH!
IT WAS A FEINT!
SERA!
GOT 'IM!
WSH

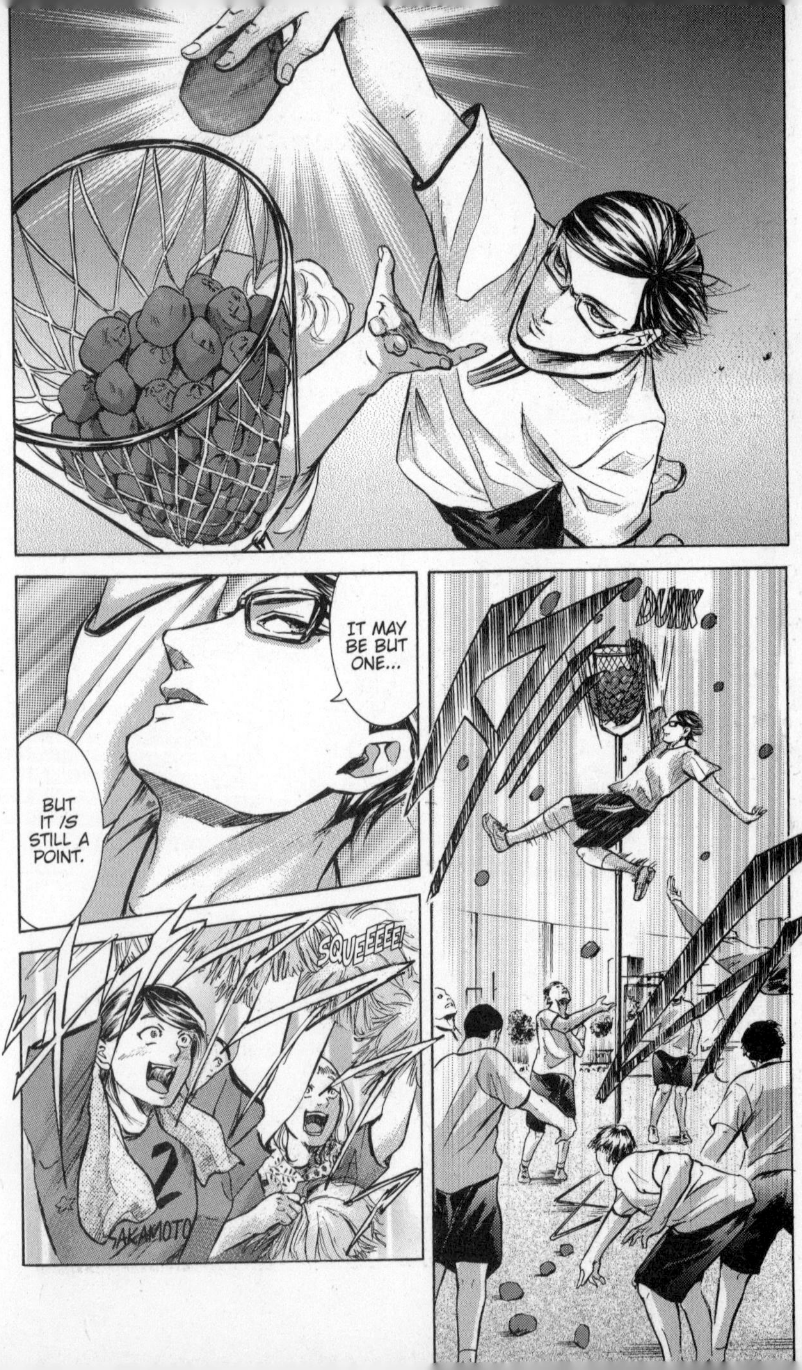
DUNK
IT MAY BE BUT ONE...
BUT IT IS STILL A POINT.
SQUEEEEE!

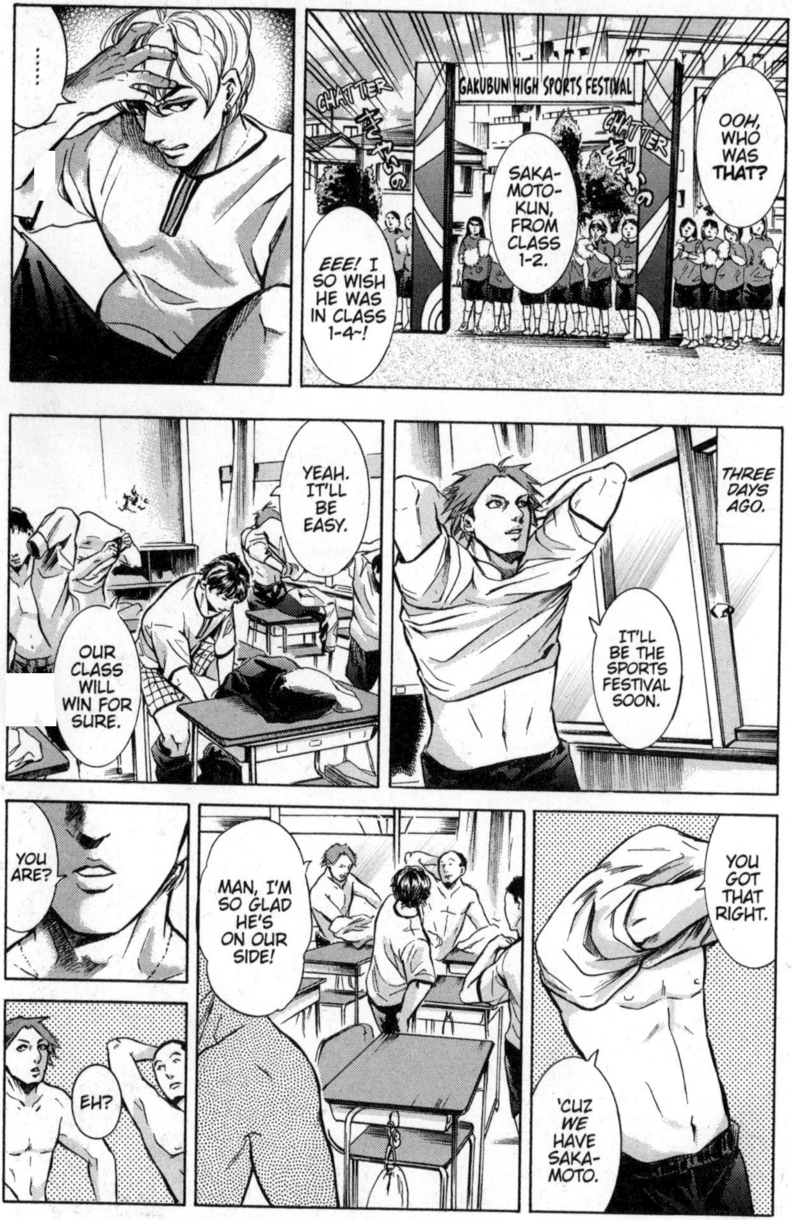
OOH, WHO WAS THAT?
CHATTER
GAKUBUN HIGH SPORTS FESTIVAL
CHATTER
SAKA-MOTO-KUN, FROM CLASS 1-2.
EEE! I SO WISH HE WAS IN CLASS 1-4~!
......
THREE DAYS AGO.
IT'LL BE THE SPORTS FESTIVAL SOON.
YEAH. IT'LL BE EASY.
OUR CLASS WILL WIN FOR SURE.
YOU GOT THAT RIGHT.
'CUZ WE HAVE SAKA-MOTO.
MAN, I'M SO GLAD HE'S ON OUR SIDE!
YOU ARE?
EH?

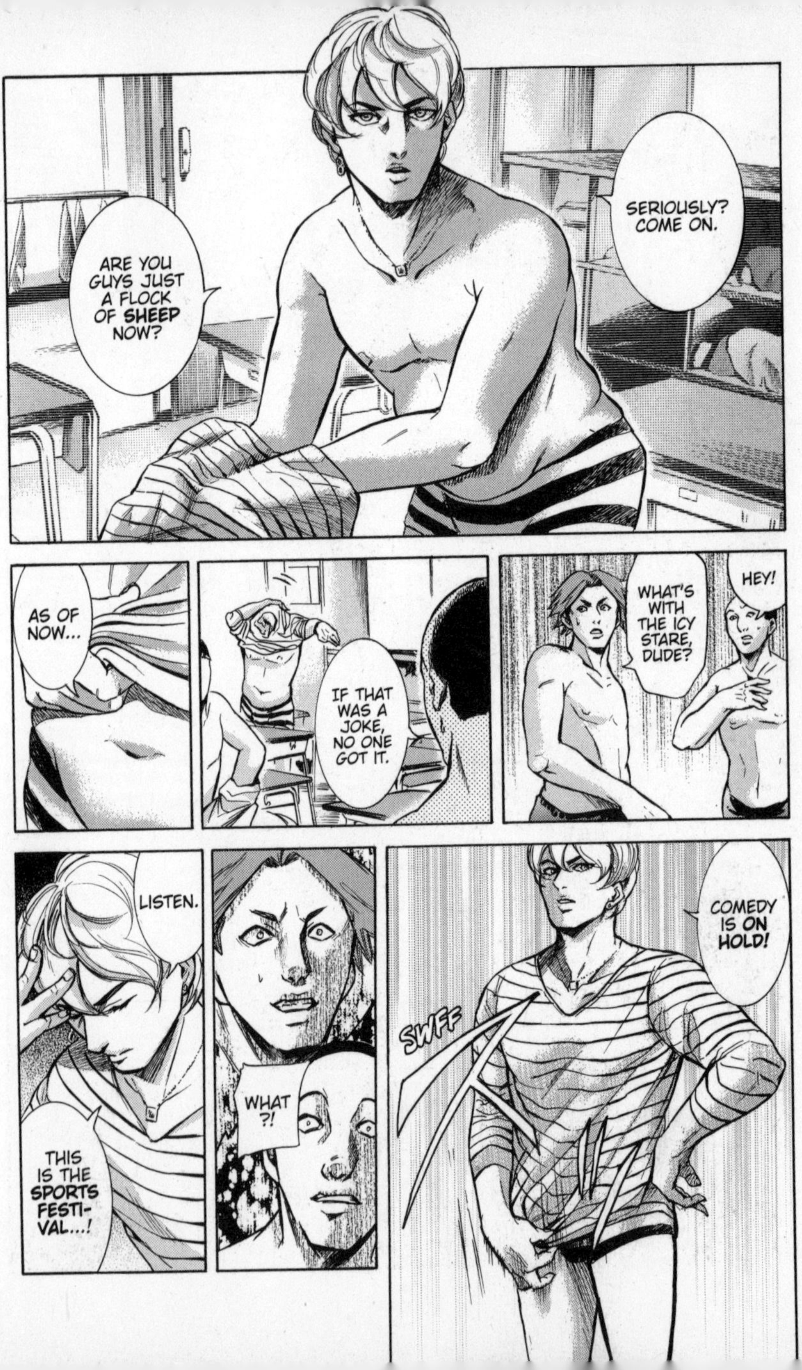
SERIOUSLY? COME ON.
ARE YOU GUYS JUST A FLOCK OF SHEEP NOW?
HEY!
WHAT'S WITH THE ICY STARE, DUDE?
IF THAT WAS A JOKE, NO ONE GOT IT.
AS OF NOW...
COMEDY IS ON HOLD!
SWFF
WHAT ?!
LISTEN.
THIS IS THE SPORTS FESTIVAL...!

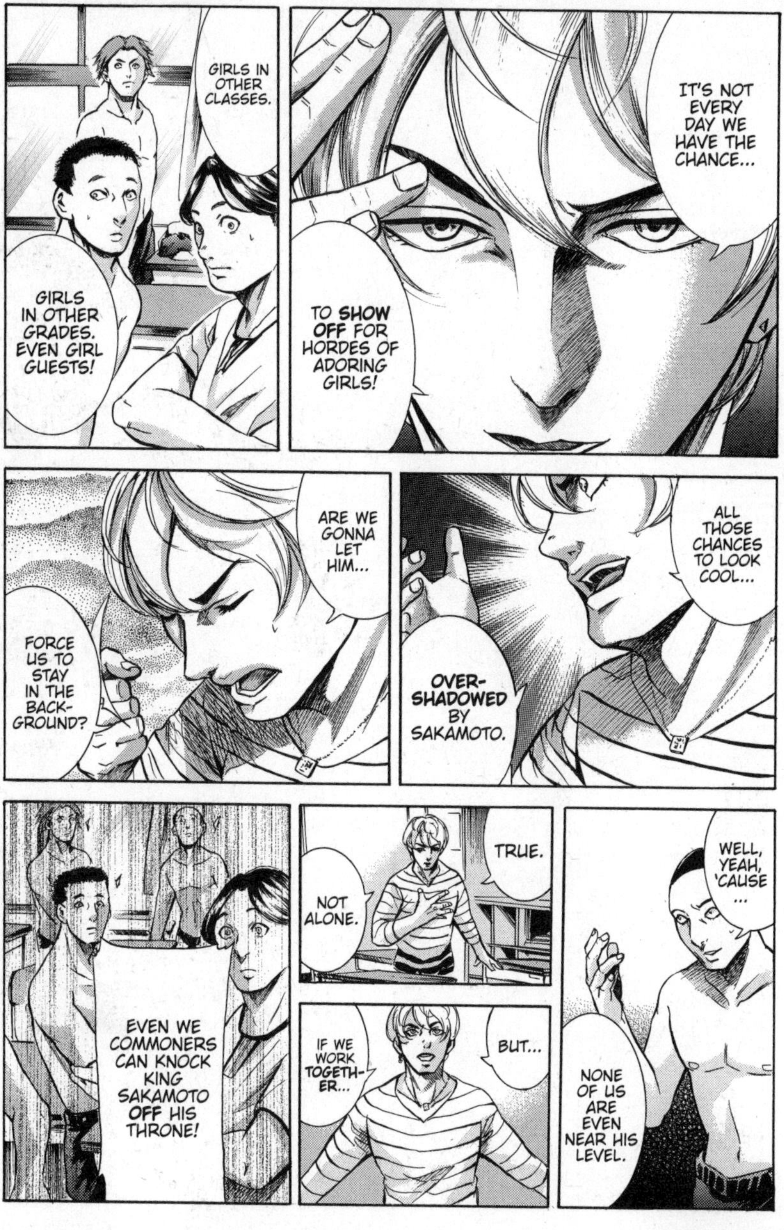
IT'S NOT EVERY DAY WE HAVE THE CHANCE...
TO **SHOW OFF** FOR HORDES OF ADORING GIRLS!
GIRLS IN OTHER CLASSES.
GIRLS IN OTHER GRADES. EVEN GIRL GUESTS!
ALL THOSE CHANCES TO LOOK COOL...
OVER-SHADOWED BY SAKAMOTO.
ARE WE GONNA LET HIM...
FORCE US TO STAY IN THE BACK-GROUND?
WELL, YEAH, 'CAUSE...
NONE OF US ARE EVEN NEAR HIS LEVEL.
TRUE.
NOT ALONE.
BUT...
IF WE WORK **TOGETHER**...
EVEN WE COMMONERS CAN KNOCK KING SAKAMOTO **OFF** HIS THRONE!

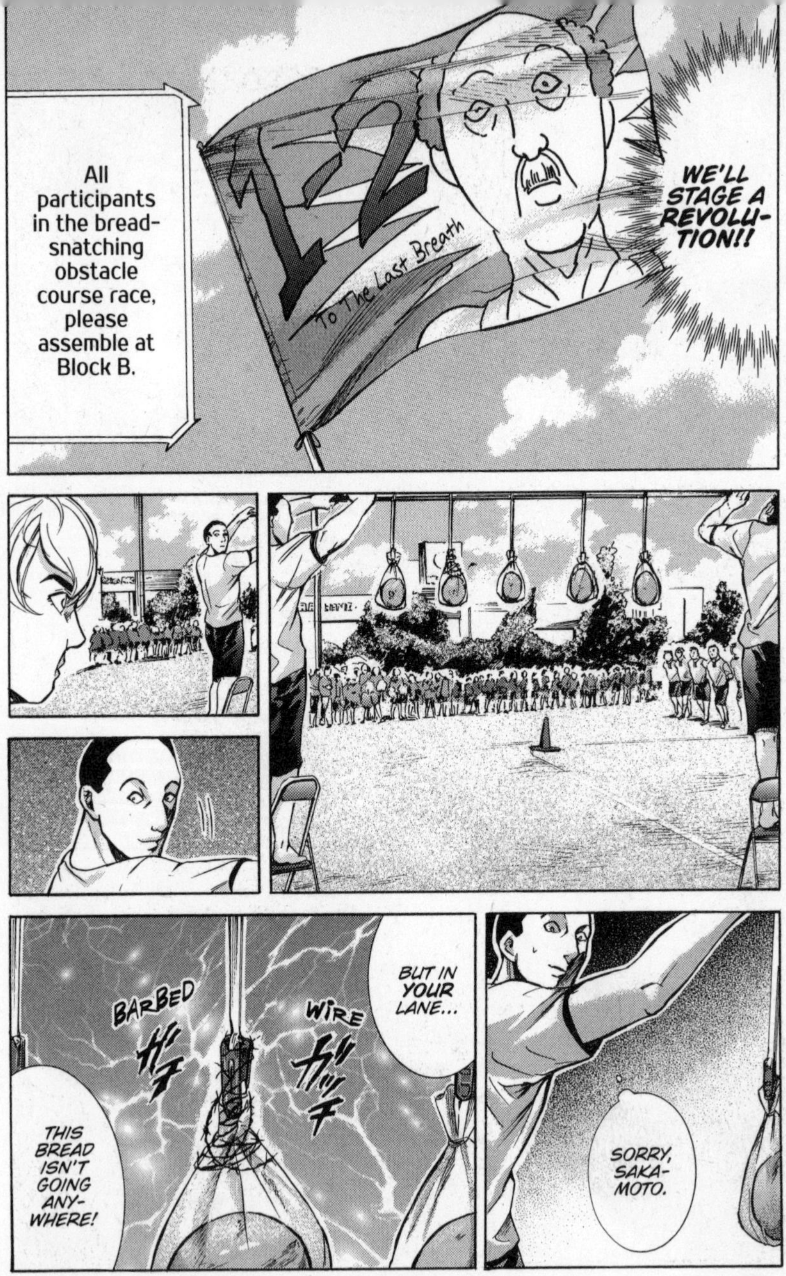
WE'LL STAGE A REVOLUTION!!
To The Last Breath
All participants in the bread-snatching obstacle course race, please assemble at Block B.
SORRY, SAKAMOTO.
BUT IN YOUR LANE...
WIRE
BARBED
THIS BREAD ISN'T GOING ANYWHERE!

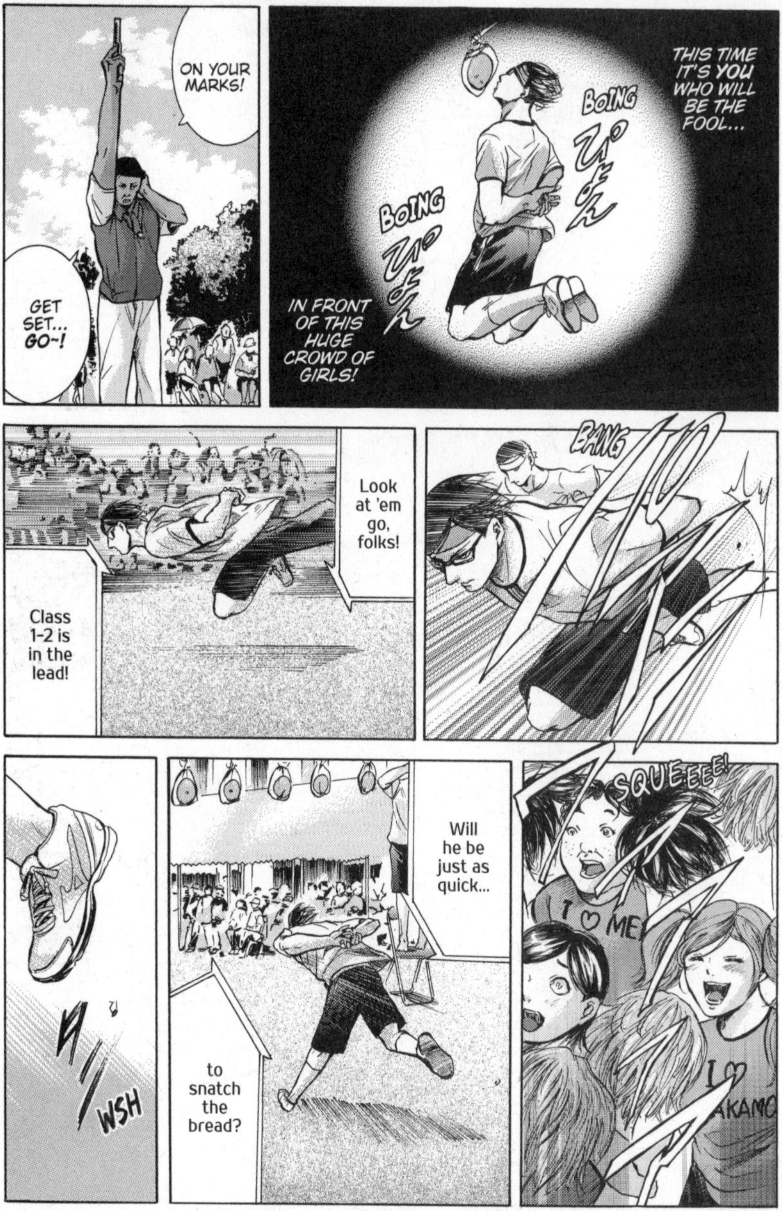

THIS TIME IT'S YOU WHO WILL BE THE FOOL...
BOING
BOING
IN FRONT OF THIS HUGE CROWD OF GIRLS!
ON YOUR MARKS!
GET SET... GO~!
BANG
Look at 'em go, folks!
Class 1-2 is in the lead!
SQUEEEE!
Will he be just as quick...
to snatch the bread?
WSH

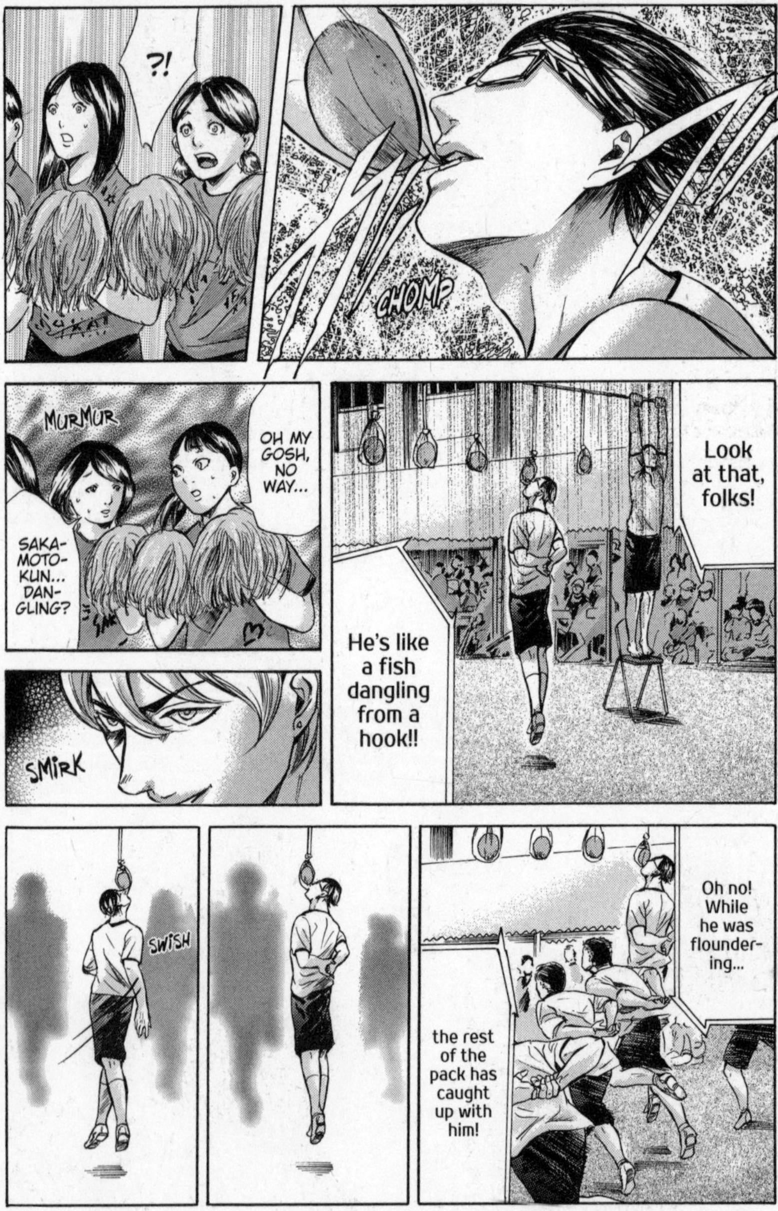
CHOMP
?!
Look at that, folks!
He's like a fish dangling from a hook!!
OH MY GOSH, NO WAY...
MURMUR
SAKAMOTO-KUN... DANGLING?
SMIRK
Oh no! While he was floundering...
the rest of the pack has caught up with him!
SWISH

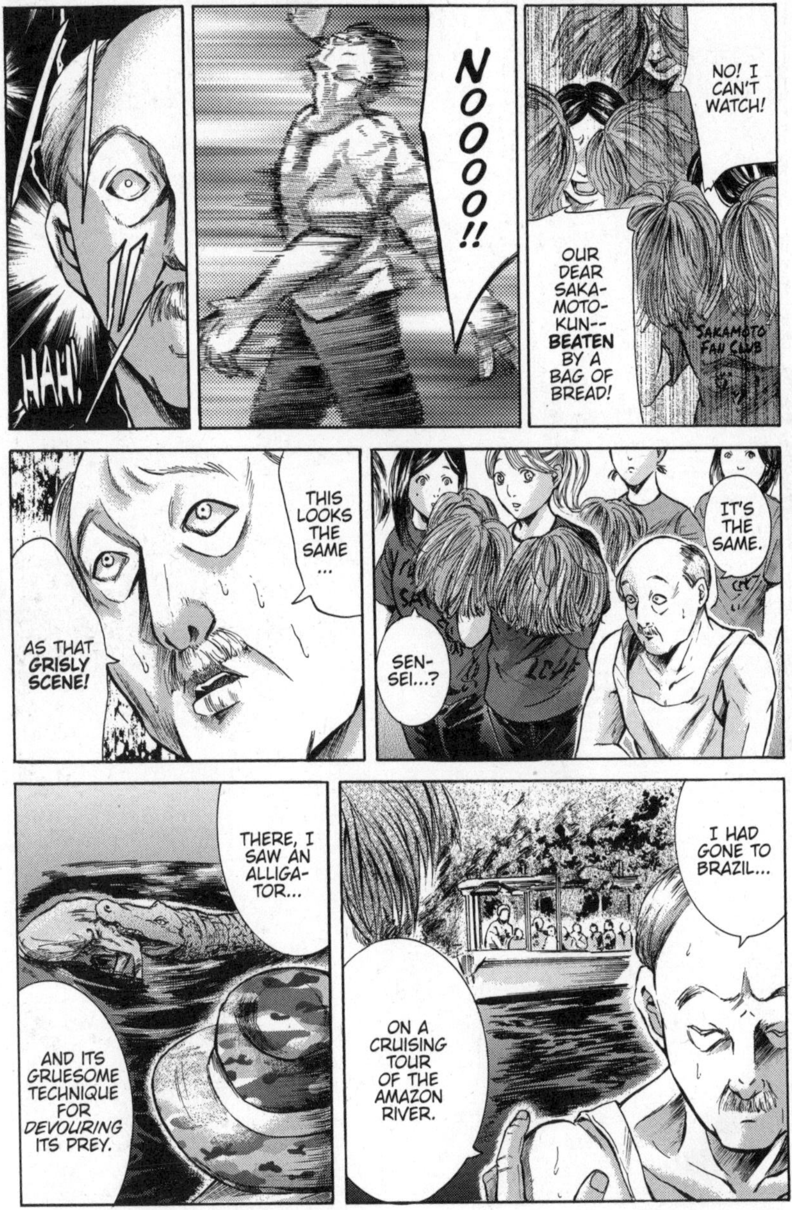
NO! I CAN'T WATCH!
OUR DEAR SAKAMOTO-KUN-- **BEATEN** BY A BAG OF BREAD!
SAKAMOTO FAN CLUB
NOOOOO!!
HAH!
IT'S THE SAME.
SEN-SEI...?
THIS LOOKS THE SAME...
AS THAT **GRISLY** SCENE!
I HAD GONE TO BRAZIL...
ON A CRUISING TOUR OF THE AMAZON RIVER.
THERE, I SAW AN ALLIGATOR...
AND ITS GRUESOME TECHNIQUE FOR *DEVOURING* ITS PREY.

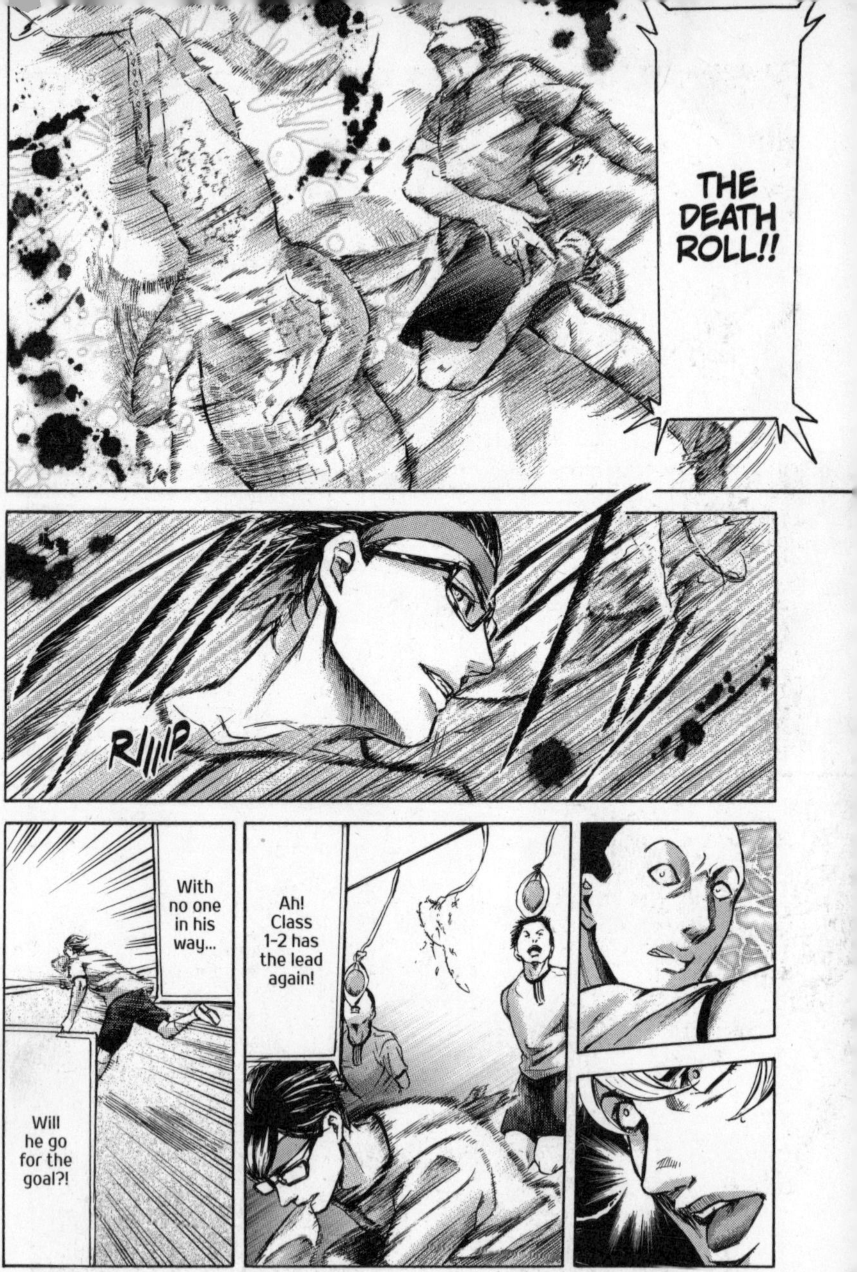
THE DEATH ROLL!!
RIIIIP
Ah! Class 1-2 has the lead again!
With no one in his way...
Will he go for the goal?!

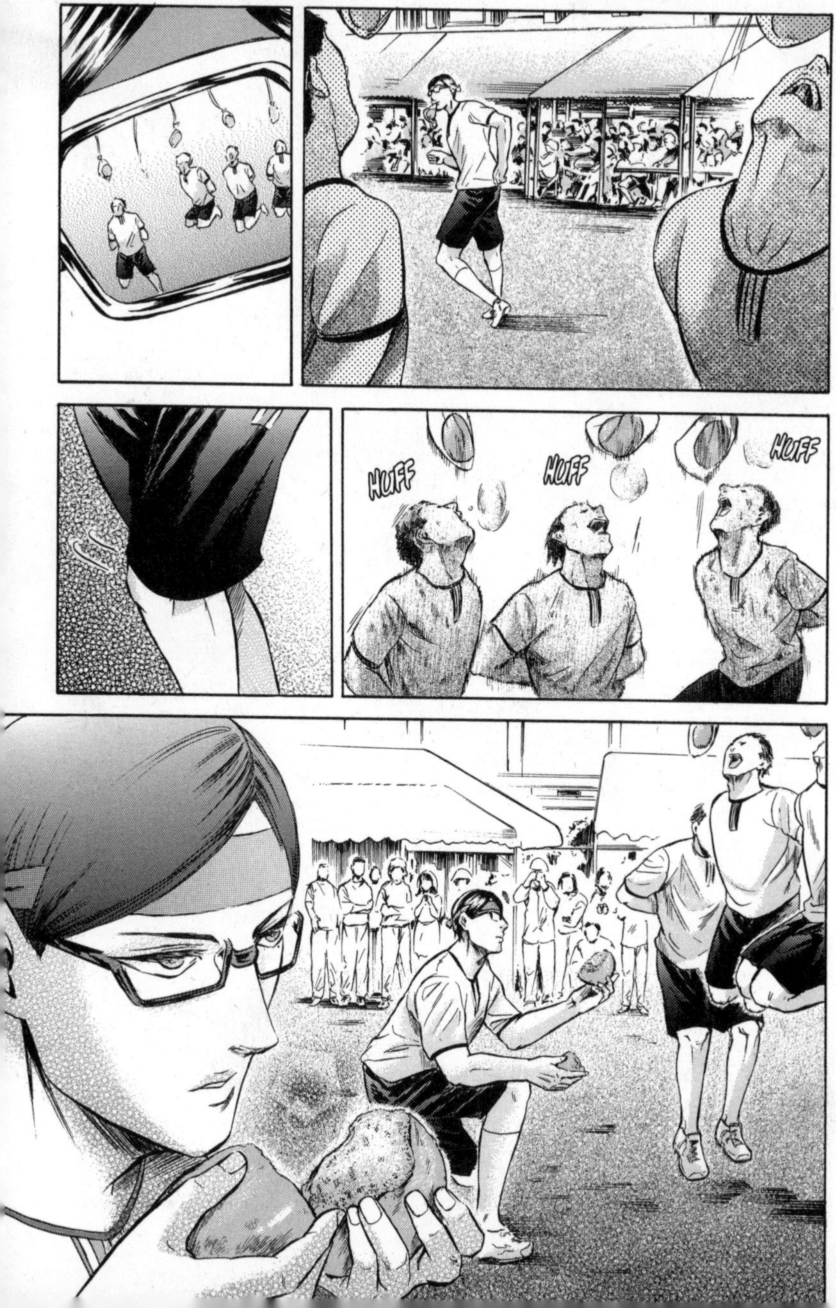
HUFF
HUFF
HUFF

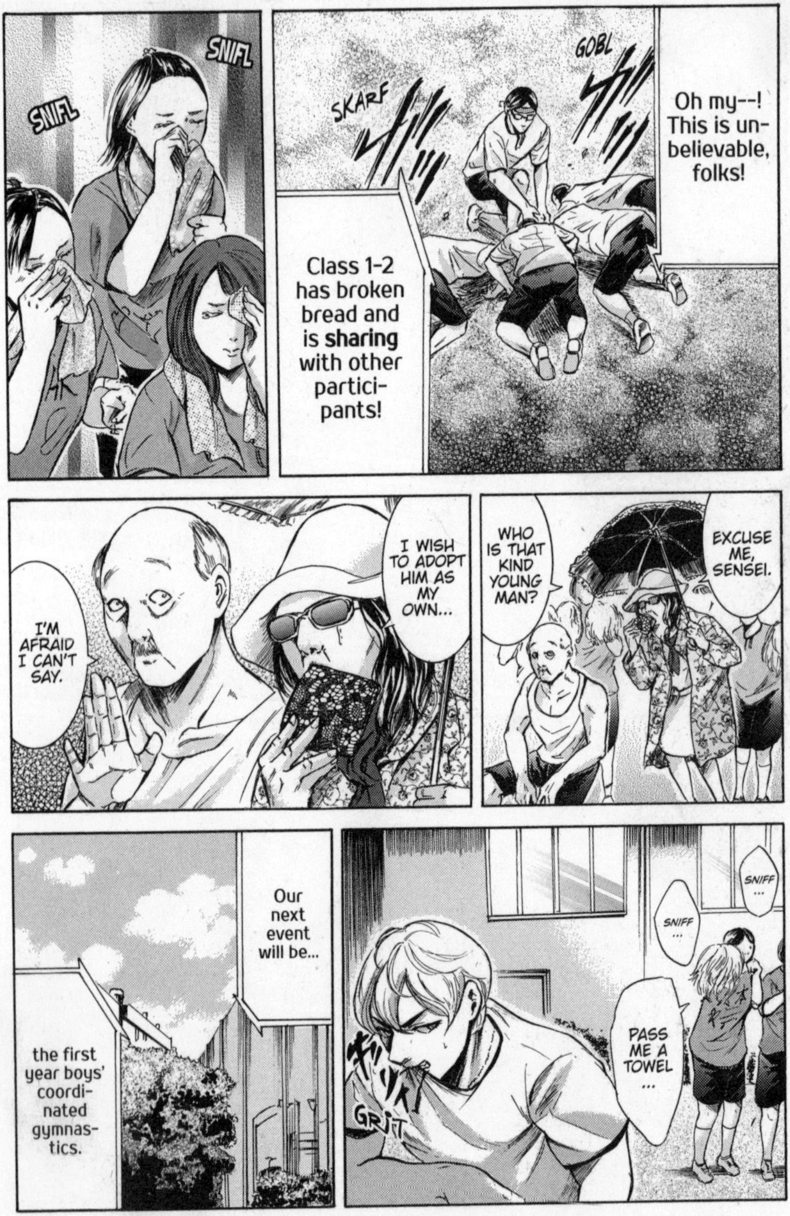
Oh my--! This is un-believable, folks!
GOBL
SKARF
Class 1-2 has broken bread and is **sharing** with other partici-pants!
SNIFL
SNIFL
EXCUSE ME, SENSEI.
WHO IS THAT KIND YOUNG MAN?
I WISH TO ADOPT HIM AS MY OWN...
I'M AFRAID I CAN'T SAY.
SNIFF...
SNIFF...
PASS ME A TOWEL...
GRIT
Our next event will be...
the first year boys' coordi-nated gymnas-tics.

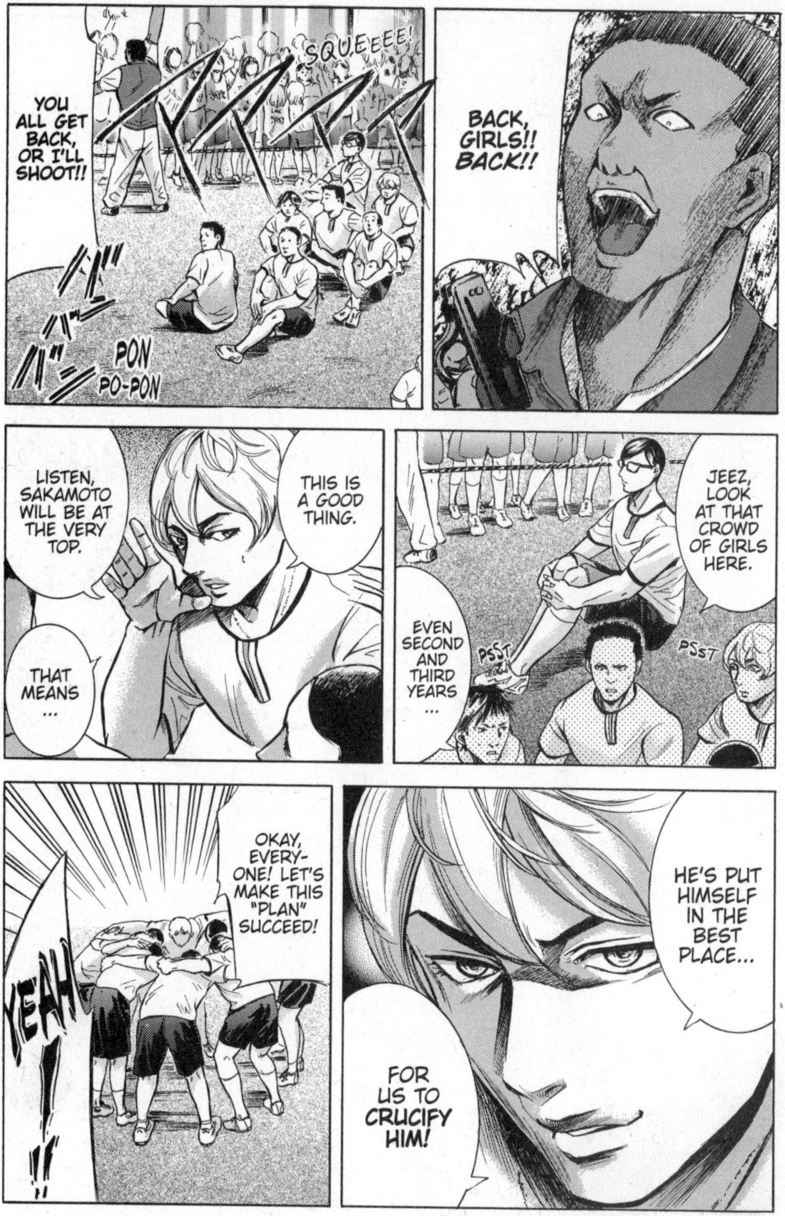
BACK, GIRLS!! BACK!!
SQUEEEEE!
YOU ALL GET BACK, OR I'LL SHOOT!!
PON PO-PON
JEEZ, LOOK AT THAT CROWD OF GIRLS HERE.
EVEN SECOND AND THIRD YEARS ...
PSST
PSST
THIS IS A GOOD THING.
LISTEN, SAKAMOTO WILL BE AT THE VERY TOP.
THAT MEANS ...
HE'S PUT HIMSELF IN THE BEST PLACE...
FOR US TO CRUCIFY HIM!
OKAY, EVERY-ONE! LET'S MAKE THIS "PLAN" SUCCEED!
YEAH!!!

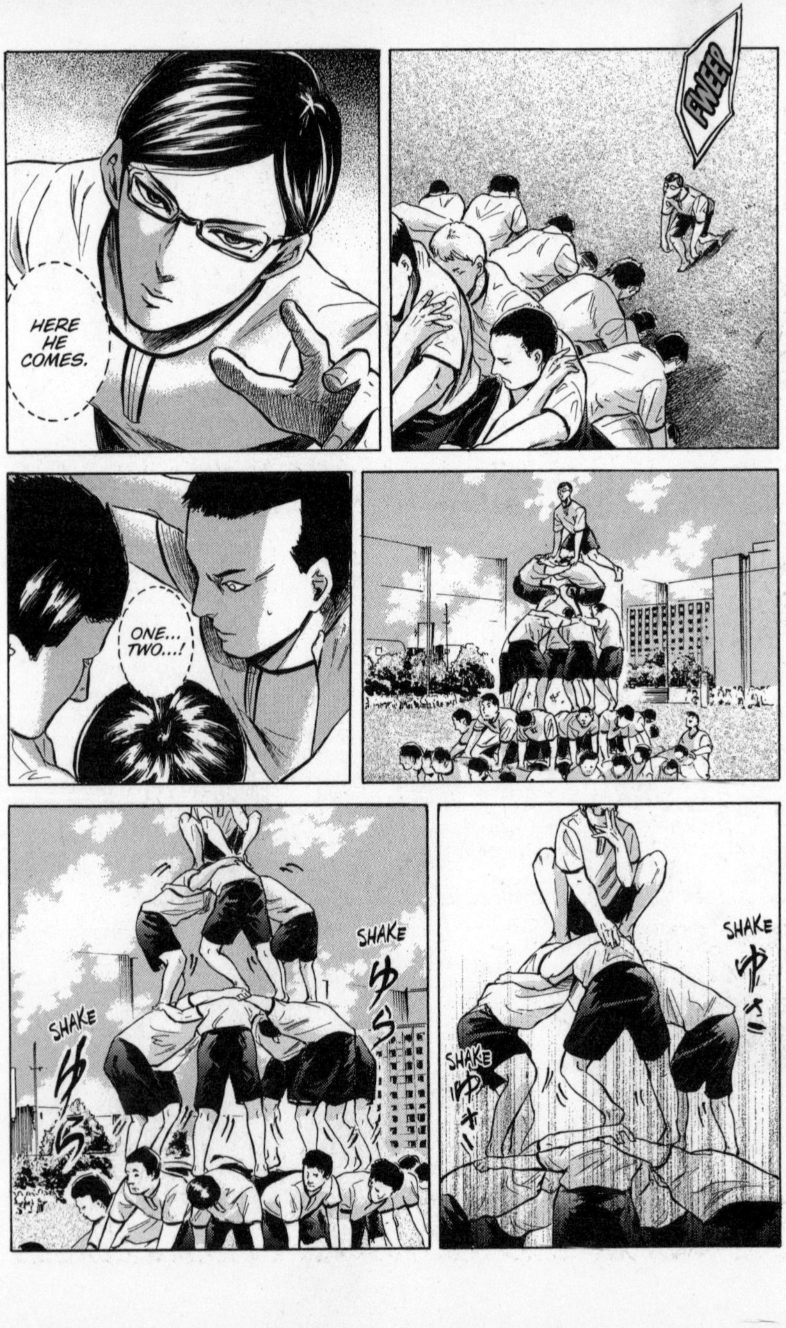
FWEEP
HERE HE COMES.
ONE... TWO...!
SHAKE
ゆさ
SHAKE
ゆさ
SHAKE
ゆら
SHAKE
ゆら

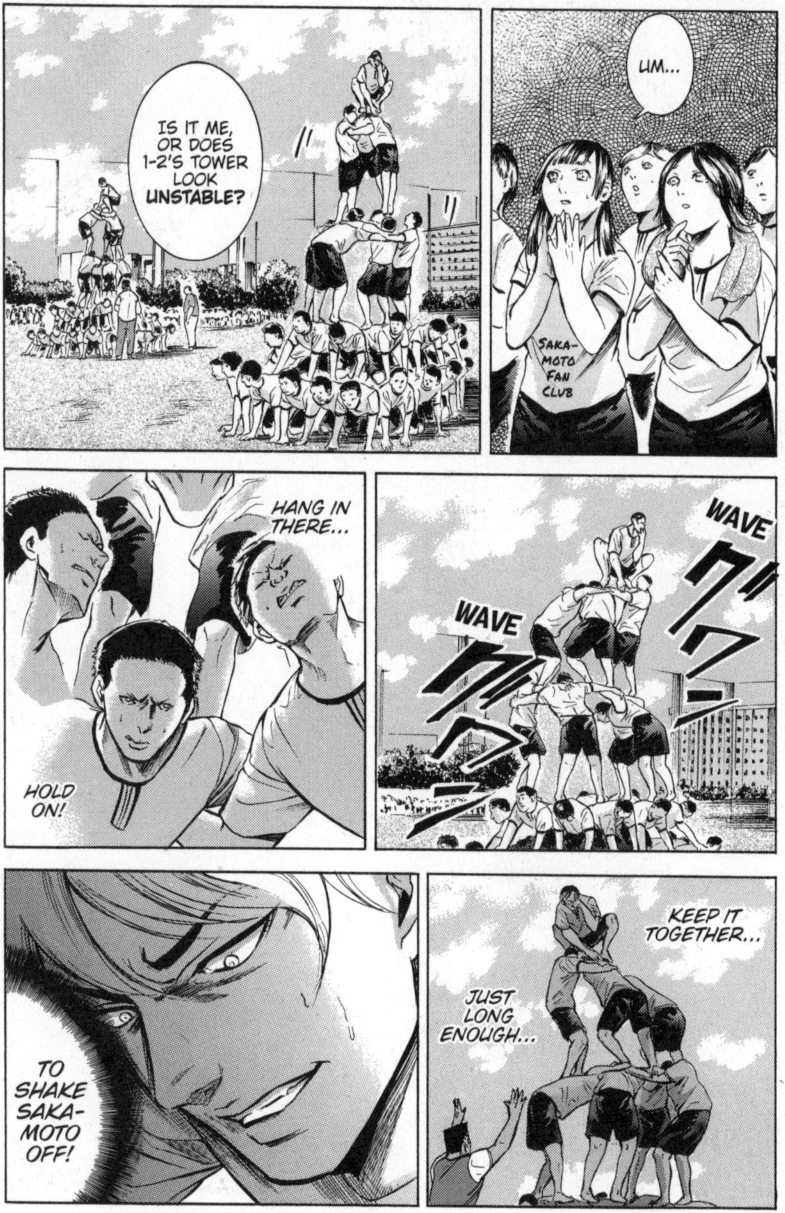
UM...
SAKA-
MOTO
FAN
CLUB
IS IT ME, OR DOES 1-2'S TOWER LOOK UNSTABLE?
WAVE
WAVE
HANG IN THERE...
HOLD ON!
KEEP IT TOGETHER...
JUST LONG ENOUGH...
TO SHAKE SAKA-MOTO OFF!

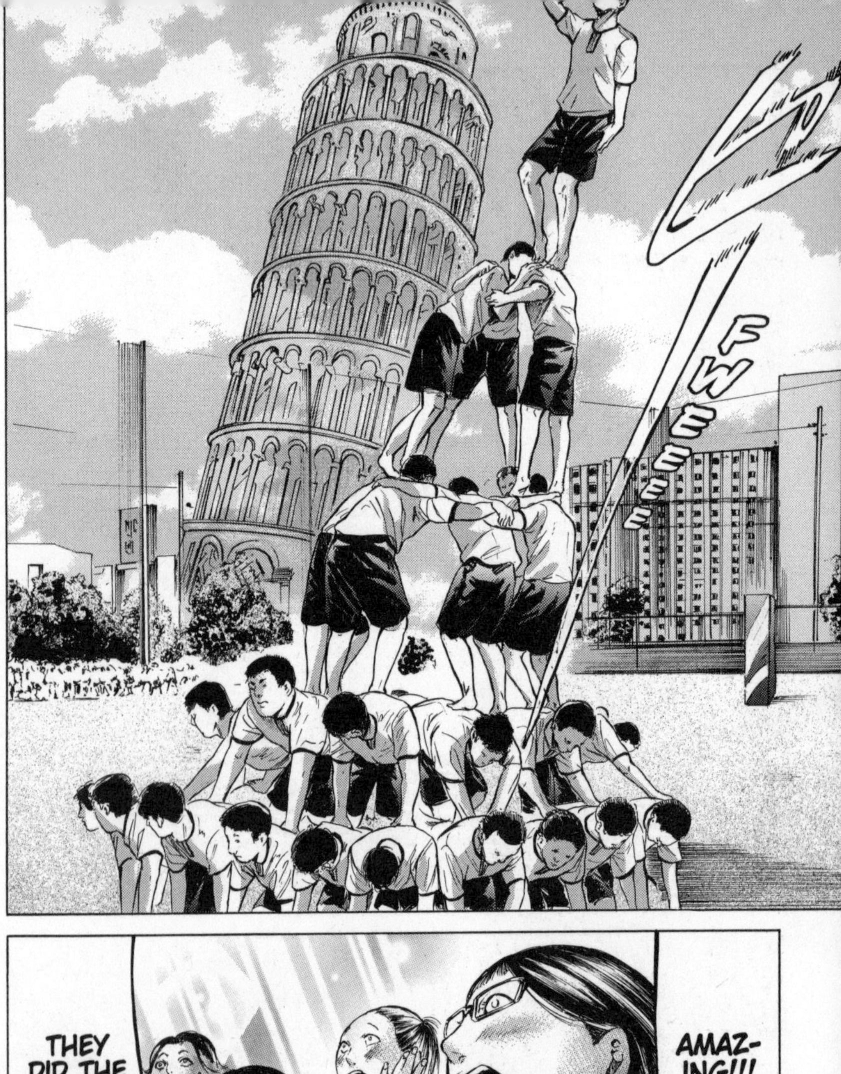
FWEEEEE
AMAZ-ING!!!
THEY DID THE LEANING TOWER OF PISA!!

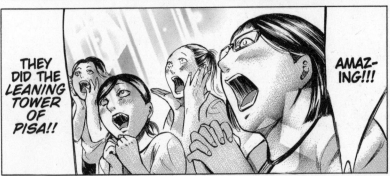

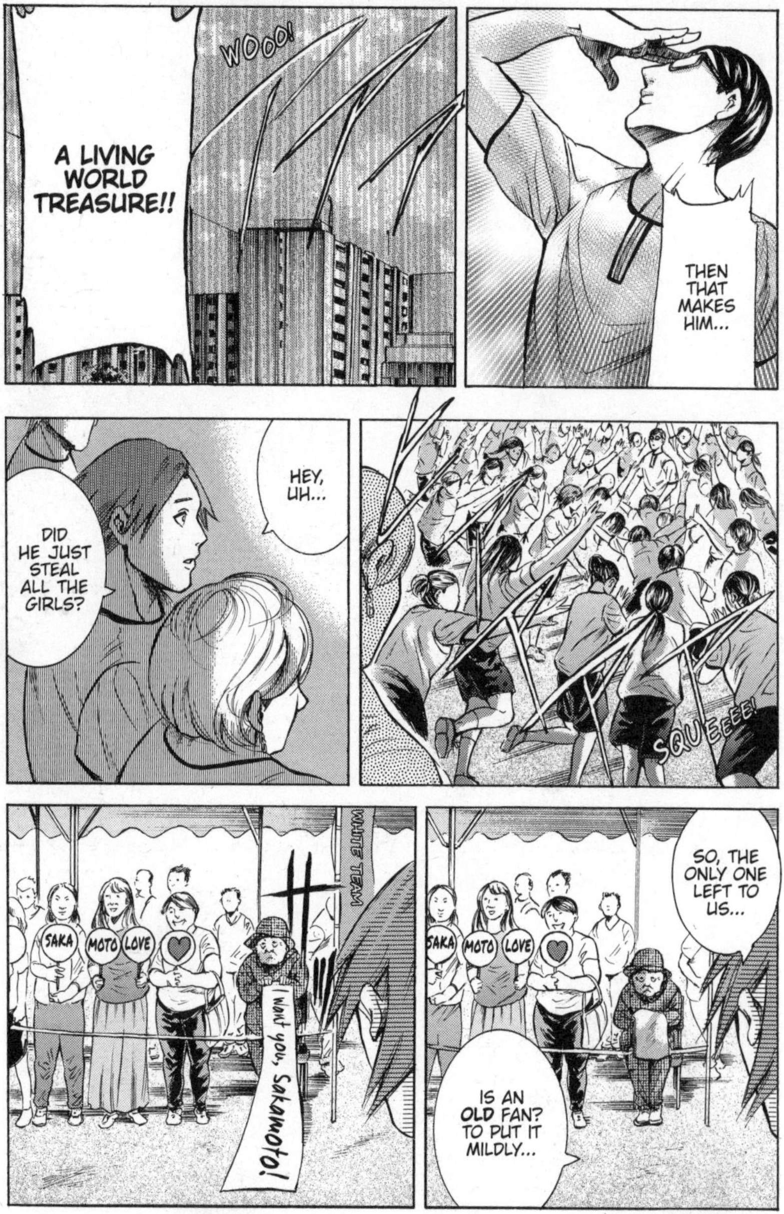
THEN THAT MAKES HIM...
WOOO!
A LIVING WORLD TREASURE!!
SQUEEEEE!
HEY, UH...
DID HE JUST STEAL ALL THE GIRLS?
SO, THE ONLY ONE LEFT TO US...
SAKA MOTO LOVE
IS AN OLD FAN? TO PUT IT MILDLY...
WHITE TEAM
SAKA MOTO LOVE
I want you, Sakamoto!

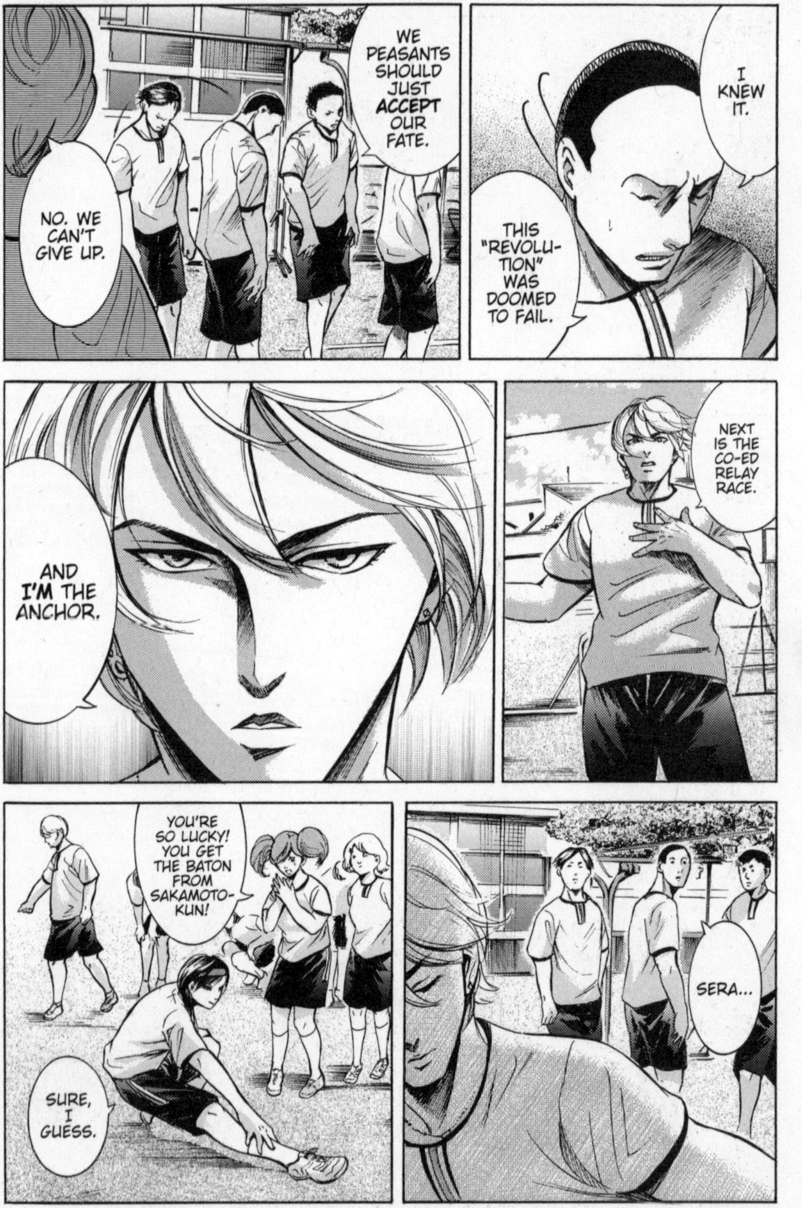
I KNEW IT.
THIS "REVOLUTION" WAS DOOMED TO FAIL.
WE PEASANTS SHOULD JUST ACCEPT OUR FATE.
NO. WE CAN'T GIVE UP.
NEXT IS THE CO-ED RELAY RACE.
AND I'M THE ANCHOR.
SERA...
YOU'RE SO LUCKY! YOU GET THE BATON FROM SAKAMOTO-KUN!
SURE, I GUESS.

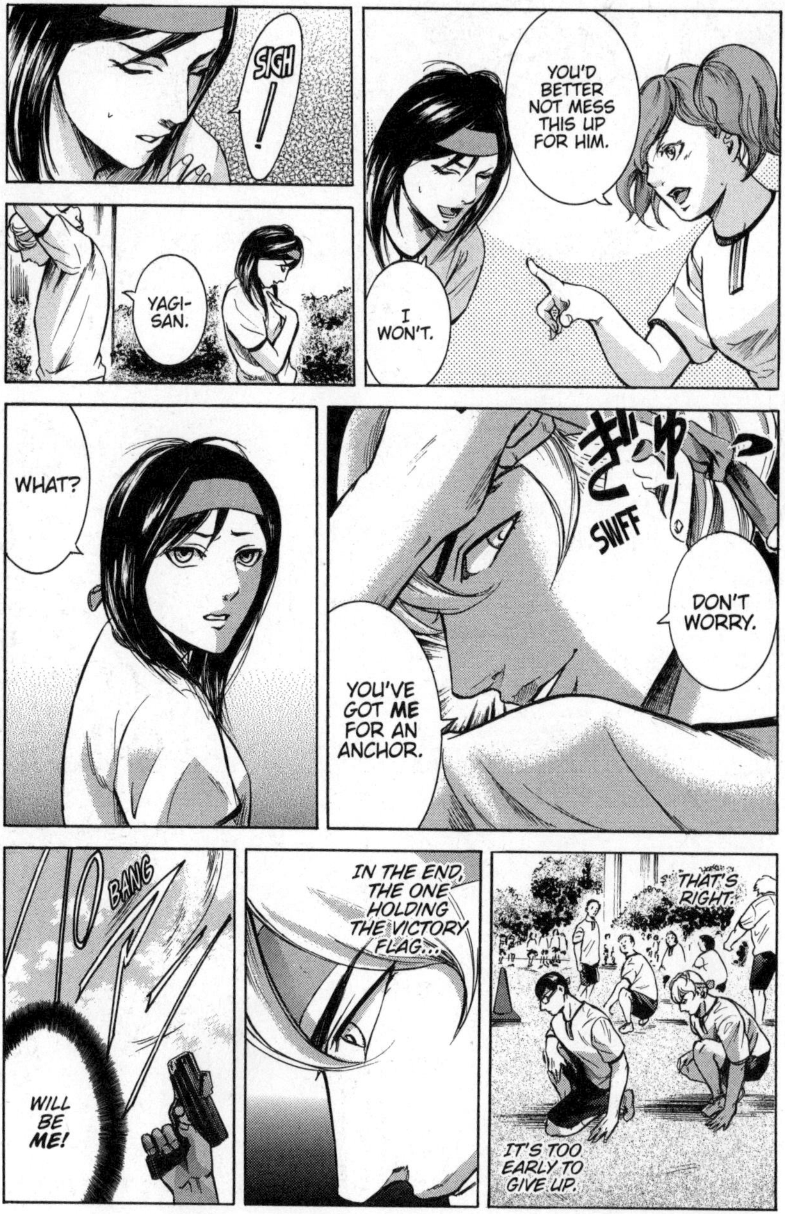
YOU'D BETTER NOT MESS THIS UP FOR HIM.
I WON'T.
SIGH!
YAGI-SAN.
ぎゅっ
SWFF
DON'T WORRY.
YOU'VE GOT ME FOR AN ANCHOR.
WHAT?
THAT'S RIGHT.
IT'S TOO EARLY TO GIVE UP.
IN THE END, THE ONE HOLDING THE VICTORY FLAG...
BANG
WILL BE ME!

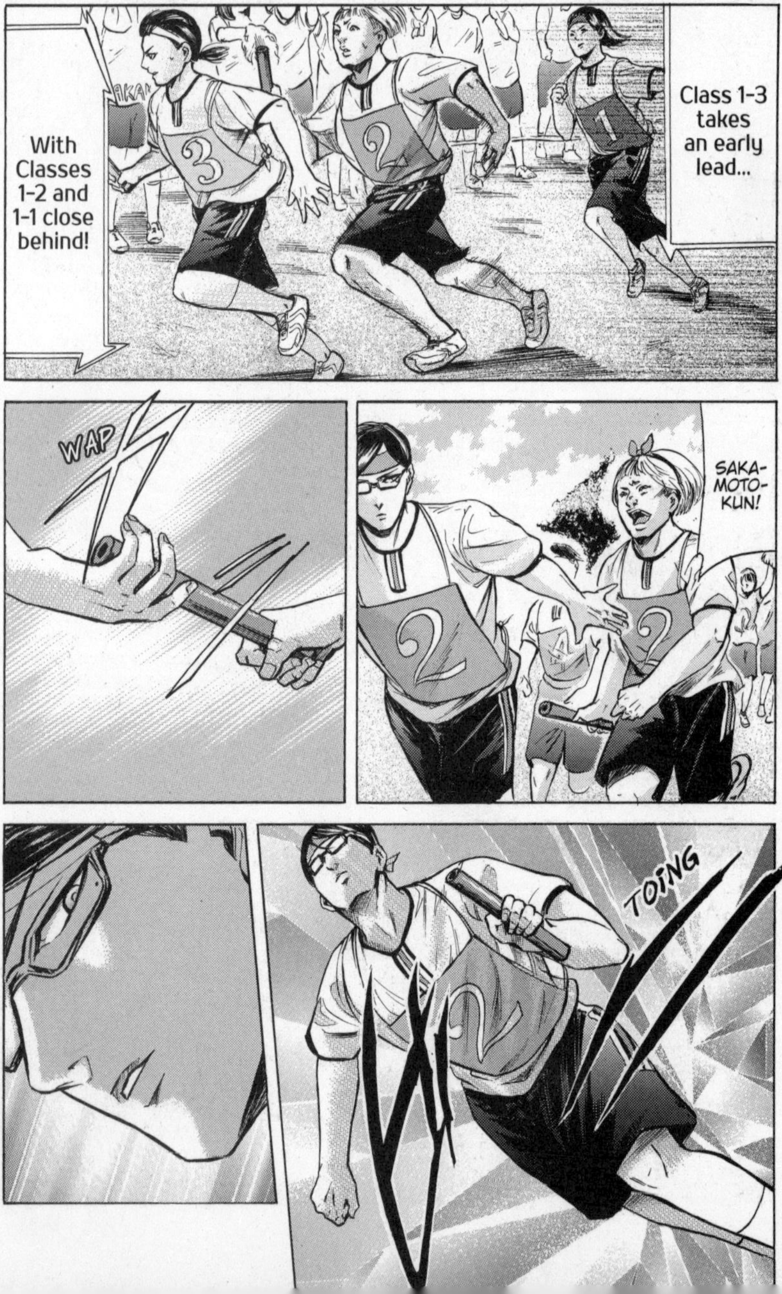
Class 1-3 takes an early lead...
With Classes 1-2 and 1-1 close behind!
SAKA-MOTO-KUN!
WAP
TOING

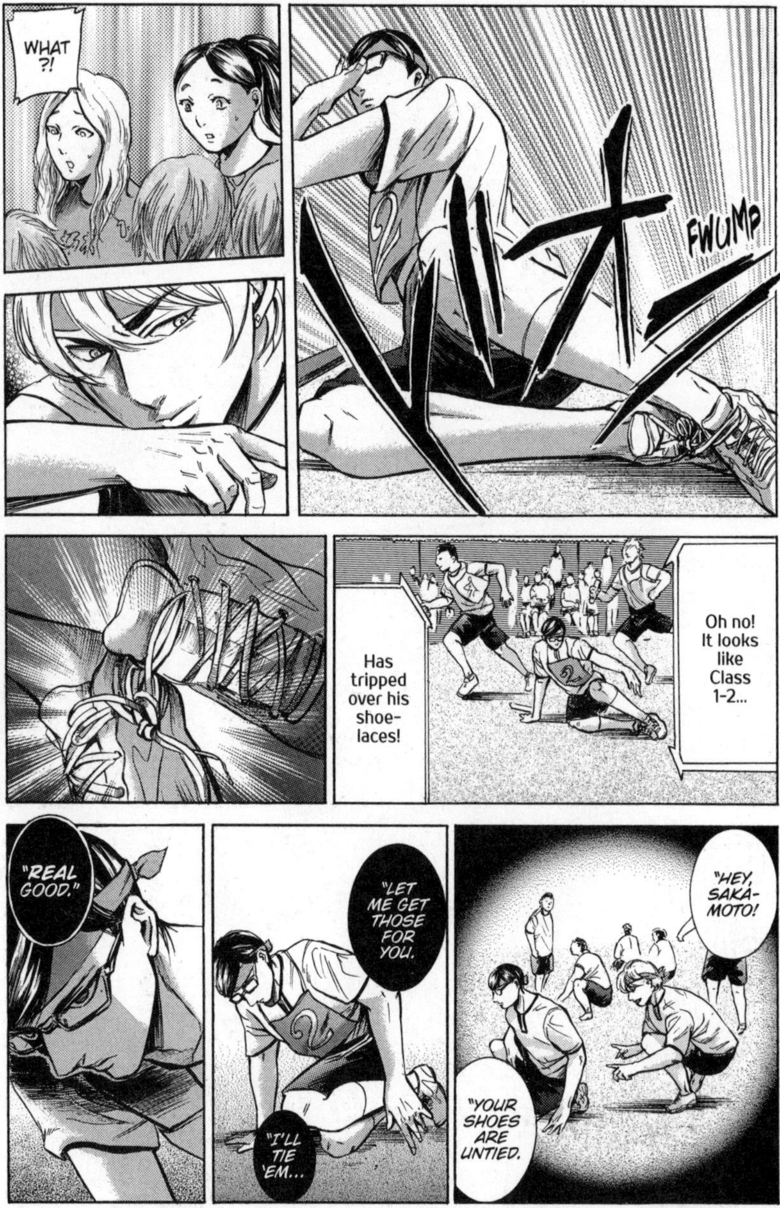
FWUMP
WHAT ?!
Oh no! It looks like Class 1-2...
Has tripped over his shoelaces!
"HEY, SAKAMOTO!
"YOUR SHOES ARE UNTIED.
"LET ME GET THOSE FOR YOU.
"I'LL TIE 'EM...
"REAL GOOD."

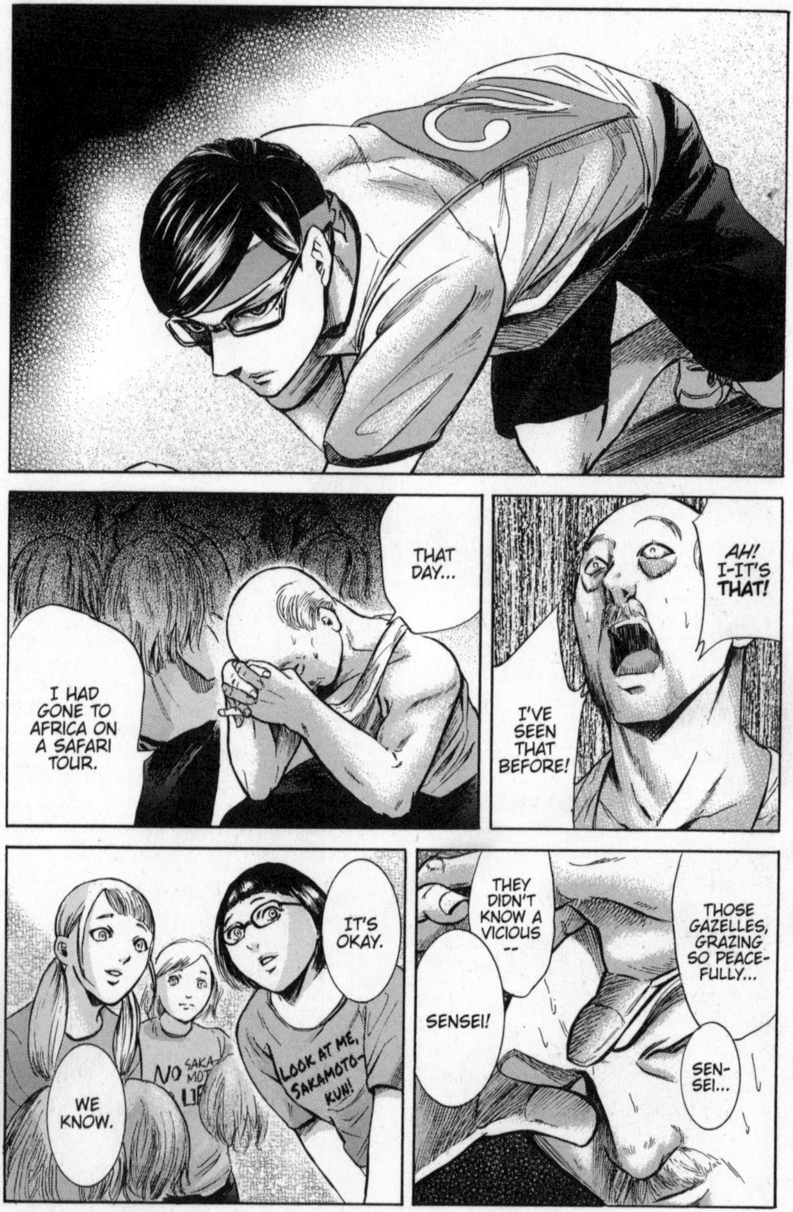
AH! I-IT'S THAT!
I'VE SEEN THAT BEFORE!
THAT DAY...
I HAD GONE TO AFRICA ON A SAFARI TOUR.
THOSE GAZELLES, GRAZING SO PEACE-FULLY...
THEY DIDN'T KNOW A VICIOUS --
SEN-SEI...
SENSEI!
IT'S OKAY.
LOOK AT ME, SAKAMOTO-KUN!
WE KNOW.

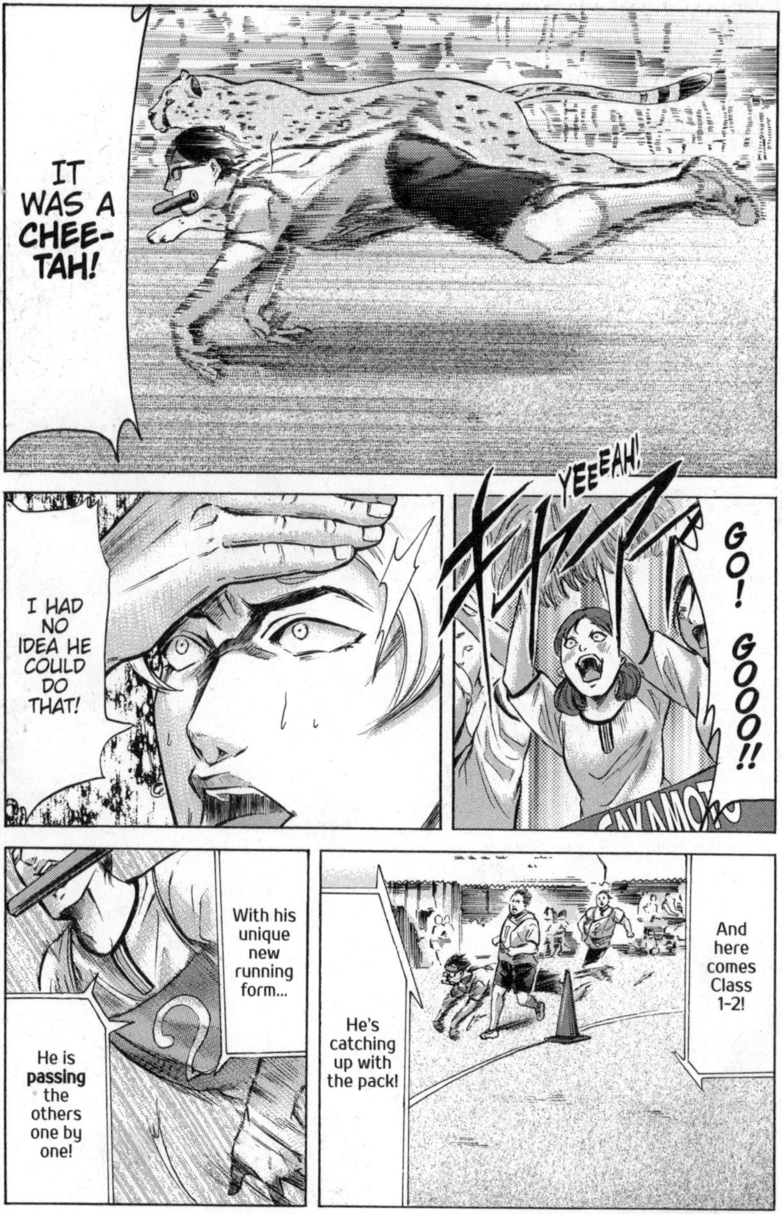
IT WAS A CHEE-TAH!
YEEEAH!
GO! GOOOO!!
I HAD NO IDEA HE COULD DO THAT!
And here comes Class 1-2!
He's catching up with the pack!
With his unique new running form...
He is **passing** the others one by one!

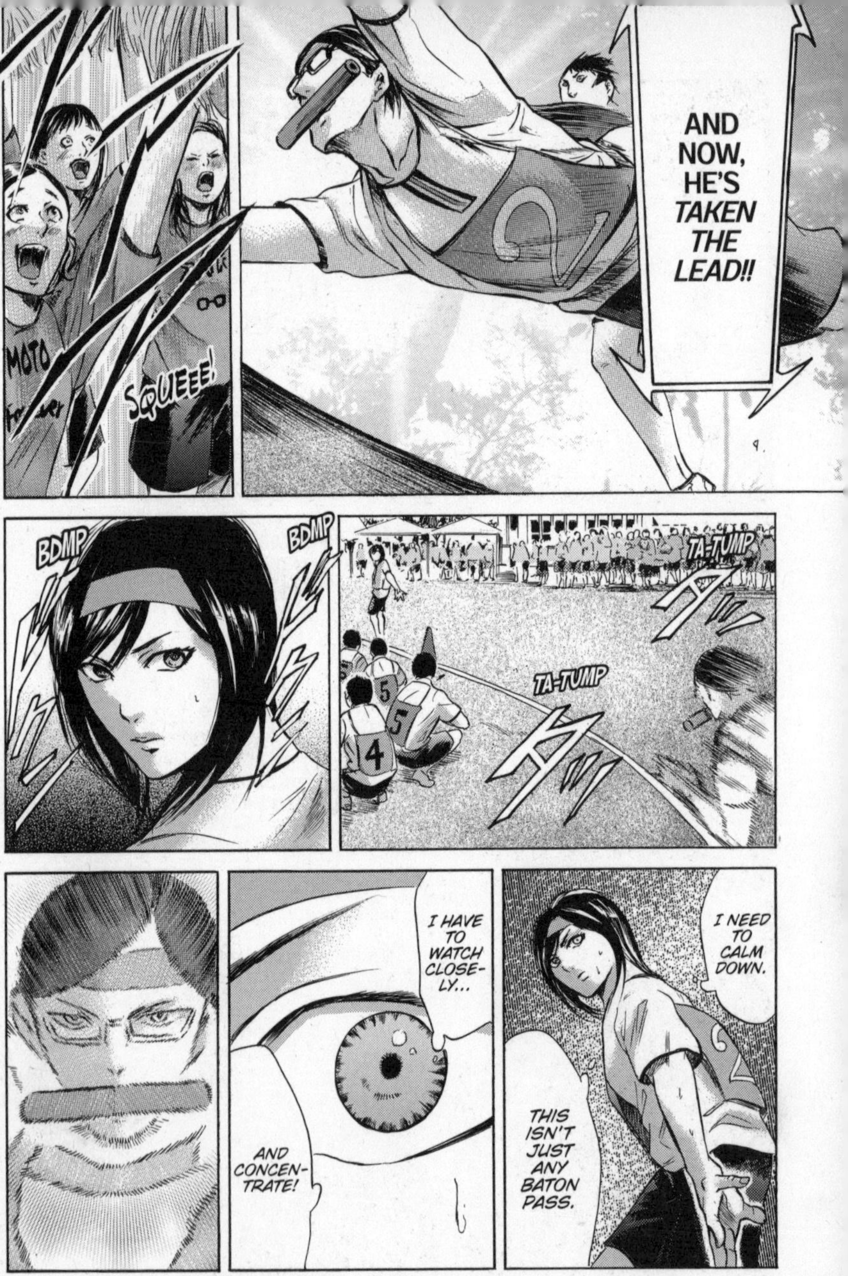
AND NOW, HE'S TAKEN THE LEAD!!
SQUEEEE!
TA-TUMP
TA-TUMP
BDMP
BDMP
I NEED TO CALM DOWN.
THIS ISN'T JUST ANY BATON PASS.
I HAVE TO WATCH CLOSELY...
AND CONCENTRATE!

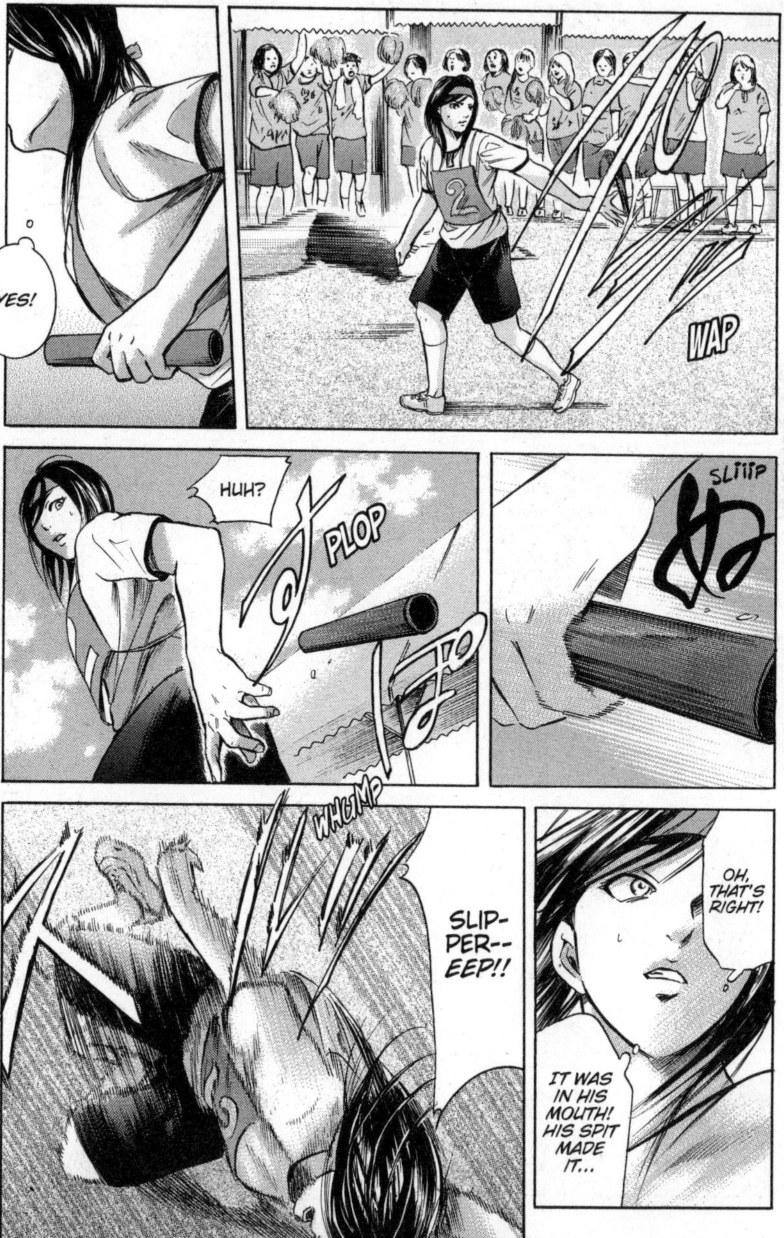
WAP
YES!
SLIIIP
HUH?
PLOP
OH, THAT'S RIGHT!
IT WAS IN HIS MOUTH! HIS SPIT MADE IT...
WHUMP
SLIP-PER--EEP!!

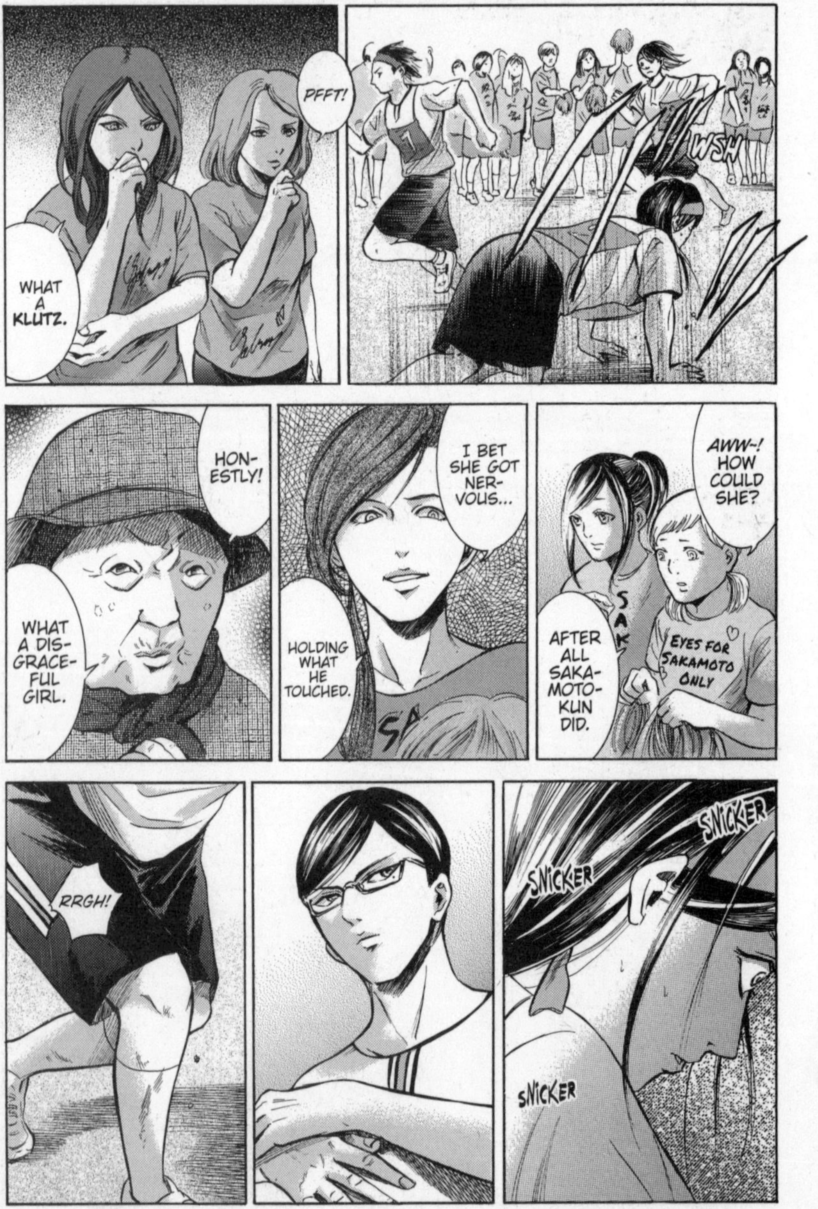
WSH
PFFT!
WHAT A KLUTZ.
AWW-! HOW COULD SHE?
AFTER ALL SAKAMOTO-KUN DID.
EYES FOR SAKAMOTO ONLY
I BET SHE GOT NERVOUS...
HOLDING WHAT HE TOUCHED.
HONESTLY!
WHAT A DISGRACEFUL GIRL.
SNICKER
SNICKER
SNICKER
RRGH!

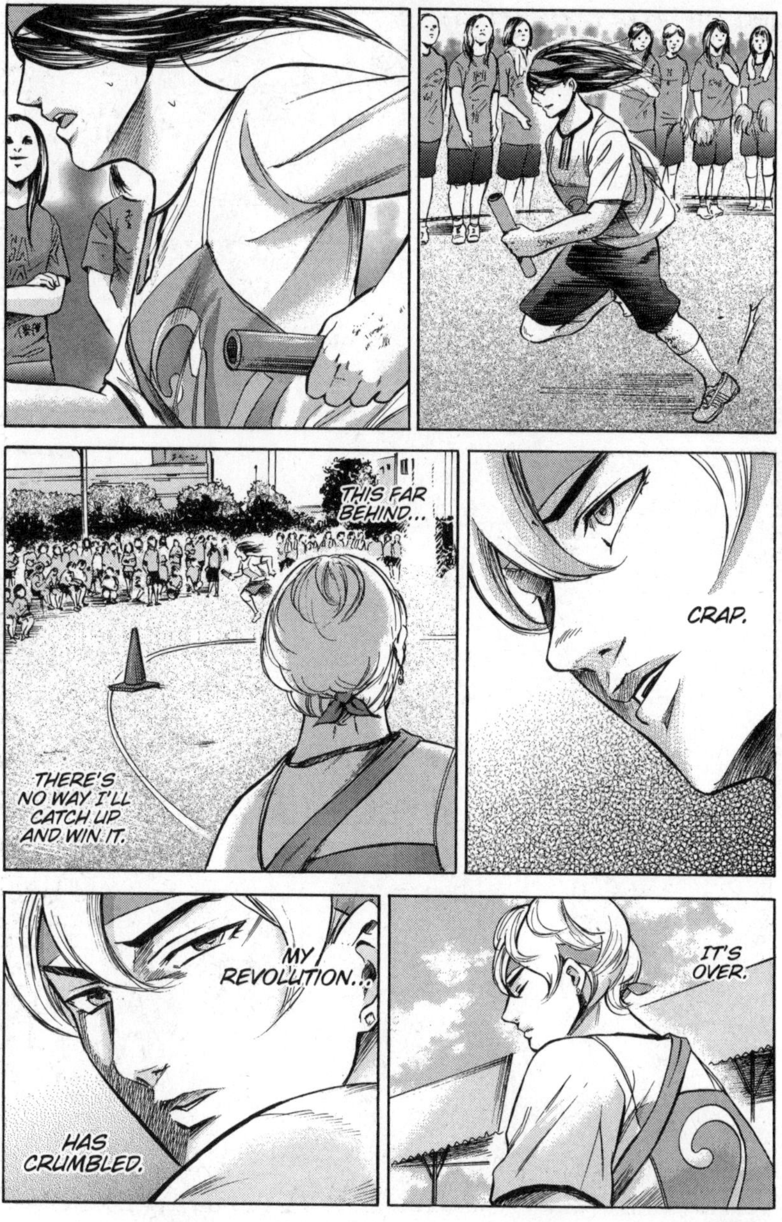
CRAP.
THIS FAR BEHIND...
THERE'S NO WAY I'LL CATCH UP AND WIN IT.
IT'S OVER.
MY REVOLUTION...
HAS CRUMBLED.

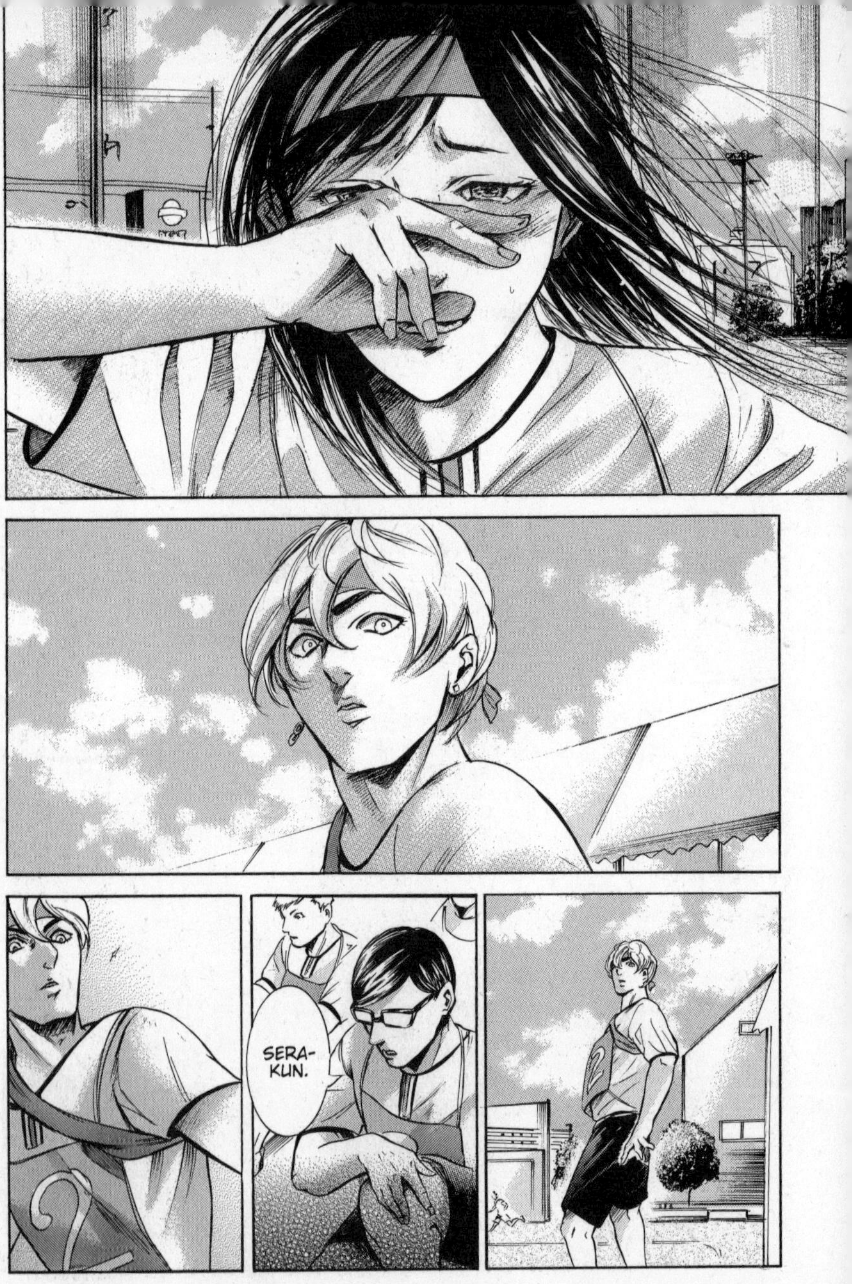
SERA-KUN.

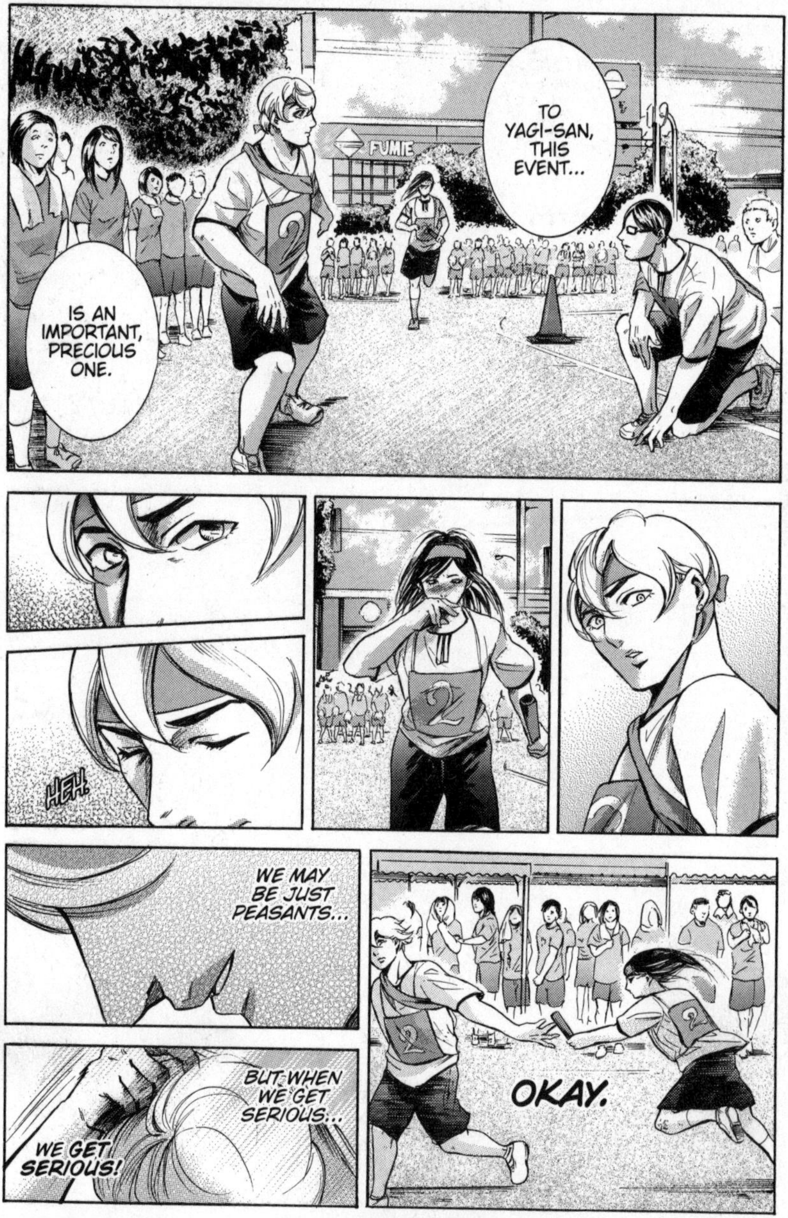
TO YAGI-SAN, THIS EVENT...
IS AN IMPORTANT, PRECIOUS ONE.
HEH.
OKAY.
WE MAY BE JUST PEASANTS...
BUT WHEN WE GET SERIOUS...
WE GET SERIOUS!

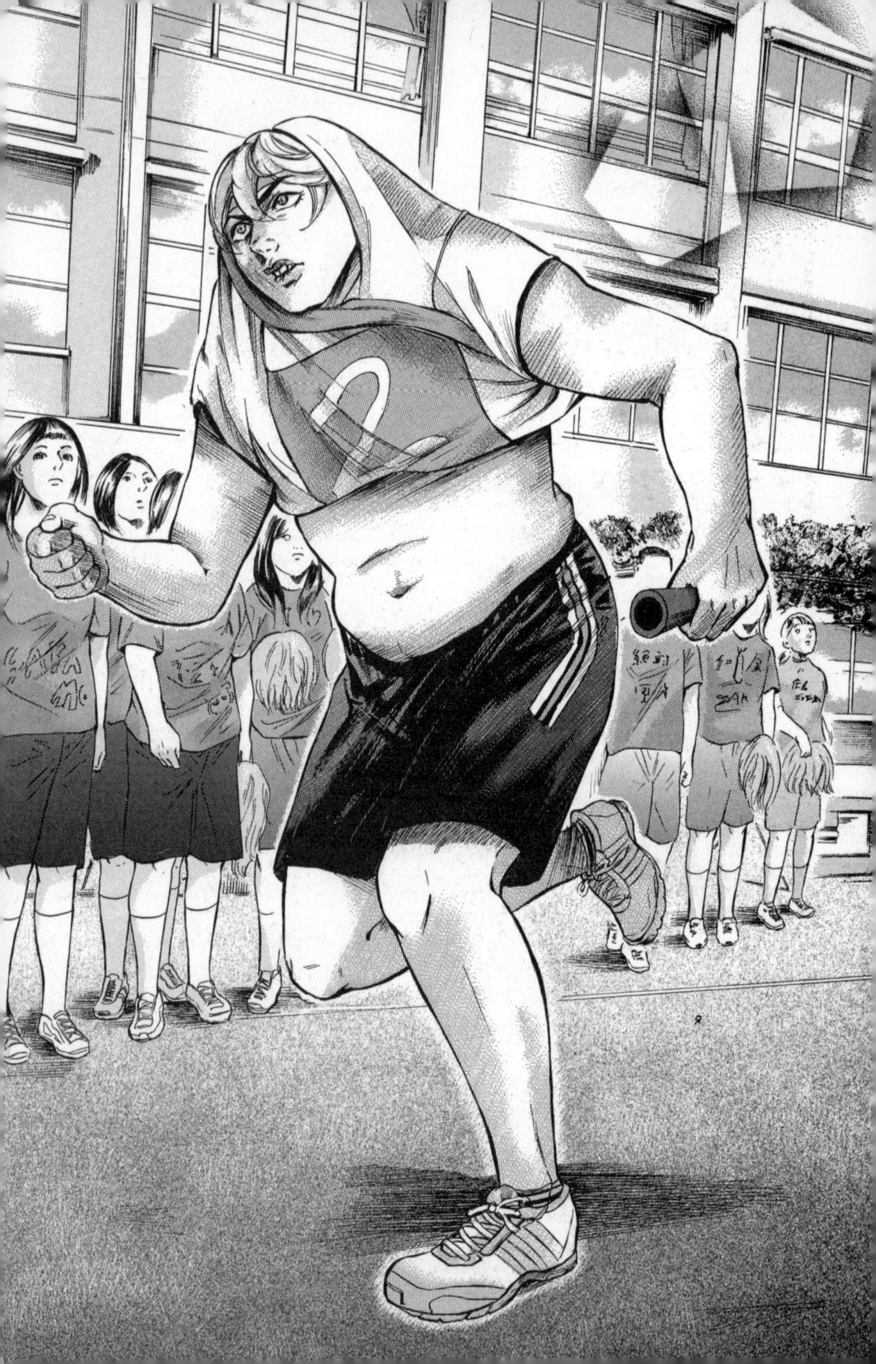

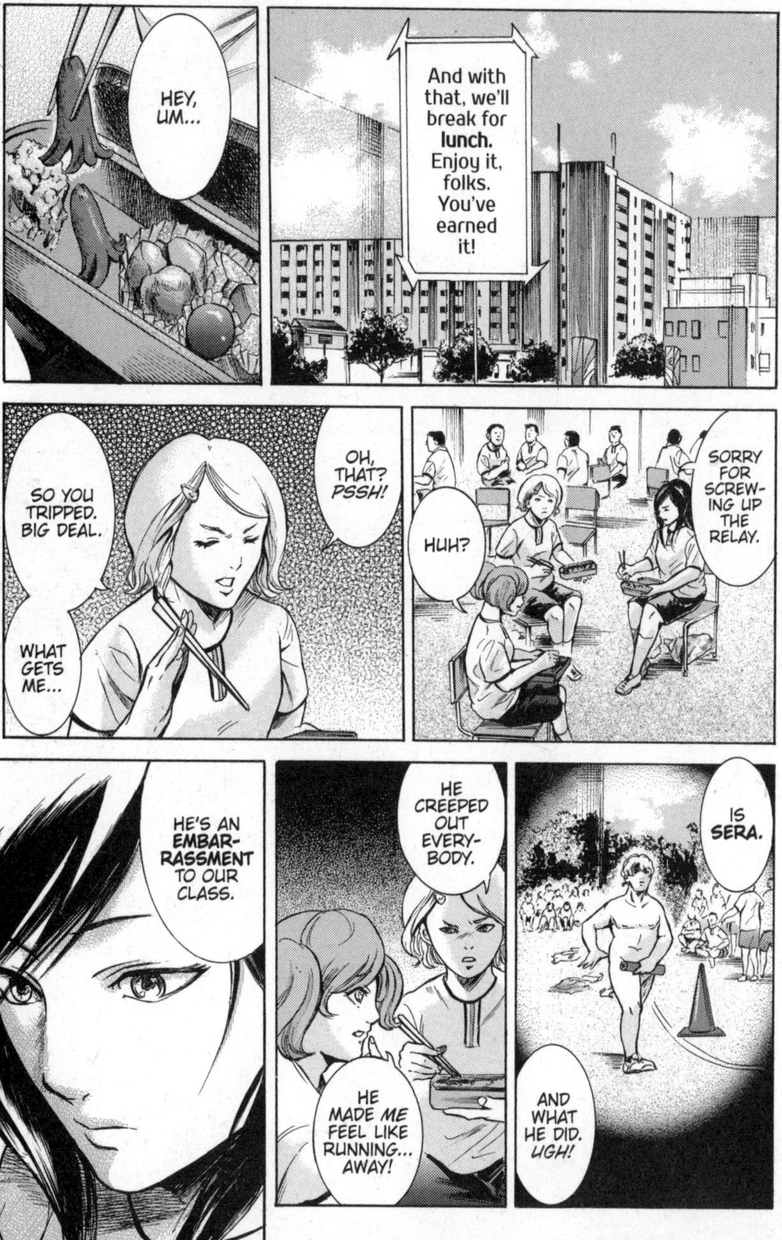
And with that, we'll break for **lunch.** Enjoy it, folks. You've earned it!
HEY, UM...
SORRY FOR SCREWING UP THE RELAY.
HUH?
OH, THAT? *PSSH!*
SO YOU TRIPPED. BIG DEAL.
WHAT GETS ME...
IS **SERA.**
AND WHAT HE DID. *UGH!*
HE CREEPED OUT EVERYBODY.
HE MADE *ME* FEEL LIKE RUNNING... AWAY!
HE'S AN **EMBARRASSMENT** TO OUR CLASS.

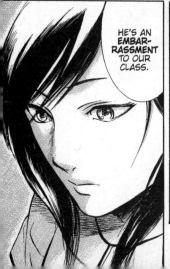

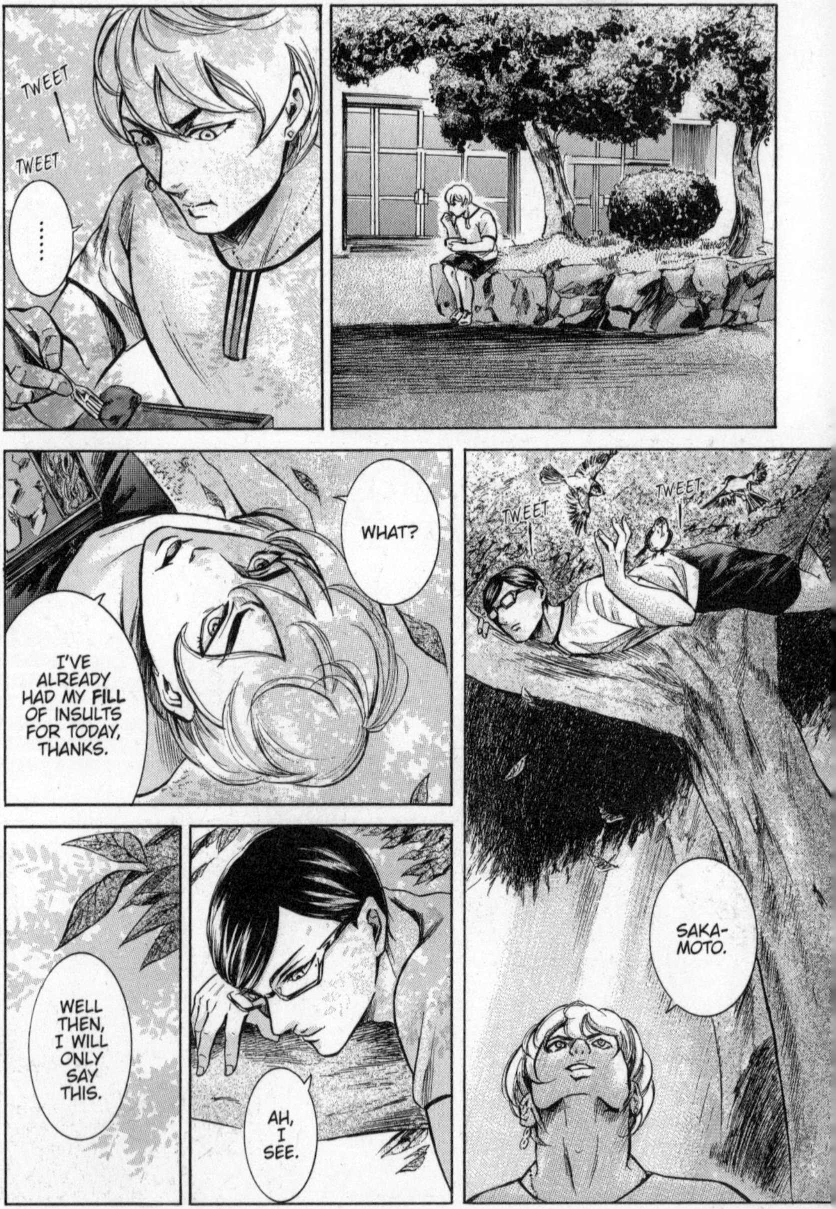
TWEET
TWEET
....
TWEET
TWEET
SAKA-MOTO.
WHAT?
I'VE ALREADY HAD MY **FILL** OF INSULTS FOR TODAY, THANKS.
AH, I SEE.
WELL THEN, I WILL ONLY SAY THIS.

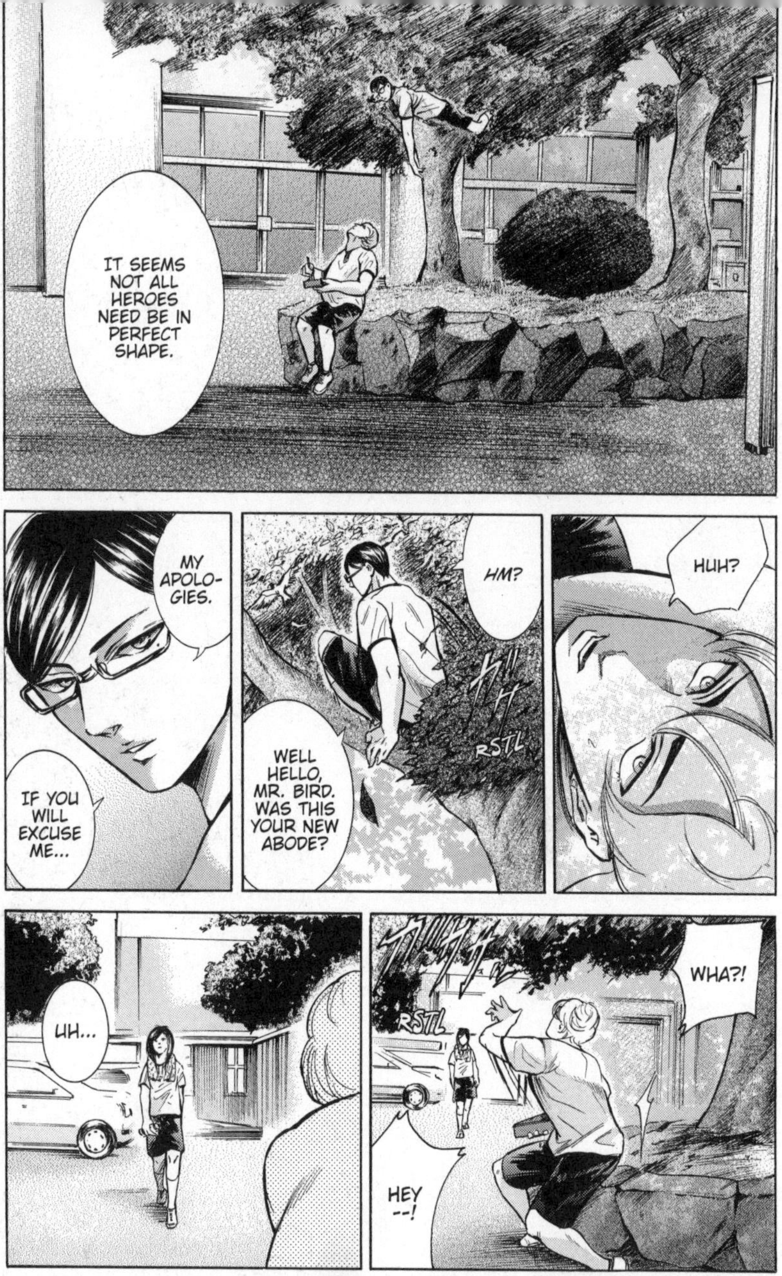
IT SEEMS NOT ALL HEROES NEED BE IN PERFECT SHAPE.
HUH?
HM?
RSTL
WELL HELLO, MR. BIRD. WAS THIS YOUR NEW ABODE?
MY APOLOGIES.
IF YOU WILL EXCUSE ME...
WHA?!
RSTL
HEY--!
UH...

OH.

UH, SURE.

NEVER MIND. I'M JUST GOING TO THE BATHROOM.

......

I NEVER NOTICED BEFORE, BUT...

YOU'RE ACTUALLY KINDA COOL.

Y'KNOW ...

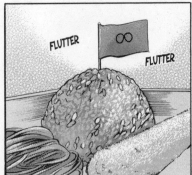

FLUTTER

FLUTTER

BUH?

Break Time #4:
Science Lab

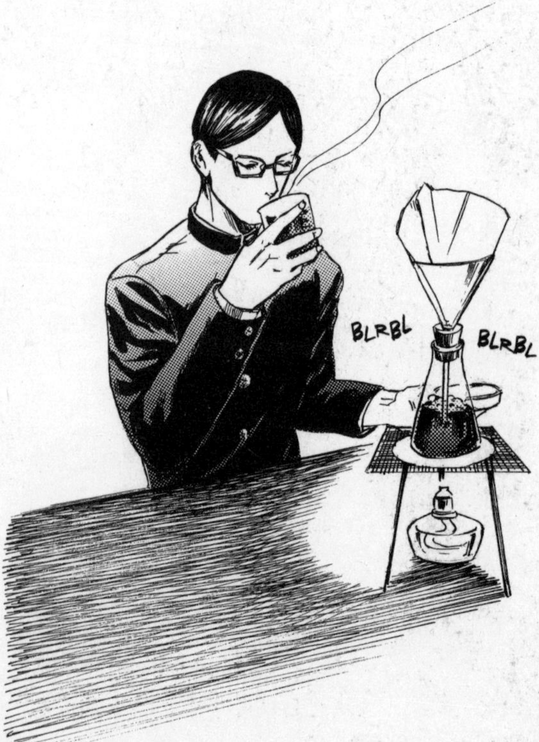
BLRBL
BLRBL

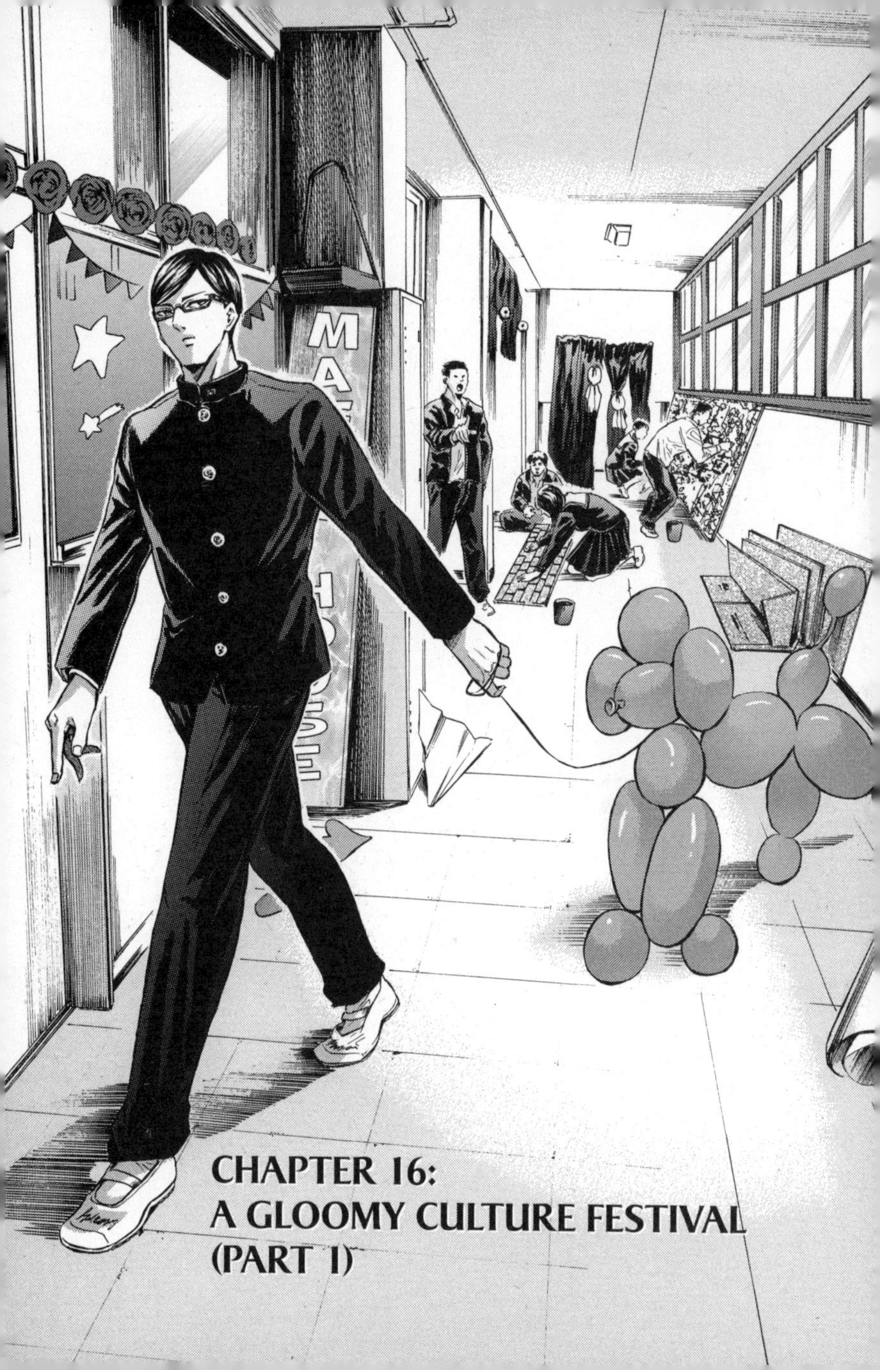

CHAPTER 16: A GLOOMY CULTURE FESTIVAL (PART 1)

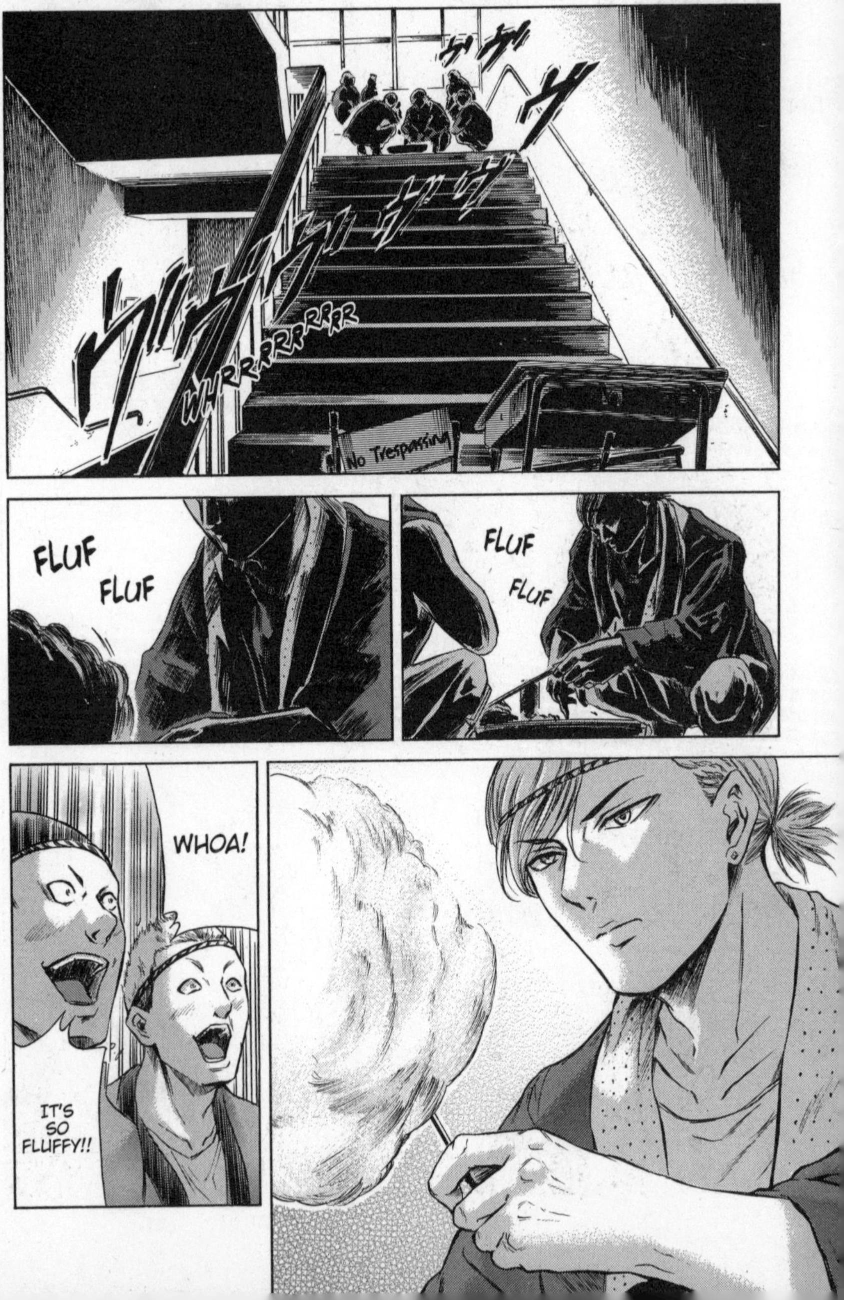
WHRRRRRRRRRR
No Trespassing
FLUF
FLUF
FLUF
FLUF
WHOA!
IT'S SO FLUFFY!!

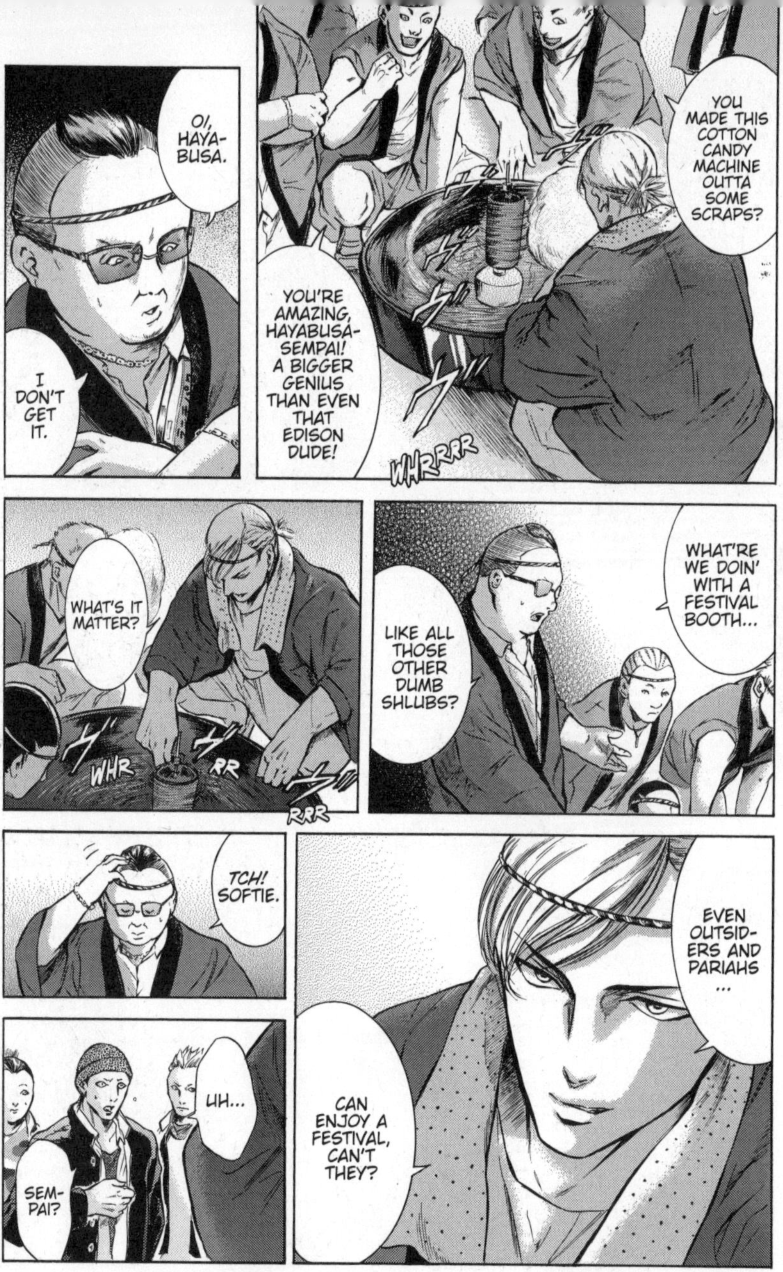
YOU MADE THIS COTTON CANDY MACHINE OUTTA SOME SCRAPS?
YOU'RE AMAZING, HAYABUSA-SEMPAI! A BIGGER GENIUS THAN EVEN THAT EDISON DUDE!
WHRRRR
OI, HAYABUSA.
I DON'T GET IT.
WHAT'RE WE DOIN' WITH A FESTIVAL BOOTH...
LIKE ALL THOSE OTHER DUMB SHLUBS?
WHAT'S IT MATTER?
WHR
RR
RRR
EVEN OUTSIDERS AND PARIAHS ...
CAN ENJOY A FESTIVAL, CAN'T THEY?
TCH! SOFTIE.
UH...
SEM-PAI?

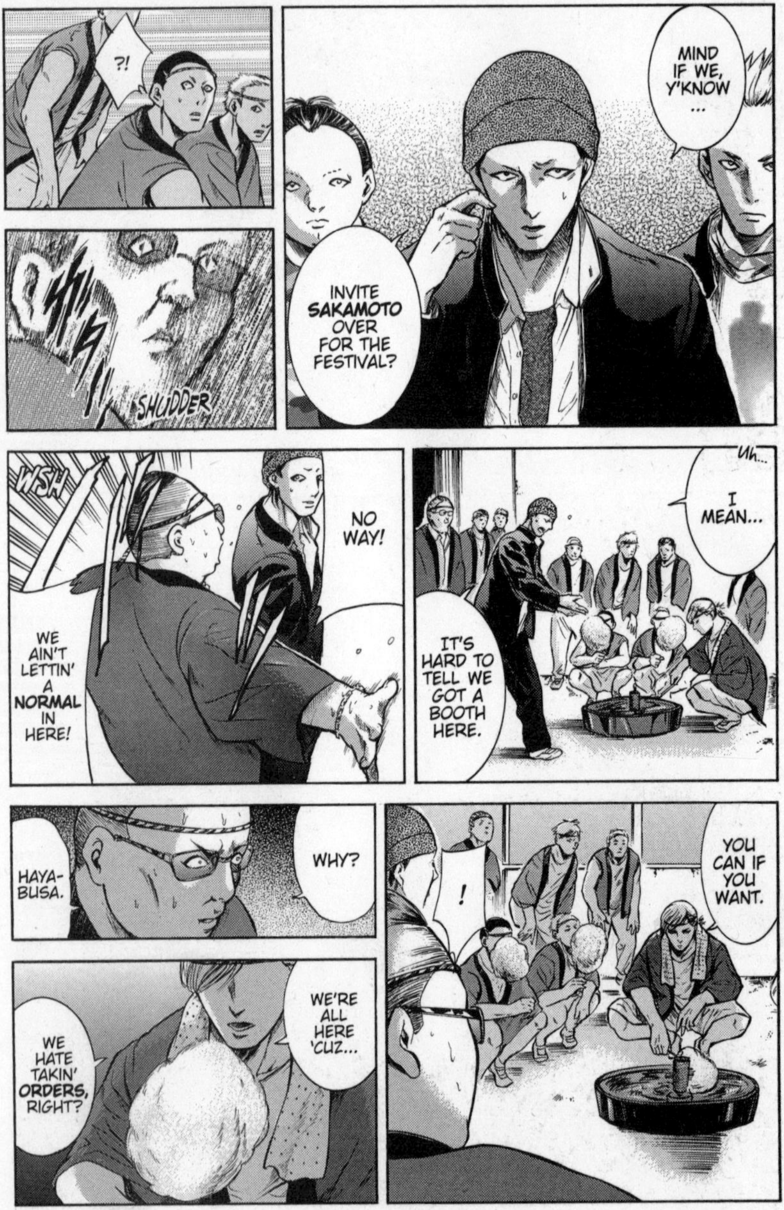
MIND IF WE, Y'KNOW ...
INVITE SAKAMOTO OVER FOR THE FESTIVAL?
?!
SHUDDER
Uh...
I MEAN...
IT'S HARD TO TELL WE GOT A BOOTH HERE.
WSH
NO WAY!
WE AIN'T LETTIN' A NORMAL IN HERE!
YOU CAN IF YOU WANT.
!
WHY?
HAYA-BUSA.
WE'RE ALL HERE 'CUZ...
WE HATE TAKIN' ORDERS, RIGHT?

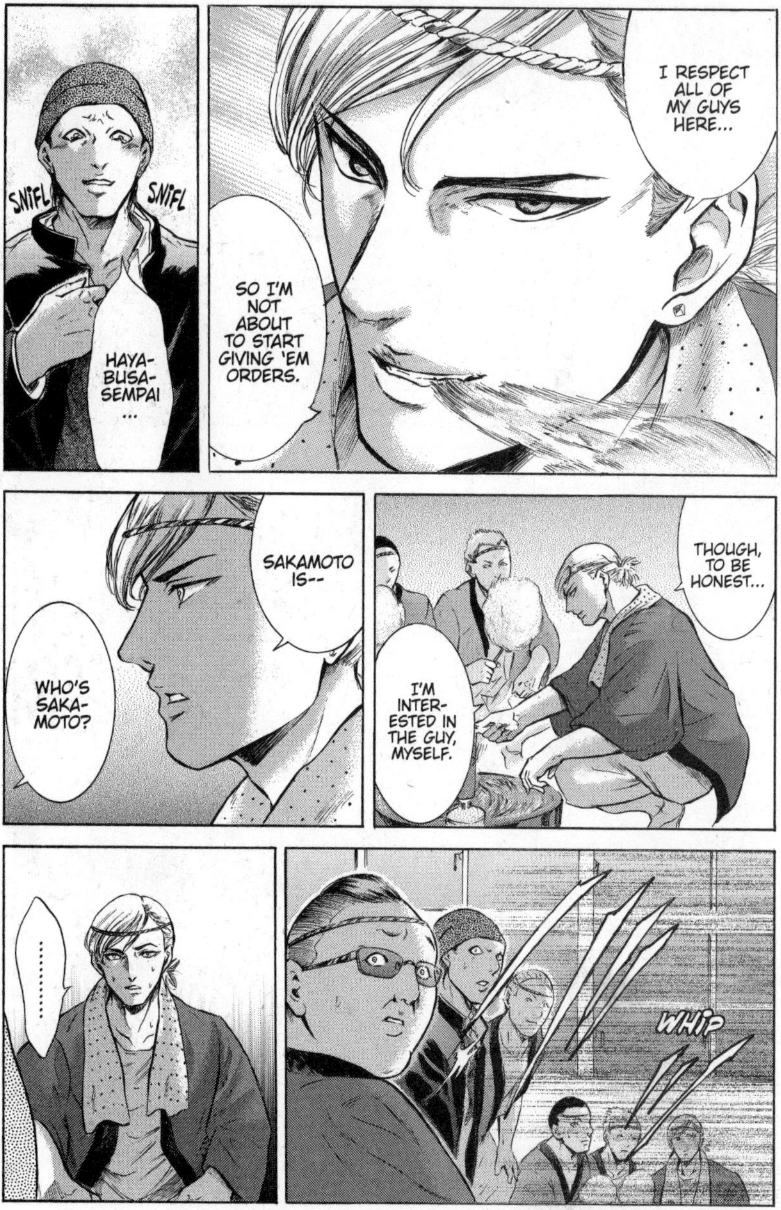
I RESPECT ALL OF MY GUYS HERE...
SO I'M NOT ABOUT TO START GIVING 'EM ORDERS.
SNIFL
SNIFL
HAYA-BUSA-SEMPAI ...
THOUGH, TO BE HONEST...
I'M INTER-ESTED IN THE GUY, MYSELF.
SAKAMOTO IS--
WHO'S SAKA-MOTO?
WHIP
......

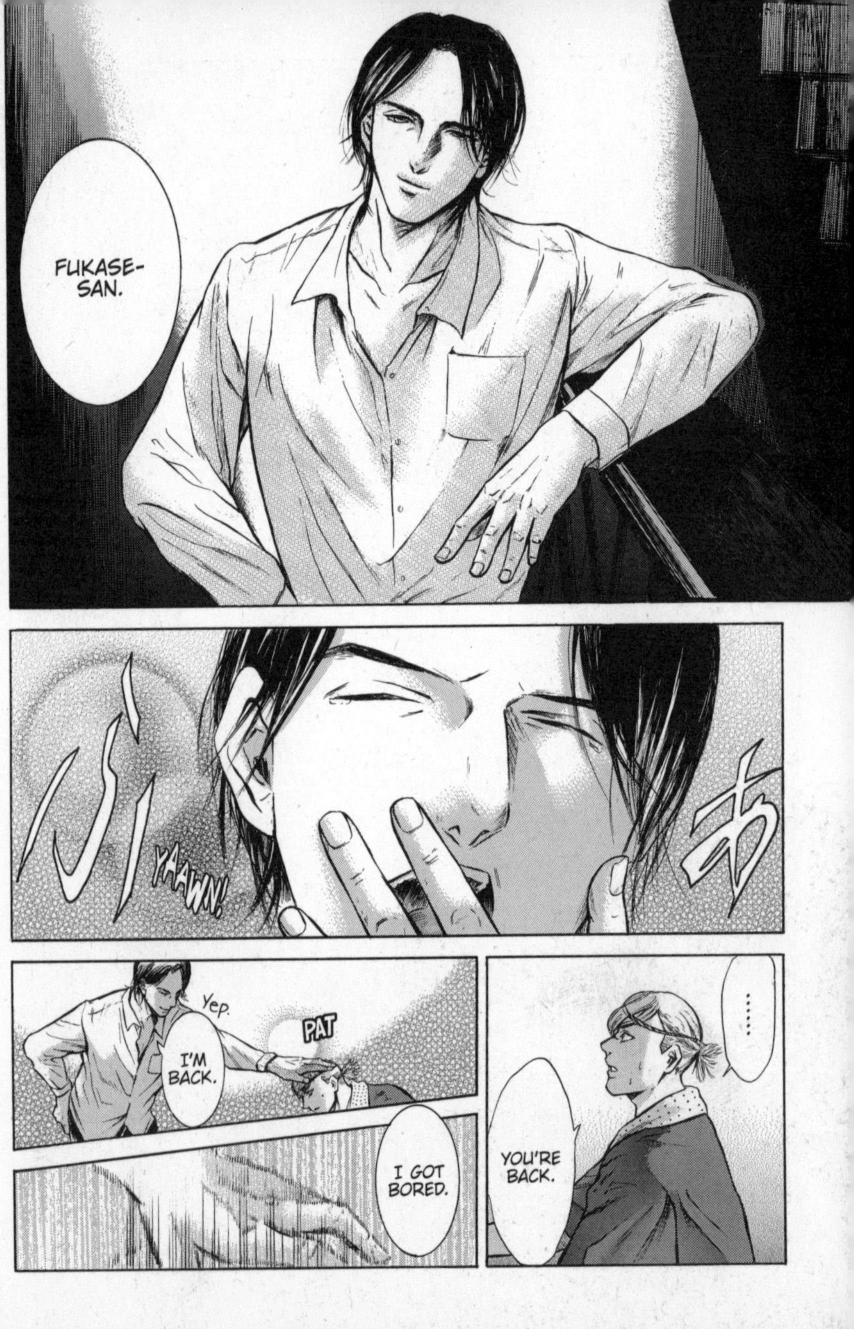
FUKASE-SAN.
ふ
あ
YAAWN!
......
YOU'RE BACK.
Yep.
PAT
I'M BACK.
I GOT BORED.

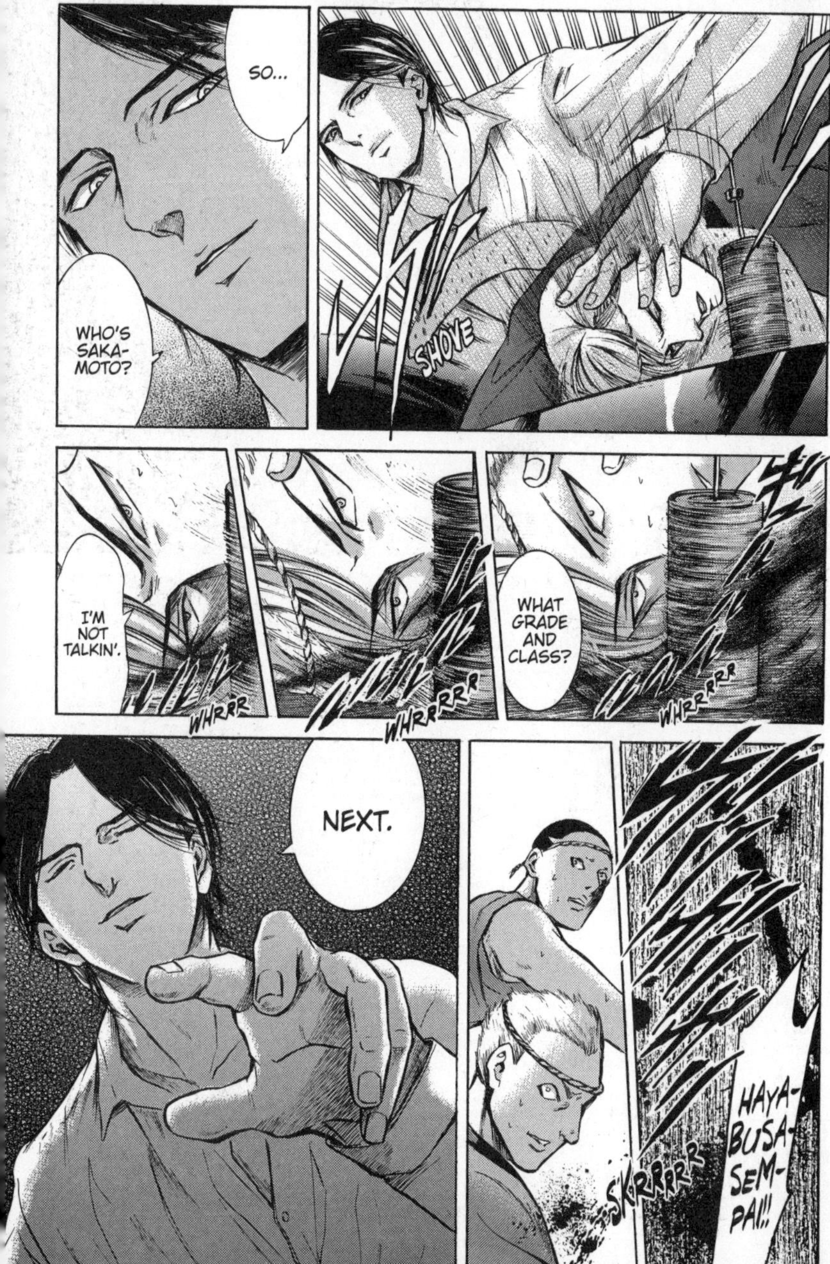
SHOVE
SO...
WHO'S SAKA-MOTO?
WHAT GRADE AND CLASS?
WHRRRRR
WHRRRR
I'M NOT TALKIN'.
WHRRR
SKRRRRR
HAYA-BUSA-SEM-PAI!!
NEXT.

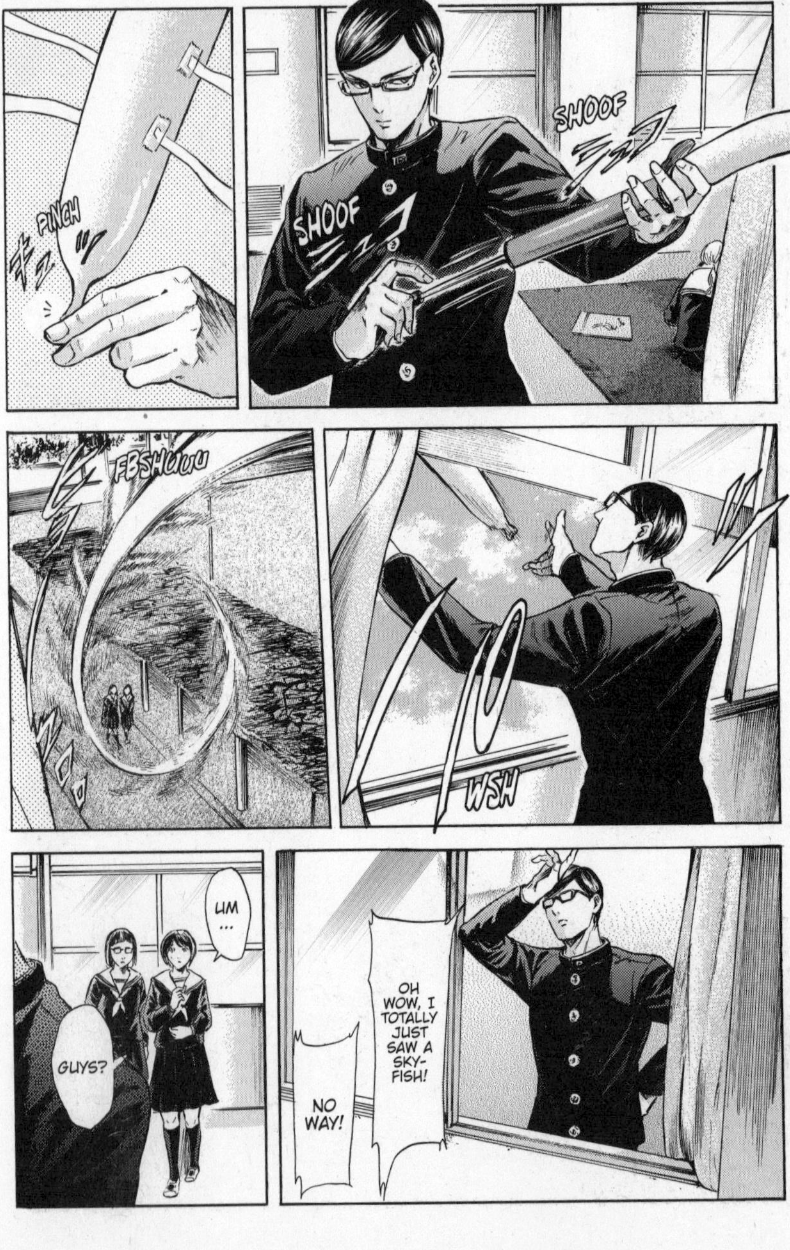
SHOOF
SHOOF
PINCH
WSH
FBSHUUU
OH WOW, I TOTALLY JUST SAW A SKY-FISH!
NO WAY!
UM...
GUYS?

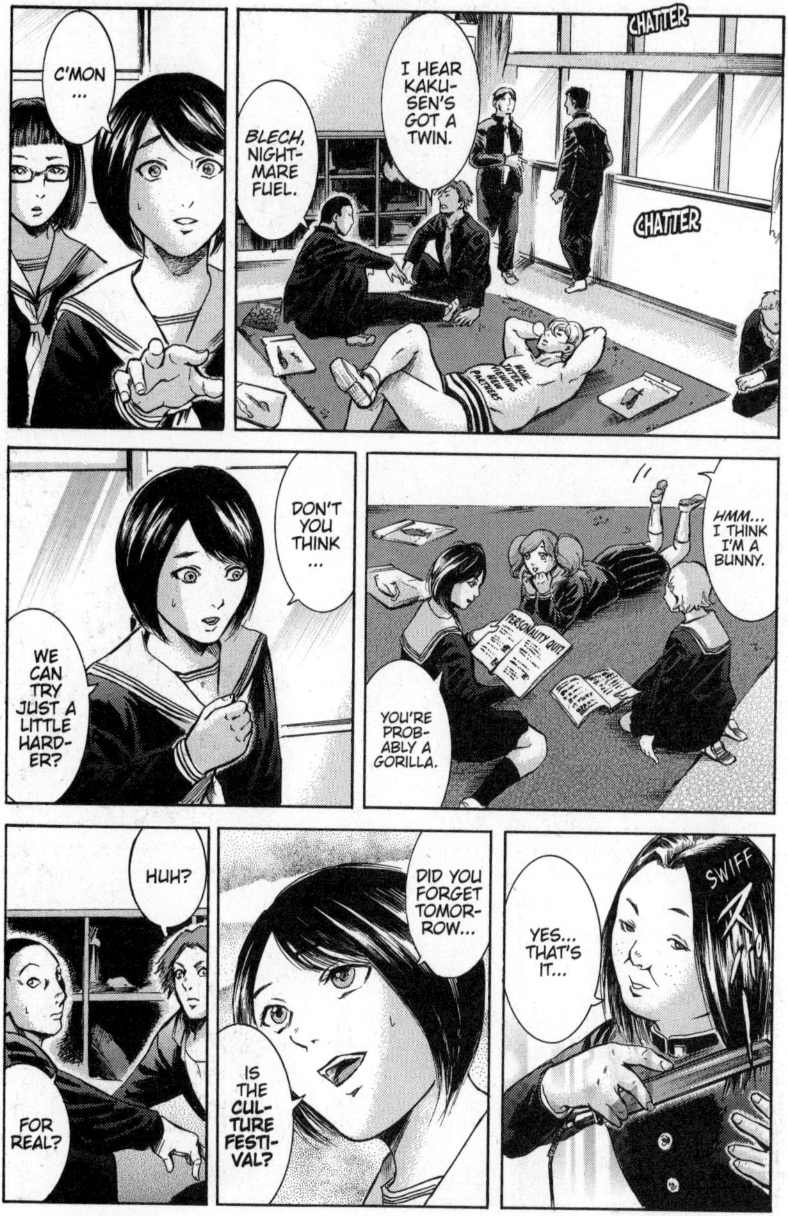
CHATTER
I HEAR KAKU-SEN'S GOT A TWIN.
BLECH, NIGHT-MARE FUEL.
CHATTER
NOW INTER-VIEWING NEW PARTNERS
C'MON ...
HMM... I THINK I'M A BUNNY.
PERSONALITY QUIZ
YOU'RE PROB-ABLY A GORILLA.
DON'T YOU THINK ...
WE CAN TRY JUST A LITTLE HARD-ER?
SWIFF
YES... THAT'S IT...
DID YOU FORGET TOMOR-ROW...
IS THE CUL-TURE FESTI-VAL?
HUH?
FOR REAL?

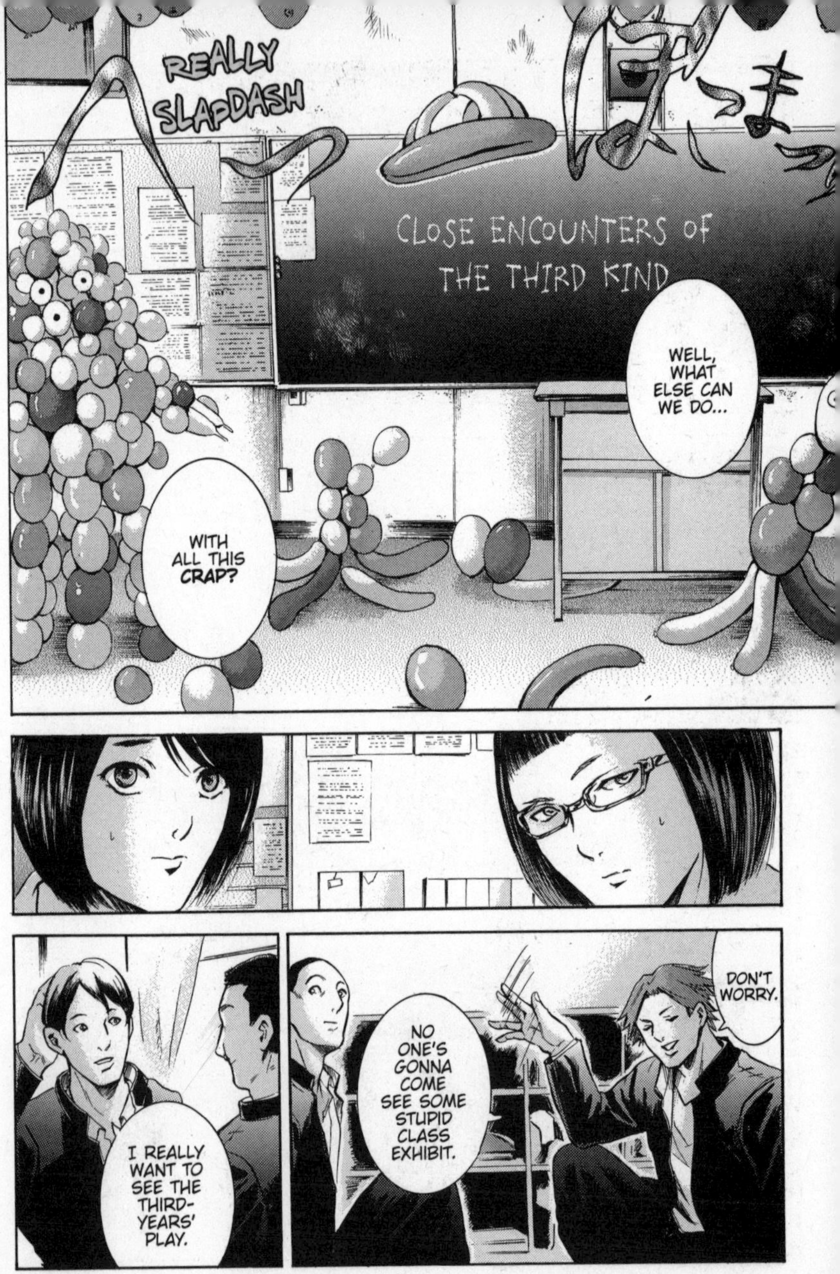
REALLY SLAPDASH
CLOSE ENCOUNTERS OF THE THIRD KIND
WELL, WHAT ELSE CAN WE DO...
WITH ALL THIS CRAP?
DON'T WORRY.
NO ONE'S GONNA COME SEE SOME STUPID CLASS EXHIBIT.
I REALLY WANT TO SEE THE THIRD-YEARS' PLAY.

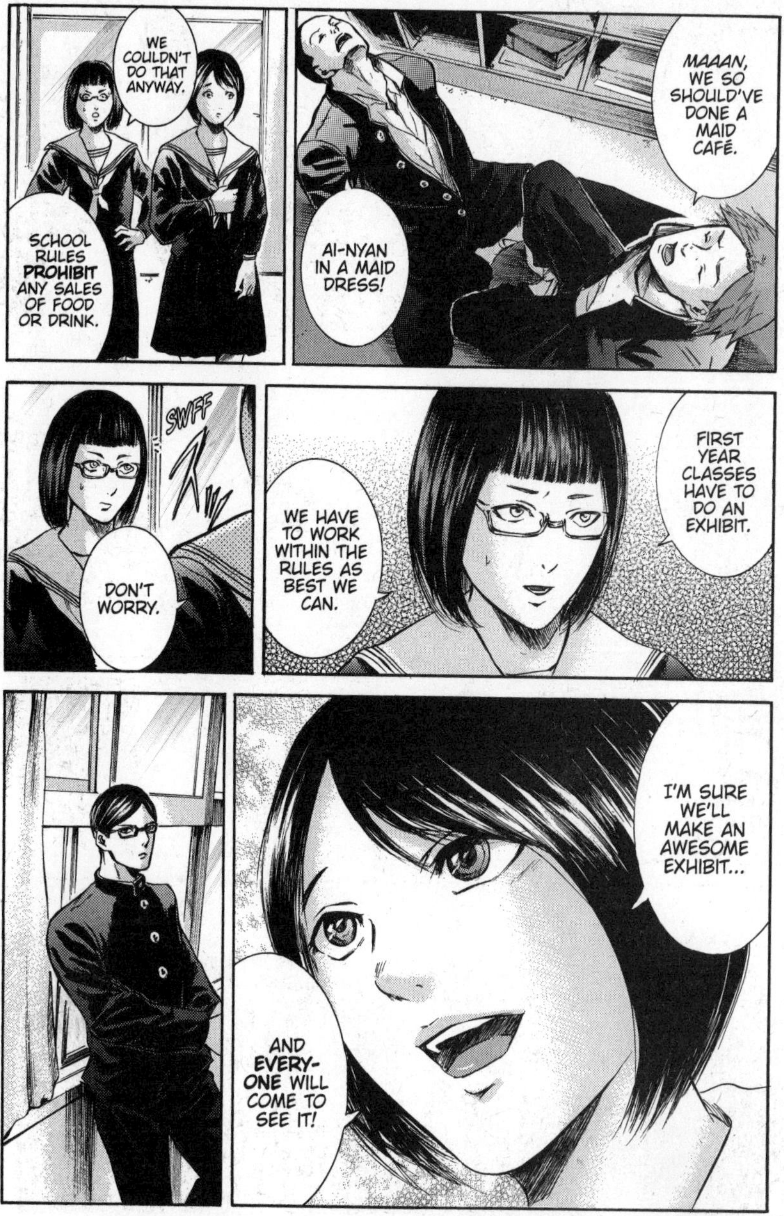
MAAAN, WE SO SHOULD'VE DONE A MAID CAFÉ.
AI-NYAN IN A MAID DRESS!
WE COULDN'T DO THAT ANYWAY.
SCHOOL RULES **PROHIBIT** ANY SALES OF FOOD OR DRINK.
FIRST YEAR CLASSES HAVE TO DO AN EXHIBIT.
WE HAVE TO WORK WITHIN THE RULES AS BEST WE CAN.
SWFF
DON'T WORRY.
I'M SURE WE'LL MAKE AN AWESOME EXHIBIT...
AND **EVERY-ONE** WILL COME TO SEE IT!

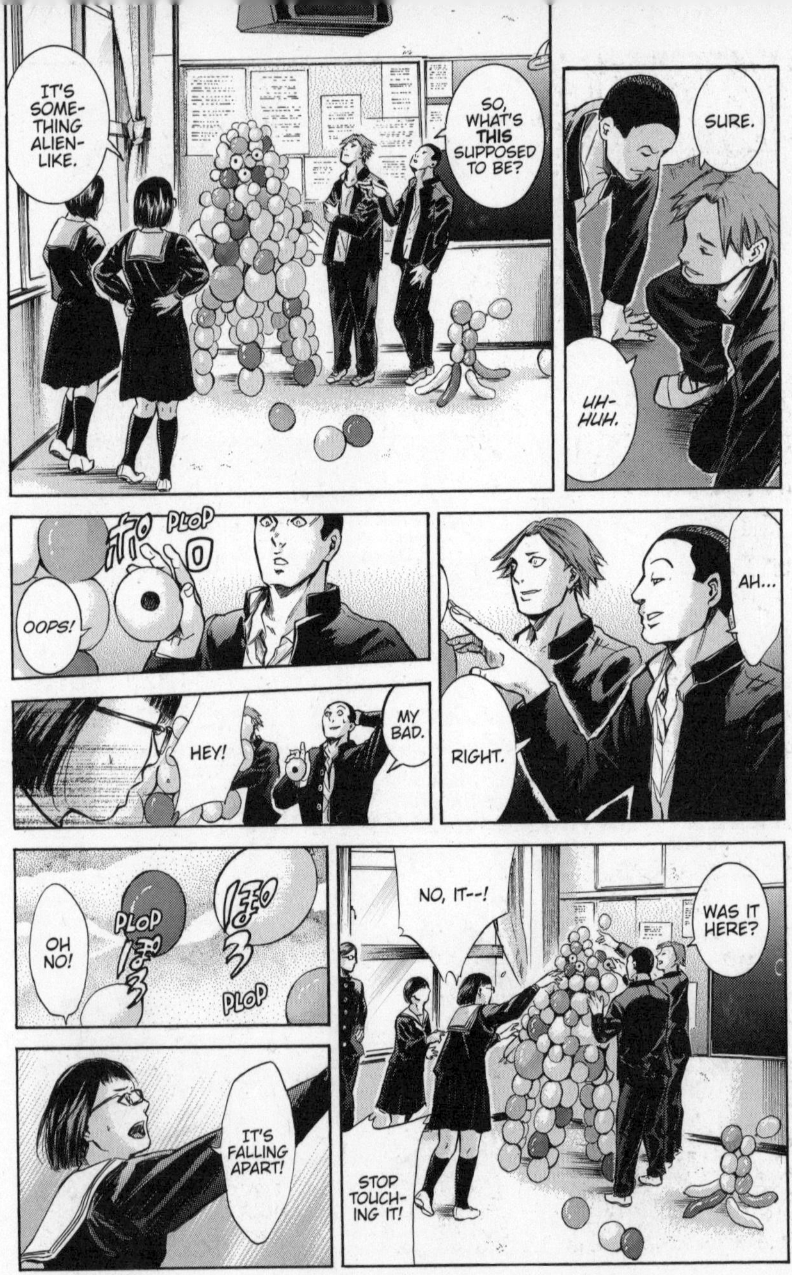
SURE.
UH-HUH.
SO, WHAT'S **THIS** SUPPOSED TO BE?
IT'S SOMETHING ALIEN-LIKE.
AH...
RIGHT.
PLOP
ポロ
OOPS!
MY BAD.
HEY!
WAS IT HERE?
NO, IT--!
STOP TOUCHING IT!
ぽろ
PLOP
ぽろ
PLOP
OH NO!
IT'S FALLING APART!

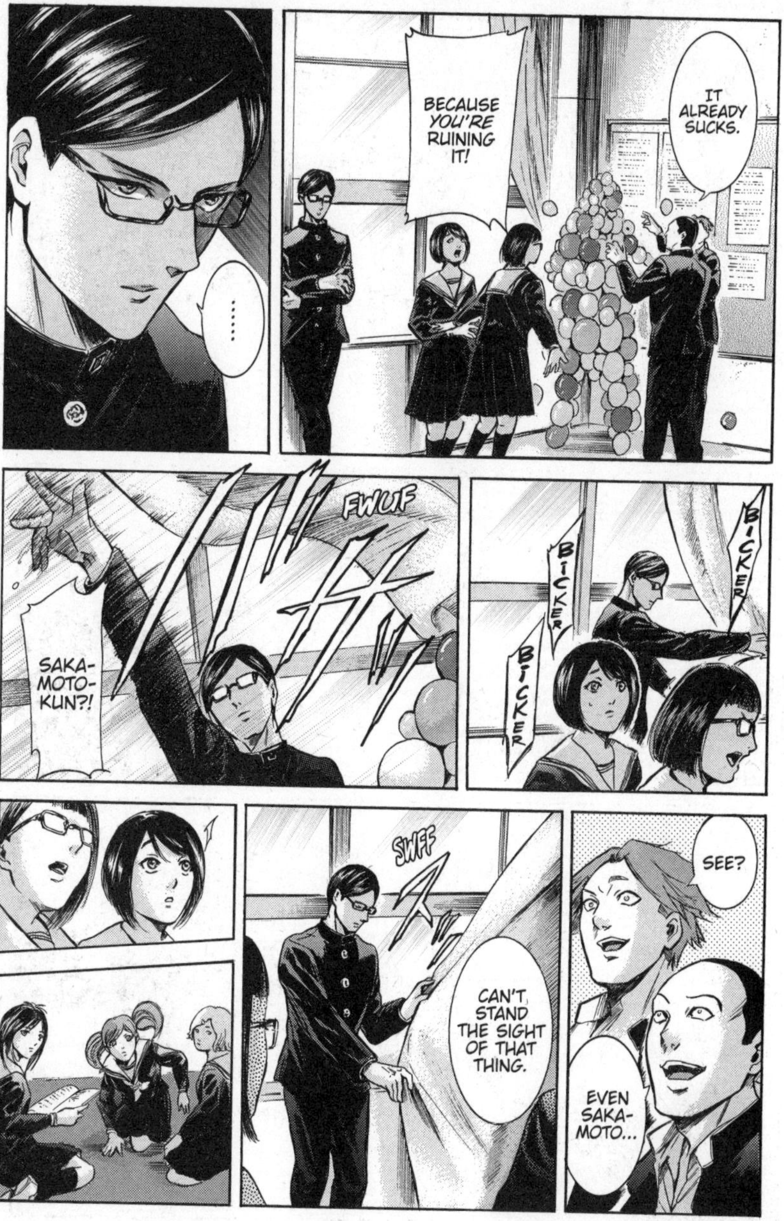
IT ALREADY SUCKS.
BECAUSE YOU'RE RUINING IT!
......
BICKER
BICKER
BICKER
FWUF
SAKA-MOTO-KUN?!
SEE?
EVEN SAKA-MOTO...
SWFF
CAN'T STAND THE SIGHT OF THAT THING.

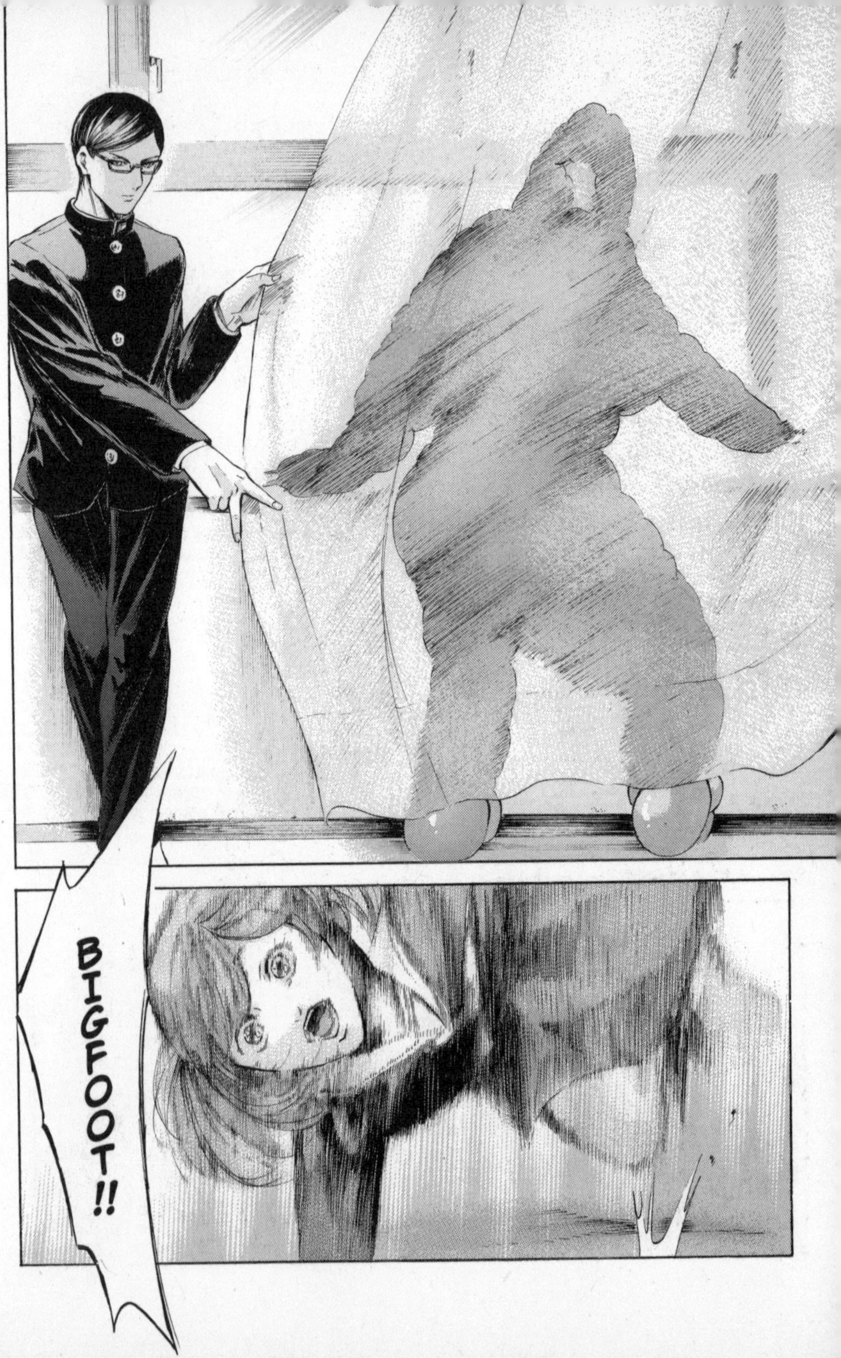
BIGFOOT!!

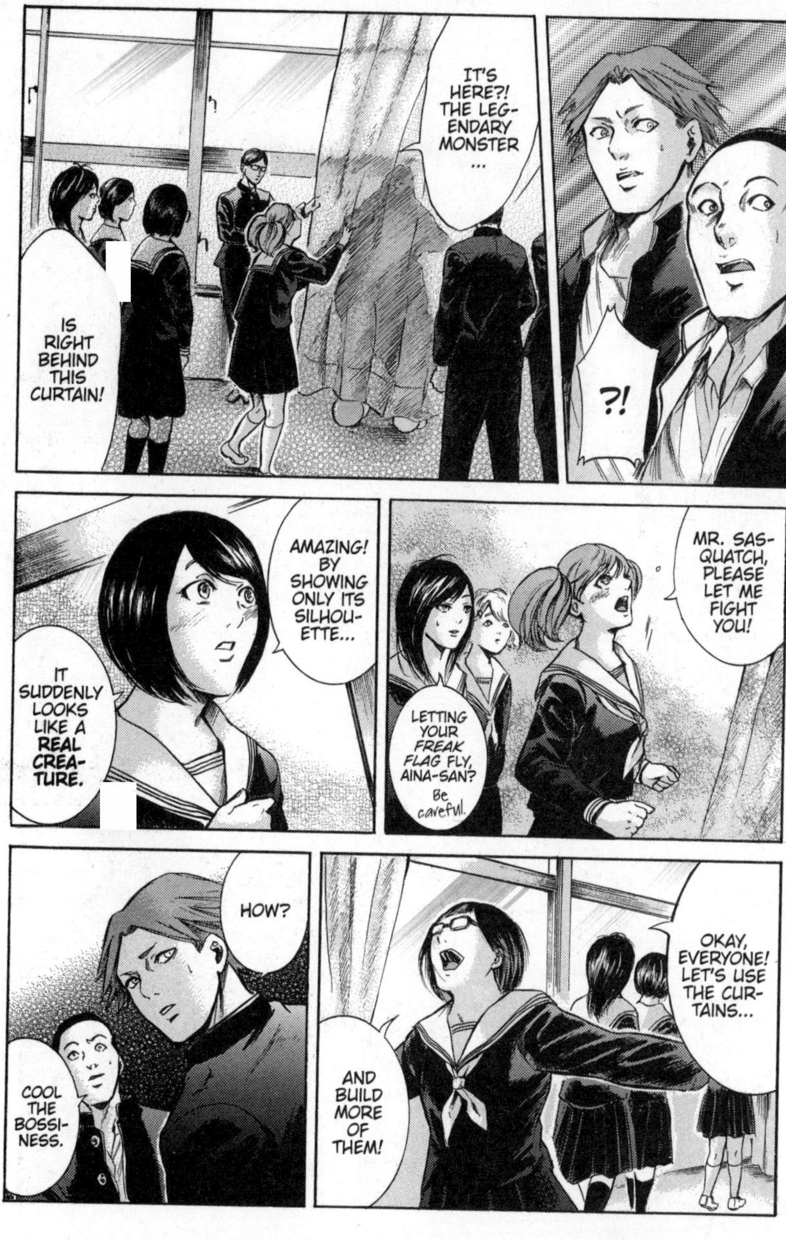
?!
IT'S HERE?! THE LEGENDARY MONSTER...
IS RIGHT BEHIND THIS CURTAIN!
MR. SASQUATCH, PLEASE LET ME FIGHT YOU!
LETTING YOUR FREAK FLAG FLY, AINA-SAN?
Be careful.
AMAZING! BY SHOWING ONLY ITS SILHOUETTE...
IT SUDDENLY LOOKS LIKE A REAL CREATURE.
OKAY, EVERYONE! LET'S USE THE CURTAINS...
AND BUILD MORE OF THEM!
HOW?
COOL THE BOSSINESS.

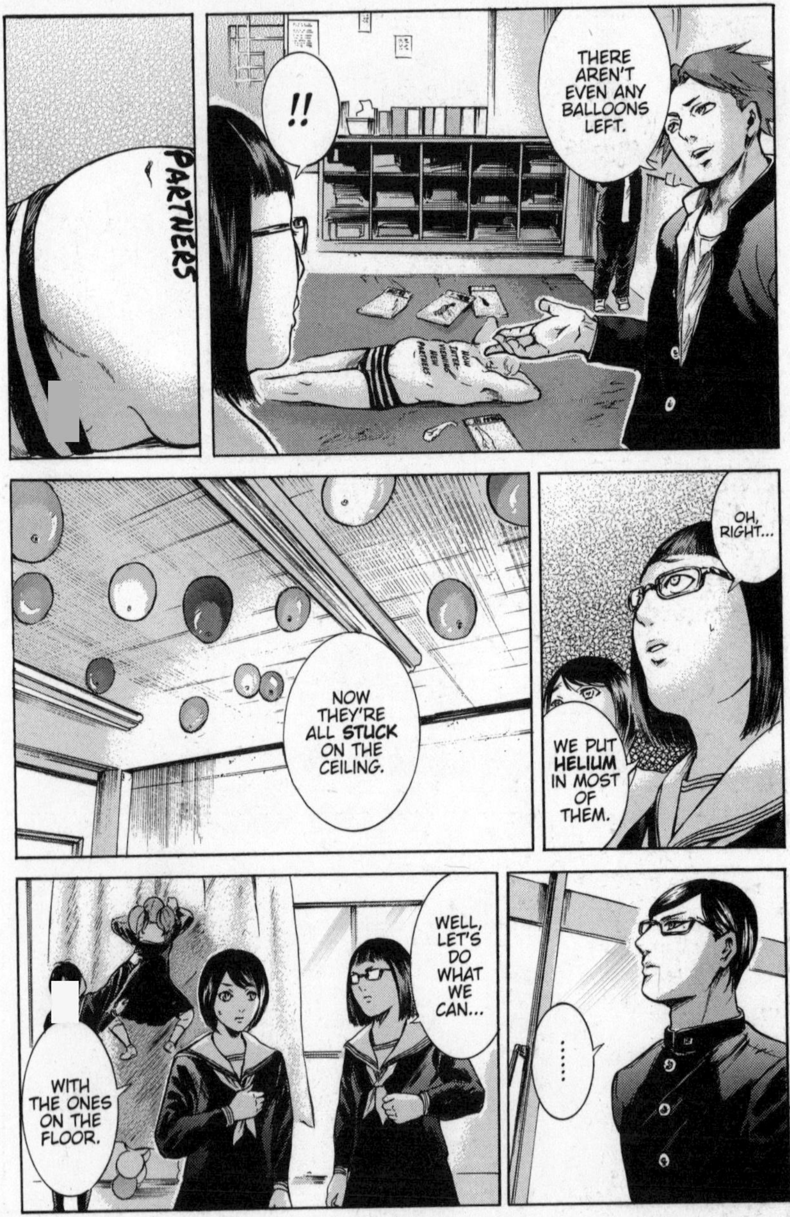
THERE AREN'T EVEN ANY BALLOONS LEFT.
!!
NOW INTER-VIEWING NEW PARTNERS
PARTNERS
OH, RIGHT...
WE PUT HELIUM IN MOST OF THEM.
NOW THEY'RE ALL STUCK ON THE CEILING.
......
WELL, LET'S DO WHAT WE CAN...
WITH THE ONES ON THE FLOOR.

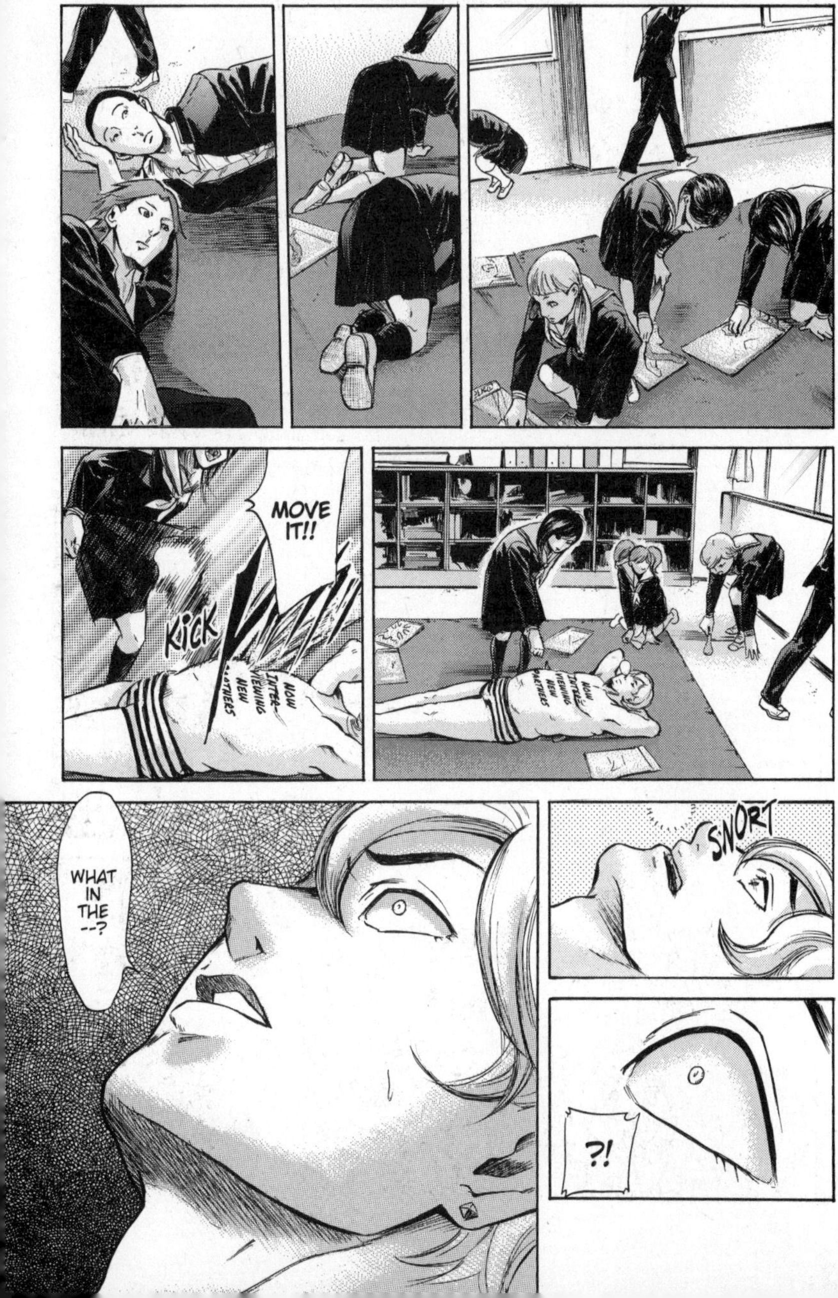
NOW INTER-VIEWING NEW PARTNERS
MOVE IT!!
KICK
NOW INTER-VIEWING NEW
SNORT
?!
WHAT IN THE --?

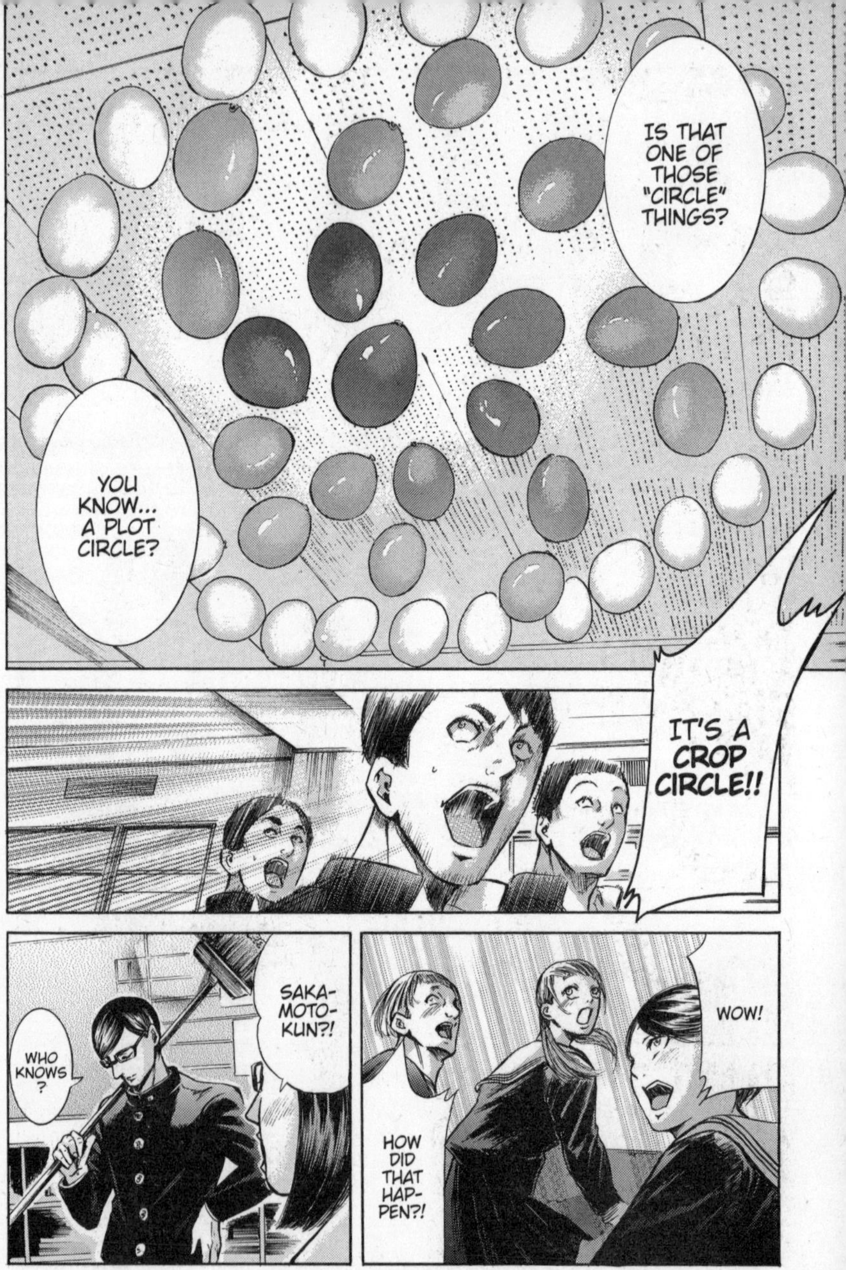
IS THAT ONE OF THOSE "CIRCLE" THINGS?
YOU KNOW... A PLOT CIRCLE?
IT'S A CROP CIRCLE!!
WOW!
HOW DID THAT HAP-PEN?!
SAKA-MOTO-KUN?!
WHO KNOWS?

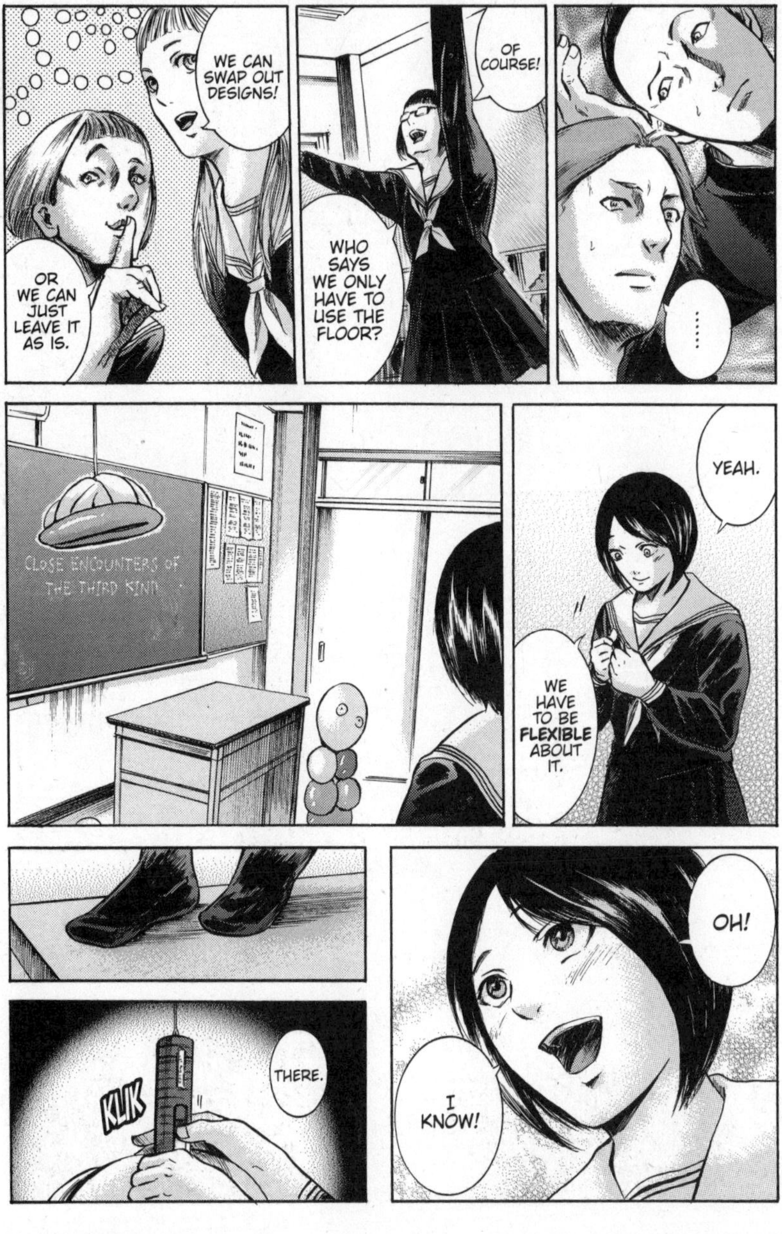
......
OF COURSE!
WHO SAYS WE ONLY HAVE TO USE THE FLOOR?
WE CAN SWAP OUT DESIGNS!
OR WE CAN JUST LEAVE IT AS IS.
YEAH.
WE HAVE TO BE **FLEXIBLE** ABOUT IT.
CLOSE ENCOUNTERS OF THE THIRD KIND
OH!
I KNOW!
KLIK
THERE.

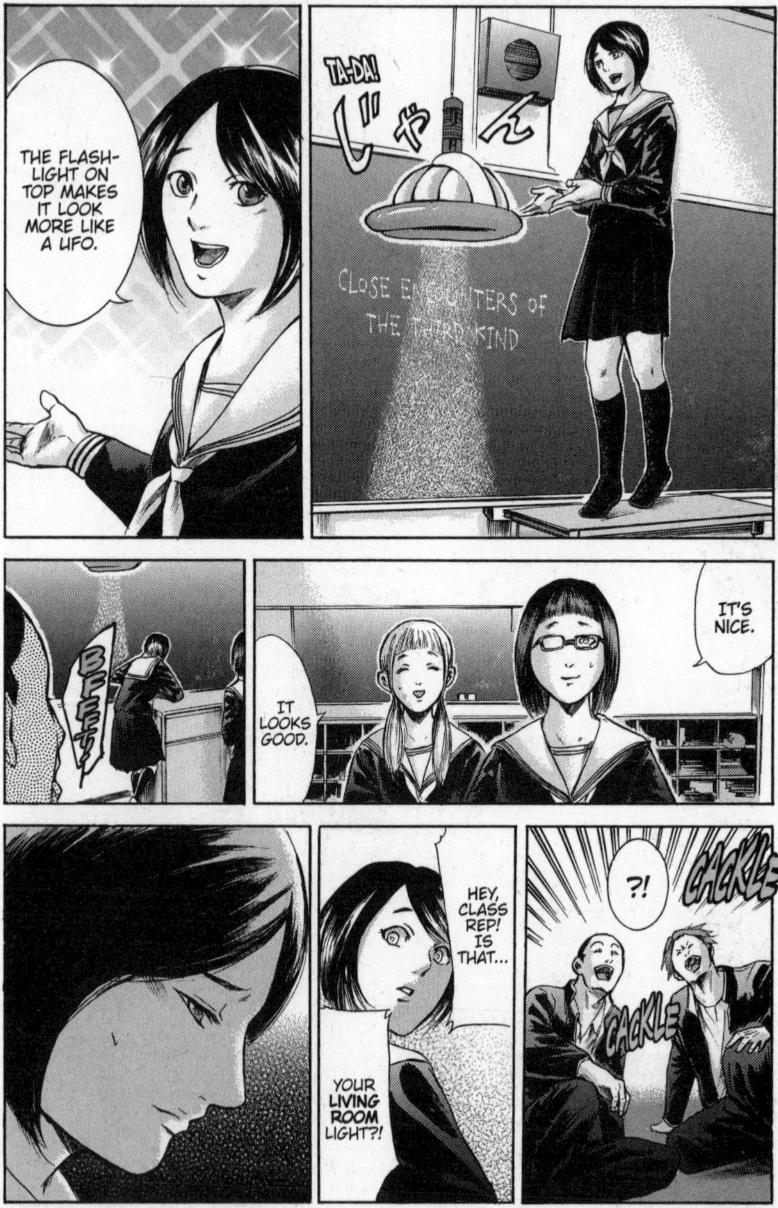
TA-DA!
じゃん
CLOSE ENCOUNTERS OF THE THIRD KIND
THE FLASH-LIGHT ON TOP MAKES IT LOOK MORE LIKE A UFO.
IT'S NICE.
IT LOOKS GOOD.
BFFFT!
CACKLE
?!
CACKLE
HEY, CLASS REP! IS THAT...
YOUR LIVING ROOM LIGHT?!

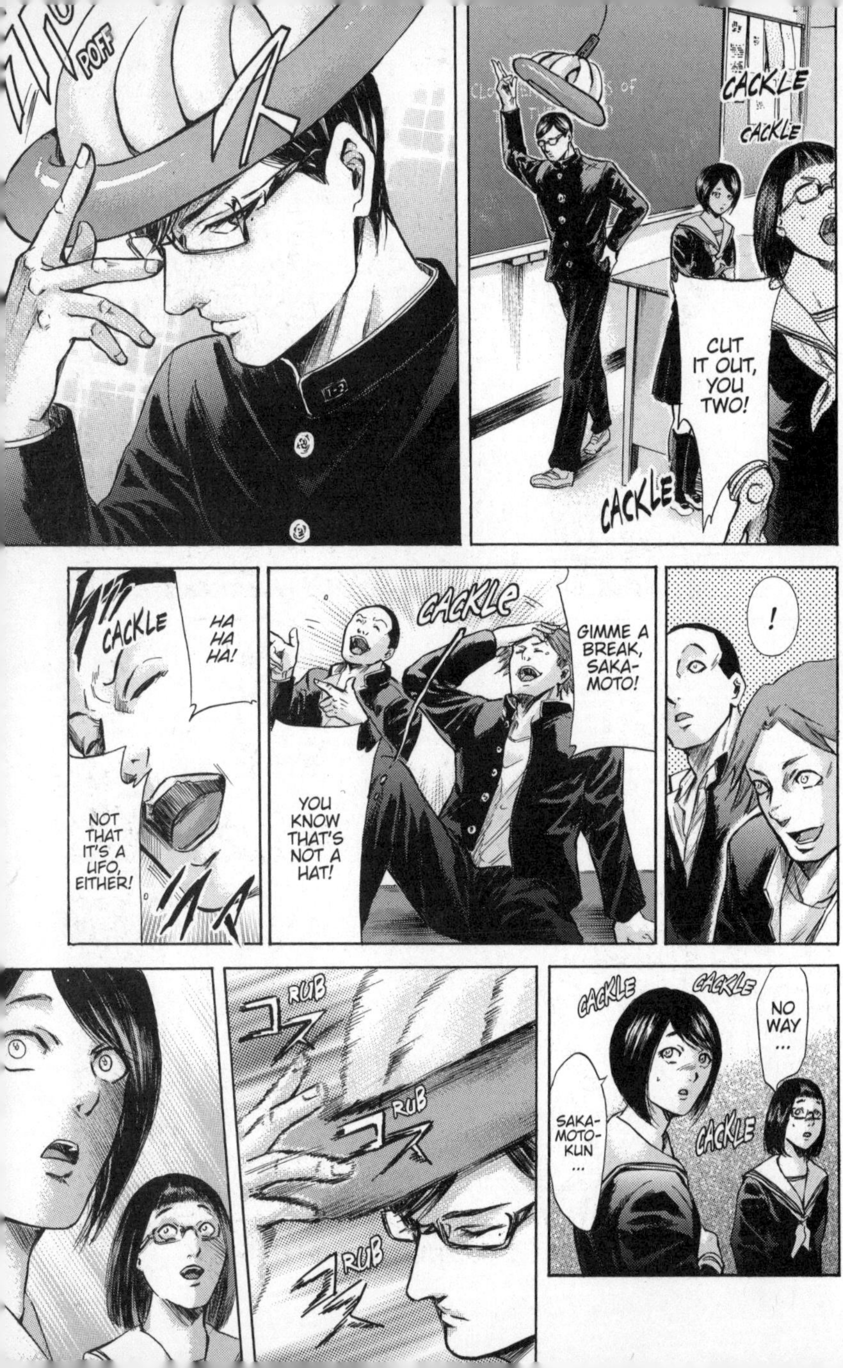
CACKLE
CACKLE
CUT IT OUT, YOU TWO!
CACKLE
POFF
!
CACKLE
GIMME A BREAK, SAKAMOTO!
YOU KNOW THAT'S NOT A HAT!
HA HA HA!
CACKLE
NOT THAT IT'S A UFO, EITHER!
NO WAY ...
CACKLE
CACKLE
SAKAMOTO-KUN ...
CACKLE
RUB
RUB
RUB

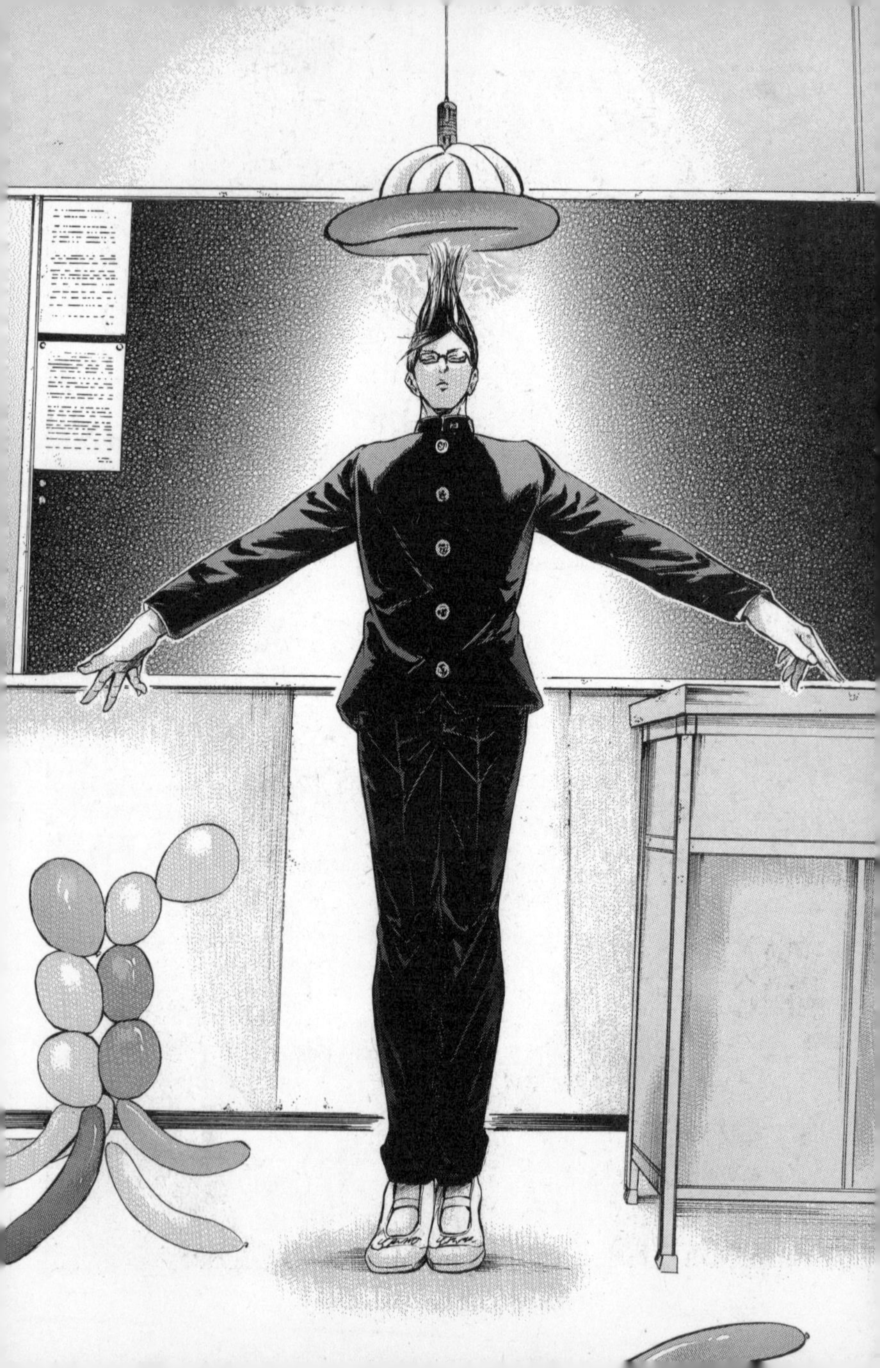

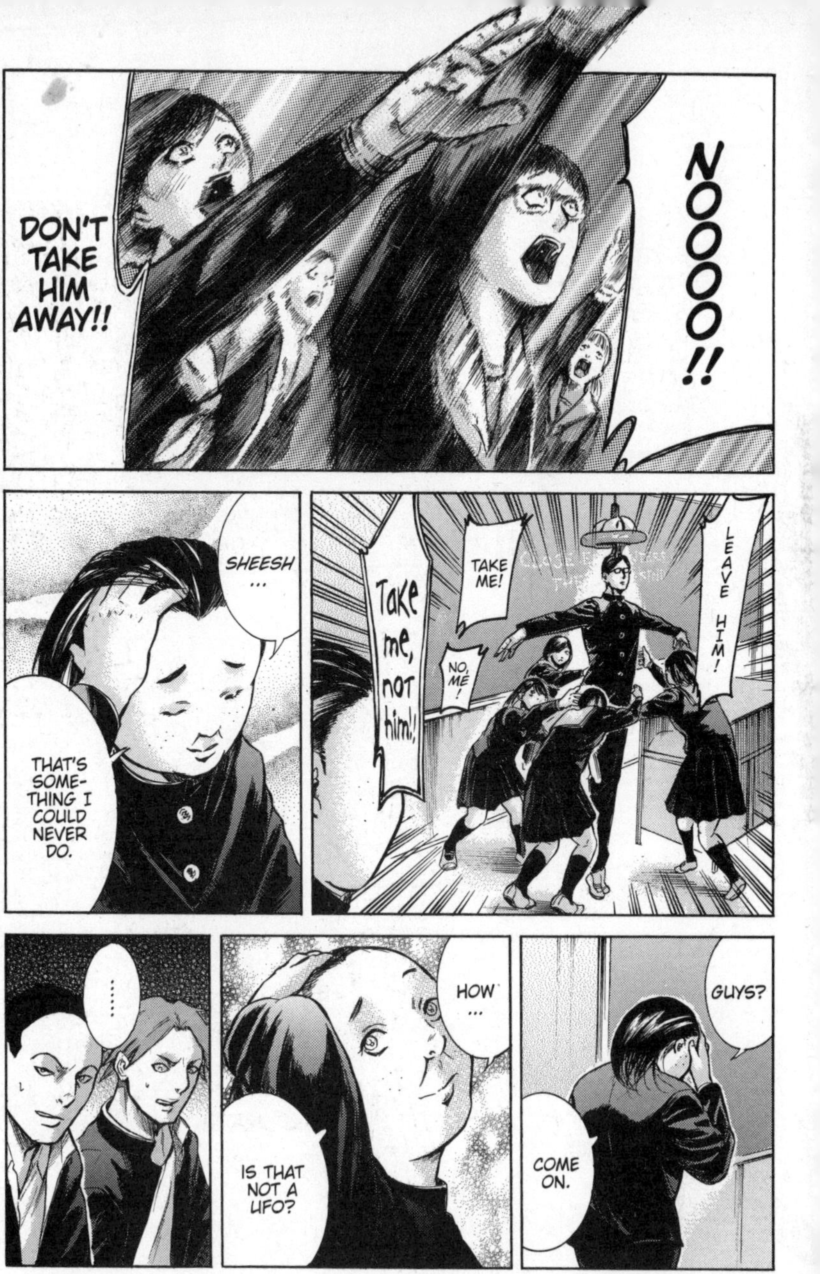
NOOOOO!!
DON'T TAKE HIM AWAY!!
LEAVE HIM!
TAKE ME!
NO, ME!
Take me, not him!!
SHEESH ...
THAT'S SOMETHING I COULD NEVER DO.
GUYS?
COME ON.
HOW ...
IS THAT NOT A UFO?
......

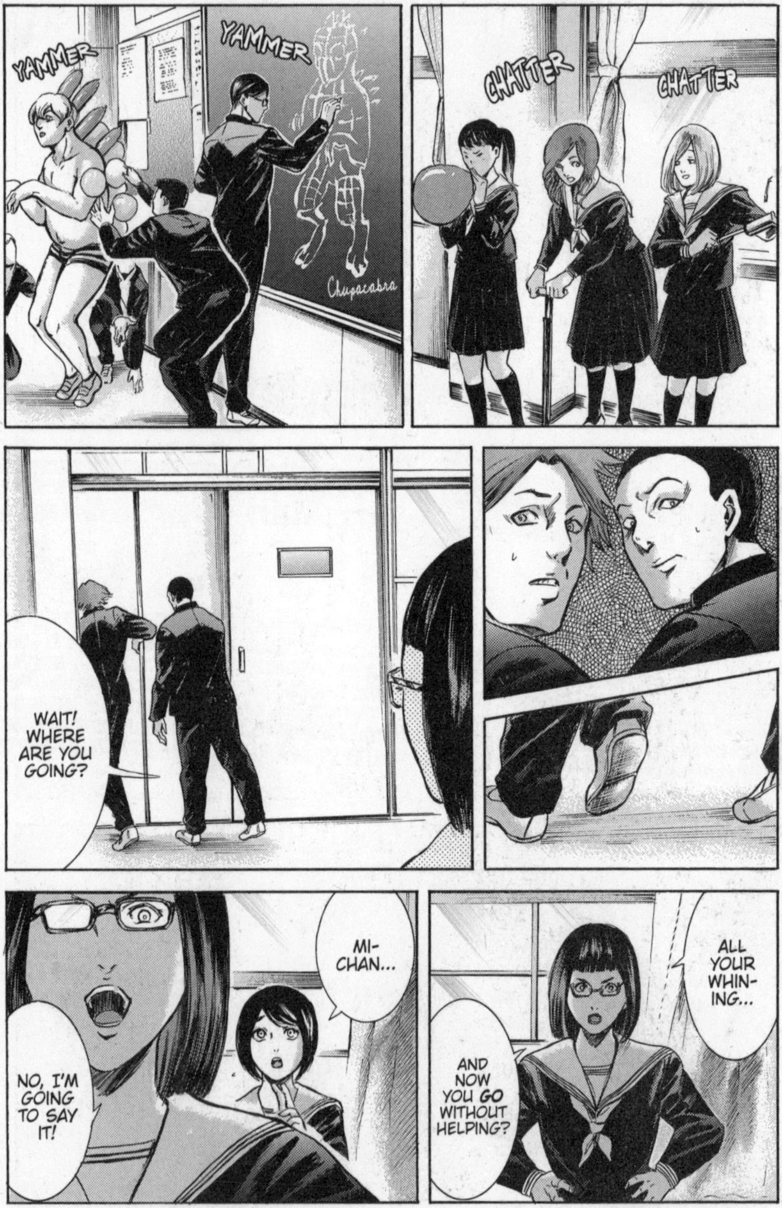
CHATTER
CHATTER
YAMMER
YAMMER
Chupacabra
WAIT! WHERE ARE YOU GOING?
ALL YOUR WHIN-ING...
AND NOW YOU **GO** WITHOUT HELPING?
MI-CHAN...
NO, I'M GOING TO SAY IT!

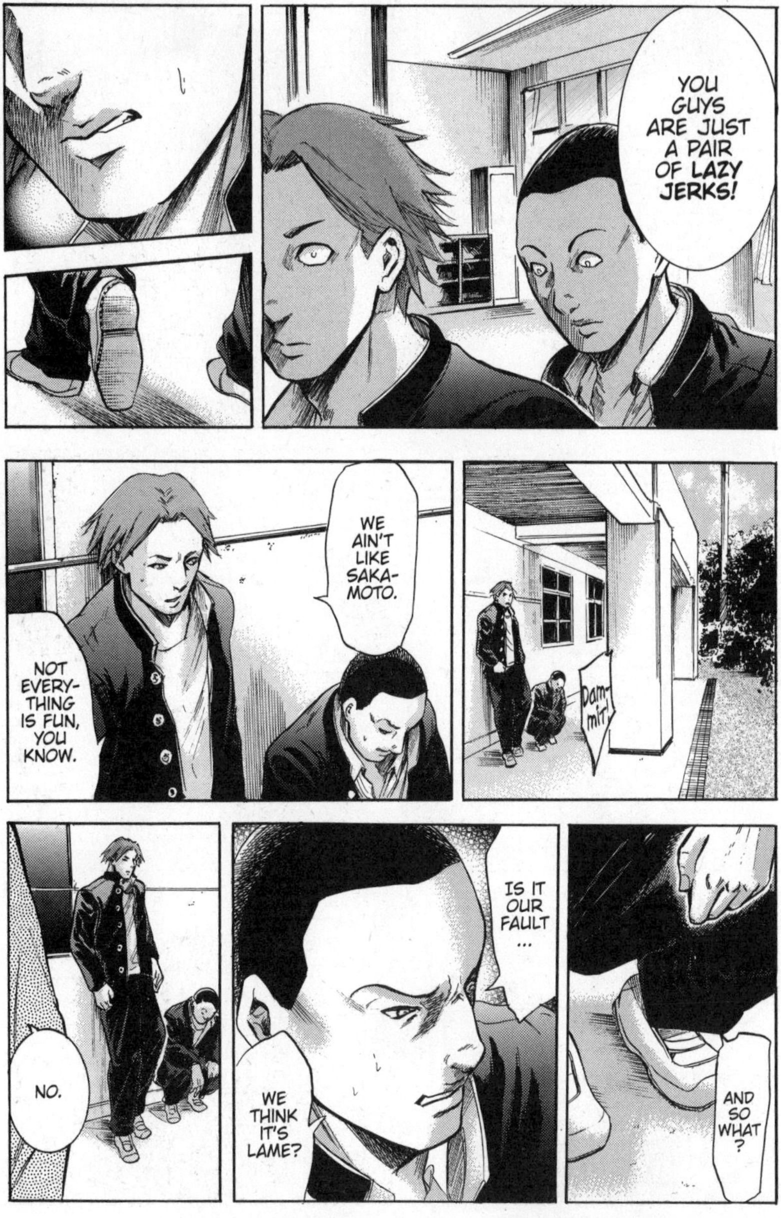
YOU GUYS ARE JUST A PAIR OF LAZY JERKS!
Dam-mit!
WE AIN'T LIKE SAKA-MOTO.
NOT EVERY-THING IS FUN, YOU KNOW.
AND SO WHAT?
IS IT OUR FAULT ...
WE THINK IT'S LAME?
NO.

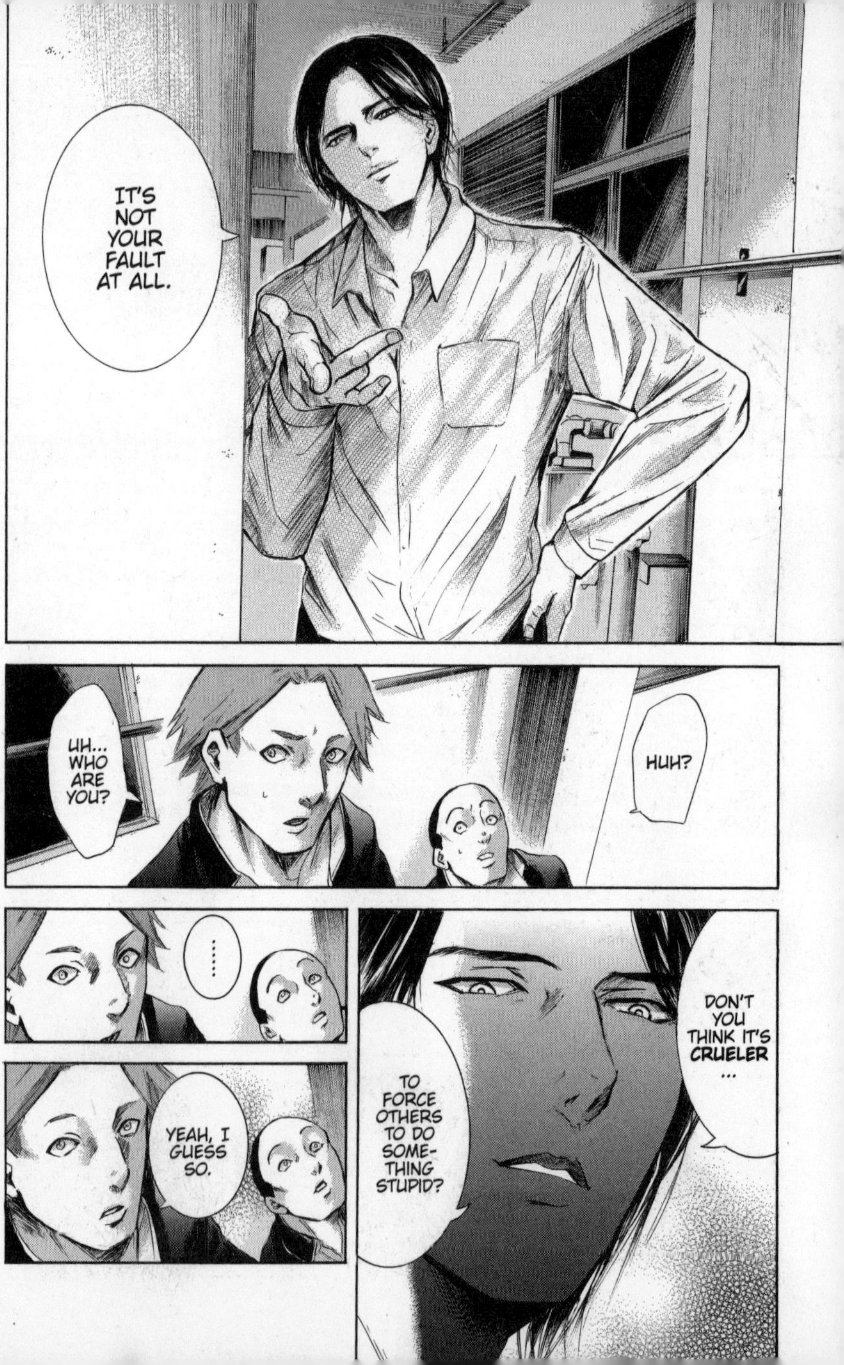
IT'S NOT YOUR FAULT AT ALL.
HUH?
UH... WHO ARE YOU?
DON'T YOU THINK IT'S CRUELER ...
TO FORCE OTHERS TO DO SOME-THING STUPID?
......
YEAH, I GUESS SO.

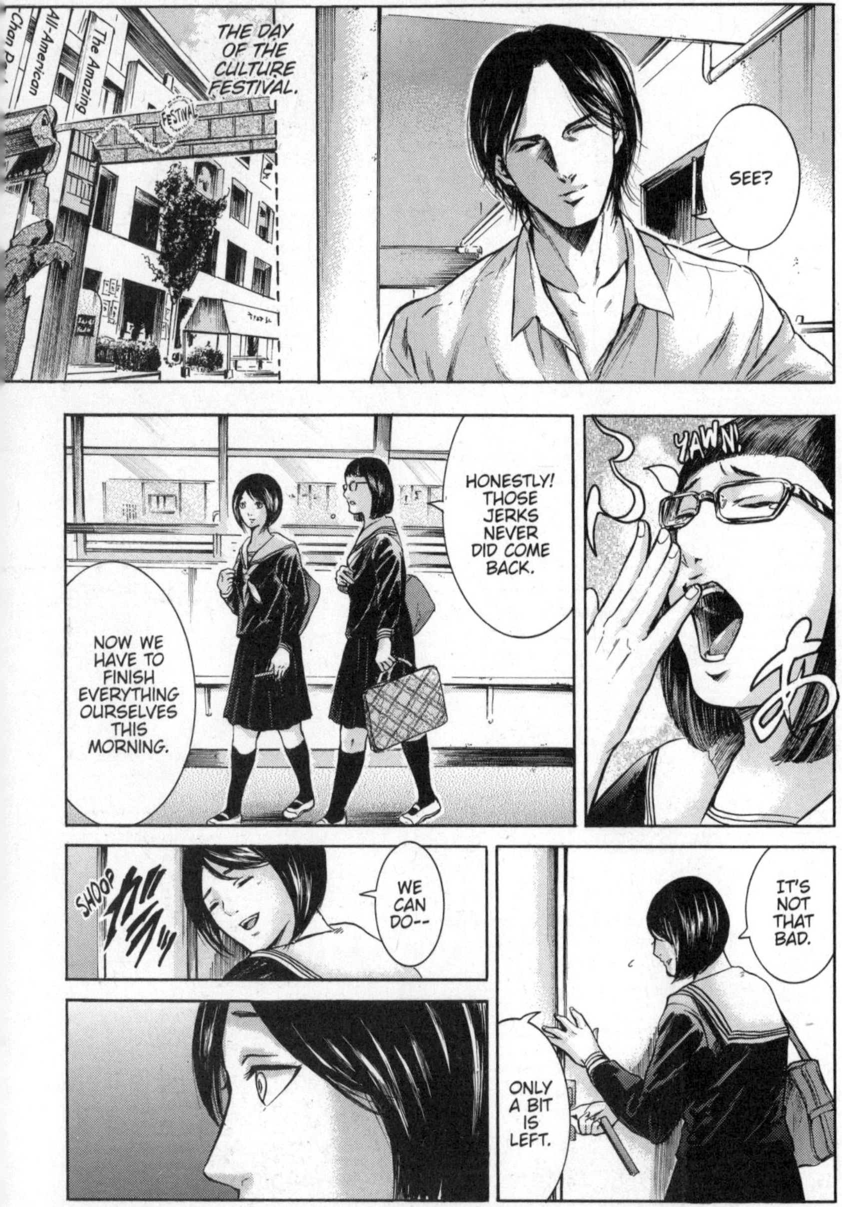
SEE?
THE DAY OF THE CULTURE FESTIVAL.
The Amazing
All-American
FESTIVAL
YAWN!
あ
HONESTLY! THOSE JERKS NEVER DID COME BACK.
NOW WE HAVE TO FINISH EVERYTHING OURSELVES THIS MORNING.
IT'S NOT THAT BAD.
ONLY A BIT IS LEFT.
WE CAN DO--
SHOOP

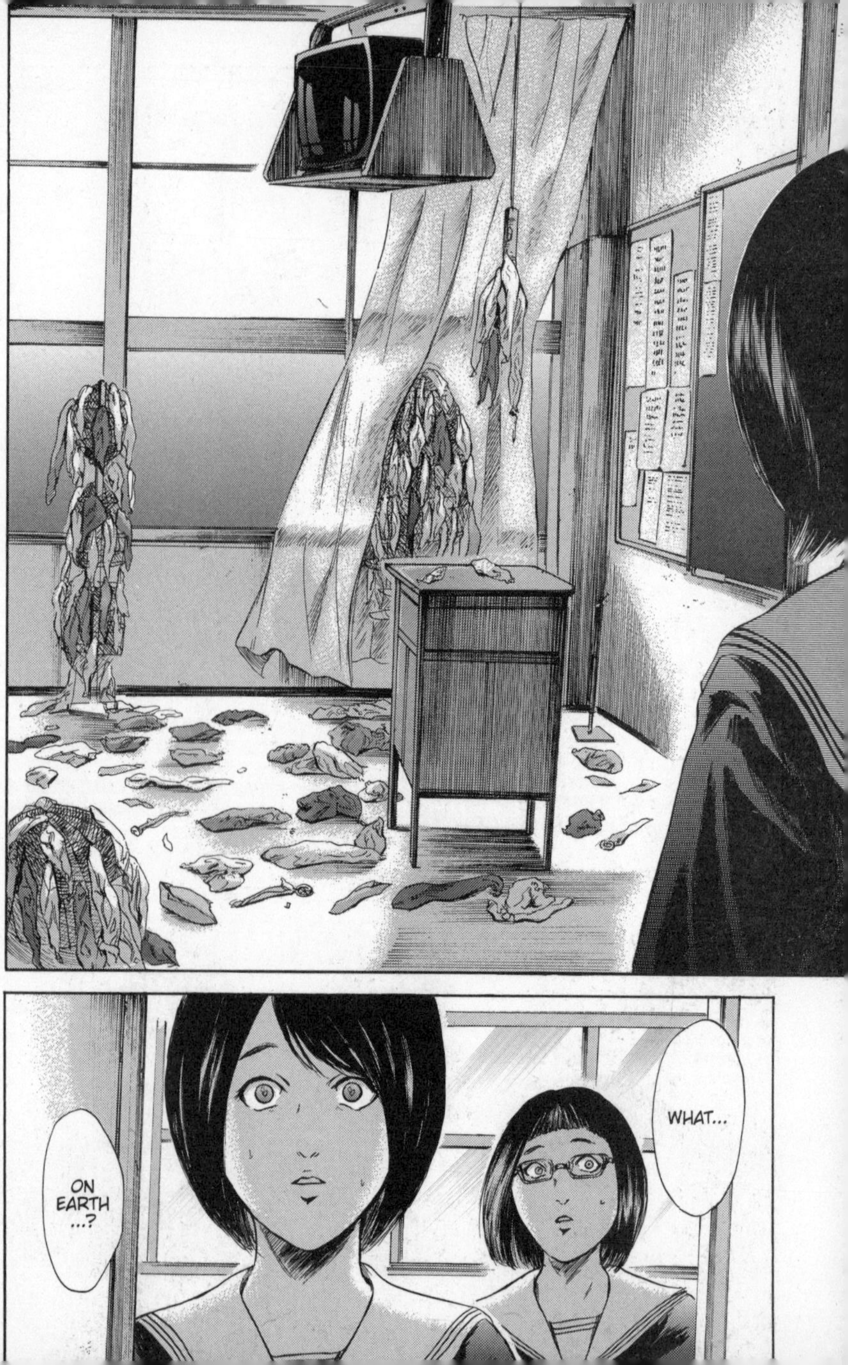
WHAT...
ON EARTH ...?

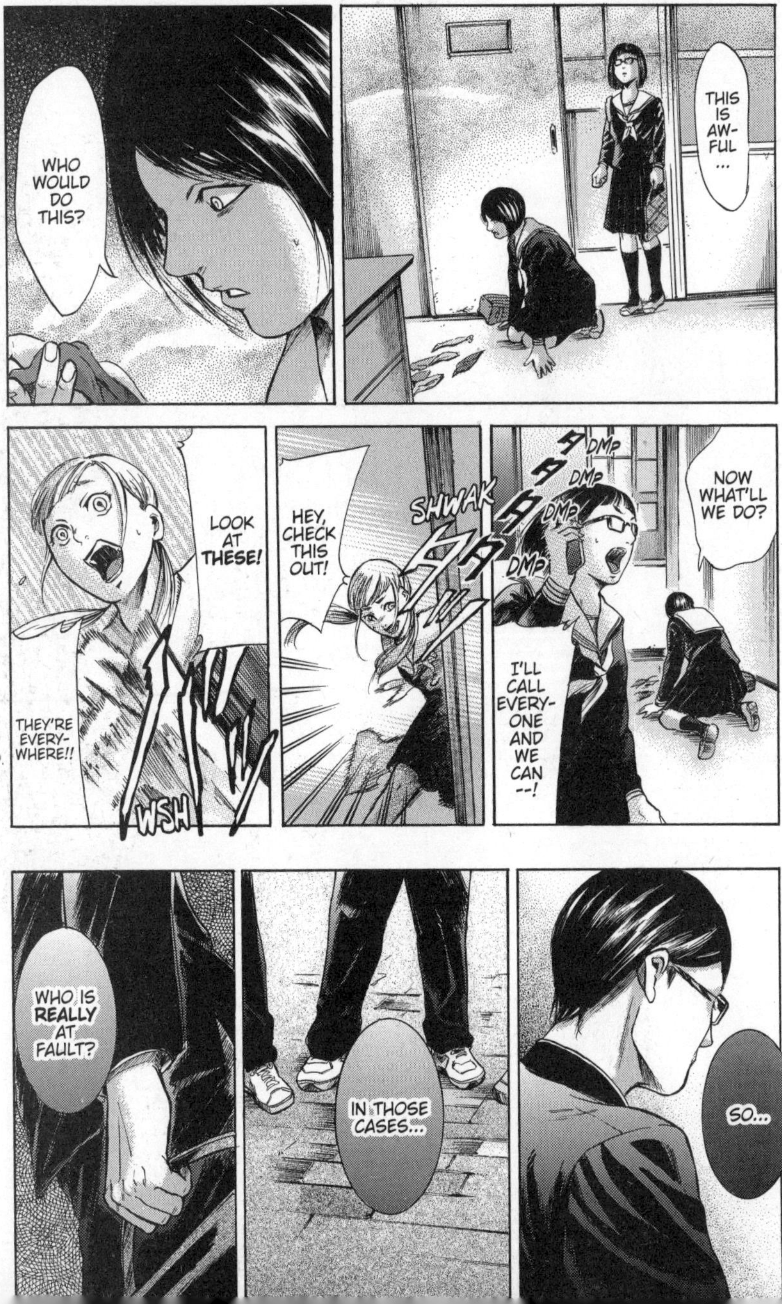
THIS IS AWFUL...
WHO WOULD DO THIS?
NOW WHAT'LL WE DO?
DMP DMP DMP DMP
I'LL CALL EVERYONE AND WE CAN--!
SHWAK
HEY, CHECK THIS OUT!
LOOK AT **THESE!**
THEY'RE EVERYWHERE!!
WSH
SO...
IN THOSE CASES...
WHO IS **REALLY** AT FAULT?

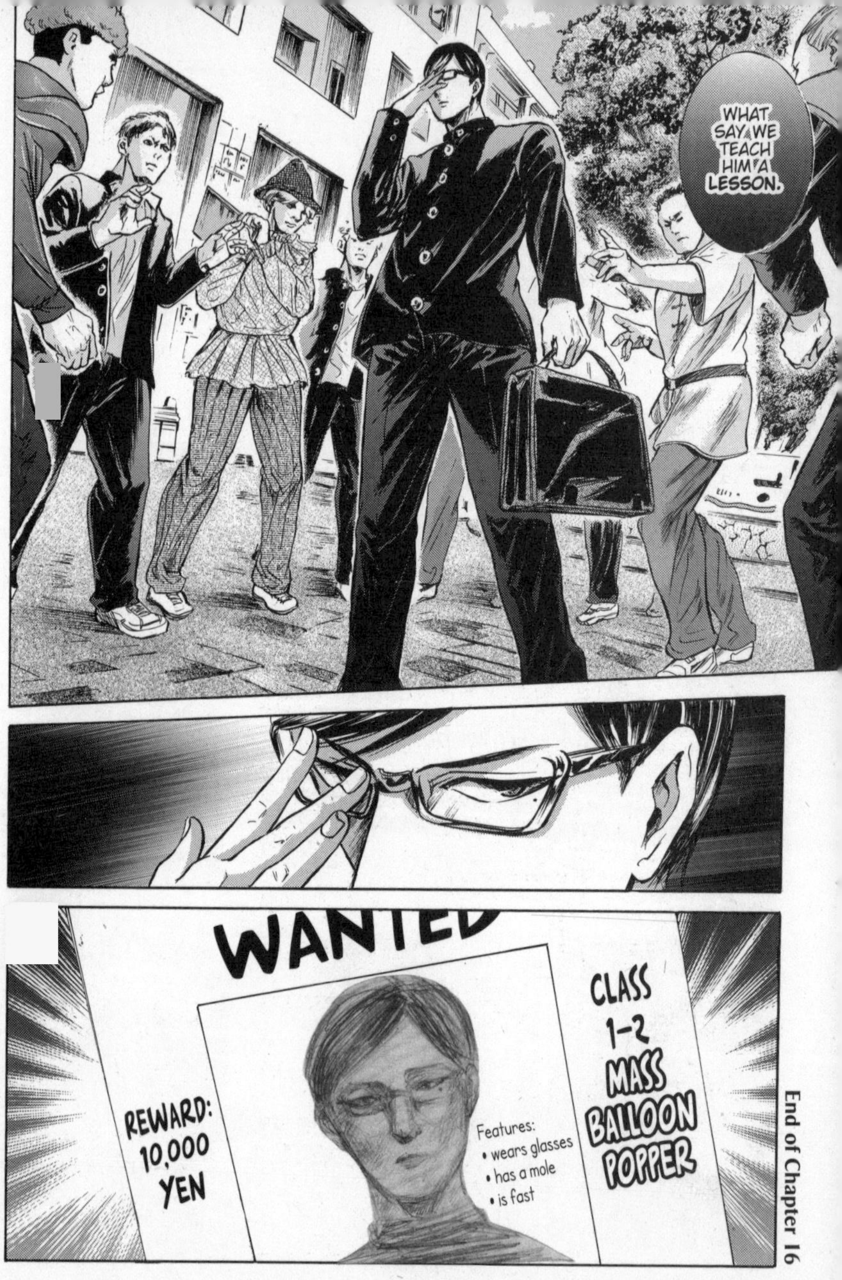
WHAT SAY WE TEACH HIM A LESSON.
WANTED
CLASS 1-2 MASS BALLOON POPPER
Features:
• wears glasses
• has a mole
• is fast
REWARD: 10,000 YEN

End of Chapter 16

Break Time #5:
Classroom

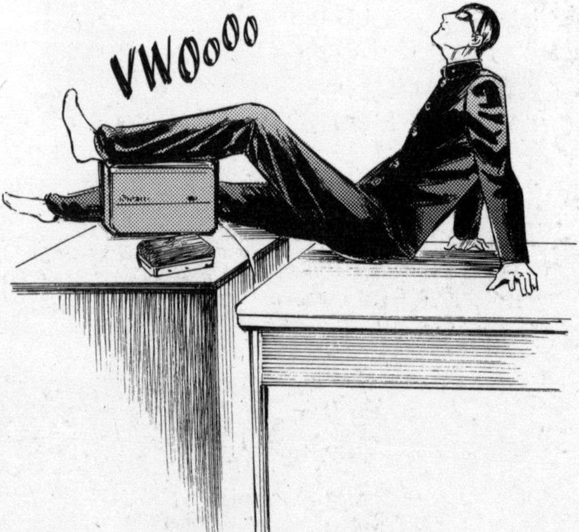
VWOoOo

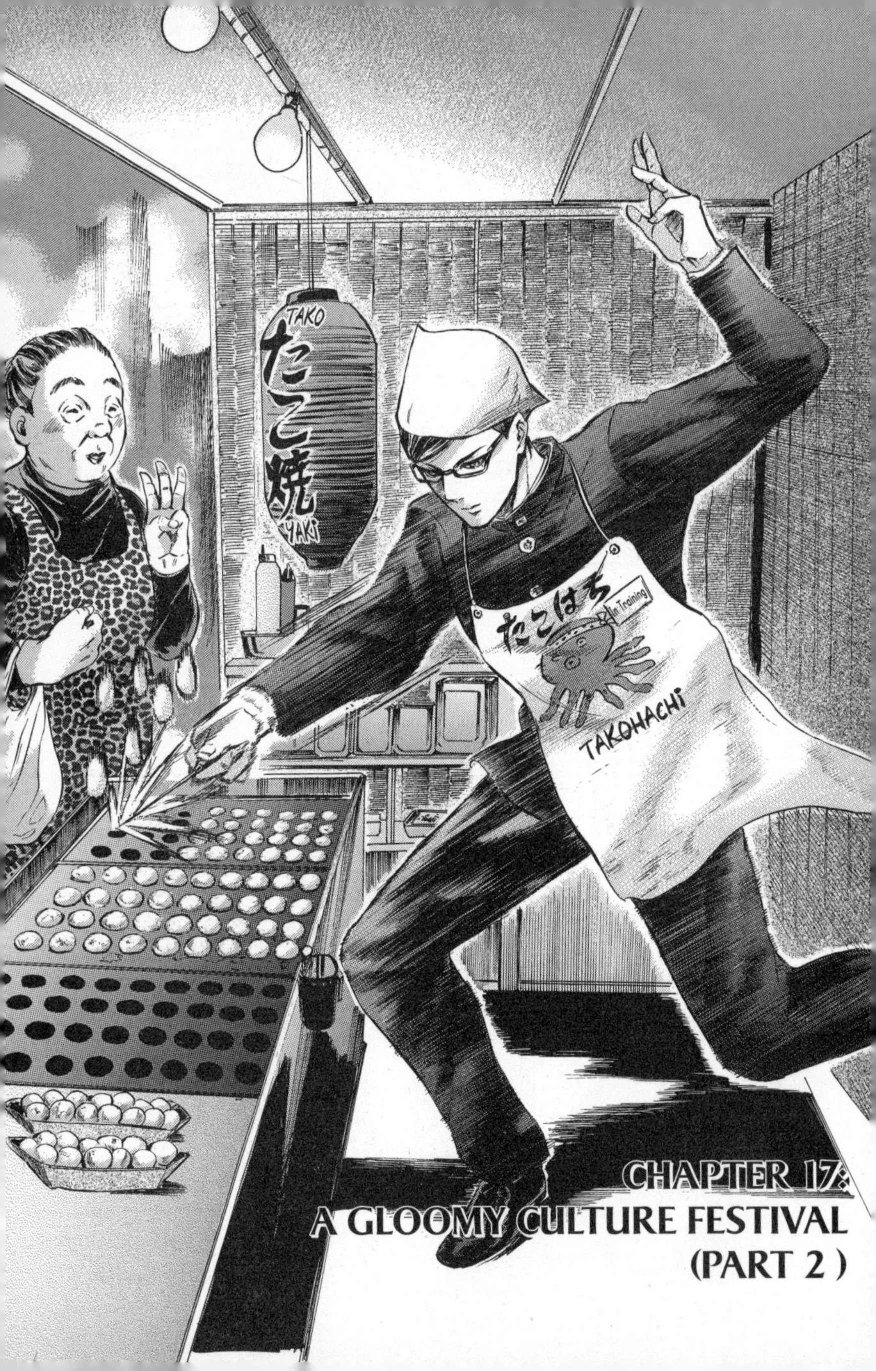
TAKO
たこ焼
YAKI
たこはち
In-Training
TAKOHACHI
TAKOHACHI
CHAPTER 17:
A GLOOMY CULTURE FESTIVAL
(PART 2)

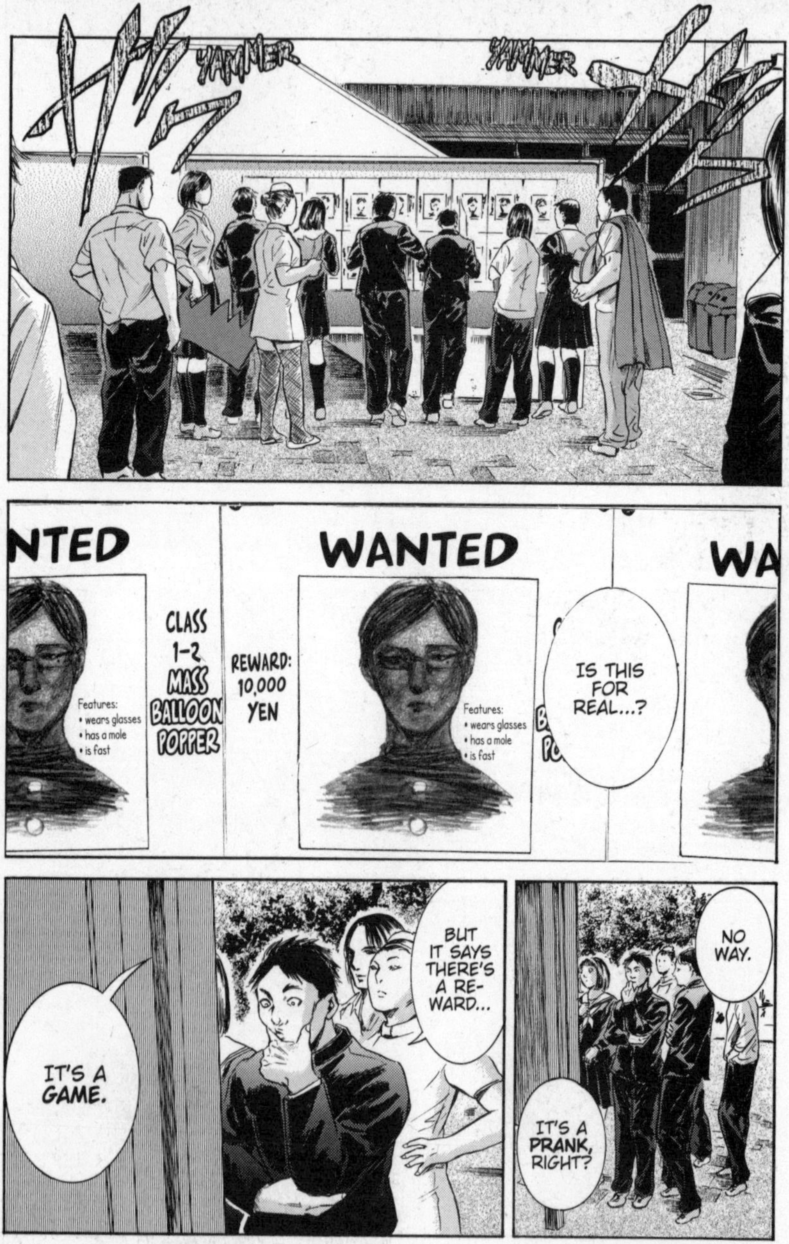
YAMMER YAMMER
YAMMER
IS THIS FOR REAL...?
WANTED
Features:
• wears glasses
• has a mole
• is fast
REWARD: 10,000 YEN
CLASS 1-2 MASS BALLOON POPPER
Features:
• wears glasses
• has a mole
• is fast
NO WAY.
IT'S A PRANK, RIGHT?
BUT IT SAYS THERE'S A RE-WARD...
IT'S A GAME.

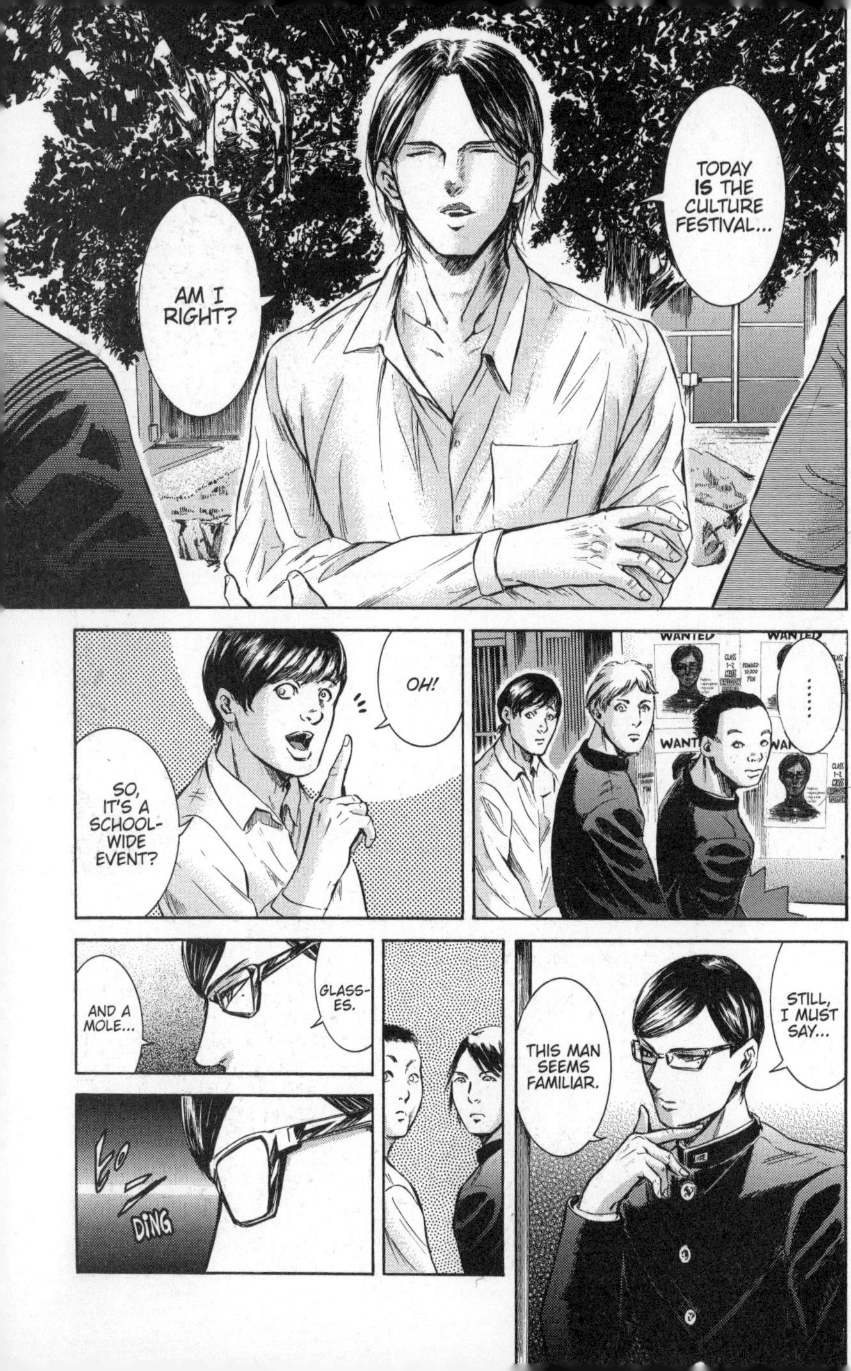
TODAY IS THE CULTURE FESTIVAL...
AM I RIGHT?
WANTED
......
OH!
SO, IT'S A SCHOOL-WIDE EVENT?
STILL, I MUST SAY...
THIS MAN SEEMS FAMILIAR.
GLASS-ES.
AND A MOLE...
DING

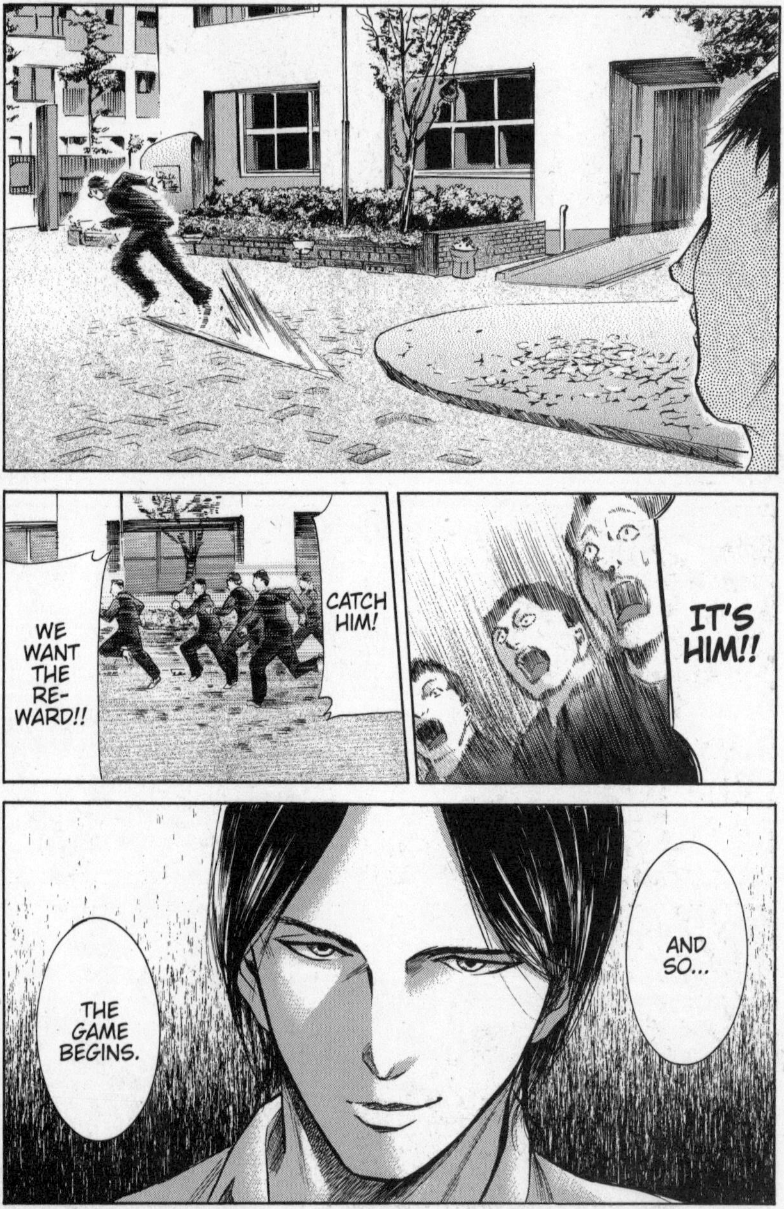
IT'S HIM!!
CATCH HIM!
WE WANT THE RE-WARD!!
AND SO...
THE GAME BEGINS.

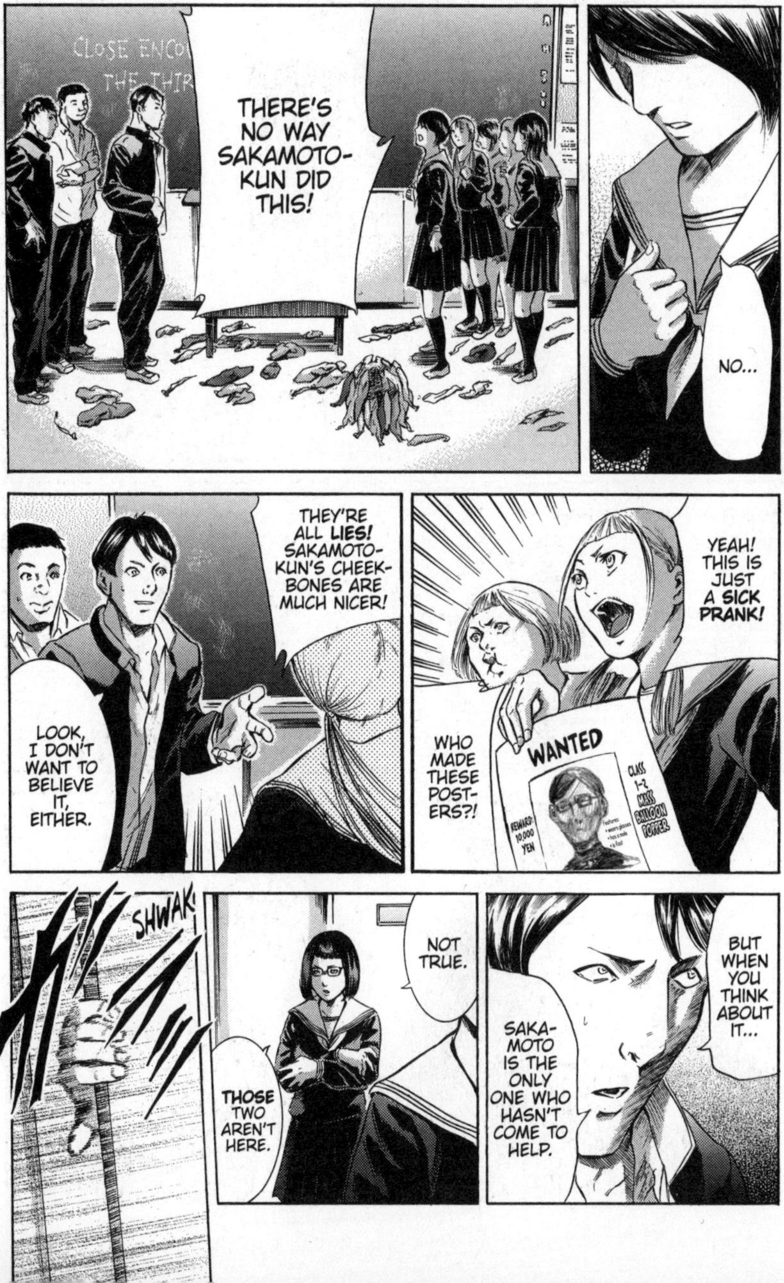
NO...
THERE'S NO WAY SAKAMOTO-KUN DID THIS!
YEAH! THIS IS JUST A **SICK PRANK!**
WHO MADE THESE POSTERS?!
WANTED
CLASS 1-2 MASS BALLOON POPPER
REWARD: 10,000 YEN
THEY'RE ALL **LIES!** SAKAMOTO-KUN'S CHEEKBONES ARE MUCH NICER!
LOOK, I DON'T WANT TO BELIEVE IT, EITHER.
BUT WHEN YOU THINK ABOUT IT...
SAKAMOTO IS THE ONLY ONE WHO HASN'T COME TO HELP.
NOT TRUE.
THOSE TWO AREN'T HERE.
SHWAK!

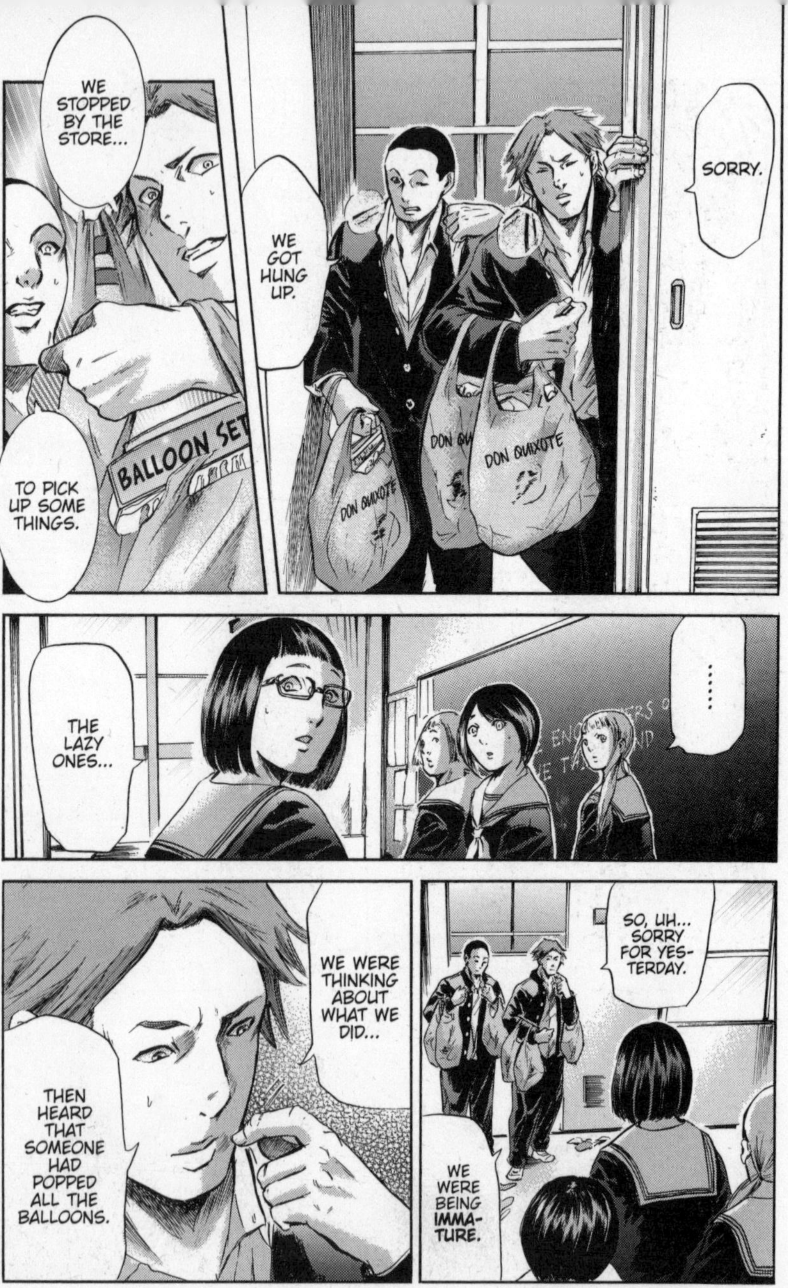
SORRY.
WE GOT HUNG UP.
DON QUIXOTE
DON QUIXOTE
DON QUIXOTE
WE STOPPED BY THE STORE...
BALLOON SET
TO PICK UP SOME THINGS.
......
THE LAZY ONES...
SO, UH... SORRY FOR YES-TERDAY.
WE WERE BEING IMMA-TURE.
WE WERE THINKING ABOUT WHAT WE DID...
THEN HEARD THAT SOMEONE HAD POPPED ALL THE BALLOONS.

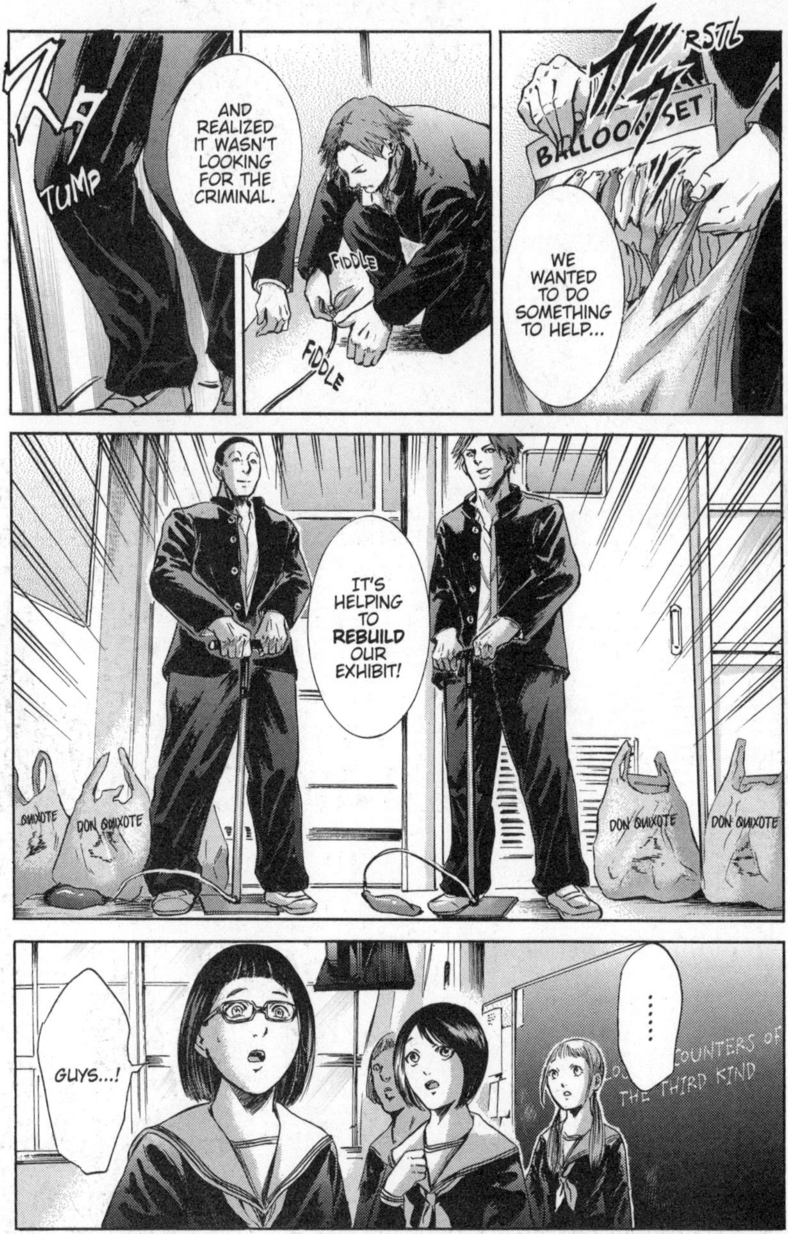

RSTL
BALLOON SET
WE WANTED TO DO SOMETHING TO HELP...
AND REALIZED IT WASN'T LOOKING FOR THE CRIMINAL.
FIDDLE
FIDDLE
TUMP
IT'S HELPING TO **REBUILD** OUR EXHIBIT!
DON QUIXOTE
DON QUIXOTE
DON QUIXOTE
QUIXOTE
......
THE THIRD KIND
GUYS...!

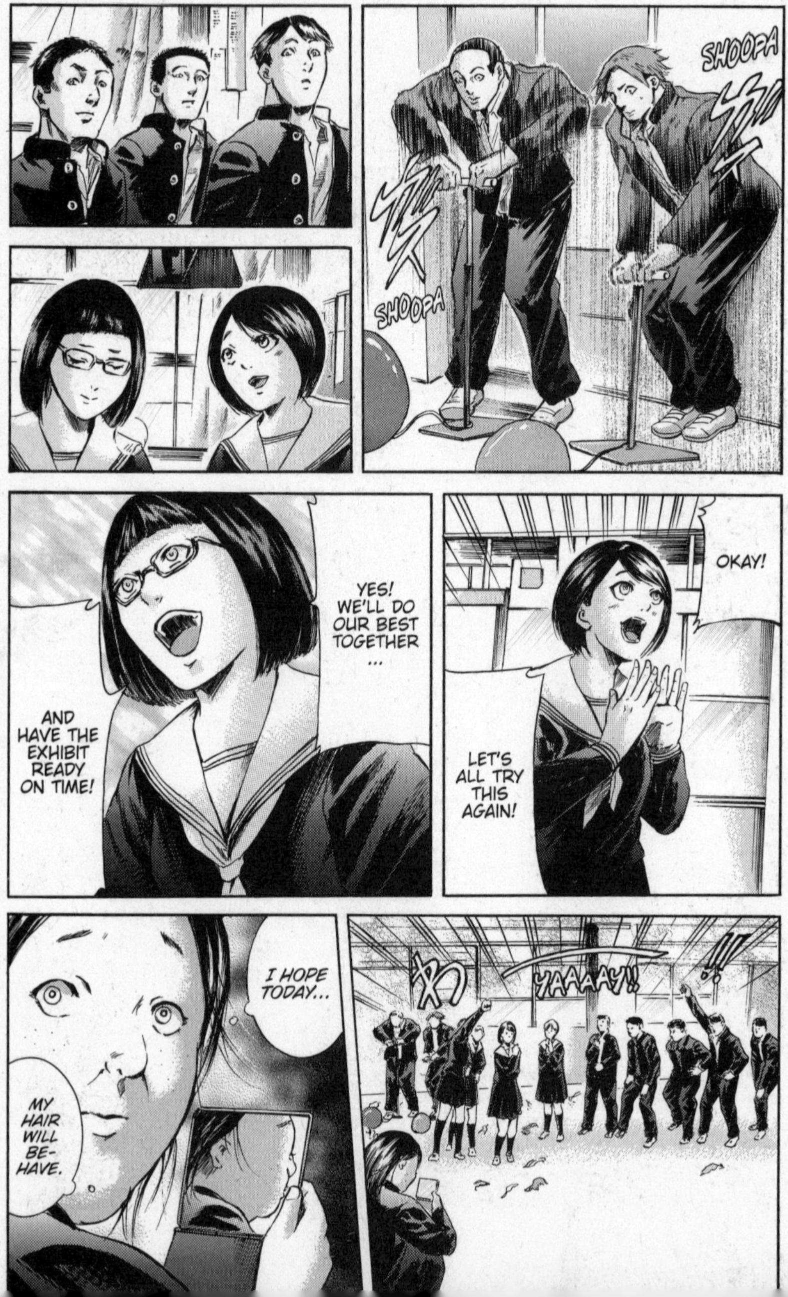
SHOOPA
SHOOPA
OKAY!
LET'S ALL TRY THIS AGAIN!
YES! WE'LL DO OUR BEST TOGETHER ...
AND HAVE THE EXHIBIT READY ON TIME!
YAAAAY!!
I HOPE TODAY...
MY HAIR WILL BE-HAVE.

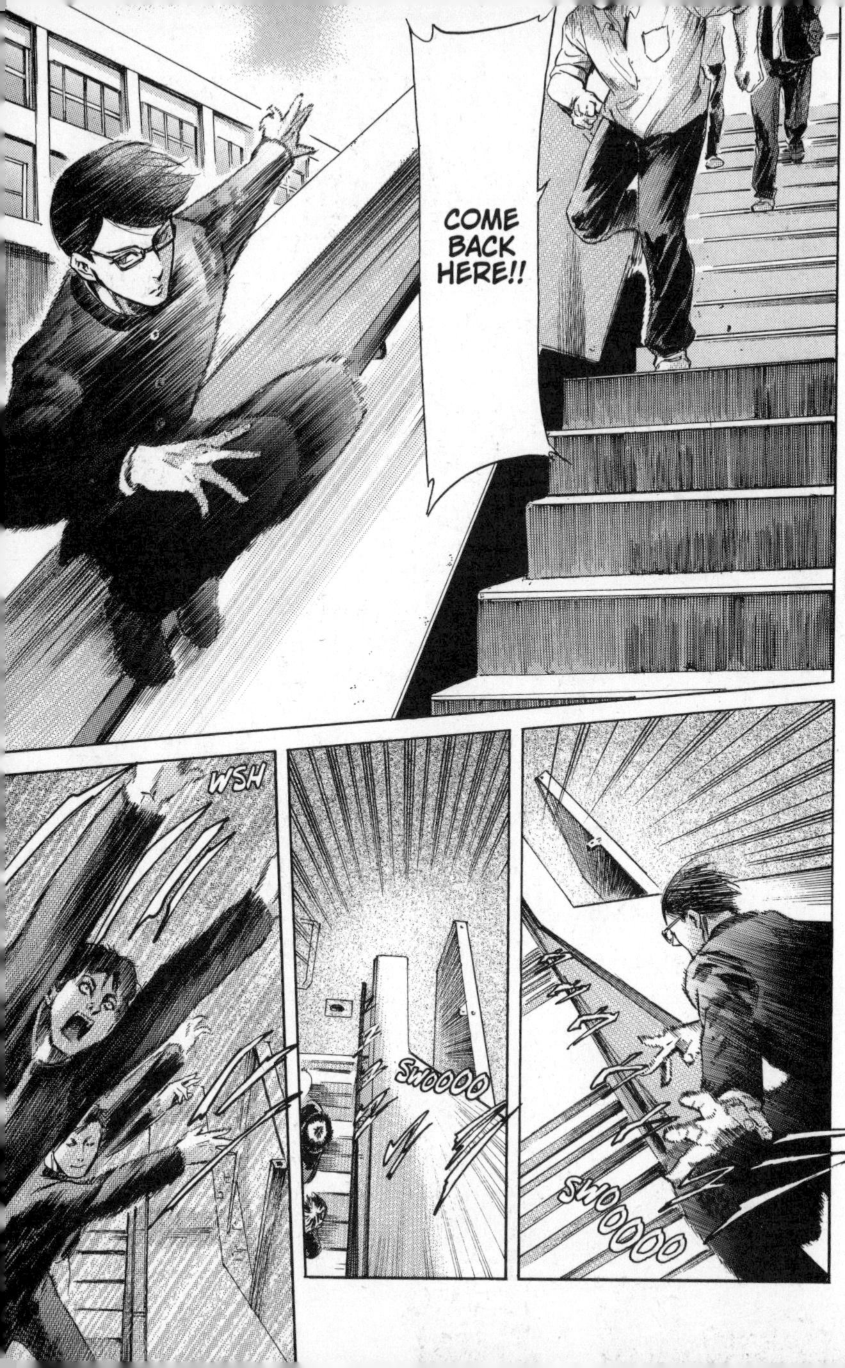
COME BACK HERE!!
SWOOOOO
SWOOOO
WSH

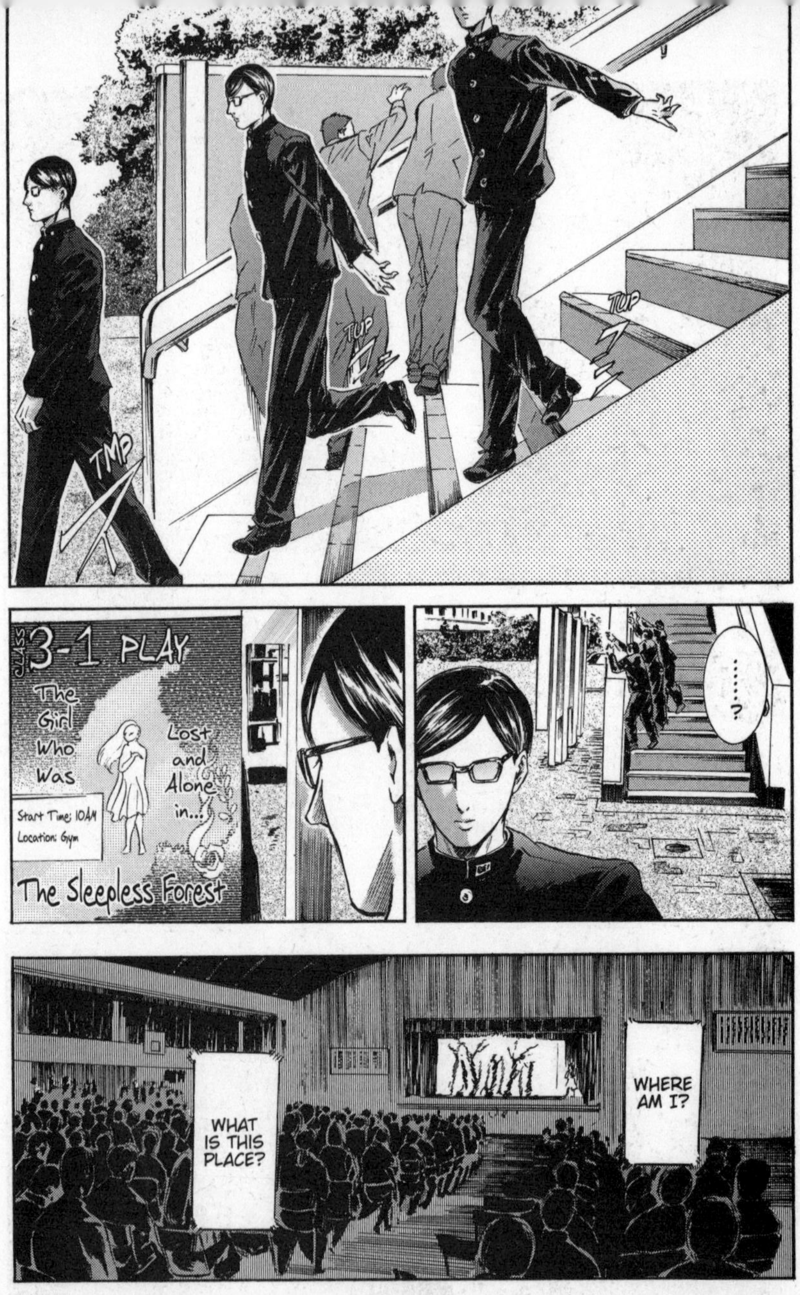
TUP
TUP
TMP
?......
CLASS 3-1 PLAY
The Girl Who Was Lost and Alone in...
The Sleepless Forest
Start Time: 10AM
Location: Gym
WHERE AM I?
WHAT IS THIS PLACE?

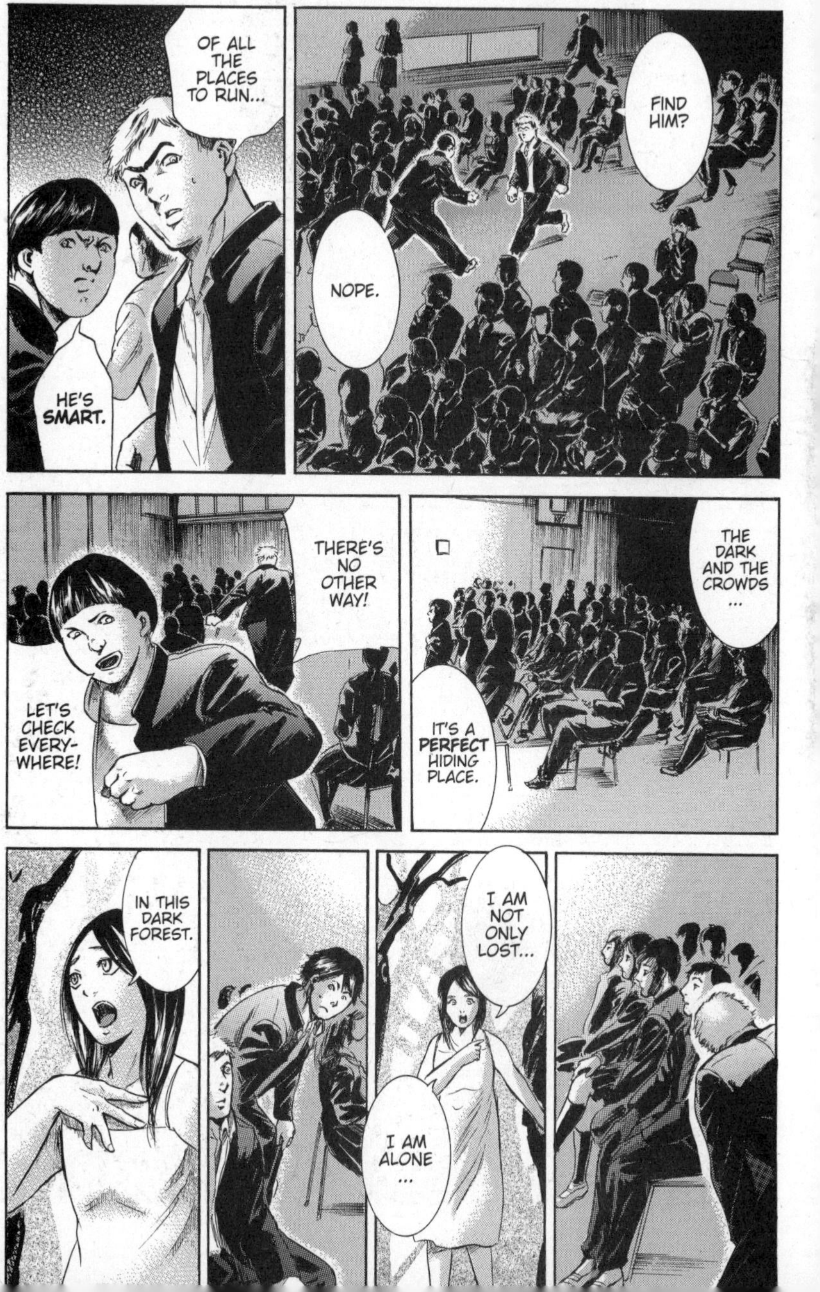
FIND HIM?
NOPE.
OF ALL THE PLACES TO RUN...
HE'S SMART.
THE DARK AND THE CROWDS...
IT'S A PERFECT HIDING PLACE.
THERE'S NO OTHER WAY!
LET'S CHECK EVERY-WHERE!
I AM NOT ONLY LOST...
I AM ALONE...
IN THIS DARK FOREST.

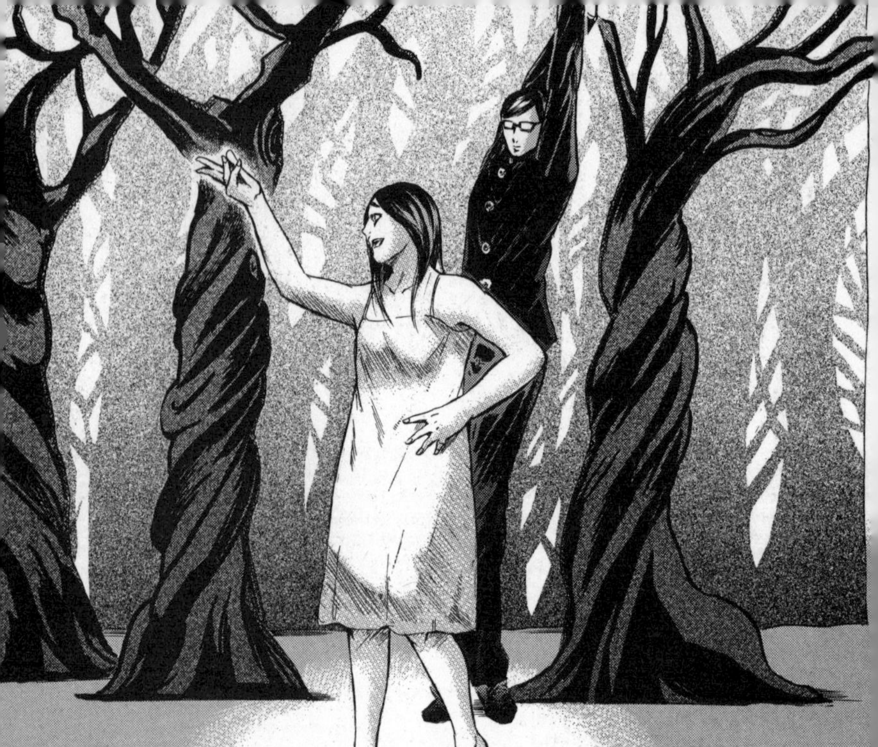

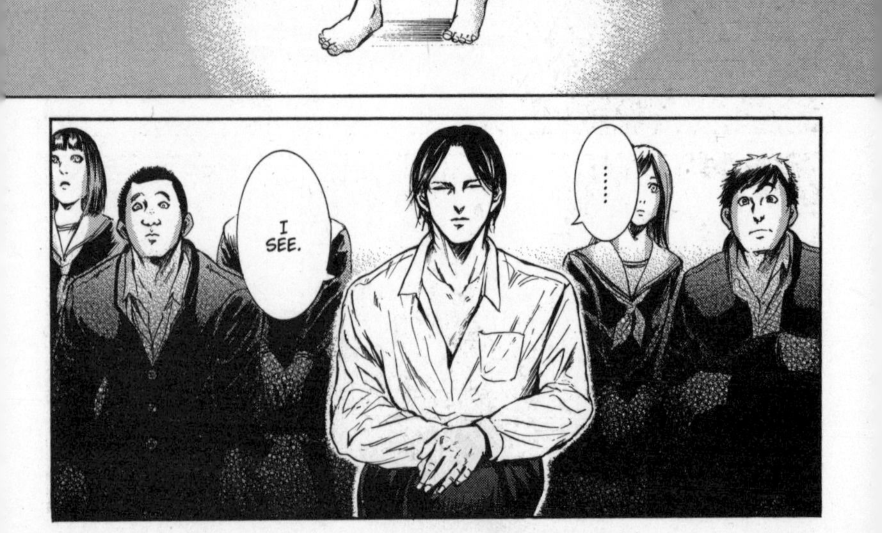
……
I SEE.

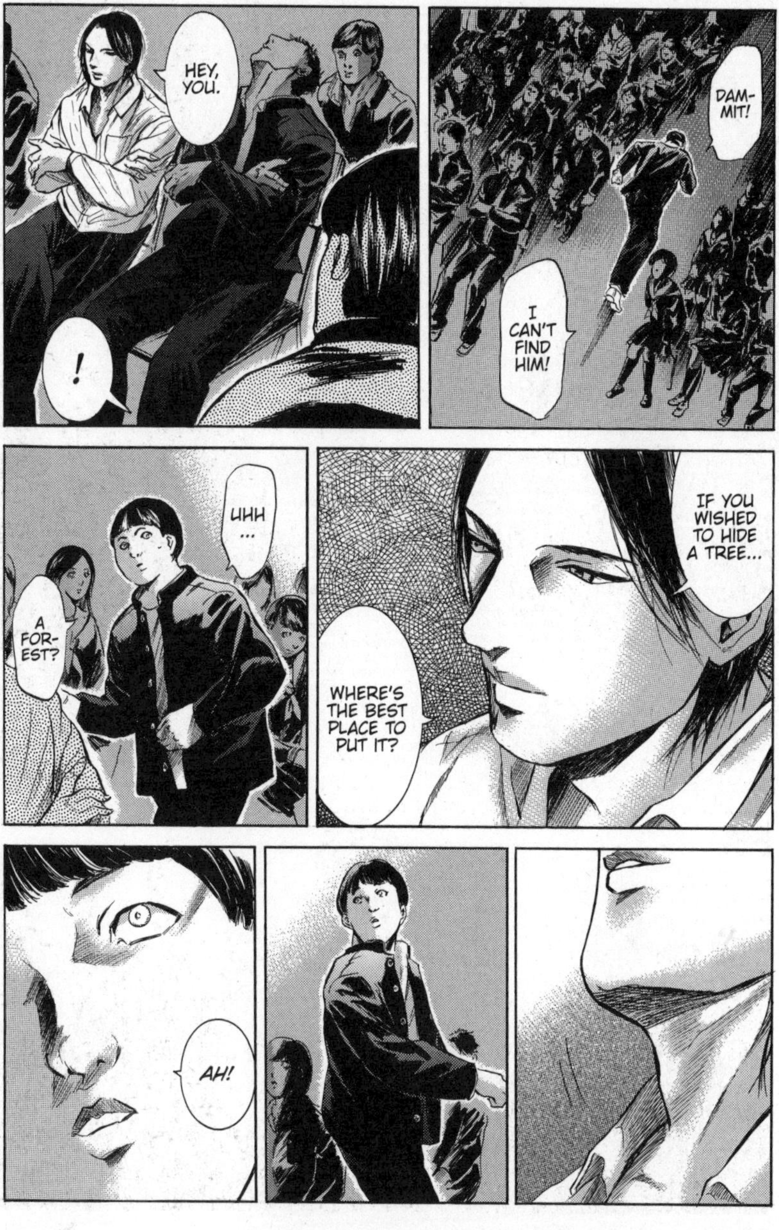
DAM-MIT!
I CAN'T FIND HIM!
HEY, YOU.
!
IF YOU WISHED TO HIDE A TREE...
WHERE'S THE BEST PLACE TO PUT IT?
UHH ...
A FOR-EST?
AH!

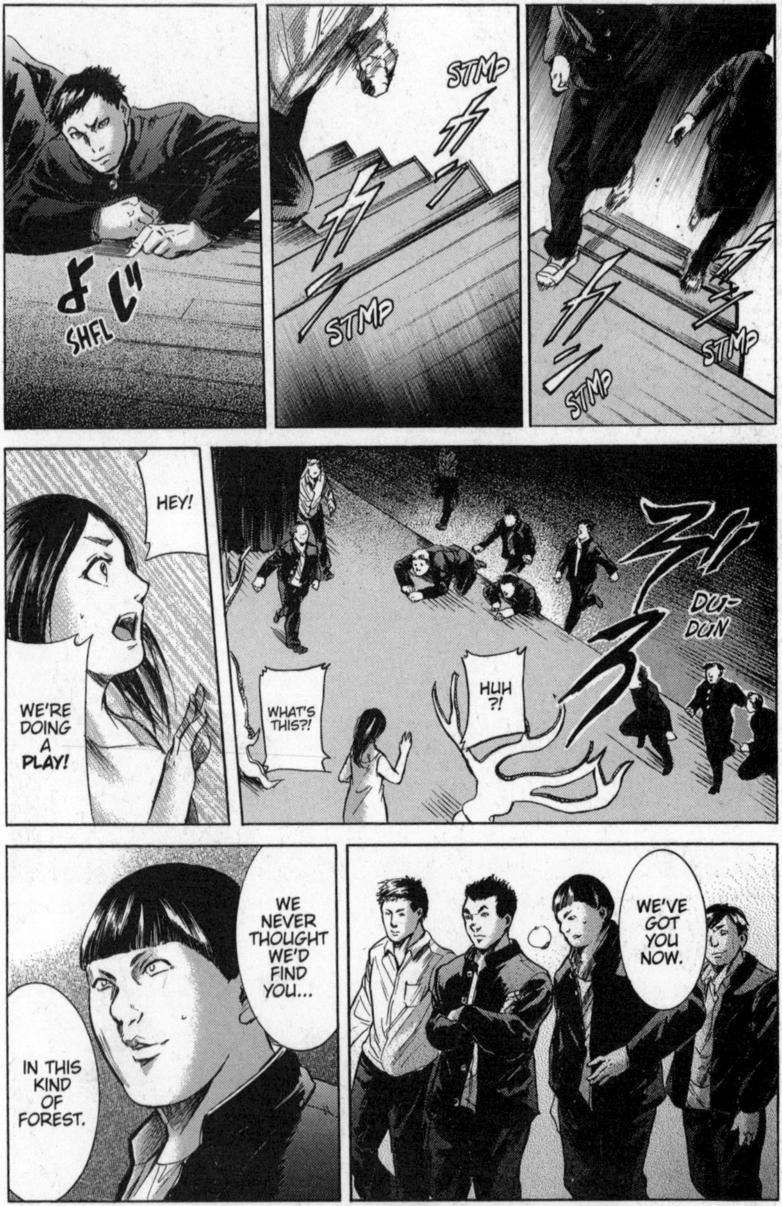
STMP
STMP
STMP
STMP
よじ
SHFL
DU-DUN
HUH?!
WHAT'S THIS?!
HEY!
WE'RE DOING A PLAY!
WE'VE GOT YOU NOW.
WE NEVER THOUGHT WE'D FIND YOU...
IN THIS KIND OF FOREST.

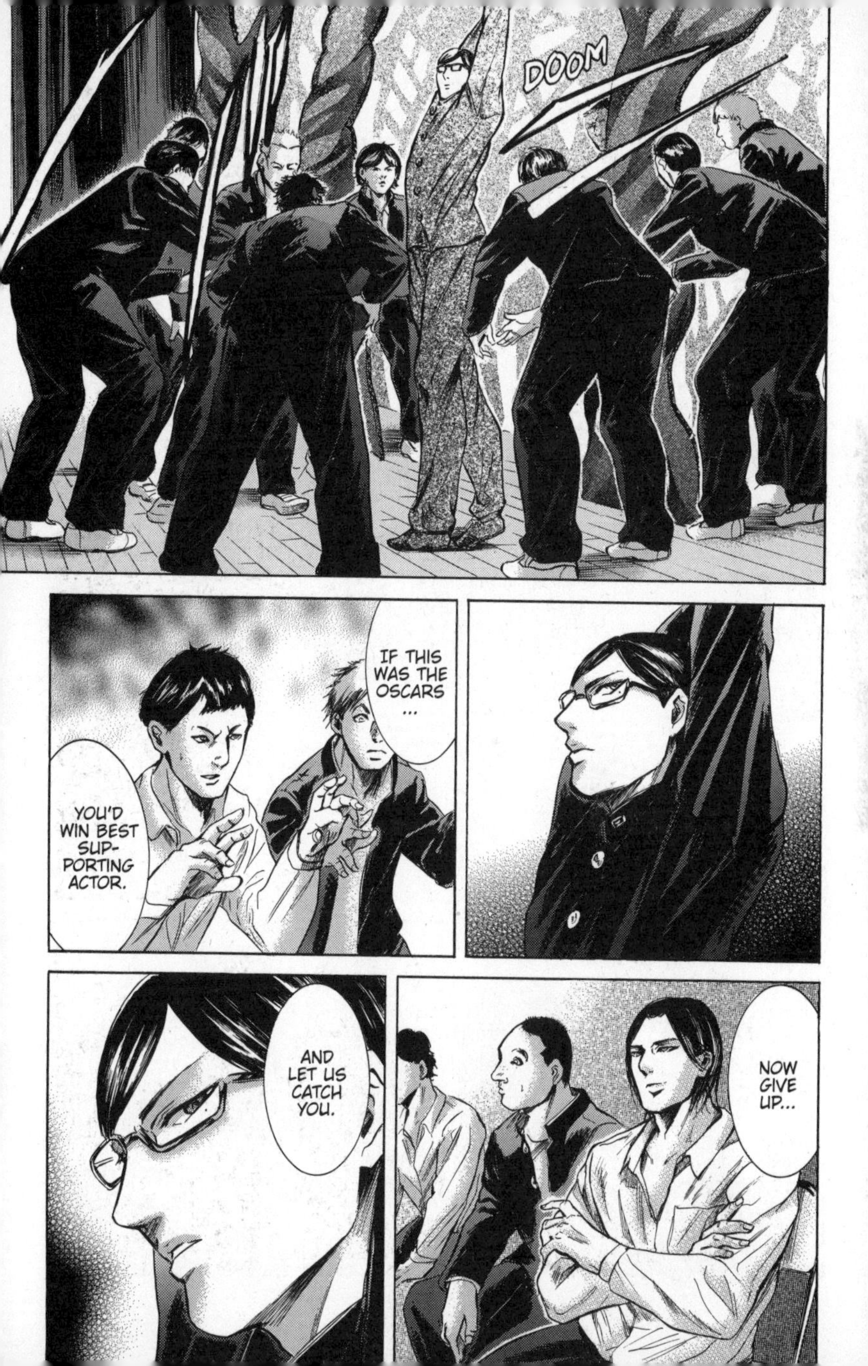
DOOM
IF THIS WAS THE OSCARS...
YOU'D WIN BEST SUP-PORTING ACTOR.
NOW GIVE UP...
AND LET US CATCH YOU.

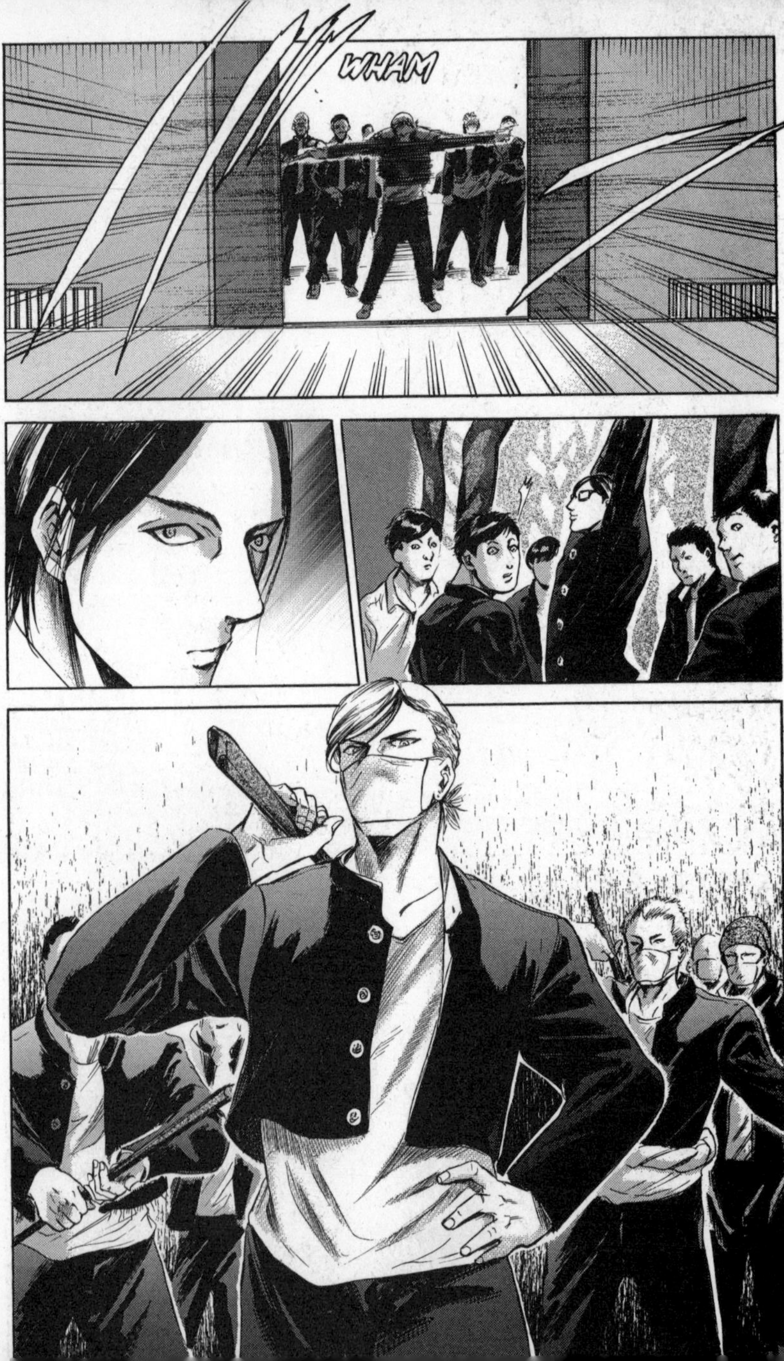
WHAM

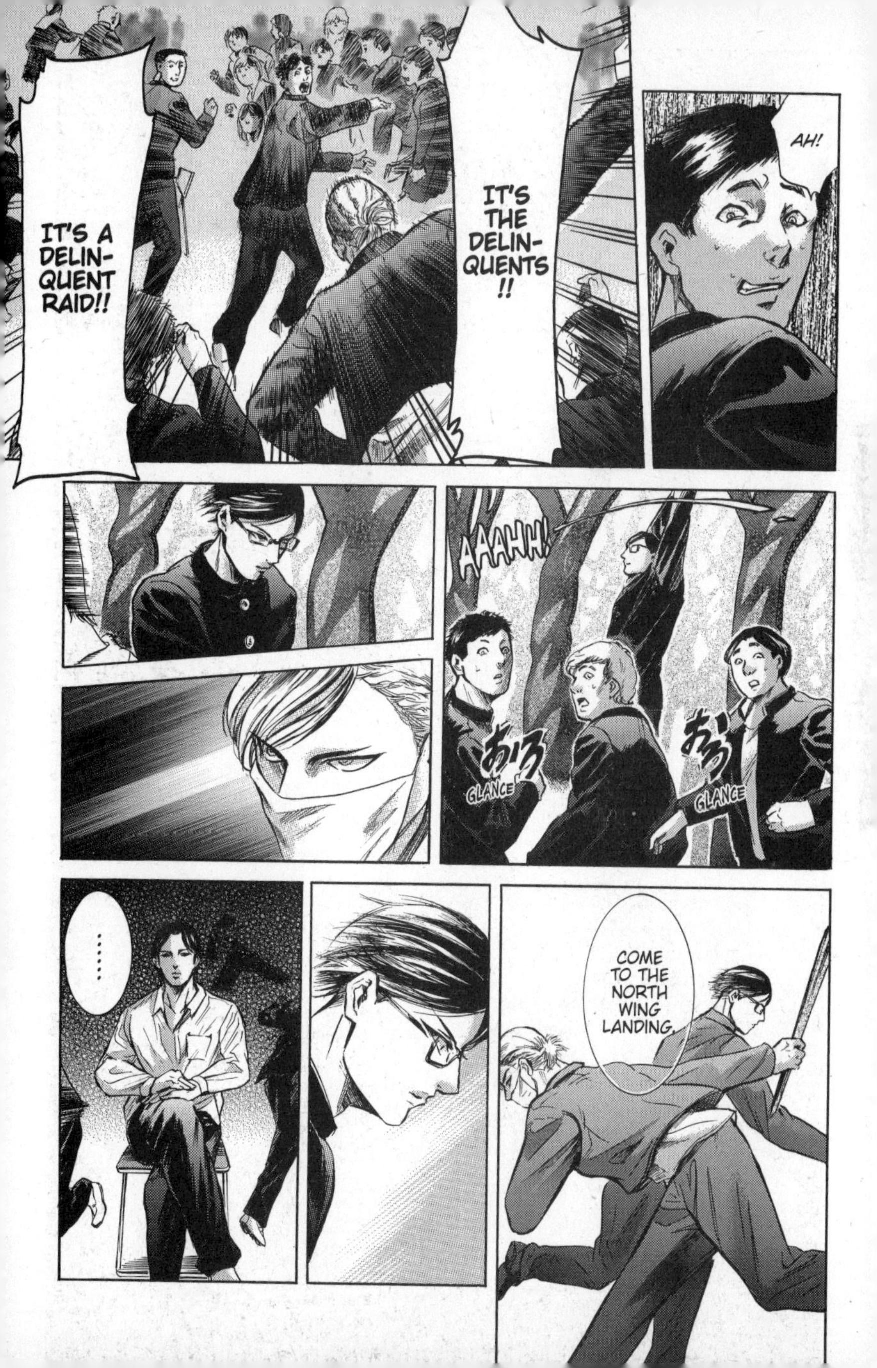

AH!
IT'S THE DELIN-QUENTS!!
IT'S A DELIN-QUENT RAID!!
AAAHH!
おろ
GLANCE
あろ
GLANCE
COME TO THE NORTH WING LANDING.
......

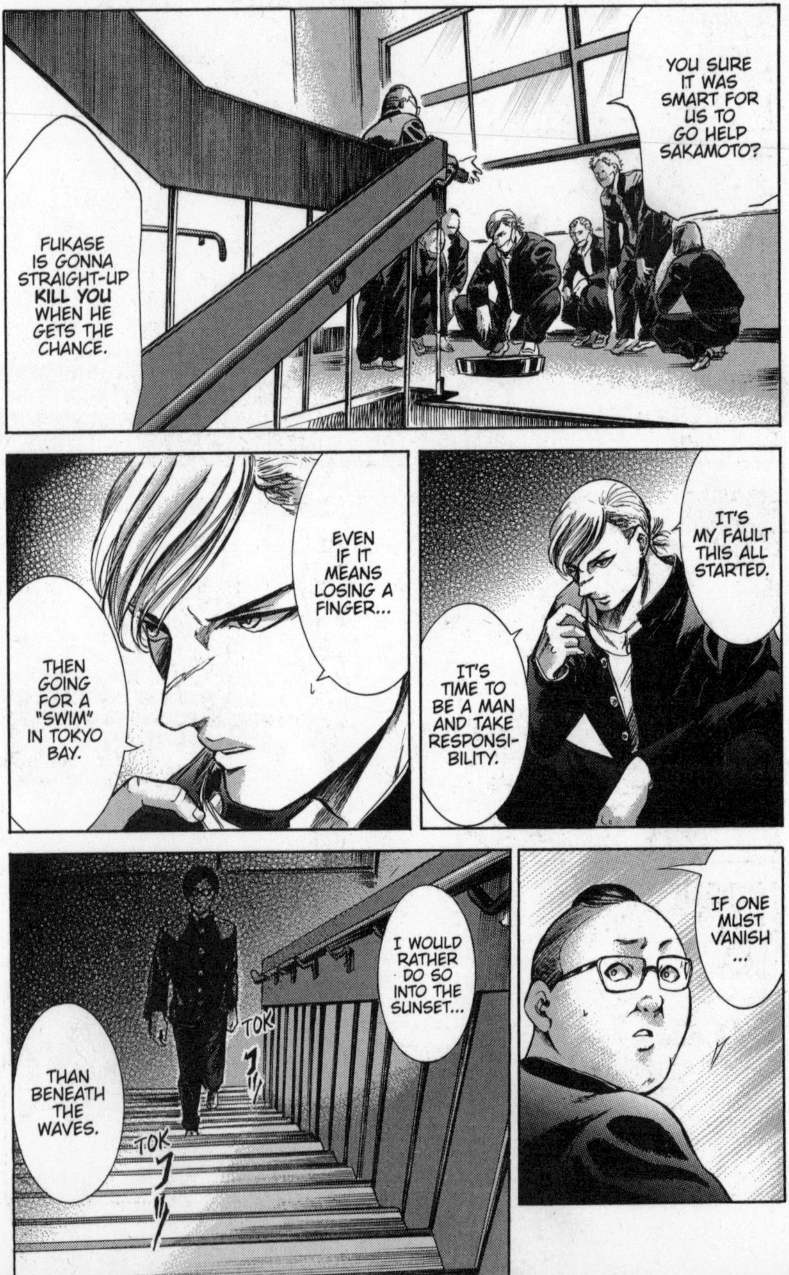
YOU SURE IT WAS SMART FOR US TO GO HELP SAKAMOTO?
FUKASE IS GONNA STRAIGHT-UP **KILL YOU** WHEN HE GETS THE CHANCE.
IT'S MY FAULT THIS ALL STARTED.
IT'S TIME TO BE A MAN AND TAKE RESPONSI-BILITY.
EVEN IF IT MEANS LOSING A FINGER...
THEN GOING FOR A "SWIM" IN TOKYO BAY.
IF ONE MUST VANISH ...
I WOULD RATHER DO SO INTO THE SUNSET...
TOK
THAN BENEATH THE WAVES.
TOK

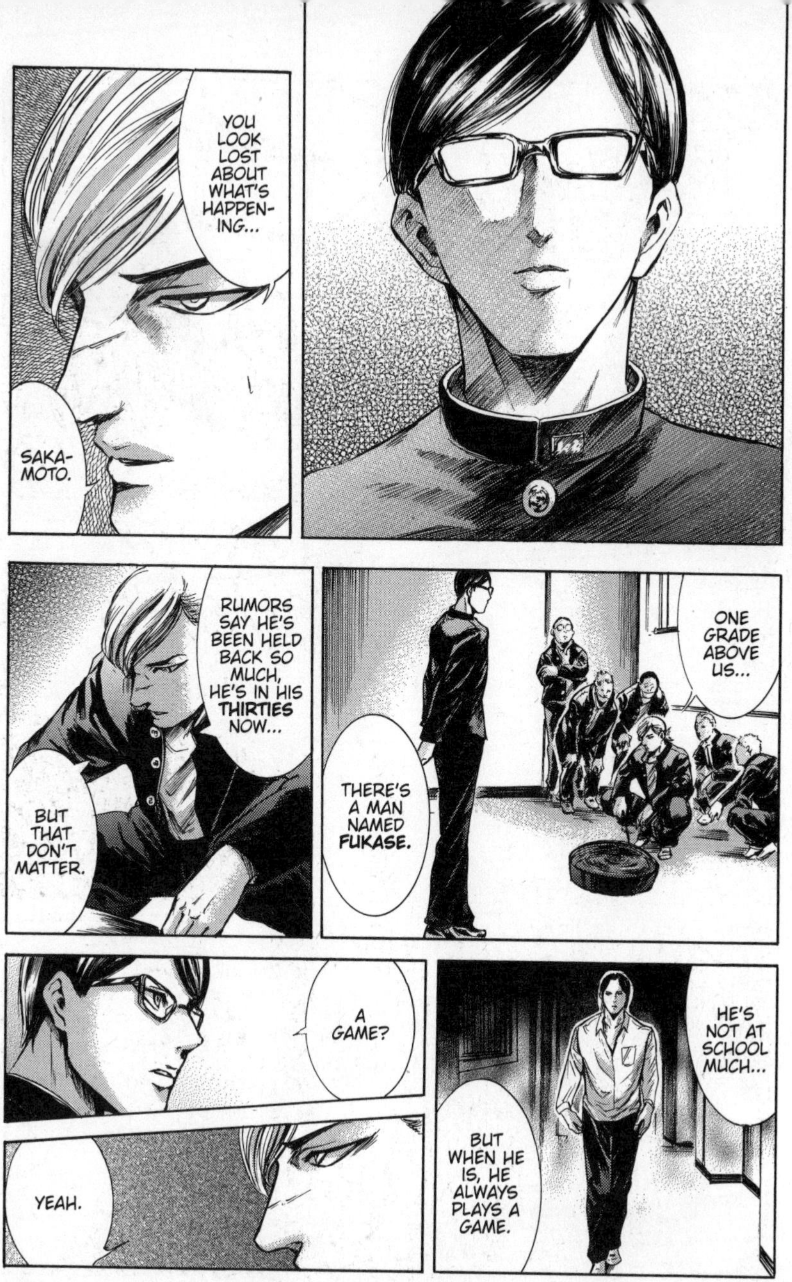
YOU LOOK LOST ABOUT WHAT'S HAPPEN-ING...
SAKA-MOTO.
ONE GRADE ABOVE US...
THERE'S A MAN NAMED **FUKASE.**
RUMORS SAY HE'S BEEN HELD BACK SO MUCH, HE'S IN HIS **THIRTIES** NOW...
BUT THAT DON'T MATTER.
HE'S NOT AT SCHOOL MUCH...
BUT WHEN HE IS, HE ALWAYS PLAYS A GAME.
A GAME?
YEAH.

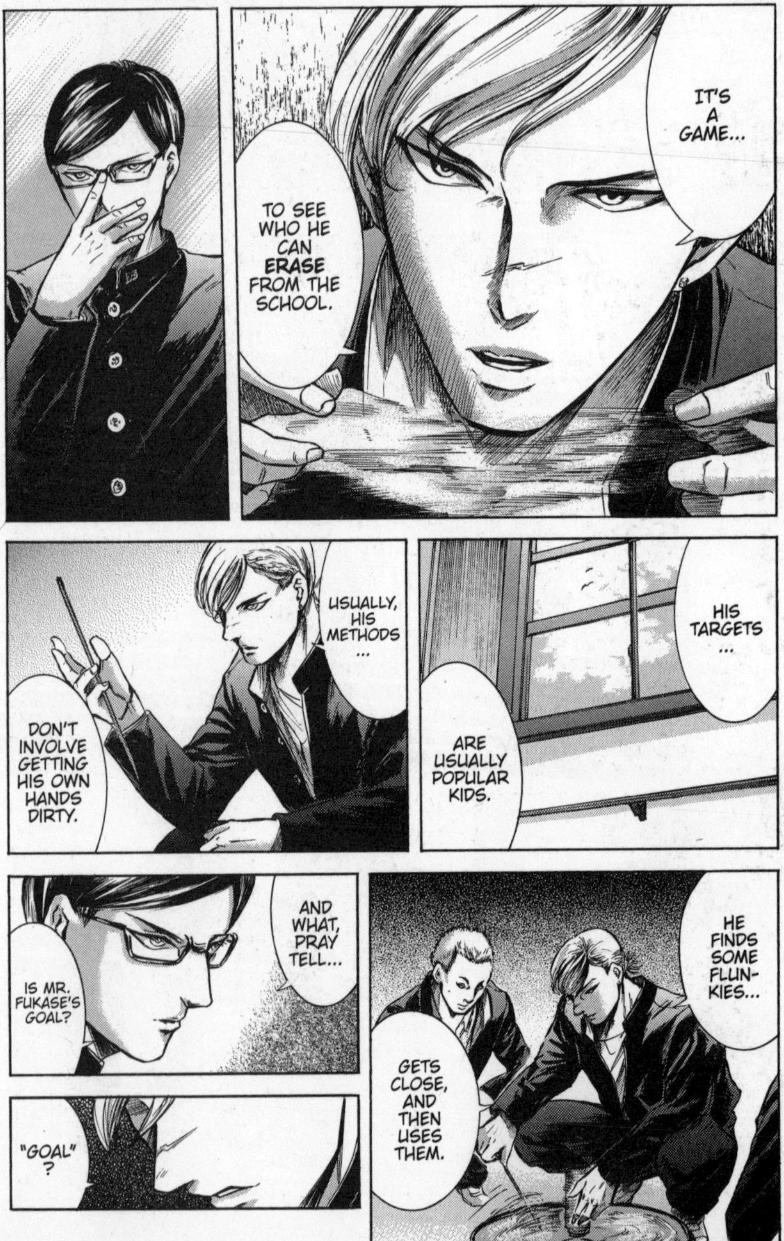
IT'S A GAME...
TO SEE WHO HE CAN **ERASE** FROM THE SCHOOL.
HIS TARGETS...
ARE USUALLY POPULAR KIDS.
USUALLY, HIS METHODS...
DON'T INVOLVE GETTING HIS OWN HANDS DIRTY.
HE FINDS SOME FLUNKIES...
GETS CLOSE, AND THEN USES THEM.
AND WHAT, PRAY TELL...
IS MR. FUKASE'S GOAL?
"GOAL"?

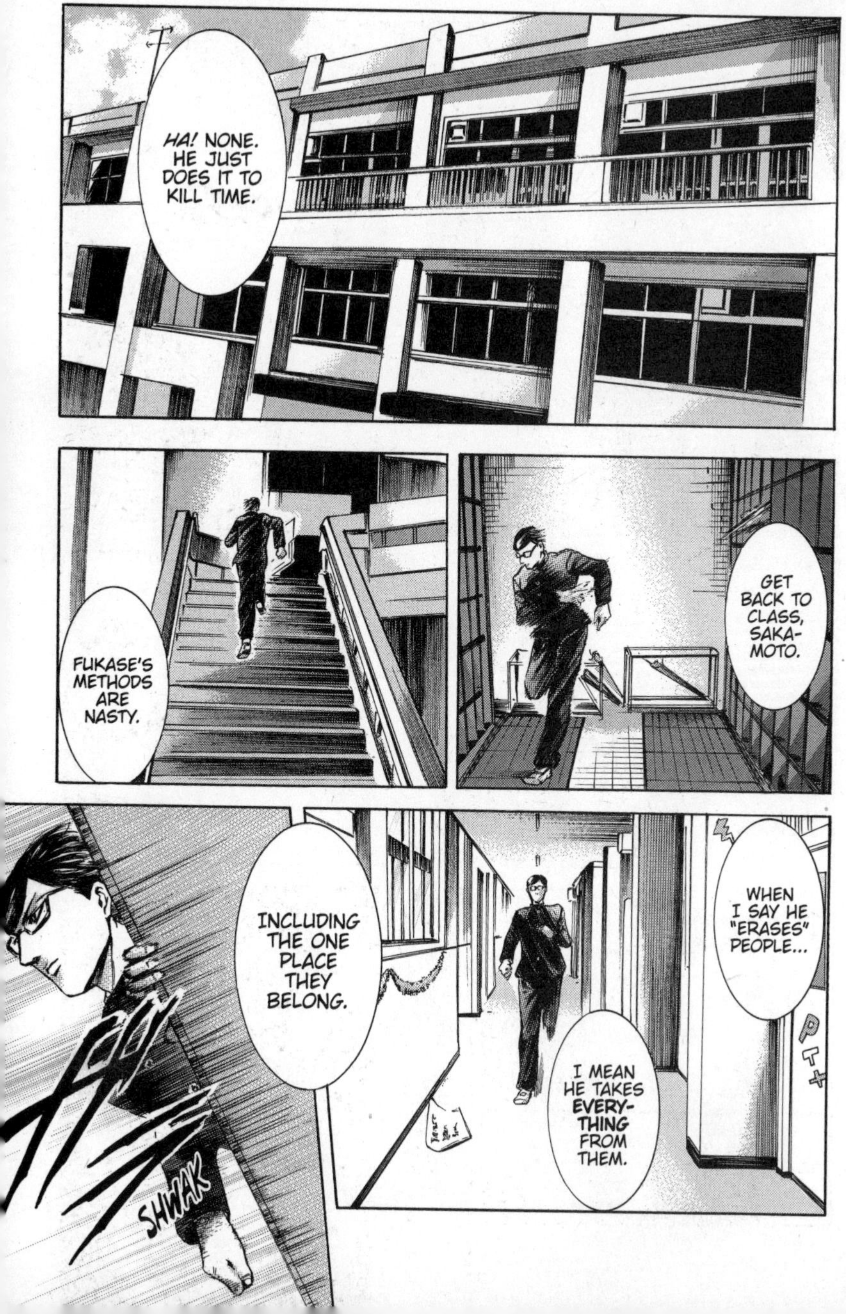
HA! NONE. HE JUST DOES IT TO KILL TIME.
GET BACK TO CLASS, SAKAMOTO.
FUKASE'S METHODS ARE NASTY.
WHEN I SAY HE "ERASES" PEOPLE...
I MEAN HE TAKES EVERYTHING FROM THEM.
INCLUDING THE ONE PLACE THEY BELONG.
SHWAK

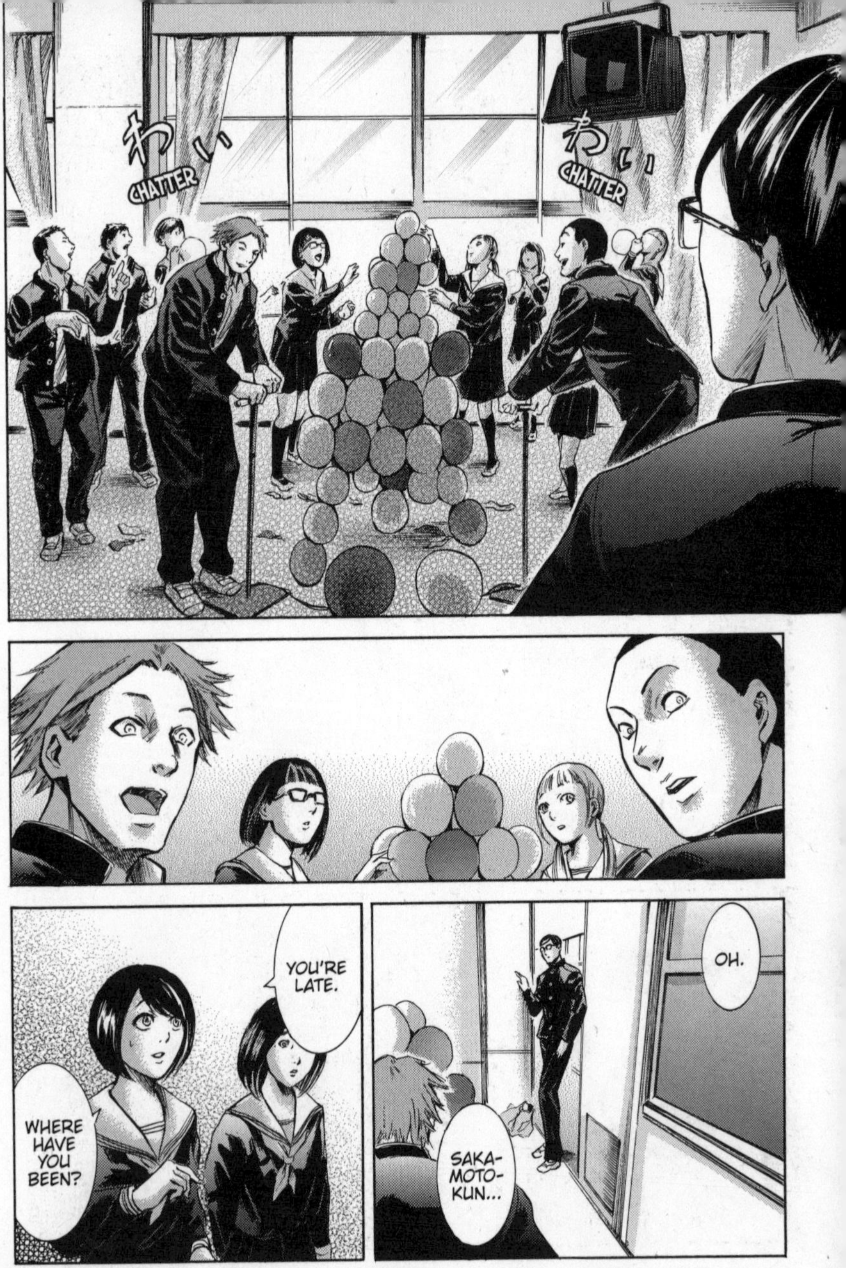
わい
CHATTER
わい
CHATTER
OH.
SAKA-MOTO-KUN...
YOU'RE LATE.
WHERE HAVE YOU BEEN?

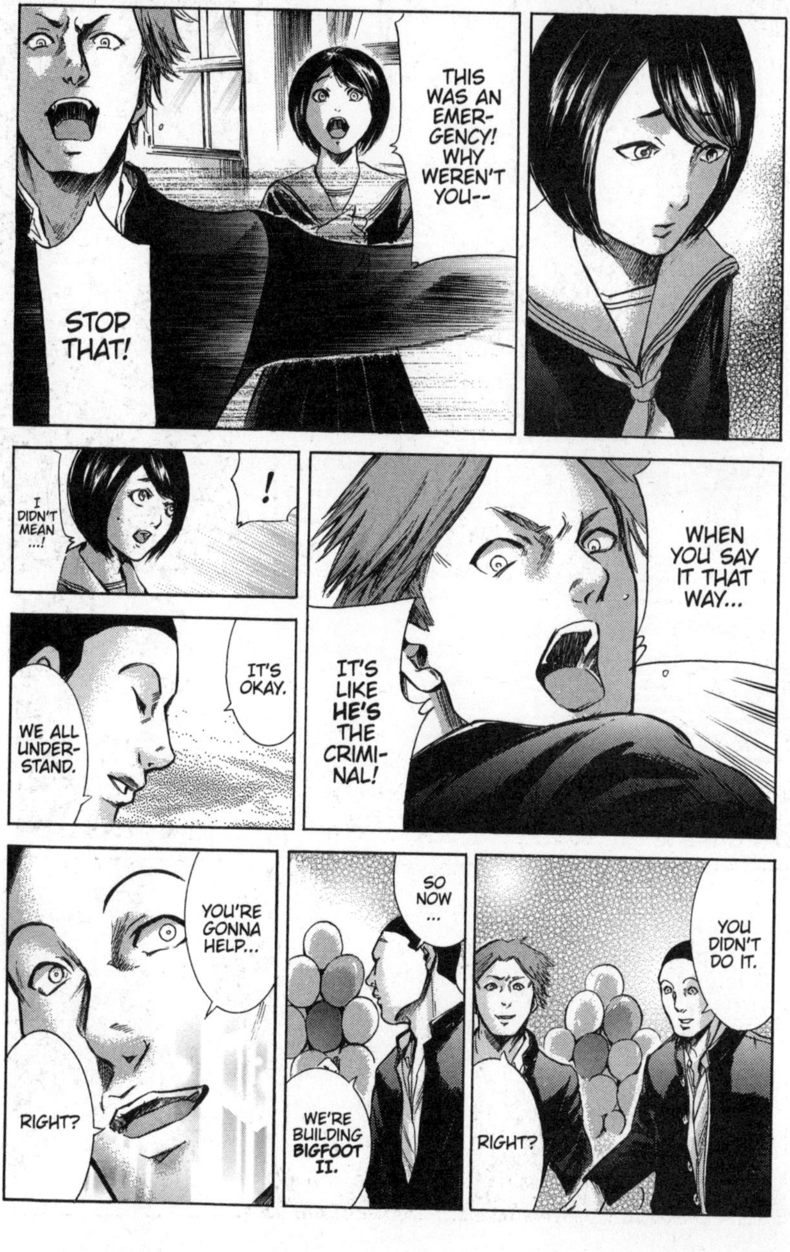
THIS WAS AN EMERGENCY! WHY WEREN'T YOU--
STOP THAT!
WHEN YOU SAY IT THAT WAY...
IT'S LIKE HE'S THE CRIMINAL!
!
I DIDN'T MEAN ...!
IT'S OKAY.
WE ALL UNDERSTAND.
YOU DIDN'T DO IT.
RIGHT?
SO NOW ...
WE'RE BUILDING BIGFOOT II.
YOU'RE GONNA HELP...
RIGHT?

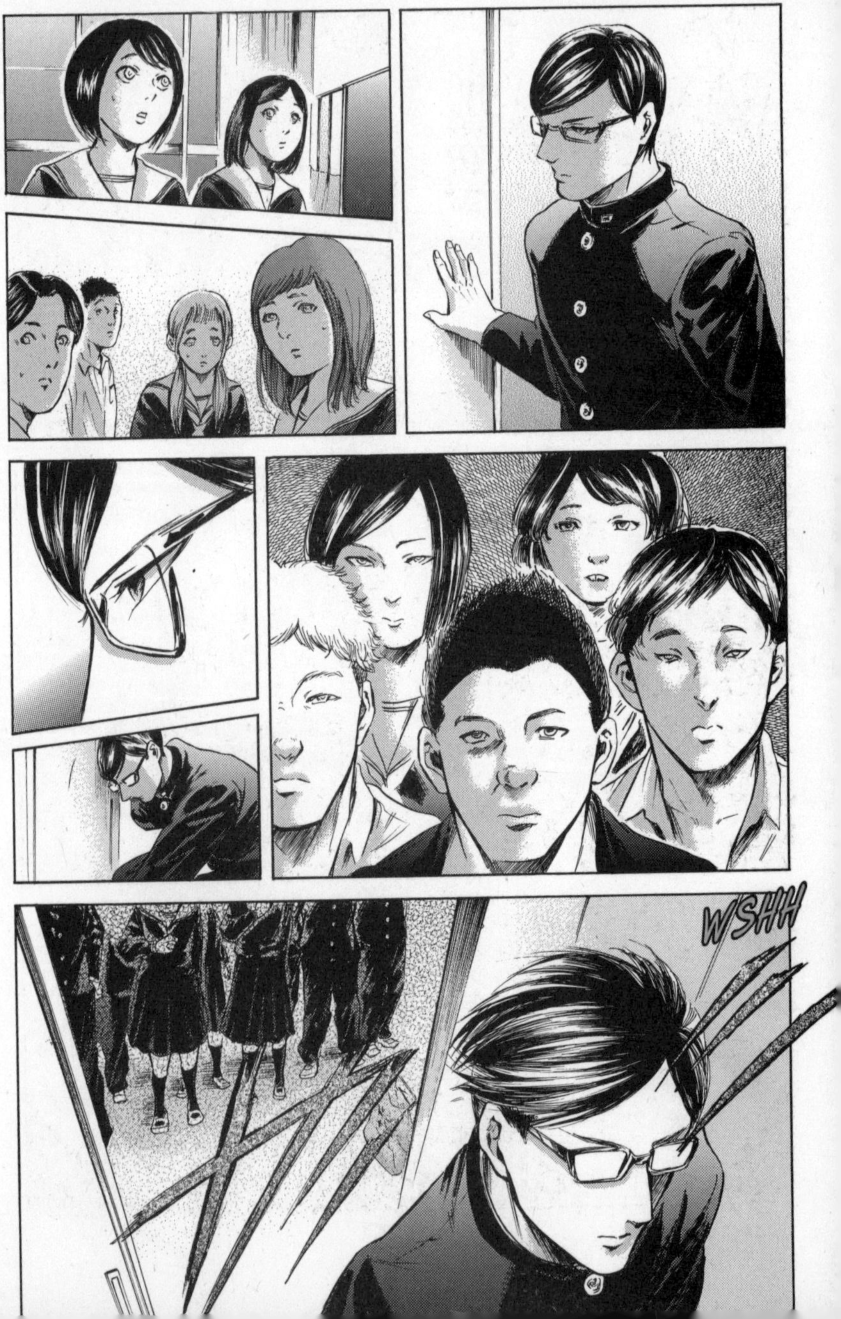
WSHH

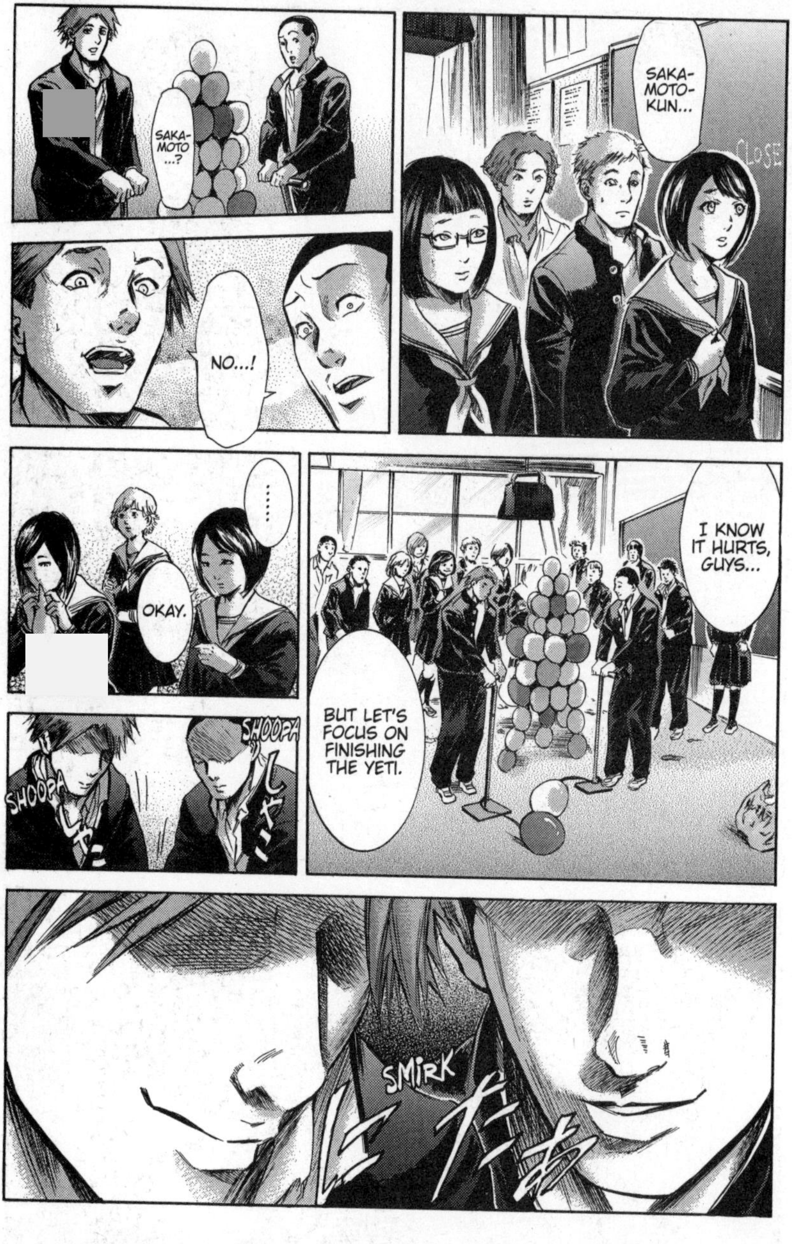
SAKA-MOTO-KUN...
CLOSE
SAKA-MOTO ...?
NO...!
I KNOW IT HURTS, GUYS...
BUT LET'S FOCUS ON FINISHING THE YETI.
......
OKAY.
SHOOPA
SHOOPA
SMIRK

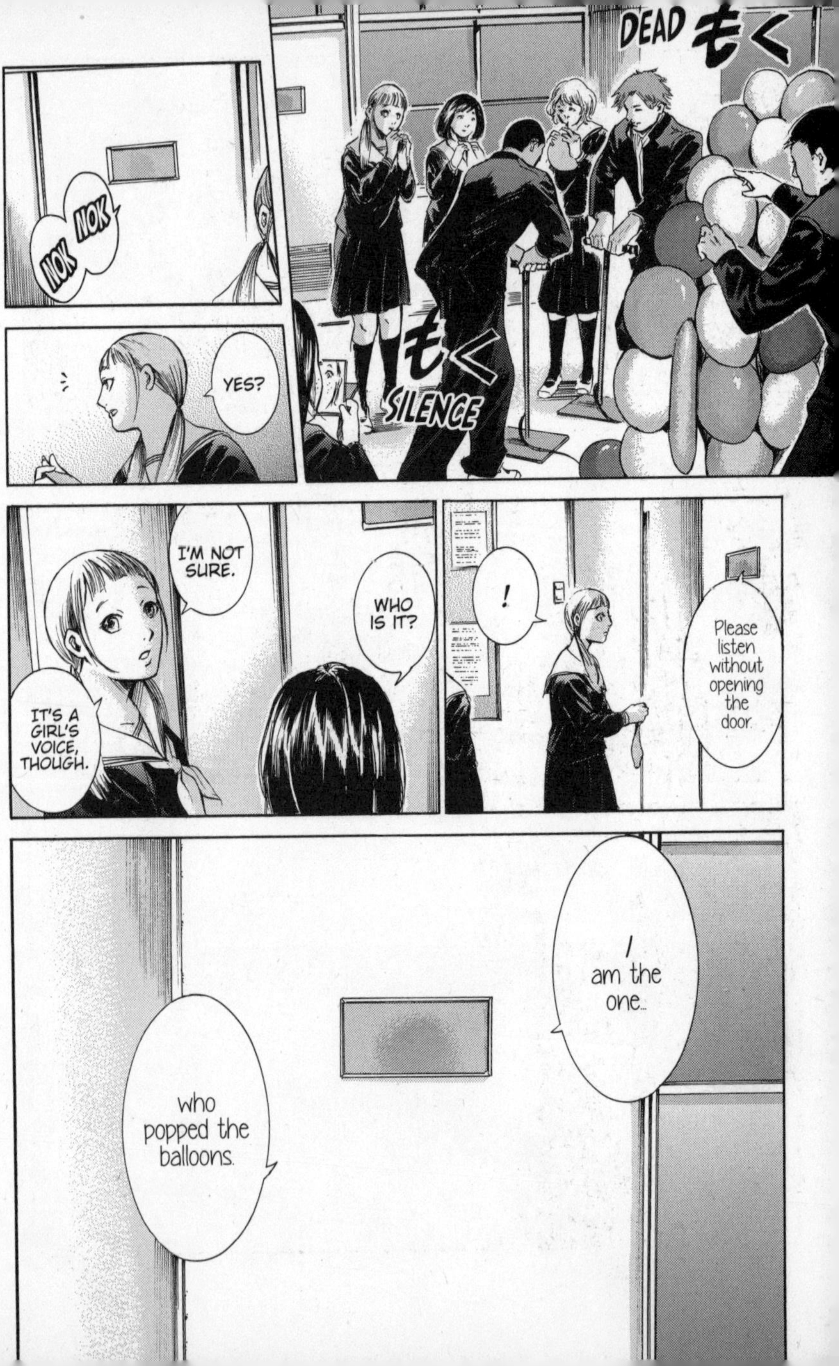
DEAD もく
もく
SILENCE
NOK NOK
YES?
!
Please listen without opening the door.
WHO IS IT?
I'M NOT SURE.
IT'S A GIRL'S VOICE, THOUGH.
I am the one...
who popped the balloons.

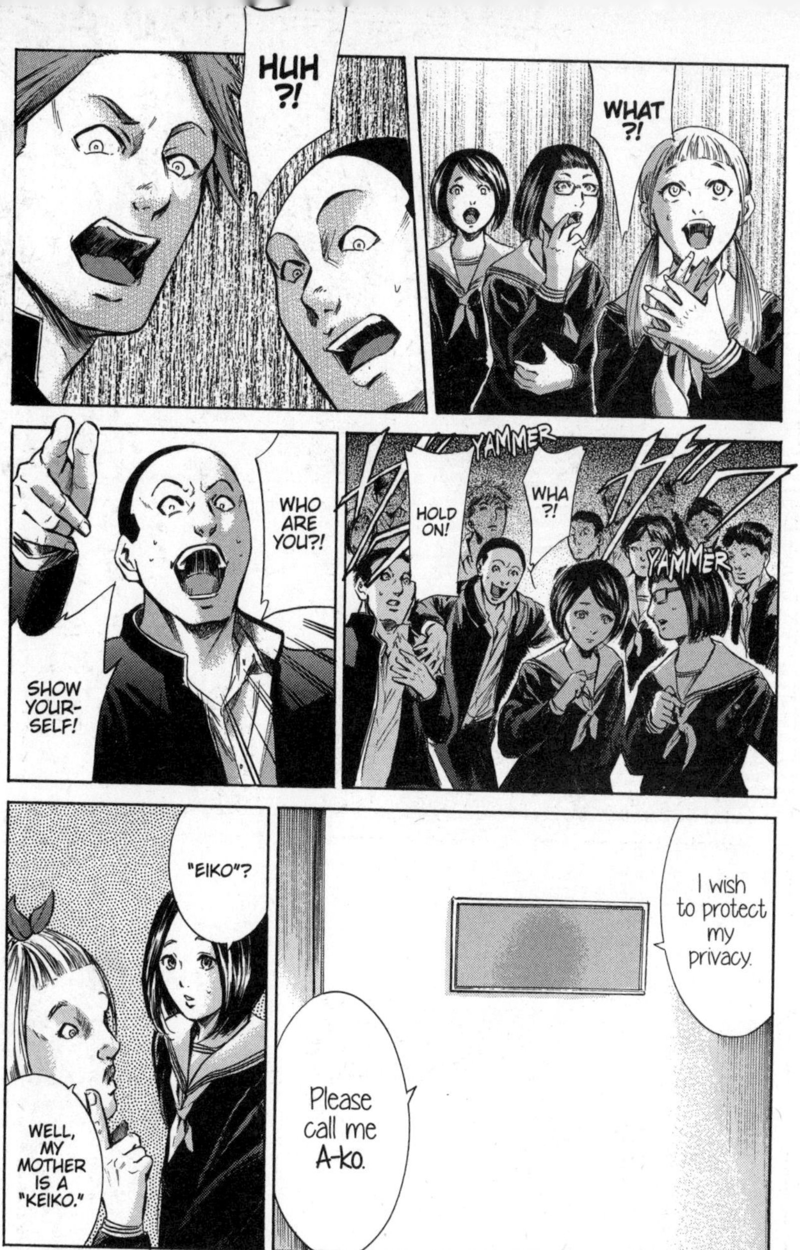
WHAT ?!
HUH ?!
YAMMER
WHA ?!
HOLD ON!
YAMMER
WHO ARE YOU?!
SHOW YOUR-SELF!
I wish to protect my privacy.
Please call me A-ko.
"EIKO"?
WELL, MY MOTHER IS A "KEIKO."

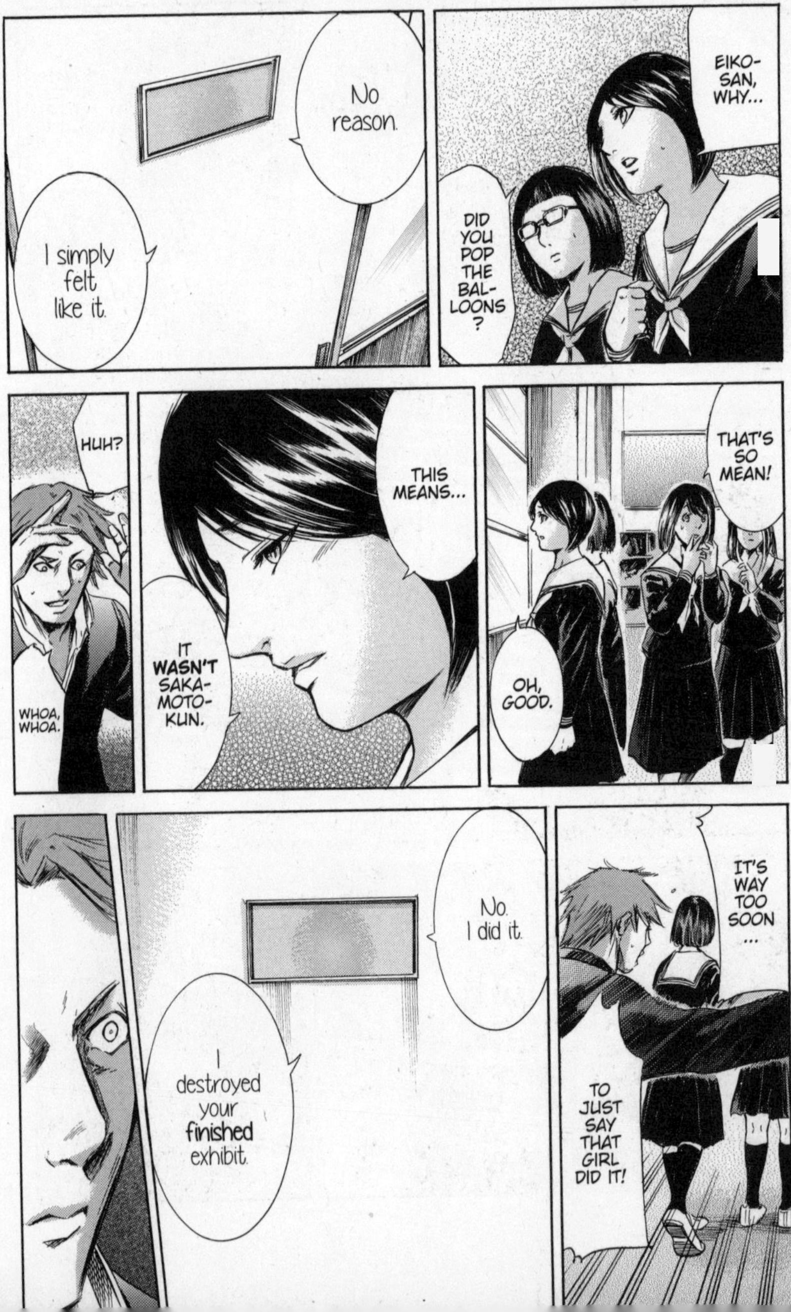
EIKO-SAN, WHY...
DID YOU POP THE BALLOONS?
No reason.
I simply felt like it.
THAT'S SO MEAN!
OH, GOOD.
THIS MEANS...
IT WASN'T SAKAMOTO-KUN.
HUH?
WHOA, WHOA.
IT'S WAY TOO SOON...
TO JUST SAY THAT GIRL DID IT!
No. I did it.
I destroyed your finished exhibit.

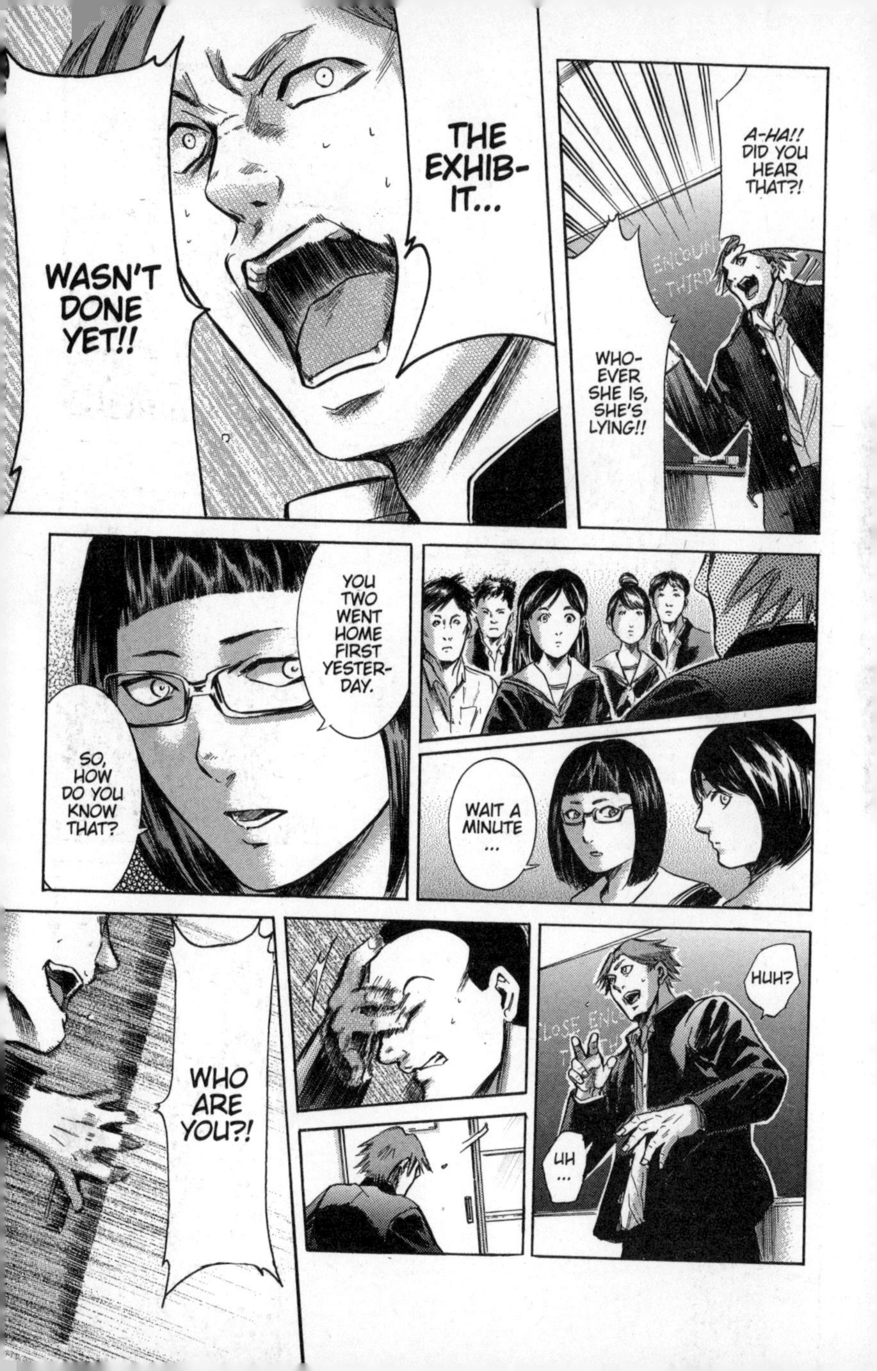
A-HA!! DID YOU HEAR THAT?!
WHO-EVER SHE IS, SHE'S LYING!!
THE EXHIB-IT...
WASN'T DONE YET!!
WAIT A MINUTE ...
YOU TWO WENT HOME FIRST YESTER-DAY.
SO, HOW DO YOU KNOW THAT?
HUH?
UH ...
WHO ARE YOU?!

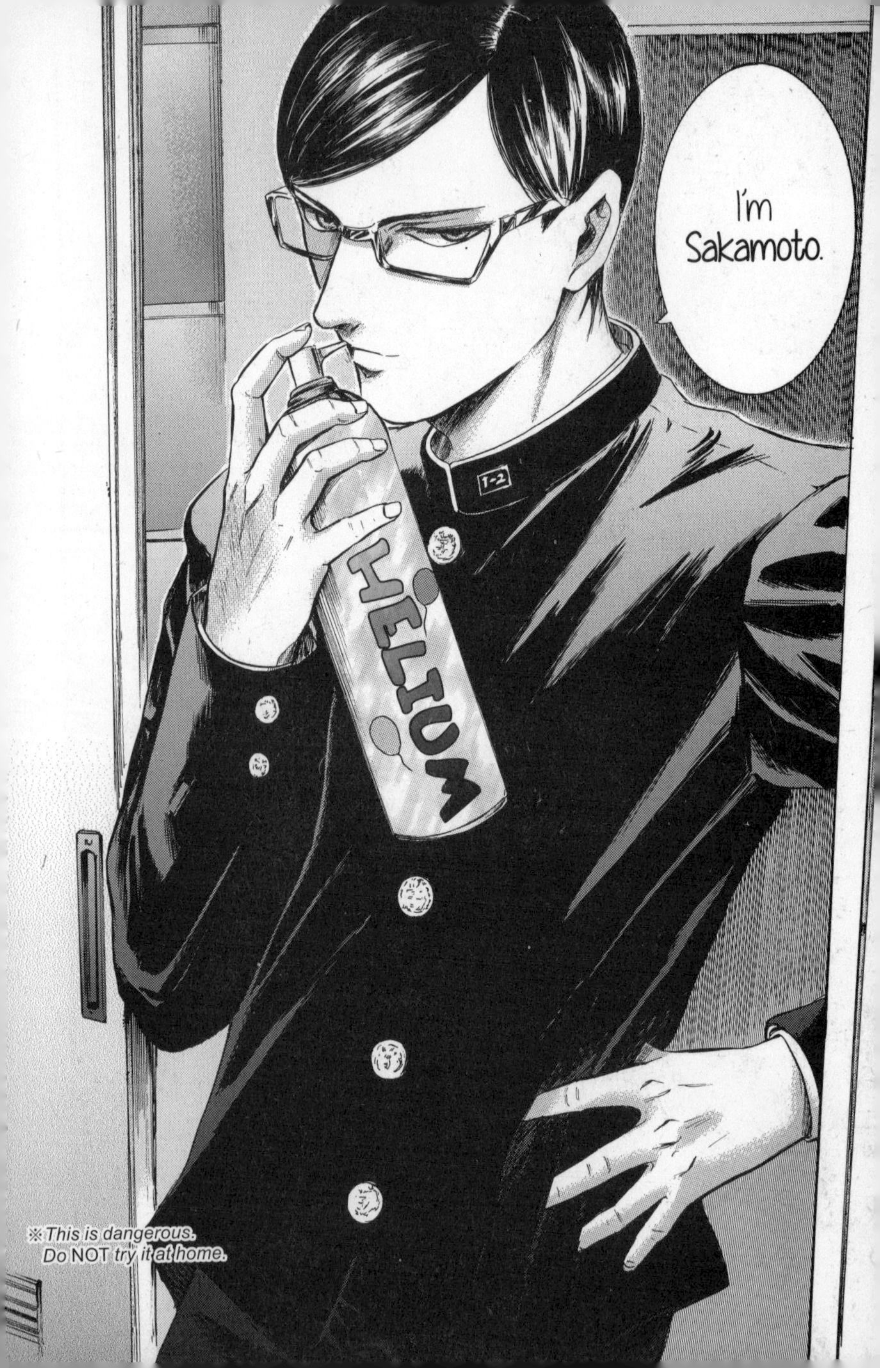
I'm Sakamoto.
HELIUM
1-2
※This is dangerous. Do NOT try it at home.

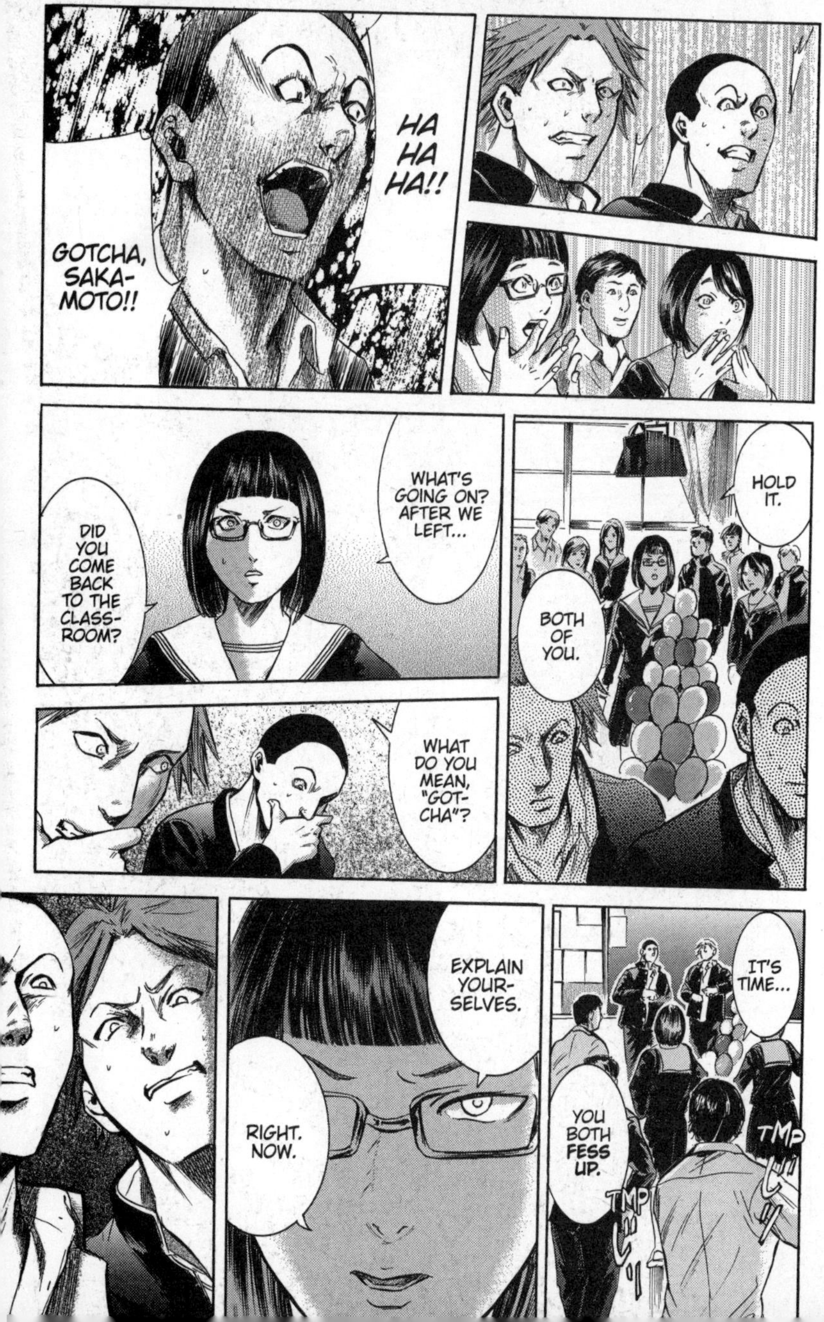
HA HA HA!!
GOTCHA, SAKAMOTO!!
HOLD IT.
BOTH OF YOU.
WHAT'S GOING ON? AFTER WE LEFT...
DID YOU COME BACK TO THE CLASSROOM?
WHAT DO YOU MEAN, "GOTCHA"?
IT'S TIME...
YOU BOTH FESS UP.
TMP
TMP
EXPLAIN YOURSELVES.
RIGHT. NOW.

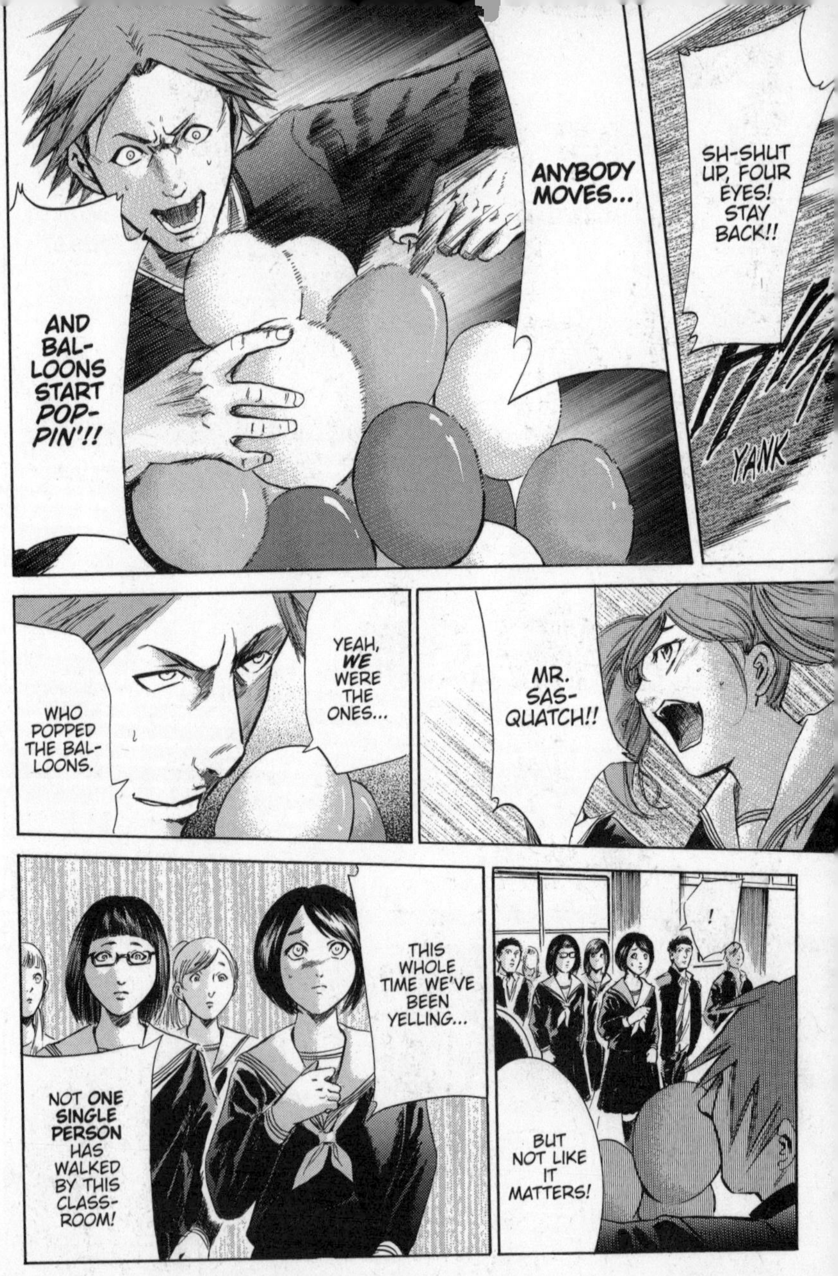
SH-SHUT UP, FOUR EYES! STAY BACK!!
YANK
ANYBODY MOVES...
AND BALLOONS START POPPIN'!!
MR. SASQUATCH!!
YEAH, WE WERE THE ONES...
WHO POPPED THE BALLOONS.
!
BUT NOT LIKE IT MATTERS!
THIS WHOLE TIME WE'VE BEEN YELLING...
NOT ONE SINGLE PERSON HAS WALKED BY THIS CLASSROOM!

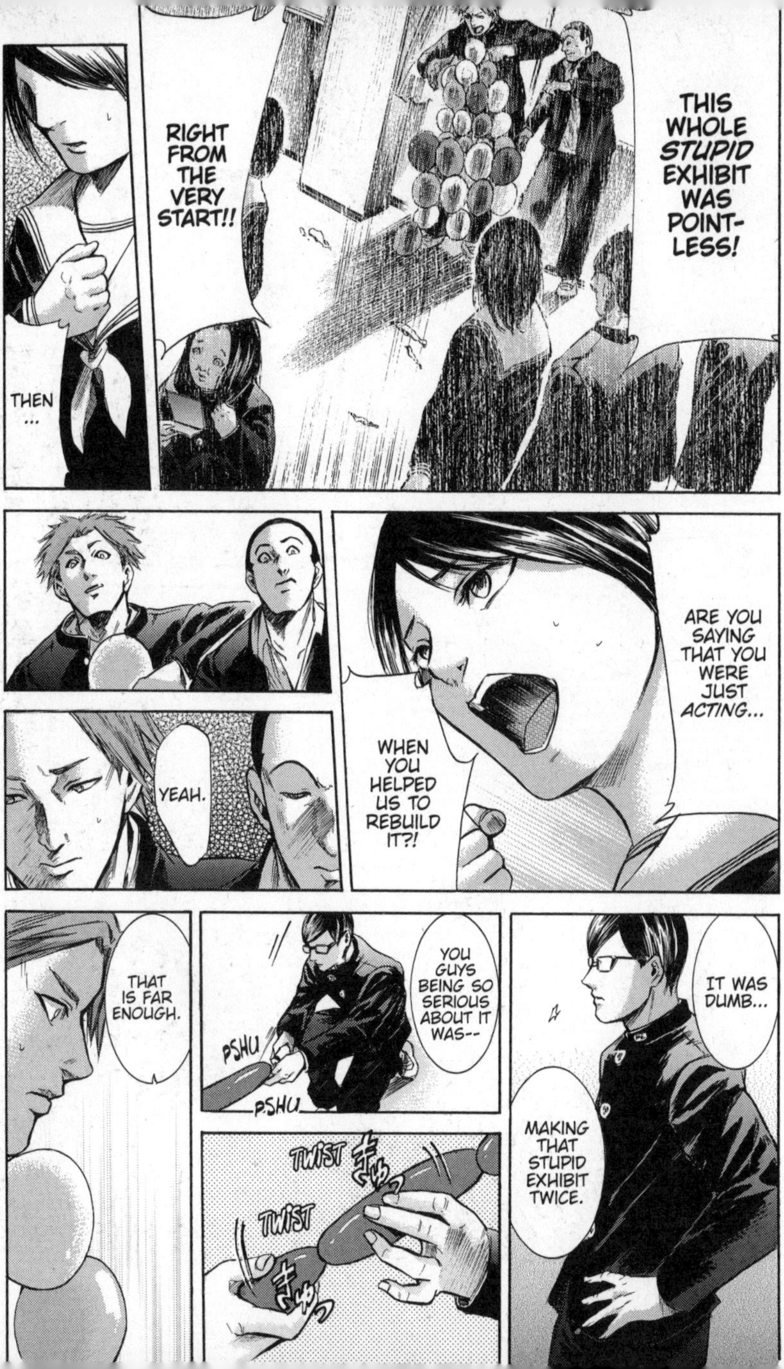
THIS WHOLE STUPID EXHIBIT WAS POINT-LESS!
RIGHT FROM THE VERY START!!
THEN ...
ARE YOU SAYING THAT YOU WERE JUST ACTING...
WHEN YOU HELPED US TO REBUILD IT?!
YEAH.
IT WAS DUMB...
MAKING THAT STUPID EXHIBIT TWICE.
YOU GUYS BEING SO SERIOUS ABOUT IT WAS--
PSHU
PSHU
TWIST
TWIST
THAT IS FAR ENOUGH.

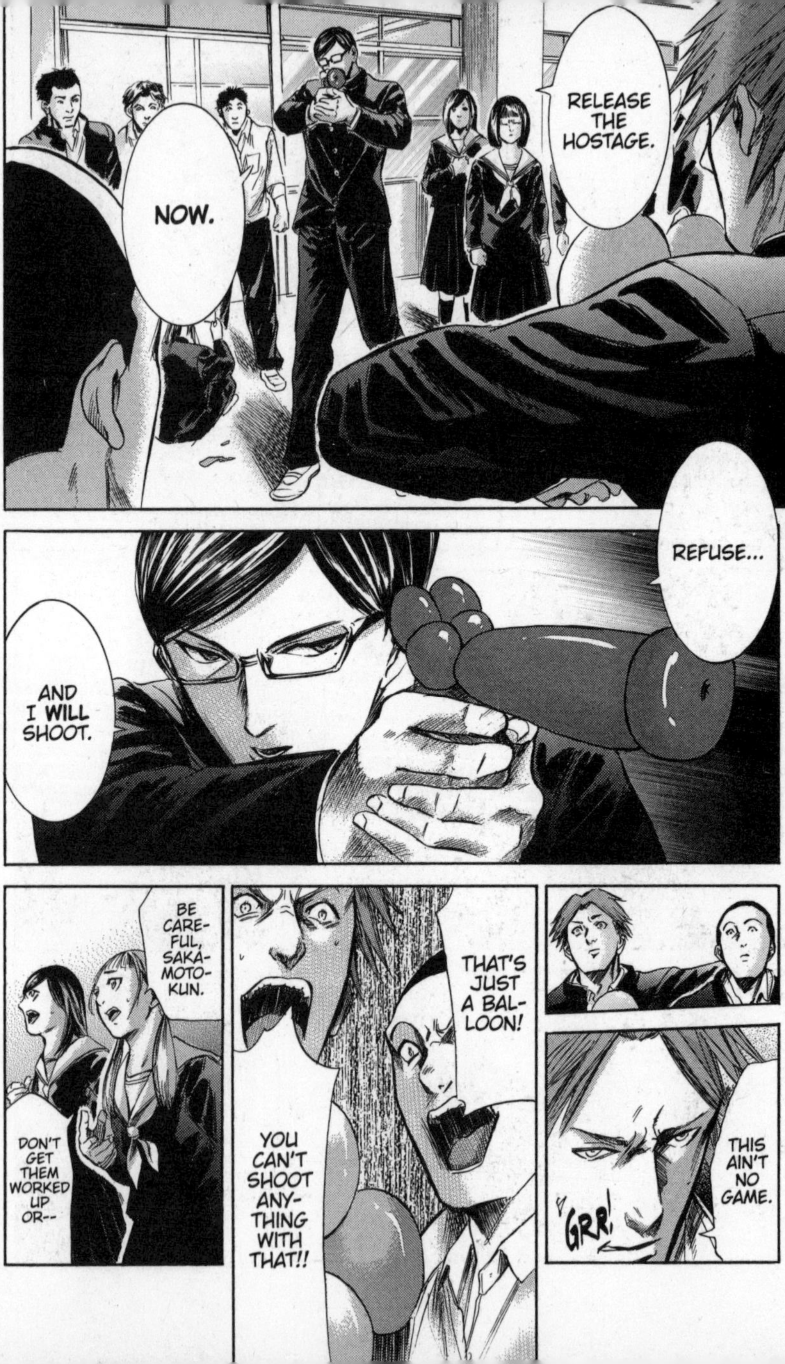
RELEASE THE HOSTAGE.
NOW.
REFUSE...
AND I WILL SHOOT.
THIS AIN'T NO GAME.
GRR!
THAT'S JUST A BALLOON!
YOU CAN'T SHOOT ANYTHING WITH THAT!!
BE CAREFUL, SAKAMOTO-KUN.
DON'T GET THEM WORKED UP OR--

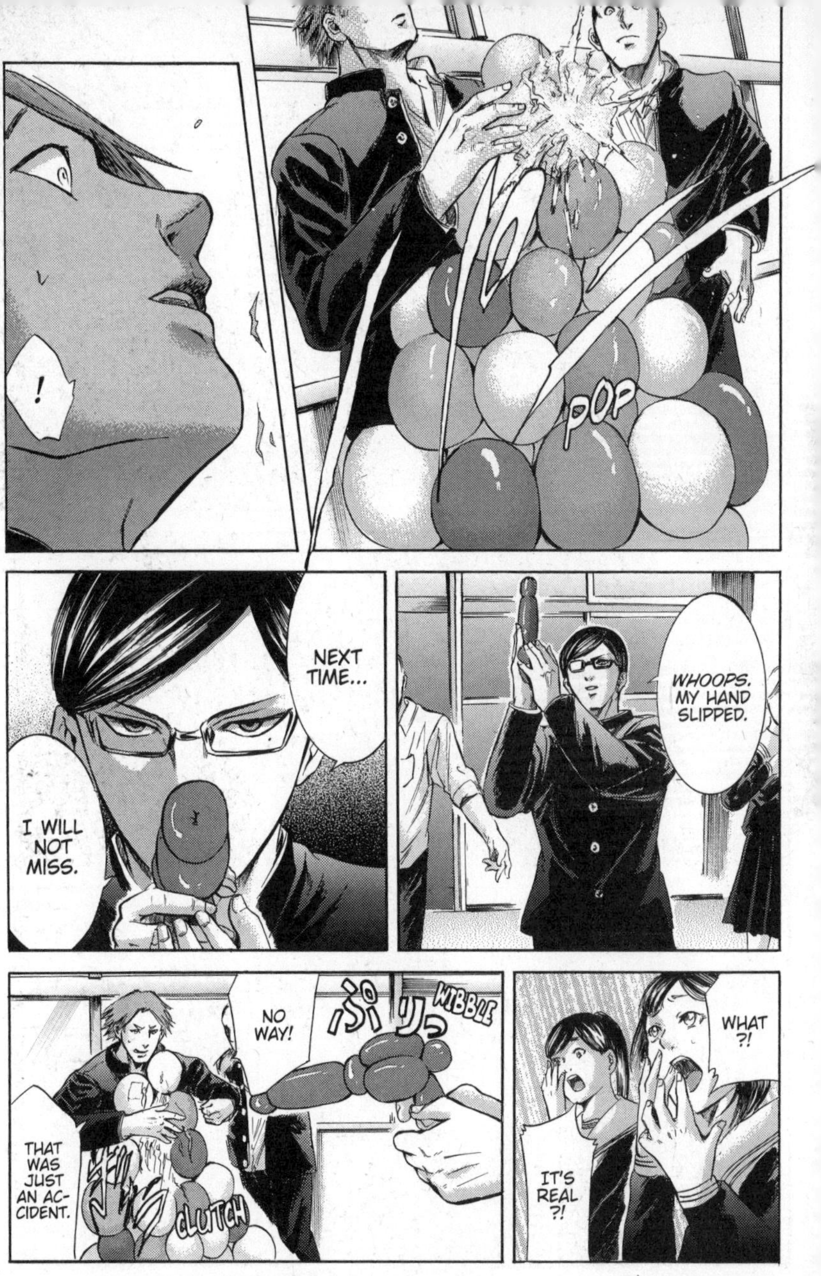
POP
!
WHOOPS. MY HAND SLIPPED.
NEXT TIME...
I WILL NOT MISS.
WHAT?!
IT'S REAL?!
NO WAY!
WIBBLE
THAT WAS JUST AN ACCIDENT.
CLUTCH

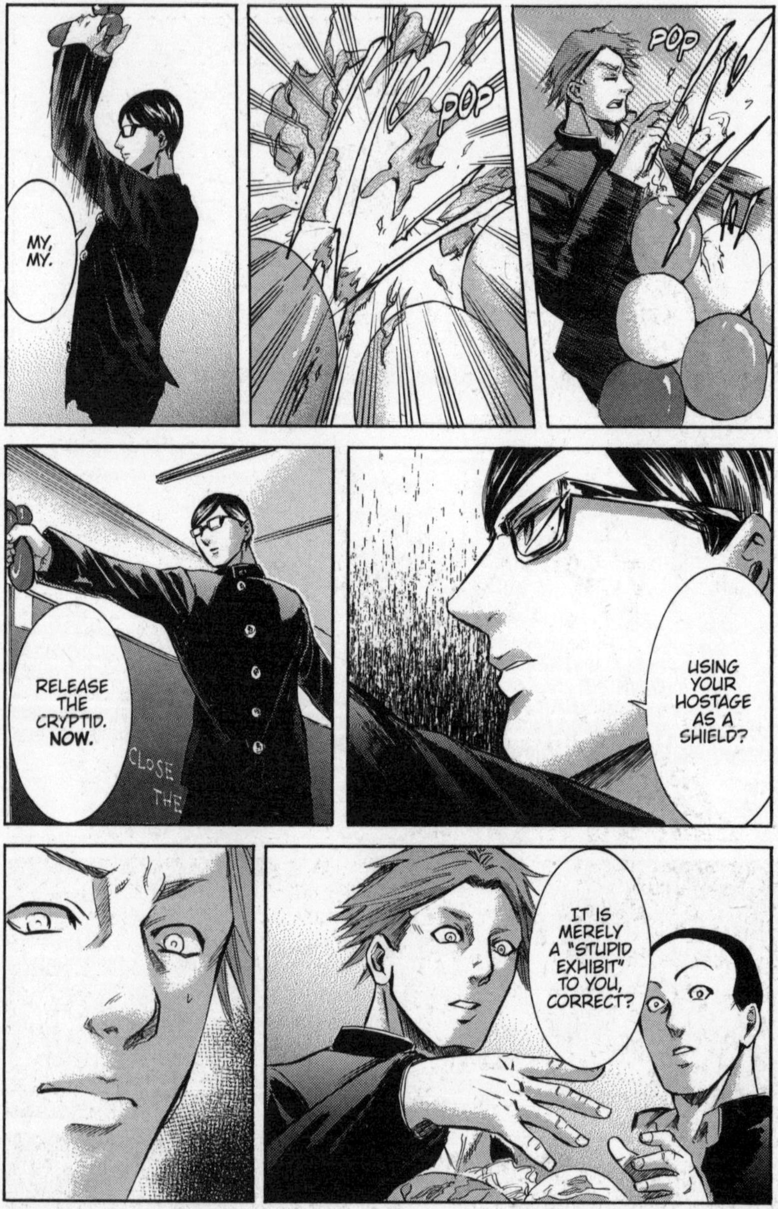
POP
POP
MY, MY.
USING YOUR HOSTAGE AS A SHIELD?
RELEASE THE CRYPTID. NOW.
CLOSE THE
IT IS MERELY A "STUPID EXHIBIT" TO YOU, CORRECT?

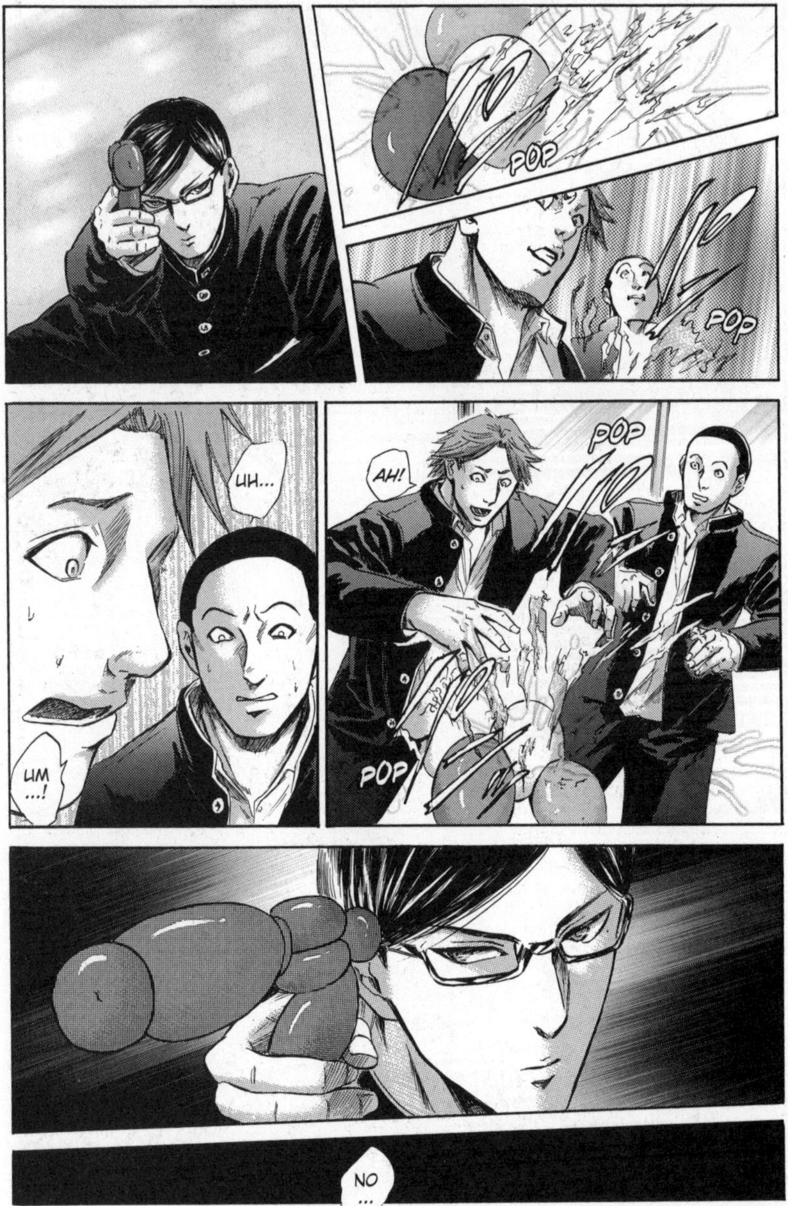
POP
POP
POP
AH!
POP
UH...
UM ...!
NO ...

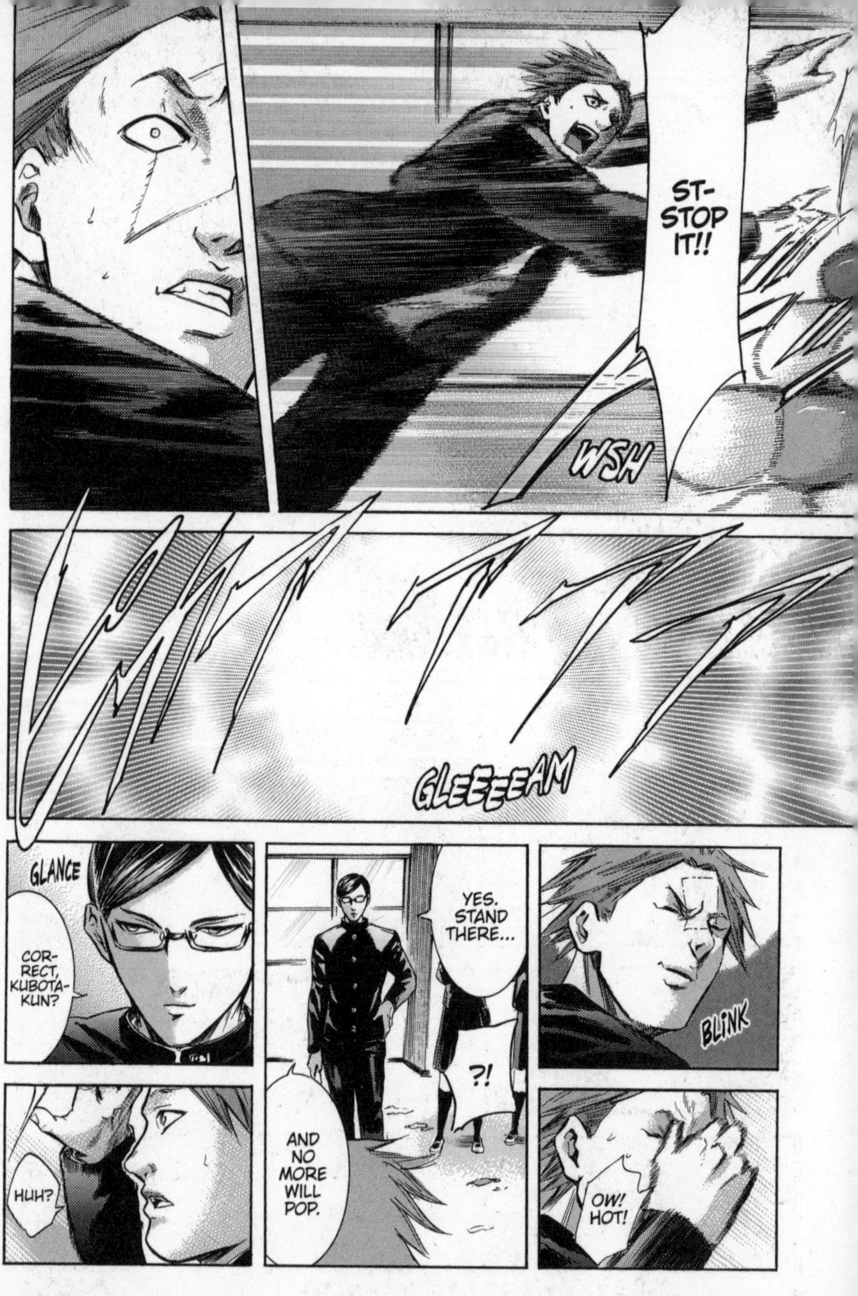
ST-STOP IT!!
WSH
GLEEEEEAM
BLINK
OW! HOT!
YES. STAND THERE...
?!
AND NO MORE WILL POP.
GLANCE
CORRECT, KUBOTA-KUN?
HUH?

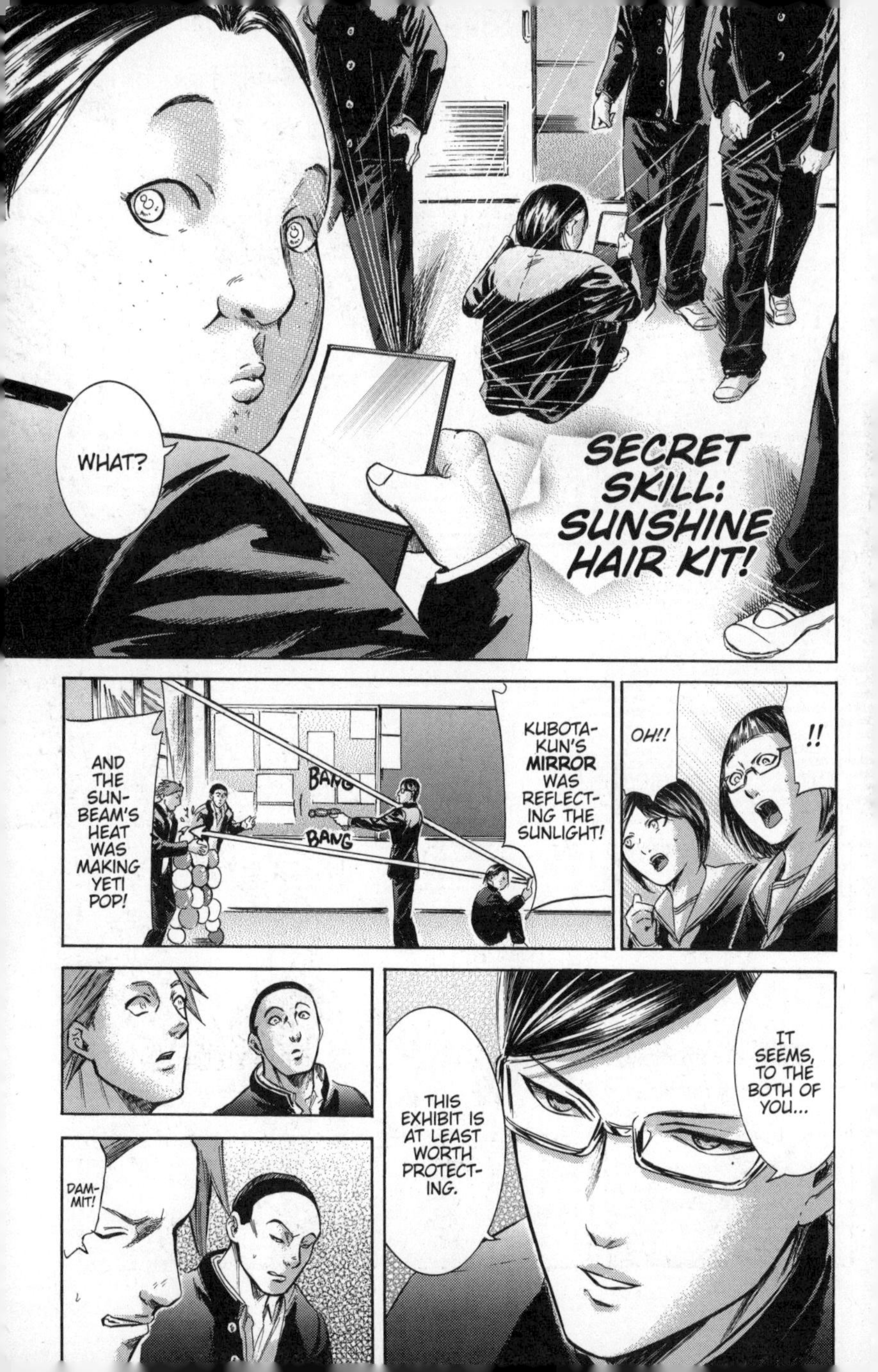

SECRET SKILL: SUNSHINE HAIR KIT!
WHAT?
!!
OH!!
KUBOTA-KUN'S MIRROR WAS REFLECTING THE SUNLIGHT!
BANG
BANG
AND THE SUN-BEAM'S HEAT WAS MAKING YETI POP!
IT SEEMS, TO THE BOTH OF YOU...
THIS EXHIBIT IS AT LEAST WORTH PROTECT-ING.
DAM-MIT!

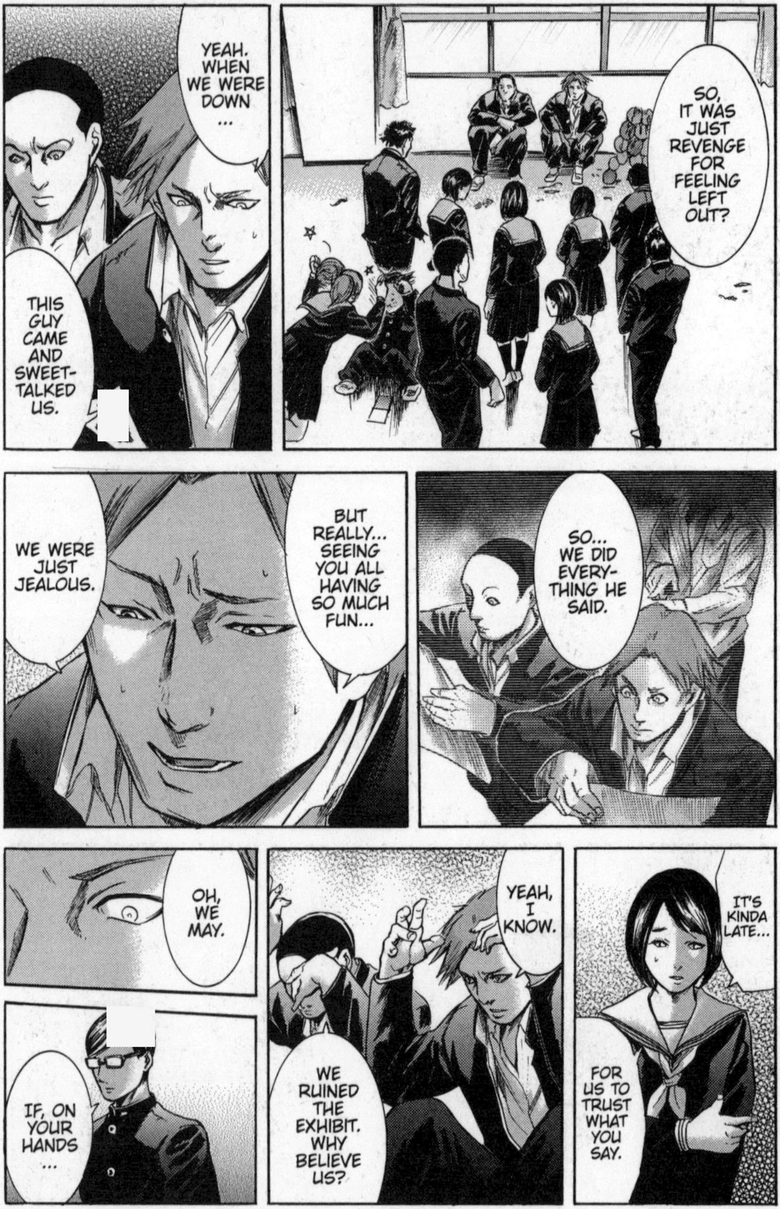
SO, IT WAS JUST REVENGE FOR FEELING LEFT OUT?
YEAH. WHEN WE WERE DOWN ...
THIS GUY CAME AND SWEET-TALKED US.
SO... WE DID EVERY-THING HE SAID.
BUT REALLY... SEEING YOU ALL HAVING SO MUCH FUN...
WE WERE JUST JEALOUS.
IT'S KINDA LATE...
FOR US TO TRUST WHAT YOU SAY.
YEAH, I KNOW.
WE RUINED THE EXHIBIT. WHY BELIEVE US?
OH, WE MAY.
IF, ON YOUR HANDS ...

YOU HAVE
YOUR OWN
LITTLE
BALLOONS
GROWING.

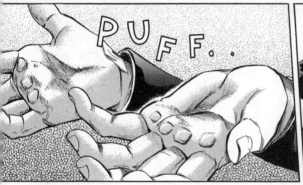

P U F F . .

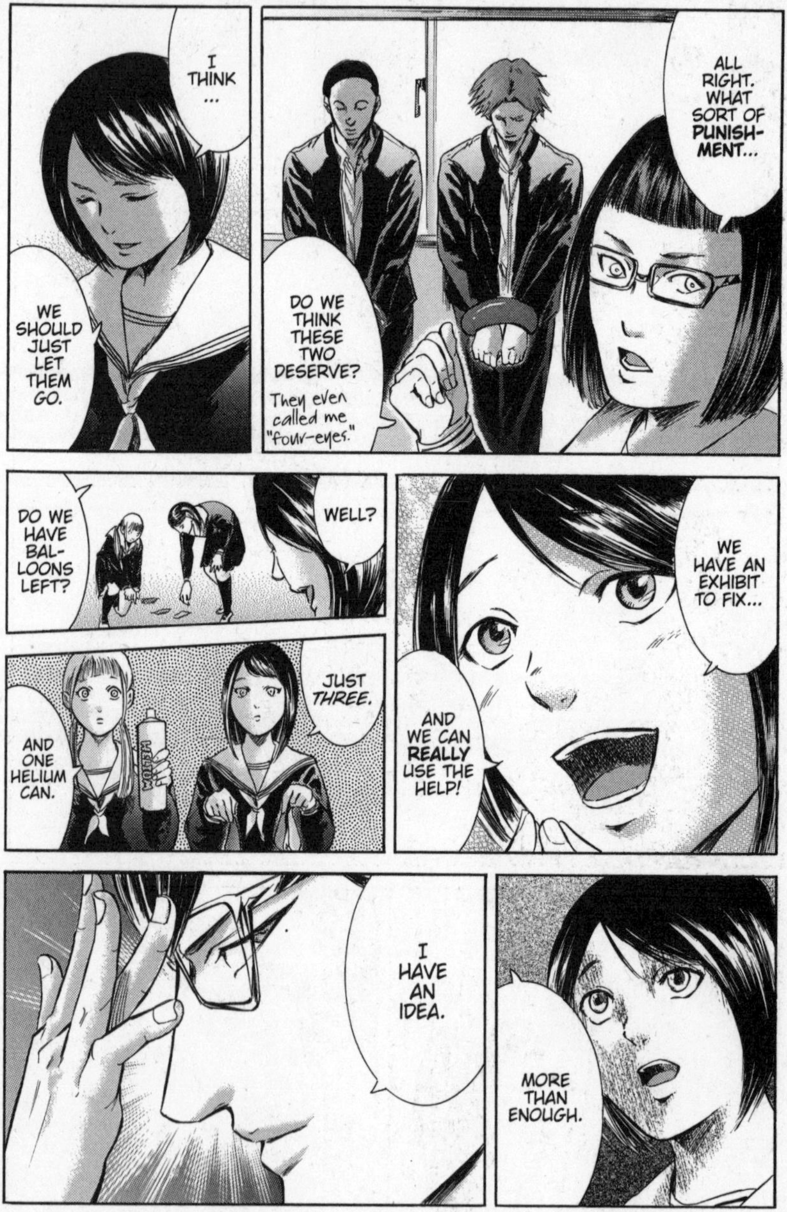
ALL RIGHT. WHAT SORT OF PUNISHMENT...
DO WE THINK THESE TWO DESERVE?
They even called me "four-eyes."
I THINK...
WE SHOULD JUST LET THEM GO.
WE HAVE AN EXHIBIT TO FIX...
AND WE CAN REALLY USE THE HELP!
WELL?
DO WE HAVE BALLOONS LEFT?
JUST THREE.
AND ONE HELIUM CAN.
MORE THAN ENOUGH.
I HAVE AN IDEA.

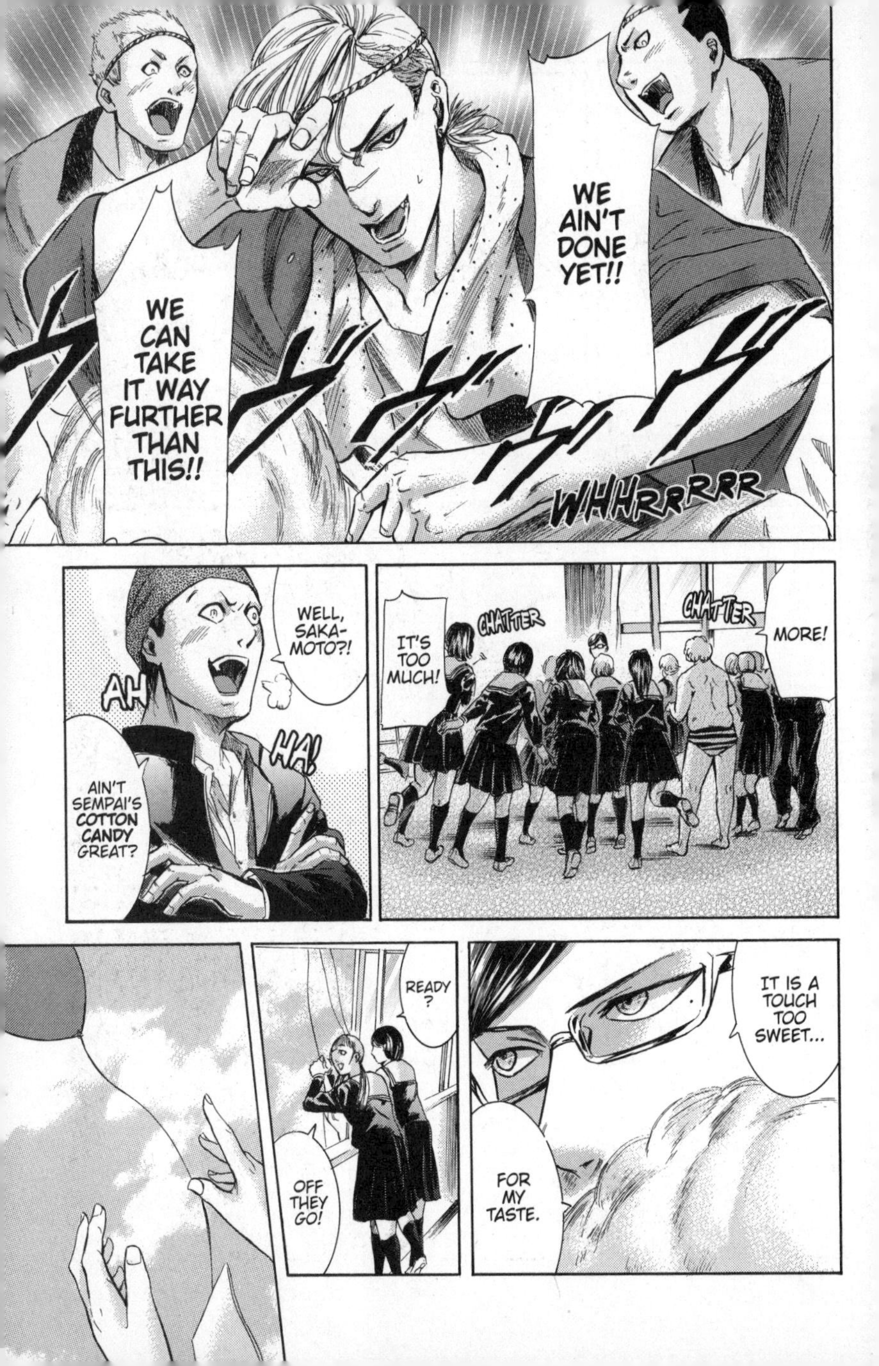
WE AIN'T DONE YET!!
WE CAN TAKE IT WAY FURTHER THAN THIS!!
WHHRRRRR
MORE!
CHATTER
IT'S TOO MUCH!
CHATTER
WELL, SAKA-MOTO?!
AH
HA!
AIN'T SEMPAI'S COTTON CANDY GREAT?
IT IS A TOUCH TOO SWEET...
FOR MY TASTE.
READY?
OFF THEY GO!

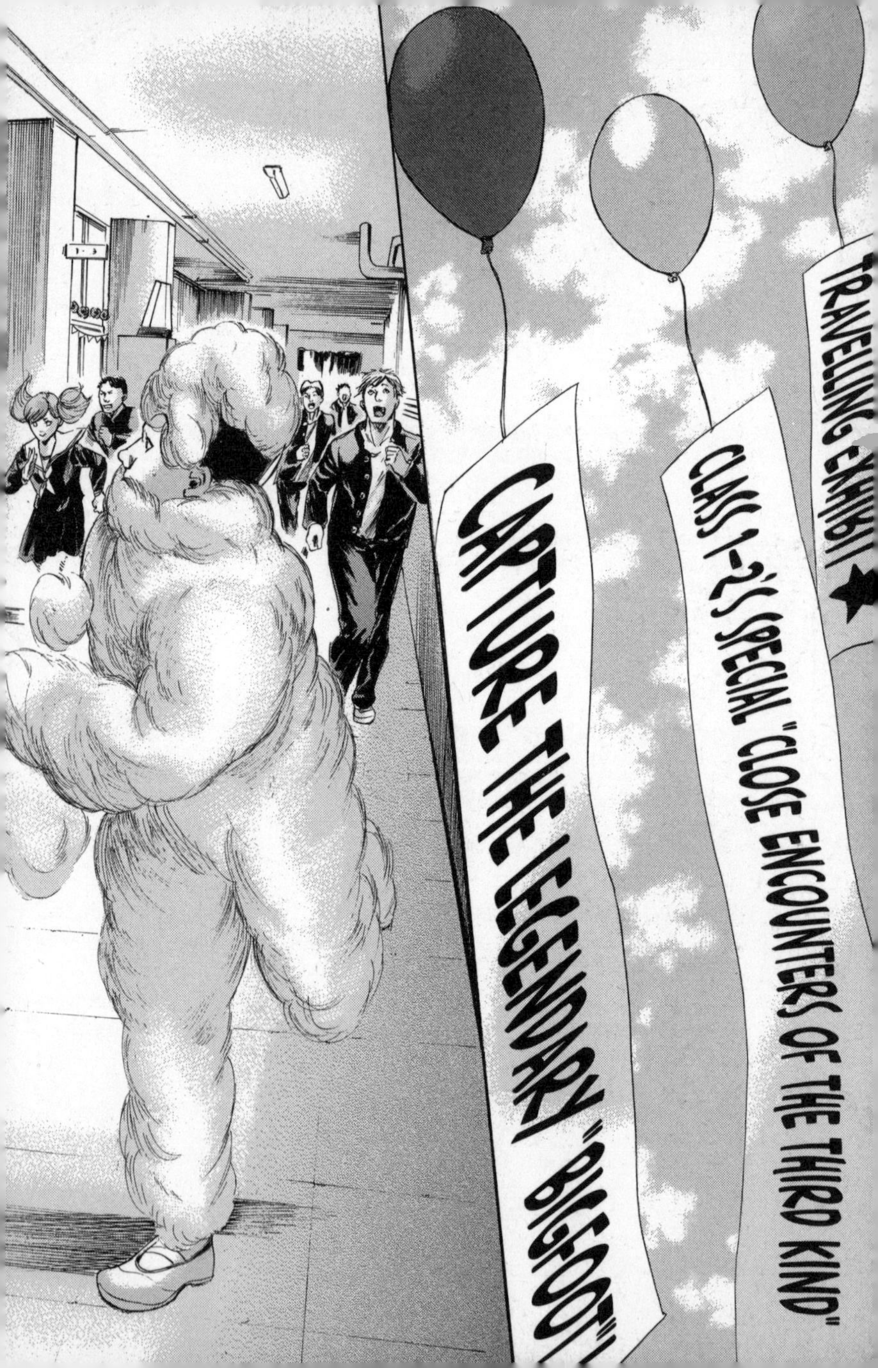
TRAVELLING EXHIBIT!! ★
CLASS 1-2'S SPECIAL "CLOSE ENCOUNTERS OF THE THIRD KIND"
CAPTURE THE LEGENDARY "BIGFOOT"!

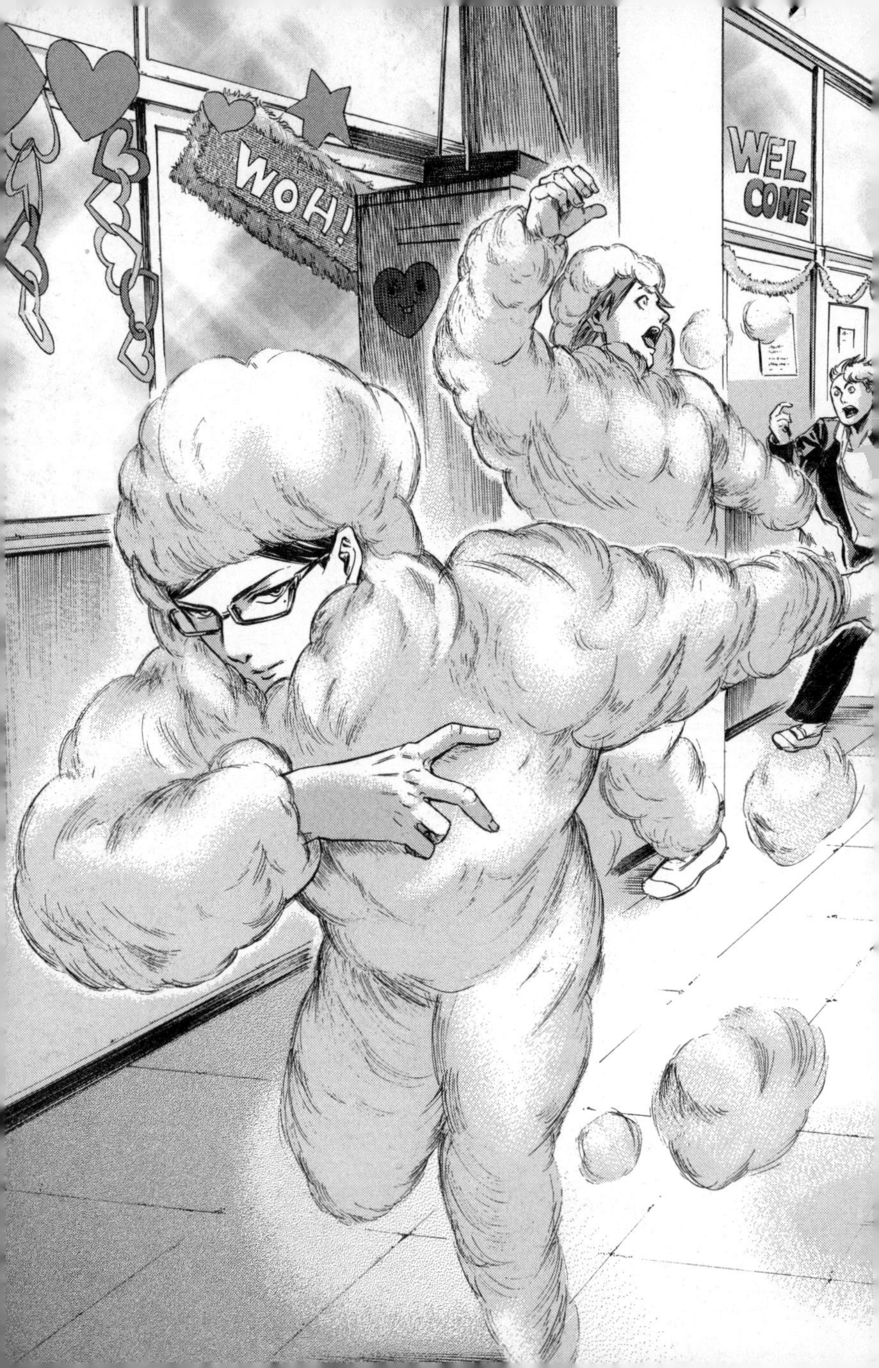
WOH!
WEL
COME

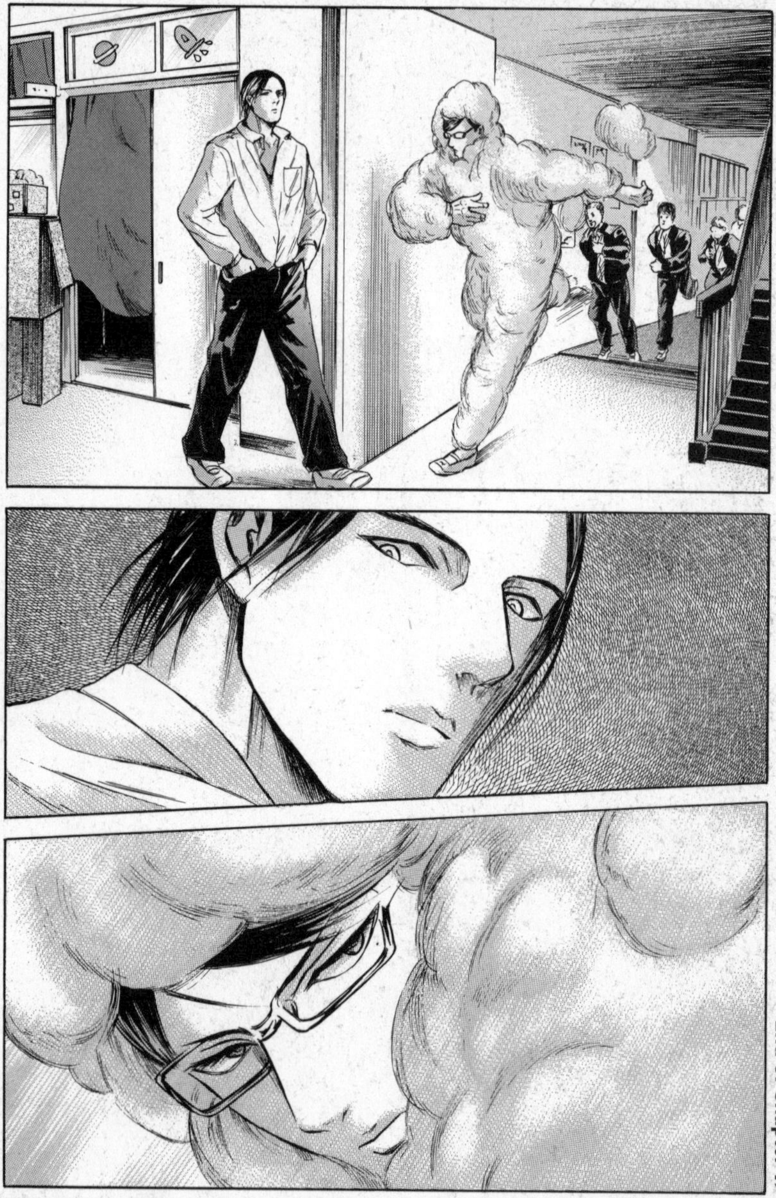

End of Chapter 17

Haven't You Heard?
I'M SAKAMOTO

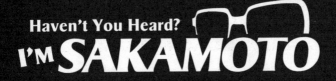

Haven't You Heard?
I'M SAKAMOTO

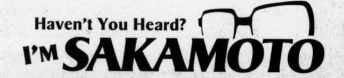

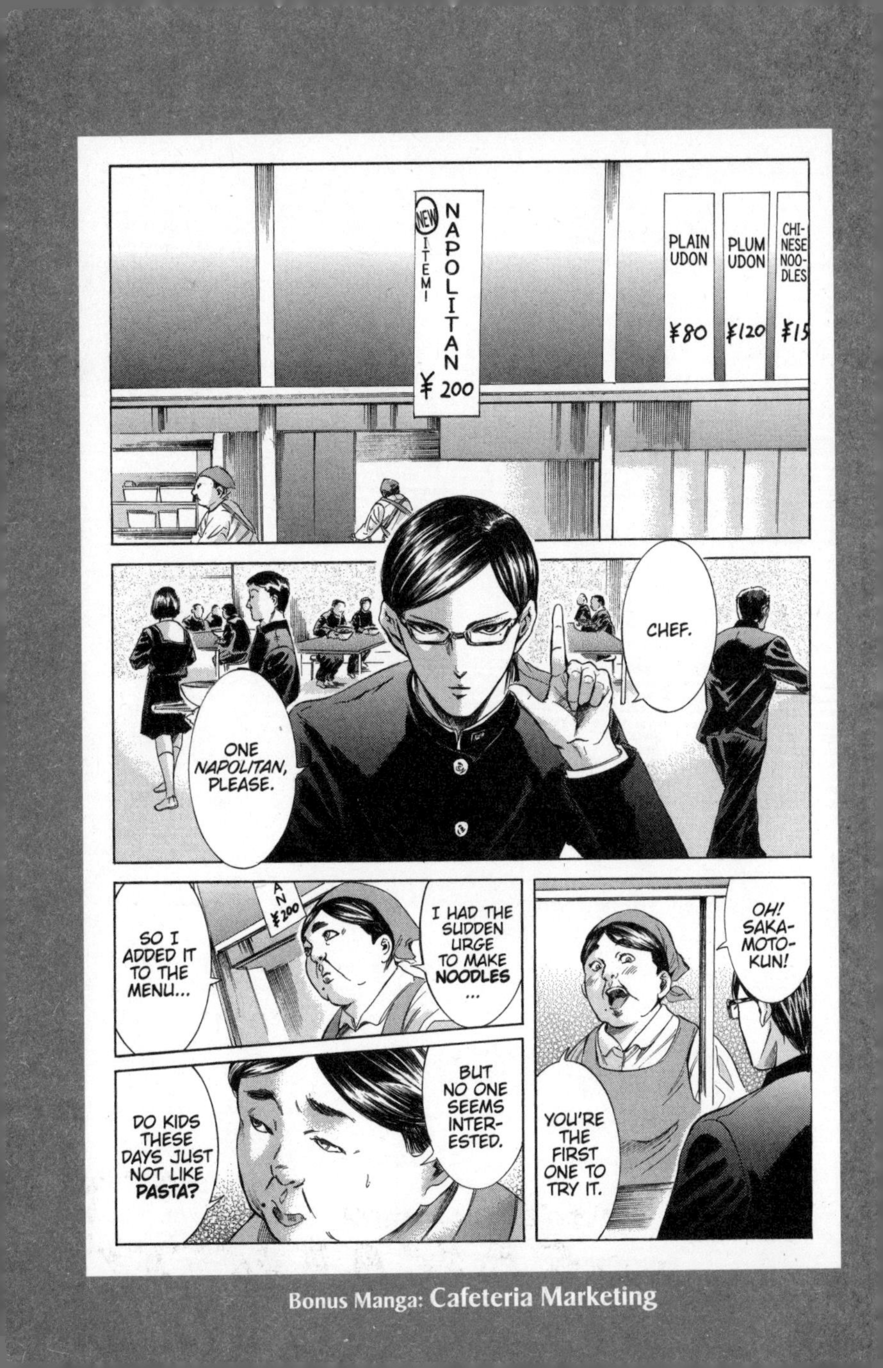
CHINESE NOODLES ¥15
PLUM UDON ¥120
PLAIN UDON ¥80
NEW ITEM! NAPOLITAN ¥200
CHEF.
ONE NAPOLITAN, PLEASE.
OH! SAKAMOTO-KUN!
YOU'RE THE FIRST ONE TO TRY IT.
I HAD THE SUDDEN URGE TO MAKE NOODLES ...
SO I ADDED IT TO THE MENU...
BUT NO ONE SEEMS INTERESTED.
DO KIDS THESE DAYS JUST NOT LIKE PASTA?

Bonus Manga: Cafeteria Marketing

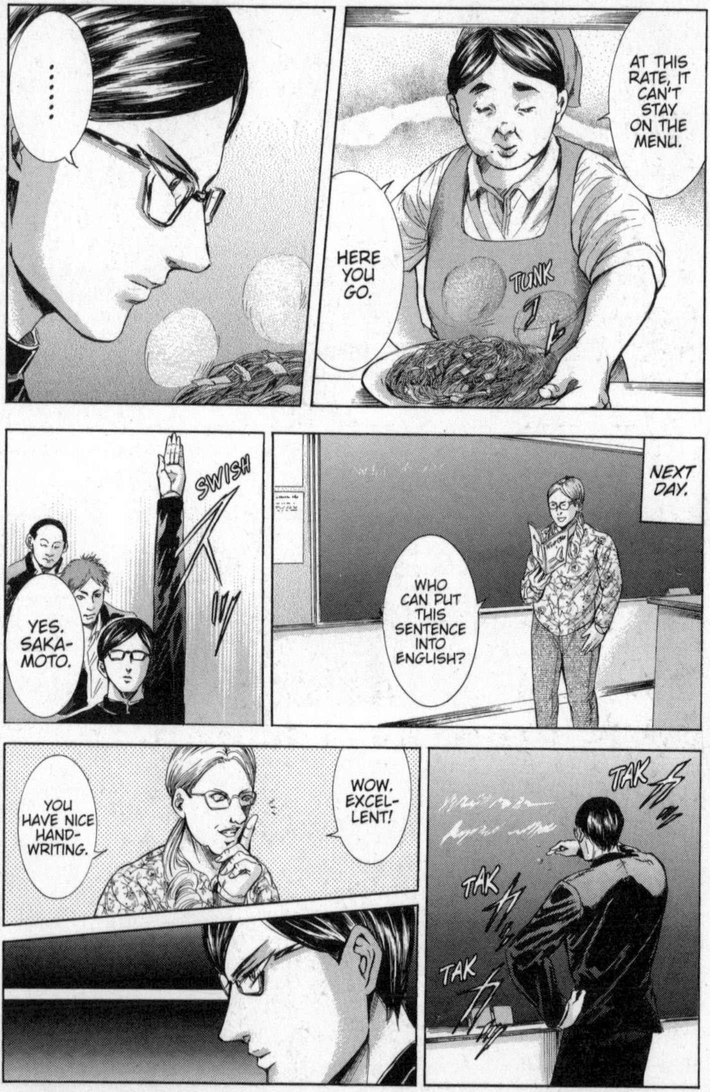
AT THIS RATE, IT CAN'T STAY ON THE MENU.
HERE YOU GO.
TUNK
......
NEXT DAY.
WHO CAN PUT THIS SENTENCE INTO ENGLISH?
SWISH
YES. SAKAMOTO.
TAK
TAK
TAK
WOW. EXCELLENT!
YOU HAVE NICE HANDWRITING.

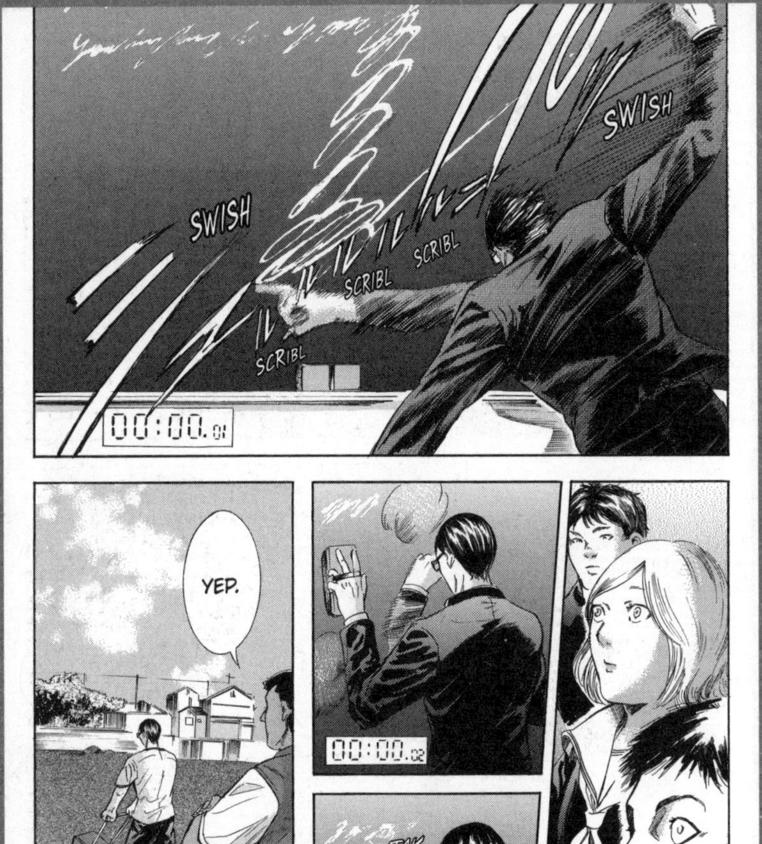
SWISH
SWISH
SCRIBL
SCRIBL
SCRIBL
00:00.01
00:00.02
TAK
TAK
00:00.03
YEP.
SQEEKA
SQEEKA
THAT'S IT! MAKE A NICE CURVE...

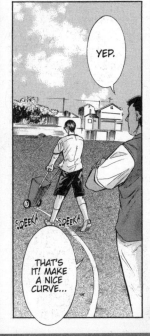

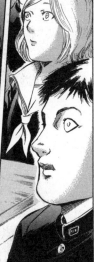

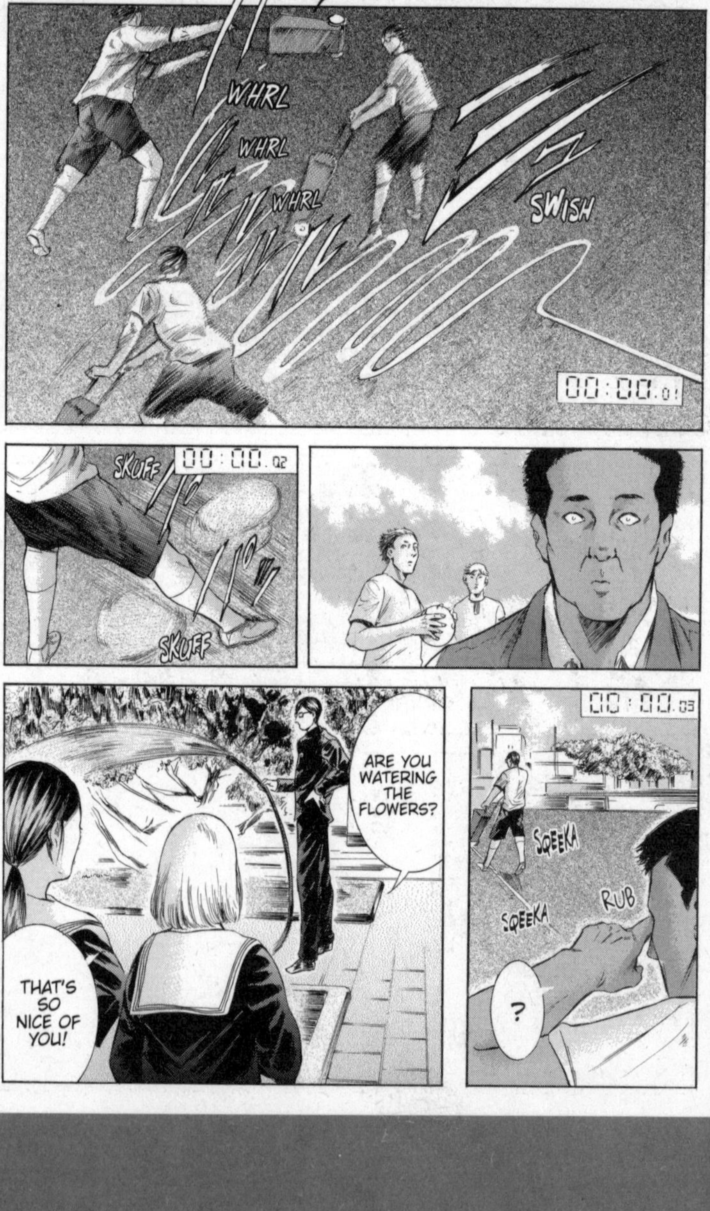
WHRL
WHRL
WHRL
SWISH
00:00.01
00:00.02
SKUFF
SKUFF
00:00.03
SQEEKA
RUB
SQEEKA
?
ARE YOU WATERING THE FLOWERS?
THAT'S SO NICE OF YOU!

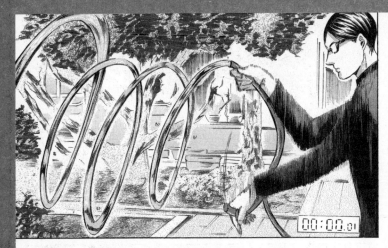

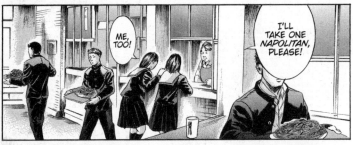

00:00.01
I'LL TAKE ONE NAPOLITAN, PLEASE!
ME, TOO!
THANK GOODNESS!
THE NAPOLITAN IS A HIT!
I GUESS MY HUNCHES ...
AREN'T SO FAR OFF, AFTER ALL.

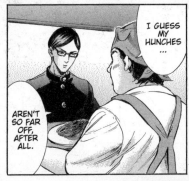

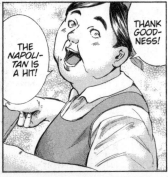

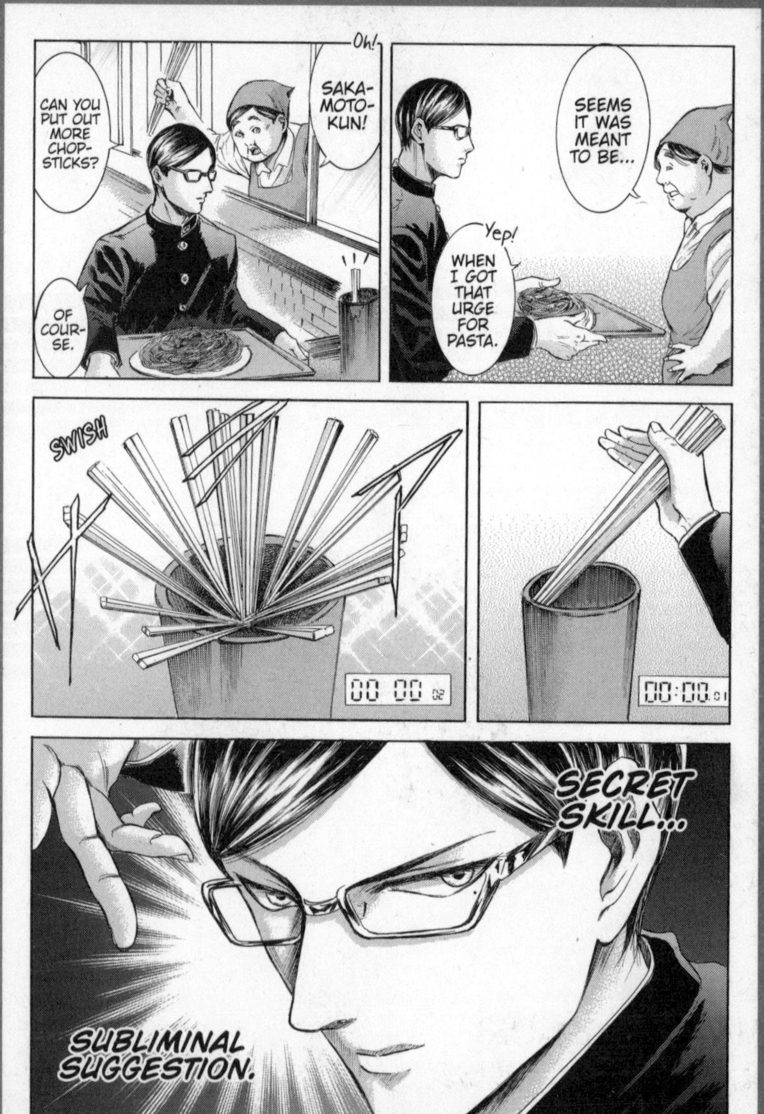
SEEMS IT WAS MEANT TO BE...
Yep!
WHEN I GOT THAT URGE FOR PASTA.
Oh!
SAKA-MOTO-KUN!
CAN YOU PUT OUT MORE CHOP-STICKS?
OF COUR-SE.
00:00.01
SWISH
00 00 02
SECRET SKILL...
SUBLIMINAL SUGGESTION.

End of Bonus Manga

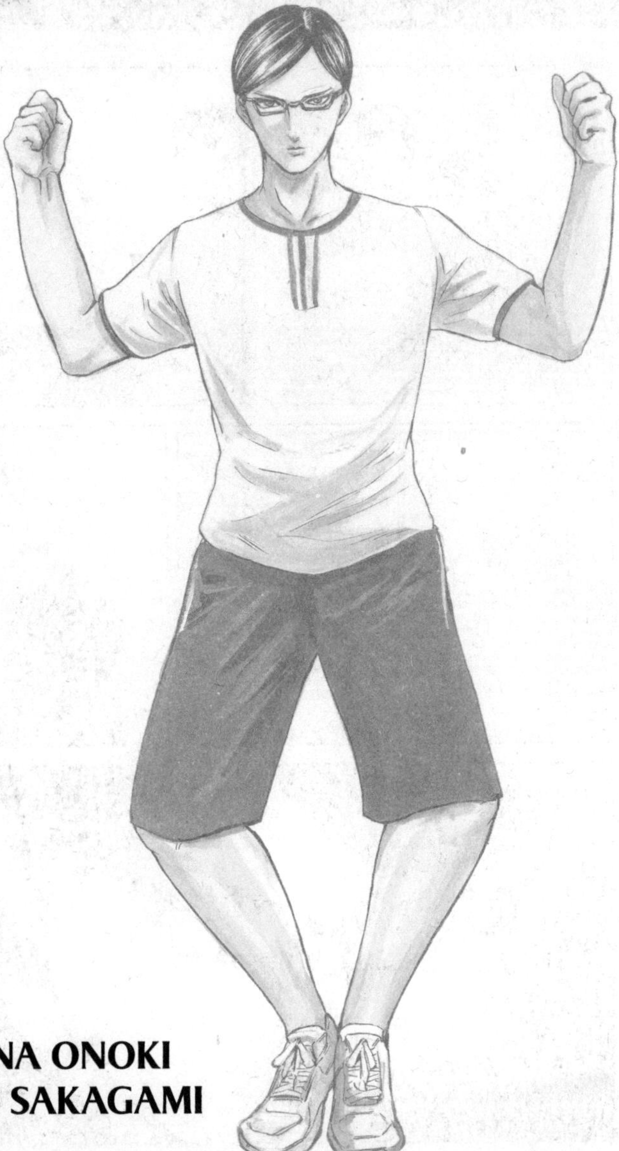

‹STAFF›

HARUNA ONOKI
KAORI SAKAGAMI

To be continued...

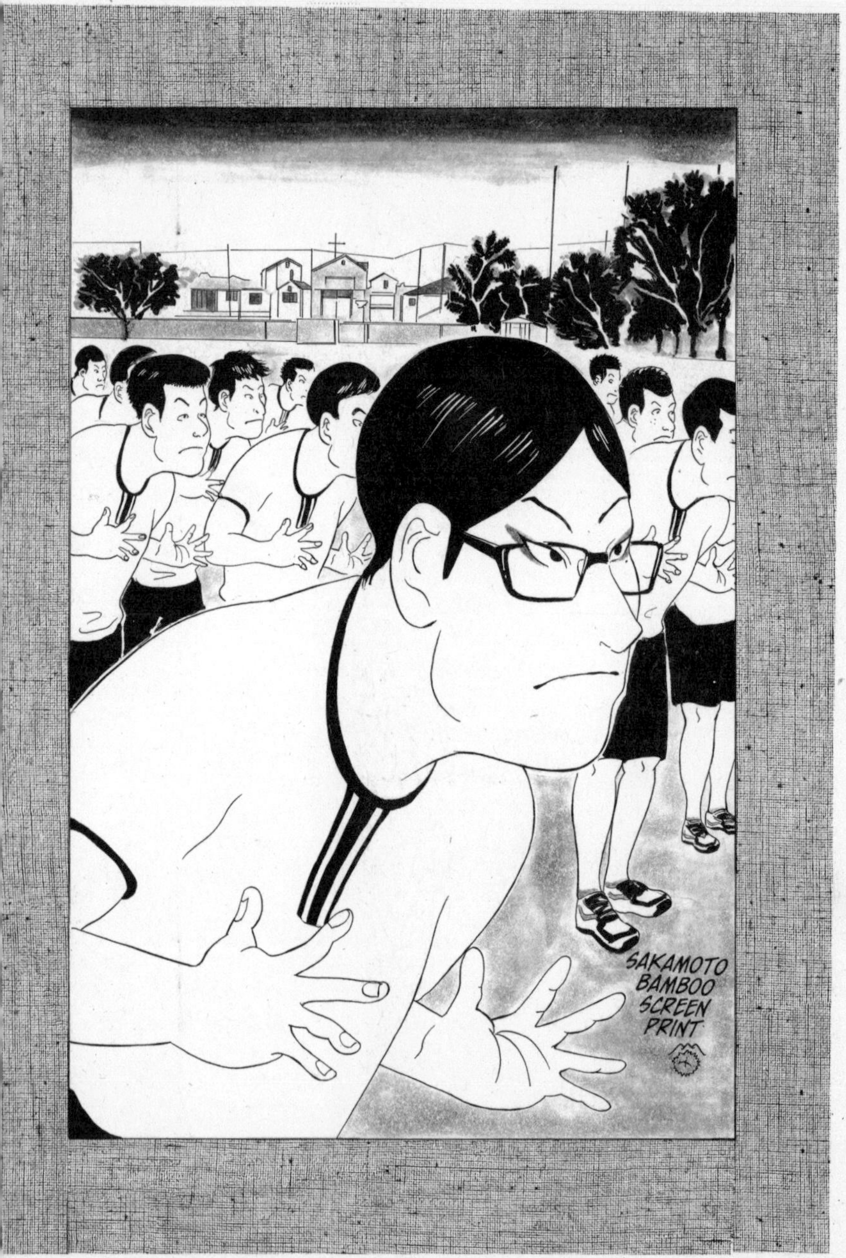
SAKAMOTO
BAMBOO
SCREEN
PRINT